Time Out

Buenos Aires

timeout.com/buenosaires

Published by Time Out Guides Ltd, a wholly owned subsidiary of Time Out Group Ltd.
Time Out and the Time Out logo are trademarks of Time Out Group Ltd.

© **Time Out Group Ltd 2006**
Previous editions 2001, 2005.

10 9 8 7 6 5 4 3 2

This edition first published in Great Britain in 2006 by Ebury Publishing
Ebury Publishing is a division of The Random House Group Ltd,
20 Vauxhall Bridge Road, London SW1V 2SA

Random House Australia Pty Limited 20 Alfred Street, Milsons Point, Sydney, New South Wales 2061, Australia
Random House New Zealand Limited 18 Poland Road, Glenfield, Auckland 10, New Zealand
Random House South Africa (Pty) Limited Isle of Houghton, Corner Boundary
Road & Carse O'Gowrie, Houghton 2198, South Africa

Random House UK Limited Reg. No. 954009

Distributed in USA by Publishers Group West
1700 Fourth Street, Berkeley, California 94710

Distributed in Canada by Penguin Canada Ltd
10 Alcorn Avenue, Toronto, Ontario, Canada M4V 3B2

For further distribution details, see www.timeout.com

ISBN 1-904978-98-3 (until January 2007)
ISBN 978-1-904978-98-5 (after January 2007)

A CIP catalogue record for this book is available from the British Library

Colour reprographics by Wyndeham Icon, 3 & 4 Maverton Road, London E3 2JE

Printed and bound by Firmengruppe APPL, aprinta druck, Wemding, Germany

Papers used by Ebury Publishing are natural, recyclable products made from wood grown in sustainable forests

Edited and designed by
Time Out Guides Limited
Universal House
251 Tottenham Court Road
London W1T 7AB
Tel +44 (0)20 7813 3000
Fax +44 (0)20 7813 6001
Email guides@timeout.com
www.timeout.com

Editorial

Editors Matt Chesterton & Fiona McCann
Managing Editor Mark Rebindaine
Consultant Editor Chris Moss
Copy Editor Lily Dunn
Listings Editor Florencia Monzani
Proofreader Patrick Mulkern
Indexer Sally Davies

Editorial/Managing Director Peter Fiennes
Series Editor Ruth Jarvis
Deputy Series Editor Lesley McCave
Business Manager Gareth Garner
Guides Co-ordinator Holly Pick
Accountant Kemi Olufuwa

Design

Art Director Buenos Aires Gonzalo Gil
Designer Buenos Aires Sofía Iturbe
Art Director Scott Moore
Art Editor Pinelope Kourmouzoglou
Senior Designer Josephine Spencer
Graphic Designer Henry Elphick
Digital Imaging Dan Conway
Ad Make-up Jenny Prichard

Picture Desk

Picture Editor Jael Marschner
Deputy Picture Editor Tracey Kerrigan
Picture Researcher Helen McFarland

Advertising

Sales Director Mark Phillips
International Sales Manager Ross Canadé
International Sales Executive Simon Davies
Advertising Sales (Buenos Aires) Gordon Wilkinson
Advertising Assistant Kate Staddon

Marketing

Group Marketing Director John Luck
Marketing & Publicity Manager, US Rosella Albanese
Marketing Manager Yvonne Poon

Production

Group Production Director Mark Lamond
Production Manager Brendan McKeown
Production Co-ordinator Caroline Bradford

Time Out Group

Chairman Tony Elliott
Managing Director Mike Hardwick
Financial Director Richard Waterlow
TO Magazine Ltd MD David Pepper
Group General Manager/Director Nichola Coulthard
TO Communications Ltd MD David Pepper
Group Art Director John Oakey
Group IT Director Simon Chappell

Contributors

Introduction Matt Chesterton, Fiona McCann. **History** Peter Hudson (*Argentina versus Inglaterra* Chris Moss; *On the money* Fiona McCann). **BA Today** Anna Norman (*Shock of the new* Matt Chesterton). **Football** Matt Chesterton (*Shock of the new* Fiona McCann). **Literary BA** Chris Moss. **Where to Stay** Ben Chappell (*A place to call home* Matt Chesterton). **Sightseeing: Introduction** Chris Moss. **The Centre** Brian Hagenbuch, Chris Moss (*Mothers of reinvention?* Fiona McCann; *Walk on* Matt Chesterton). **South of the Centre** Fiona McCann (*The other side of the tracks* Matt Chesterton); **North of the Centre** Chris Moss, Caroline Patience (*Walk on: Mind your manors* Fiona McCann; *Walk on: Step on the grass* Matt Chesterton). **West of the Centre** Declan McGarvey (*Bloom town* Brian Hagenbuch). **Along the River** Declan McGarvey (*Shock of the new* Matt Chesterton). **Further Afield** Brian Hagenbuch. **Restaurants** Emma Balch, Oliver Balch, Brian Hagenbuch, Diana Heald, Fiona McCann, Mark Rebindaine (*Get the scoop* Fiona McCann; *Shock of the new* Matt Chesterton, Chris Moss; *Beef for beginners* Kristin James Henley). **Cafés, Bars & Pubs** Harry Hastings, Fiona McCann, Emma Suttles (*Bluffer's guide to BA boozing* Fiona McCann). **Shops & Services** Emma Balch. **Festivals & Events** Matt Chesterton. **Children** Fiona McCann. **Clubs** Harry Hastings, Diana Heald (*Shock of the new* Matt Chesterton). **Film** Brian Hagenbuch (*Shock of the new* Daniel Burman). **Galleries** Matt Chesterton, Diana Heald. **Gay & Lesbian** Facundo Ulla (*Brokeback Buenos Aires* Brian Hagenbuch). **Music** Brian Hagenbuch (*Theatre of dreams* Helen Vigors). **Sport & Fitness** Mark Rebindaine (*Horse play* Alex Coidan). **Tango** Chris Moss. **Theatre & Dance** Brian Hagenbuch. **Trips Out of Town: Getting Started** Joshua Goodman. **Upriver** Chris Moss, Mark Rebindaine. **Country** Matt Chesterton. **Beach** Mark Rebindaine. **Uruguay** Gabriel Bialystocki, Mark Rebindaine. **Directory** Fiona McCann, Declan McGarvey.

Maps Nexo Servicios Gráficos, Luis Sáenz Peña 20, Piso 7 'B', Buenos Aires, Argentina (www.nexolaser.com.ar).

Photography Gonzalo Gil except: page 10 Javier Verstraten; pages 14, 15, 16, 20, 23, 198, 218, 219 Clarín Contenidos; pages 28, 209 Sofía Sanchez Barrenechea; page 33 Matías Claret; pages 49, 93, 111, 112, 127, 197 Diego Ortega; pages 53, 223 Faena Hotel + Universe; page 66, 182 Jeff Barry; page 79 Tour Experience; page 109 Persico; pages 116, 126, 139, 140, 163, 169, 171, 177, 213, 231, 232 Mark Rebindaine; artwork on page 120 by Mercedes Jáuregui, page 132 Casa Cruz; page 149 Matt Chesterton; pages 158, 161, 167 Diego Sabatini; page 161 Gustavo Sosa Pinilla; page 174 Gillian Hopgood; pages 180, 243, 244 Andrés Castro; page 181 Niceto Club; page 185 Mint; page 189 BD Cine; page 201 Alejandro Ros; page 217 Pablo Carrera Oser; page 227 De la Guarda; page 236 Temaiken; page 242 Gabriela Moltó; page 245 Yuri Rothschuh; page 248 Stéphane San Quirce.

The Editors would like to thank: Tribalwerks, Daniel Burman, Jeff Barry, Carolina Penelas, Cathy Runciman, and all contributors to the previous edition of *Time Out Buenos Aires*, whose work forms the basis for parts of this book. This book is dedicated to the memory of Chris Chesterton.

Contents

Introduction

Brash, beautiful and thrillingly incoherent, Buenos Aires is a city that above all scorns mediocrity. Excelling in the contrasting arts of boom and bust, the Argentinian capital has always been front-page news. There may once have been a headline reading, 'Buenos Aires: everything muddling along quite nicely', but it's not in the archives.

No surprise, then, when, in 2002, in the wake of the country's worst ever economic crisis, the world's press went into collective hand-wringing mode and declared the death of the 'Argentinian dream'. But the obituaries were premature. Like a stubborn boxer with a high pain threshold, Buenos Aires lurched to its feet and began to rebrand itself as one of the world's most glamourous and affordable tourist destinations. The 'BA is broken' threnodies were supplanted by 'BA is booming!' puff pieces, 'phoenix' replaced 'albatross' as the avian metaphor of choice, and now it seems no global travel itinerary is complete unless it includes a Boca Juniors versus River Plate football match, a knockout steak dinner and a tango show. Buenos Aires is so hyped it hurts.

But deservedly so. We've filled 300 pages with reasons why you'll fall in love with BA, and we could have filled 300 more. There is the tangible – great hotels for all budgets, a thriving restaurant scene, Latin America's most exciting gay nightlife, a tango resurgence; there is the intangible – the warmth, good humour and effortless style of the locals; and then there is the plain crazy – eat, drink and catch a world-class opera, and pocket change from US$50.

And, yes, there is pain too. This most civilised of cities has had barbarous interludes. History doesn't need to repeat itself here: it simply never goes away. The 1970s dictatorship, the Falklands/Malvinas war, chronic inequalities of wealth and opportunity – these are all live issues.

We haven't tried to gloss over BA's unsettling aspects, but neither have we lingered on them. In trying to strike this balance we've taken our cue from *porteños* (as the inhabitants of Buenos Aires are known), whose typical response to a bad day is to go out and have a bloody good night. It's a quixotic, hedonistic approach to life that most visitors find irresistible.

Porteños are proud of their city, determined to show tourists its best face, and wickedly adept at turning strangers in the night into close friends by dawn. So don't be surprised if the first question you're asked is a coy, 'Do you like Buenos Aires?' Answer yes, and the next question will probably be a less coy, 'Would you like to dance?'

Like we said – irresistible.

ABOUT TIME OUT GUIDES

This is the third edition of *Time Out Buenos Aires*, one of an expanding series of Time Out guides produced by the people behind the successful listings magazines in London, New York and Chicago. Our guides are all written and updated by resident experts, who have striven to provide you with all the most up-to-date information you'll need to explore the city or read up on its background, whether you're a local or a first-time visitor.

THE LIE OF THE LAND

Buenos Aires' grid system makes getting around the city relatively easy. We have divided the city into overall areas (the Centre, North of the Centre, South of the Centre, and so on), and then barrios or neighbourhoods within those (Recoleta, San Telmo, La Boca, Congreso, and so on). For more details, *see p61*. Every place is listed with its exact address – written in Spanish, to help you tell a taxi driver or ask a local. For listings of locations that are not precisely pinpointed on our street maps we have given the nearest two cross streets or intersection.

THE LOWDOWN ON THE LISTINGS

Above all, we've tried to make this book as useful as possible. Addresses, telephone numbers, websites, transport information, opening times, admission prices and credit card details are all included in our listings. And, as far as possible, we've given details of facilities, services and events, all checked and correct as we went to press. However, venues can change their arrangements, and during holiday periods some businesses and attractions have variable hours.

While every effort has been made to ensure the accuracy of information contained in this guide, the publishers cannot accept responsibility for any errors it may contain.

PRICES AND PAYMENT

The prices we have supplied should be treated as guidelines; volatile economic conditions can cause prices to change. For most services we have published prices as they were quoted to us – in either Argentinian pesos (AR$) or US dollars (US$). This allows you to identify the places that are charging tourists dollar rates for their services (and often charging lower peso prices to locals). For ease of use, and because most visitors book their accommodation in advance, we have quoted rates for hotels and other lodging in US dollars. At the time of going to press, one US dollar was worth about AR$3.

We have noted whether venues such as shops, hotels and restaurants accept the following credit cards: American Express (**AmEx**), Diners Club (**DC**), MasterCard (**MC**) and Visa (**V**). A few businesses may take travellers' cheques. If prices vary wildly from those we've quoted, ask whether there's good reason. If not, go elsewhere. We aim to give the best and most up-to-date advice, so we always want to know if you've been badly treated or overcharged.

TELEPHONE NUMBERS

To phone Buenos Aires from outside Argentina, dial your country's international code, then 54 (for Argentina) then 11 (for Buenos Aires) and finally the local eight-digit number, which we have given in all listings. If you are calling from within Argentina, but outside the city, you will need to add 011 before the eight-digit number. Within the city just dial the eight digits.

ESSENTIAL INFORMATION

For all the practical information you might need for visiting the city – including visa and customs information, emergency phone numbers, information on local weather, details of local transport, language tips and a selection of useful websites – turn to the **Directory** chapter at the back of the guide. It starts on page 249.

MAPS

The map section at the back of this book includes orientation and neighbourhood maps of the Buenos Aires area, and street maps of central BA, with a comprehensive street index. The street maps start on page 273, and now pinpoint specific locations of hotels (❶), restaurants (❶), and cafés and bars (❶).

LET US KNOW WHAT YOU THINK

We hope you enjoy *Time Out Buenos Aires*, and we'd like to know what you think of it. We welcome tips for places that you consider we should include in future editions and take note of your criticism of our choices. You can email us at guides@timeout.com.

Advertisers

There is an online version of this book, along with guides to over 100 international cities, at **www.timeout.com**.

In Context

Parque Tres de Febrero from the late 19th century.

History

Building a nation. The hard way.

One of Argentina's top-rated TV shows of 2005 was a history programme called *Algo habrán hecho* (They must have done something). With hundreds of extras in tights and stuck-on moustaches, and just the right amount of dialogue in a sire-you-must-flee-immediately vein, it assayed a broad sweep of the country's history, debunking a few myths along the way. The show's promotional poster had a telling tagline: 'They gave us plazas, cathedrals, palaces and universities. They wanted a country.'

This is a fair summation of how most *porteños* – as Buenos Aires residents are known – feel about their city and, by extension, their nation. Proud of what they have achieved, they wonder, given the human and natural resources at their disposal, why they haven't achieved more. And if not then, or now, then when?

WHEN THE REIGN WAS IN SPAIN

For most *porteños* the city's history began when the European *conquistadors* arrived in the 16th century. But the land they conquered wasn't empty. The area stretching inland from the southern shore of the estuary of the Río de la Plata (River Plate) was populated by bands of hunter-gatherer *Querandí* who eked out a nomadic existence on the vast, grassy pampas.

The first Europeans botched their entrance spectacularly. Juan Díaz de Solís, a Portuguese navigator employed by the Spanish crown,

landed in 1516, 24 years after Columbus reached the Americas. He and the rest of the landing party were killed and eaten by the indigenous tribes on the eastern bank of the Plate. Nevertheless, successive waves of Spanish and Portuguese explorers sparked a race to colonise the area.

Spaniard Pedro de Mendoza arrived with between 1,200 and 2,000 soldiers and settlers in February 1536. The Ciudad y Puerto Santa María de los Buenos Ayres that he founded was probably located near what is now Parque Lezama. But after initial friendly contact, conflicts with the indigenous inhabitants further upriver grew. Some settlers resisted, but the main force of Spanish colonisation switched northwards and, in 1541, Domingo Martínez de Irala, commander of the garrison in Asunción, ordered the abandonment of Buenos Aires.

Settlement of what is now Argentina continued with the foundation of three regional capitals in the interior: Santiago del Estero, Tucumán and Córdoba. But it became clear that a port would be necessary to service the vast area to the south of the silver deposits of Potosí, and on 11 June 1580, Lieutenant Juan de Garay replanted the Spanish flag in the soil of Buenos Aires. The city was reborn.

But with no great fanfare. Until 1610 Buenos Aires had scarcely 500 inhabitants, few of whom dared or cared to venture into the as yet unsettled and uncultivated pampas, making them dependent on supply ships for survival. Unfortunately, these were infrequent; Spain sent virtually all its goods on a circuitous route, allowing voyages to Buenos Aires only every one or two years in an attempt to cut piracy.

From these humble beginnings Buenos Aires gradually grew in importance. By the 18th century, the process of taming the pampas was under way. Hardy settlers ventured out into the fertile plains and established what would become the vast *estancias* (cattle ranches) of the province, and the resultant trade in leather and dried beef continued to flow through Buenos Aires. In 1776, in recognition of the port's strategic position and in a bid to regain commercial control, Spain created the Virreinato del Río de la Plata (Viceroyalty of the River Plate), comprised of what are today Bolivia, Paraguay, Argentina and Uruguay, and finally separating it from Peruvian command.

The new authorities immediately set up free trade agreements with Chile, Peru and Spain, and during the last two decades of the 18th century, the port boomed. The first of many waves of immigrants arrived from Europe. Buenos Aires became a bustling commercial centre, free from the strict social hierarchy that characterised its rivals in the interior. Its growing wealth funded an orphanage, a women's hospital, a shelter for the homeless and street lighting.

'The empire-building British began to cast a covetous eye on Spain's colonies.'

But the rapid growth also brought tensions. The new pro-free trade merchant class, mainly *criollos* (American-born Spanish) began to face off against the Spanish-born oligarchy which favoured Spain's monopoly. The creation of the city's first newspapers and the prospect of revolution and war in Europe also inspired heated debate about the country's future.

The empire-building British had ideas of their own and began to cast a covetous eye on Spain's colonies. In 1806, under the command of General William Carr Beresford, some 1,500 British troops entered Buenos Aires. The 'English Invasion' was a debacle, as was a second attempt in 1807 (*see p14* **Argentina versus Inglaterra**).

ADIOS MADRID

With the blundering Brits sent home with their sabres between their legs, *porteño* resentment was focused once more on their Spanish rulers. Simmering tensions in the city were heightened

by news that Napoleonic forces had triumphed in Spain. The *criollos* demanded that Santiago de Liniers' successor, Viceroy Baltasar Hidalgo de Cisneros, convene an open meeting of the city's governing body to consider the situation. Despite attempts by Spanish loyalists to restrict the size of the meeting, the vote was conclusive. The *criollos* declared the viceroy's reign to have expired and a junta (council) was elected to replace him. This marked a revolutionary transfer of power from the Spanish elite to the *criollos*. The loyalists made a last-ditch attempt at resistance, but a massive public protest backed by the *criollo* militia units on 25 May 1810 – in the square later to be named Plaza de Mayo in honour of the events that took place there – convinced them of the inevitable.

This conflict, henceforth to be known as the *Revolución de Mayo*, sparked a rise in anti-Spanish feeling. The country formally declared its independence in the northern province of Tucumán on 9 July 1816. On this day, celebrated annually as Argentina's independence day, the new nation announced its opposition to 'any other form of foreign domination'.

Emboldened by having crushed the English invaders in the previous decade, *criollos* in Buenos Aires subsequently led the movement for independence from Spain, promising to consult the provinces later. But the city had scarcely 40,000 inhabitants, and the provinces, jealous of its power, were not easily convinced. The province of Córdoba staged a counter-revolution, led by Liniers, who was executed by the junta for his trouble.

The resulting civil war lasted ten years, during which the government, constituted in various guises in Buenos Aires, sought to assume all the rights and privileges of the former Spanish colonial authorities.

This period saw the establishment of professional armed forces led by General José de San Martín and the rise of the *caudillos*, provincial strongmen who brutally defended regional autonomy. In the name of Federalism, these opposed centralised Unitarian rule. San Martín, the son of Spanish officials, ensured his place in Argentina's pantheon of national heroes by joining the revolutionary cause and leading a daring advance across the Andes to liberate Chile (*see p18* **On the money**).

In 1820 provincial forces defeated the nationalist army at Cepeda, outside Buenos Aires, and the centralist intentions of the city were scuppered. Thereafter the city suffered a period of turmoil. But by the end of 1820, order had been restored under Bernardino Rivadavia who dedicated the income from the customs house to improving the city, reorganising its government and justice system.

The intellectual, architectural and economic growth of the city, which now had over 55,000 inhabitants, contrasted with underdevelopment in the provinces. Nevertheless, relations with the rest of the country improved temporarily and Buenos Aires took on the responsibility for international relations as the new nation was recognised by the major foreign powers.

Rivadavia became the first president of a united and independent Argentina in 1826, but a year later the provinces were again up in arms. Rivadavia's constitution was rejected by most of the provincial *caudillos*, led by Juan Manuel de Rosas (*see p18* **On the money**) and Juan Facundo Quiroga.

Twice governor of Buenos Aires, Rosas consolidated his strong following in the countryside by organising an expedition to exterminate the indigenous Araucano, who competed with the wealthy ranch owners for the region's cattle. During his 17-year reign, Rosas consolidated the power of the port and province of Buenos Aires. But he also imposed rigid censorship and ruled by murder and repression. All citizens were compelled to make public their support for Rosas by wearing a red Federalist ribbon (the Unitarian colours were sky blue and/or white) and public documents, newspapers and personal letters were required to start with the forceful slogan 'Long live the Federation and death to the savage Unitarians!'

At the end of his second governorship, Rosas left a country that was isolated and economically backward. But he had also encouraged, albeit forcibly, national unity and paved the way for the federal constitution drafted in 1853, which established a republic with a strong central government and autonomous provinces.

FORGING A NATION

The next two decades saw the forging of the new nation, as successive presidents worked to create a unified state. Democracy, even imperfectly administered, represented an advance over the earlier despotism. Bartolomé Mitre, governor of Buenos Aires and the founder of *La Nación* newspaper, was succeeded by Domingo Faustino Sarmiento (*see p18* **On the money**).

Despite further uprisings, the national army successfully defended the republic and was further battle-hardened during a pointless war with Paraguay which lasted from 1865 to 1870. The controversial 'Desert Campaign' of 1879, on the other hand, led by General Julio Roca (*see p18* **On the money**), was deemed a resounding success. The campaign resolved the long-running conflict with indigenous groups, and in the process opened up 605,000 square kilometres (233,500 square miles) of land for cattle and sheep farming.

Agricultural output was not restricted to livestock. Technological advances facilitated the country's first wheat exports in 1878, and the following year saw refrigerated meat shipments arrive in their wake. Both developments would have a major economic impact in the decades to come. The bulk of the profits went to the large landowners, however, or were spent on British imports. The British also reaped handsome rewards from the construction of the railways, which grew by 2,516 kilometres (1,563 miles) from 1862 to 1880.

'Roca used his slaughter of indigenous groups as a springboard for the presidency.'

Characteristically, the city benefited the most from these economic advances, developing a cosmopolitan look and feel. Nevertheless, the absence of water and sewerage systems led to outbreaks of cholera in 1867 and yellow fever in 1871. The latter killed more than one-tenth of the city's population and encouraged its wealthiest inhabitants to relocate from the hard-hit southern sections to Barrio Norte.

In 1880 the city of Buenos Aires suffered its final assault at the hands of the provinces. Roca, like Rosas before him, used his slaughter of indigenous groups as a springboard for the presidency. Although backed by the provinces, he was resisted by Buenos Aires. The fighting that ensued killed more than 2,000, most of them *porteños*, before the national government was able to prevail. The city was then placed under central government control and separated from the province, which adopted as its capital La Plata, 60 kilometres (37 miles) to the east.

BELLE EPOQUE AND BUST

Roca was the figurehead for an oligarchy, represented by the Partido Autonomista Nacional (PAN), which held power for the next three decades, during which Buenos Aires mushroomed. Immigration, especially from Spain and Italy, had already swollen the city's population from 90,000 in 1854 to 526,000 by 1890. By 1914, it was the largest city on the continent, with 1,575,000 inhabitants.

Inspired by Haussmann's Parisian project, Buenos Aires was remodelled under Torcuato de Alvear, municipal chief from 1883-7 and considered the father of the modern city. The grand public buildings, parks and plazas date mainly from this time. British companies built tramways, gas and electricity networks, and a modern sewerage system was created. Meanwhile, Argentina established its place as the world's leading grain exporter and was second only to the US as a frozen meat exporter, creating a second boom for the port city.

But booms were fragile. A rise in British interest rates led the British Baring Brothers bank – which had funnelled vast sums into the republic – to cut off its cash supply and demand repayment. In 1890 Argentina was plunged into a sudden, massive economic crisis.

If emergency measures and the general conditions at the time – including devaluation and further credit from Britain – allowed Argentina to recover, the growing urban working class enjoyed little protection from social and economic problems. Discontent made them a ready audience for revolutionary ideas imported with European immigrants, and there was a series of strikes and armed uprisings. The government controlled these with police repression and the threat of deportation.

In 1912 Roque Sáenz Peña, leader of the PAN's liberal faction, enacted compulsory universal male suffrage. Electoral fraud had kept the party in government for three decades, but now the law signalled its own demise. Hipólito Yrigoyen, leader of the newly formed Unión Cívica Radical (the Radicals), was elected president in 1916, marking the advent of popular politics after a century of elite rule.

RADICALS ON THE RISE

The Radicals were to rule Argentina for the next 14 years. During this period, ten per cent of the rural population migrated to the cities, keen to join a vibrant, upwardly mobile middle class. Yrigoyen was equal to the party's promise of order, but did nothing to alter conservative political and economic structures. From 1914, international prices for Argentina's produce declined and growth was curtailed.

After initial conciliatory overtures to the unions, causing heated conservative protests, the government subsequently permitted brutal repression. In Buenos Aires, the terror reached its height during *La Semana Trágica* (Tragic Week) in 1919, when the government put down a metalworkers' strike with the aid of gangs organised by the employers, who also attacked Jewish immigrants. The body count, although numerous, was never established.

Nevertheless, Yrigoyen, in typical *caudillo* style, enjoyed almost reverential support as a populist demagogue who displayed a paternal interest in his supporters – especially students, for whom he opened up free university education. He also made nationalist gestures by creating the state-owned petroleum company Yacimientos Petrolíferas Fiscales to exploit the country's new oil wealth (oil had been discovered in 1907), and opposing US colonialism. But when

Statue of **José de San Martín**.

Yrigoyen was re-elected in 1928, he was in his twilight years. The worldwide Great Depression, which started in 1929, limited his ability to buy support by dipping into the state coffers. His government was overthrown in 1930 by an army that he himself had helped politicise, heralding a period of military intervention in state affairs after half a century in which the army had kept out of politics.

The coup was backed by the rural oligarchy, who were hardest hit by the global crisis and resented their removal from power in 1916. But it also owed much to the rise of fascist ideologies imported from Europe, which saw little use for democracy. General José Félix Uriburu's decision to dissolve Congress, censor the media and imprison political opponents in 1930, and the subsequent election of his military rival General Agustín Justo in 1931, inaugurated a period of what some termed 'patriotic fraud' – a populist ploy to prevent the Radicals from taking power.

Justo invested heavily in public works, including trunk roads from Buenos Aires to the provinces. Three new Subte (subway) lines – B, C and E – were inaugurated between 1930 and 1936, to supplement line A, the continent's oldest, which opened in 1913. Avenida 9 de Julio was also widened to its current size and the city's administration decided to broaden every

Argentina versus Inglaterra

There was the Hand of God and, long before that, the Spit of Rattin. On the race track, Stirling Moss never quite caught up with Juan Manuel Fangio. And in the South Atlantic Conflict, Margaret Thatcher beat up General Galtieri and some kids.

But 200 years ago these two powers – one an imperial nation, the other a largely forgotten province of Spain – fought over the ultimate prize: Argentina.

It started with a dream of booty and bravado. Commodore Home Riggs Popham, an explorer and supposedly astute diplomat, captured the Dutch Colony at the Cape of Good Hope to protect shipping lanes to the East Indies and South America. Puffed up by the easy victory, he decided to pre-empt the government's long-term intentions of securing a base in the River Plate by going ahead with a little invasion of his own.

On 25 June 1806, five destroyers and six transports under joint command of Popham and General William Carr Beresford (*pictured left*) sailed into the estuary. Three days later a flag was raised at Quilmes, then a mere village, and Beresford marched 1,635 men the 12 miles to Buenos Aires.

Viceroy Sobremonte fled the city and Beresford seized treasures and installed himself at the fort. But local nobleman Juan Martín de Pueyreddón refused to recognise the English authorities. On 31 July, leading a force of armed gauchos and natives, he attacked Beresford's outworks, but was driven back. His troops then surrounded the city and united with forces mustered by Martín de Alazaga, head of the Spanish merchants, and French-born politician

third or fourth street between Avenidas Caseros and Santa Fe, replacing the narrow colonial streets with today's busy transport arteries.

Production flourished with the start of World War II, which stemmed the tide of European imports. Argentina stayed neutral until late in the war, while maintaining its traditional alignment with Britain, but by 1943, the conservative government had lost much of its lustre and the army again intervened.

ENTER THE PERONS

The military was now installed as a de facto political party, running government for much of the rest of the century. But it had little idea what to do once in power. The issue was resolved with the emergence of another modern-day *caudillo*, army colonel Juan Domingo Perón, head of the then obscure labour department. He had a very keen understanding of the power of the masses, picked up during his time as a military attaché in late-1930s Italy, where he was impressed by Europe's burgeoning fascist movements.

Perón's genius was to recognise the growing importance of the Argentinian working class and win the support of the union movement,

which remains under his spell to this day. He was soon named vice-president and war minister and eventually presidential candidate. With Argentina's produce fetching bonanza prices, the healthy state of the economy allowed Perón considerable leeway with welfare projects, including housing and health schemes and the introduction of universal pensions.

Between 1936 and 1947, Buenos Aires' population swelled from 3,430,000 to 4,724,000. Most of the new inhabitants were poor migrants from the provinces – they increased from 12 to 29 per cent of the city's population – and they formed the bedrock of Perón's support. When the oligarchy decided, in 1945, that Perón had gone too far, and arrested him, it was this underclass (known in Peronist lore as the '*descamisados*' or 'shirtless ones') that came to his rescue. On 17 October – still celebrated by Peronists as *Día de la Lealtad* (Loyalty Day) – workers massed in the Plaza de Mayo to defend Perón. When he appeared around midnight on the balcony of the Casa Rosada, to the cheers of 300,000 supporters, it became evident that he was too powerful to be stopped, at least for the time being.

Santiago de Liniers who summoned military support from Montevideo. With the help of townspeople, who poured boiling water from their balconies and threw stones at the invaders, they retook the city on 12 August.

It took some time for the news to get back to Britain, which is why a month after Popham and Beresford had surrendered, *The Times* was proudly announcing 'our success in La Plata, where a small British detachment has taken one of the greatest and richest of the Spanish colonies'.

Bolstered by such reports and anachronistic, often hyperbolic, dispatches from the inept commanders, the British government launched a further expedition.

On the morning of 5 July 1807 7,000 men, led by Lieutenant-General John Whitelocke (*pictured right*) – already appointed by the Crown as Governor-General of South America – entered Buenos Aires. By the afternoon they had surrendered to the local militias, with around 300 British soldiers killed, 700 wounded and 200 missing in action.

In September of the same year *The Times* reported the debacle as 'perhaps the greatest which has been felt by this country since the commencement of the revolutionary war'.

Whitelocke was court-martialled and cashiered, taking the blame for a military campaign almost entirely bereft of strategy, communications and skill.

For many historians, these acts of resistance against a powerful empire – the first is known as *la reconquista*, the second as *la defensa* – steeled the creoles to reject Spain's authority, leading to Argentina's eventual independence. To this day the English are known fondly as '*piratas*'.

In February 1946 Perón won the first democratic election since Yrigoyen, launching propaganda and state welfare campaigns that converted him and his young, ambitious wife, Evita, into legends. While Perón fulfilled his duties, Evita dispensed the government's welfare budget, mixing easily with the poor, while enjoying her new wealth. As leader of the women's wing of Peronism, she took up the campaign that enacted women's suffrage in 1947.

Massive state intervention in the economy, however, was poorly handled. The railways, which were bought from the British to popular rejoicing, cost four times their official valuation. Mismanagement of the transport, gas and phone services damaged their efficiency. Nonetheless, in 1949, a new constitution was approved, guaranteeing social rights and allowing for Perón's re-election.

Perón was elected to a second term in 1951, but less than two months after retaking office, Evita died from cancer, aged 33. Although Perón remained a crucial figure until his death in 1974, the heart had gone from Peronism. Moreover, Argentina had exhausted most of its reserves of gold and foreign exchange, and two

bad harvests exposed the fragility of his welfare drive. He promptly abandoned the more radical economic policies and passed a law protecting foreign investment. Yet even as the economy recovered, Perón inexplicably launched a series of barbed attacks on the church, which had previously backed him. The move fuelled a growing opposition. In 1955 the Plaza de Mayo was bombed by naval planes during an attempted military uprising, killing more than 200 government supporters. In response, Peronists torched city churches. Argentina had begun to spin out of control.

ON THE BRINK...
The next two decades saw a fragmentation of Argentinian society that gave rise to a period of unparalleled barbarism. In December 1955 Perón was overthrown by the military – with wide support from the upper and middle classes – and went into exile. His Partido Justicialista, or PJ, was banned and persecuted.

The Radicals split, too, and Arturo Frondizi, leader of their more combative wing, was elected president in 1958. Once in power, however, Frondizi alienated those who had voted for him by reneging on campaign promises, though he won friends in the oligarchy with free-market policies. Angered by news that the president had held a secret meeting in Buenos Aires with Ernesto 'Che' Guevara, Argentinian-born hero of the Cuban revolution, the army forced his resignation in 1962.

Arturo Illia, leader of the Radicals' more conservative wing, was elected president the following year, with just 25 per cent of the vote. Although his brief rule restored economic growth, the military was once again dissatisfied and retook power in 1966. The country continued its descent into chaos with the growth of guerrilla movements, led by the Montoneros, who had Peronist origins, and, later, the Trotskyite People's Revolutionary Army (ERP).

Eventually even his opponents accepted that Perón was the only viable alternative to military rule, even though his movement was split between left-wing nationalists and conservatives. When Perón returned to Argentina in 1973, the tension erupted into bloodshed at a massive rally to welcome him. The violent conflict between the two factions left scores dead and the party split.

After his election as president the same year, Perón sided with the right, forcing the Montoneros to abandon the movement after haranguing them at the May Day rally in 1974. He died two months later at the age of 74, leaving the country in the incapable hands of his third wife, Isabel. She in turn was dominated by José López Rega, whom Perón had promoted to minister of social welfare. López Rega is famous as the founder of the Triple A, a shadowy paramilitary organisation dedicated to the murder of political opponents. As the violence spiralled and the economy collapsed, much of the population breathed a sigh of relief when Isabel was replaced in 1976 by a military junta, led by General Jorge Rafael Videla.

...AND INTO THE ABYSS

The satisfaction was short-lived. The *Proceso de Reorganización Nacional* (known as *'el Proceso'*), presided over by Videla, imposed order by eliminating the regime's opponents. Although the exact number of those killed during this time is still disputed, it may have been as great as 30,000, according to human rights groups. A minority had taken part in the

Behind every strong man... **Evita** (*left*) and **Isabel Perón**.

armed struggle, but most were trade unionists, political activists, rebellious priests and student leaders. Most were kidnapped, taken to torture centres and then 'disappeared': buried in unmarked graves or heavily sedated and thrown from planes over the River Plate. In the face of such horrors, many Argentinians emigrated or were forced into exile – although many more stayed and feigned ignorance.

The military government introduced radical free-market policies, reducing state intervention and allowing a flood of imports, much to the detriment of local industry. The deregulation of financial markets created a speculative boom, while spiralling national debt left a legacy from which Argentina has yet to recover. Inflation soared again and the regime sought ways to distract the population. The 1978 World Cup, staged in Argentina, was one such distraction.

'The badly led Argentinian forces were no match for a professional British taskforce.'

But although Argentina eventually triumphed on the football field (after what many consider a rigged match against Peru), growing opposition off it encouraged political parties and the church to raise their voices. The greatest courage was displayed by human rights groups, particularly the Madres de Plaza de Mayo, who marched in front of the Casa Rosada on a weekly basis to demand information on their missing children.

On 2 April 1982, under the leadership of General Leopoldo Galtieri, the military made one last desperate attempt to flame popular support, invading the Falkland Islands/Islas Malvinas, occupied by the British since 1833. The action unleashed a flood of nationalist fervour, but the generals had misjudged the reactions of friends and enemies alike.

Britain had earlier shown little interest in preserving the Falklands, even downgrading the British citizenship of the islands' 1,800 inhabitants. But the British prime minister Margaret Thatcher's unpopularity at home meant a tide of patriotic passion was as much in her interests as the junta's. On 1 May a British submarine attacked and sank the Argentinian cruiser *General Belgrano*, killing almost 400 crew members. The ship was outside the 200-mile 'exclusion zone' that the British had imposed around the islands and was steaming away from them, although the Admiralty claimed that it might have intercepted British ships on their way to join

the conflict. In retaliation, the Argentinians sank the British destroyer HMS *Sheffield* three days later, killing 20 of its crew.

A peaceful settlement was now impossible. Galtieri had trusted in US support, which never materialised; Washington eventually backed the British. The junta had an equally poor understanding of the military side of the conflict. After the sinking of the *Belgrano*, the navy sat out the rest of the conflict, and Argentinian forces, badly led and composed largely of ill-equipped conscripts, were no match for a professional British taskforce. The defeat was the final nail in the regime's coffin. It was also a huge shock to a society that had been convinced by its press that Argentina was winning the war, until the very moment of surrender.

Defeat brought the population back to its senses, although the issue has by no means gone away. Most Argentinians believe that *'las Malvinas son argentinas'* and the 1994 constitution ratified Argentina's claim to the islands, specifying that the recovery of sovereignty is an unwaivable goal of the Argentinian people. The islands appear on all Argentinian maps as Argentinian territory.

DEMOCRATIC PARTYING
Democracy returned in 1983 with the election of Radical leader Raúl Alfonsín, one of the few political leaders to have maintained his distance from the military and opposed the Falklands War. The momentous changes afoot were described at the time as *'una fiesta de democracia'* and a party atmosphere prevailed.

But the new president lacked a majority in Congress and faced a range of vested corporate interests. He also faced stiff military opposition to the investigation of abuses committed during the *Proceso* – although he was helped by the publication in 1984 of *Nunca Más* (*Never Again*), a harrowing report of human rights abuses during the military government, identifying 9,000 victims. In the ensuing public outcry, the three juntas that presided over the *Guerra Sucia* (Dirty War) were tried in 1985 and stiff sentences handed down, including life for Videla – one of very few cases of Latin American military leaders being imprisoned for their crimes. But in the face of military pressure, the government passed the *Punto Final* (Full Stop) law in 1986, limiting the trials.

Another military uprising during Easter Week in 1987 was met by impressive public demonstrations in support of democracy. But after persuading the rebels to lay down their arms, Alfonsín then caved in to the military's demands, passing the *Obediencia Debida*

On the money

If the idea of reading a history book makes your mouth go dry, don't worry; there's a far less strenuous way of getting acquainted with Argentina's heroes and villains. Simply rifle through your wallet. Here's a rundown of the luminaries on the lucre.

Two pesos *Bartolomé Mitre (1821-1906).* Warrior, statesman, poet and newspaper magnate, Mitre was equally in his element on the battlefield and in the library. His early years were defined by his opposition to Juan Manuel de Rosas. Later he led the revolt of BA province against Justo José de Urquiza's federal system, before becoming president of a more stable republic in 1862. After he retired from politics, he founded Argentina's *La Nación*, still considered one of Latin America's most influential newspapers. In his spare time he published poetry, several histories of the nation's founding fathers and a translation of Dante's *Divine Comedy*. He is buried in Recoleta Cemetery.

Five pesos General José de San Martín (1778-1850). Argentina's most revered hero, who, along with Simón Bolívar, led Latin America's revolutionary struggle against the Spanish crown. The son of Spanish officials, he joined the Argentinian revolutionary cause in 1812. His finest hour was in 1817 when he led an army of 5,000 troops over the Andes to liberate Chile, a fiendishly difficult operation which bears comparison with Hannibal's crossing of the Alps. Then it was on to Peru for more of the same. Once Peruvian independence was secured, San Martín and Bolívar met in secret to discuss the region's future. Soon after this mysterious reunion, San Martín unlaced his marching boots and retired to France. His body was returned to Buenos Aires in 1880 and interred in the city's cathedral.

Ten pesos *Manuel Belgrano (1770-1820).* Celebrated as much for his graphic design skills (he conceived the Argentinian flag) as his military prowess, Belgrano was one of the key figures behind the 1816 Declaration of Independence from Spain and subsequent revolutionary wars. A romantic hero in the broadest sense, he lost his heart to a young woman from Tucumán, but before he could make an honest woman of her was whisked away to cross swords with the Spanish loyalists. His love was left behind, carrying his child, and her irate

(Due Obedience) law, which excused the vast majority of the accused officers on the ground that they were only following orders.

Among the trade unions Alfonsín initially attracted hostility with a failed attempt to introduce new labour laws. But 13 general strikes later, he capitulated and appointed a senior union leader as labour minister. He did little better with the economy. After initial economic stabilisation as a result of the Plan Austral in 1985, the government's nerve again failed when faced with serious restructuring.

With the Peronist opposition gaining strength, Alfonsín finished his term in rout. His successor, Carlos Menem, was forced to take office five months early as the economy spun out of control, monthly inflation hit 197 per cent and looters raided supermarkets. Once in office, Menem abandoned his electoral promises and embraced neo-liberalism.

Under convertibility, introduced by Finance Minister Domingo Cavallo in 1991, the peso was pegged to the dollar at one-to-one. Privatisation resolved the problem of a bloated state sector, with handsome rewards for the business oligarchy. International capital was appreciative too; the brisk opening of the economy left virtually all leading companies and financial institutions in foreign hands. After ten years of negative growth, Menem's decade in office saw total growth of around 35 per cent, and inflation was vanquished.

parents forced her into wedlock with another man in order to protect her honour. She was eventually reunited with the general, but, as she was legally married to someone else, they could never formalise their union. Belgrano died from dropsy at the age of 50.

20 pesos *Juan Manuel de Rosas (1793-1877)*. This brooding, sideburned archetype of a Latin American despot was twice governor of Buenos Aires and employed censorship, repression and murder to maintain his 17-year rule. Still a controversial figure in Argentina, Rosas first consolidated his power by waging war on the indigenous Araucano, forming his own private army for the express purpose of exterminating them. Recognised by some historians as a clever nationalist politician with a finger on the gaucho pulse, he is despised by others for the atrocities carried out by his henchmen. He died in exile in Southampton, England, to which he fled after his defeat at the Battle of Caseros in 1852.

50 pesos *Domingo Faustino Sarmiento (1811-1888)*. The only Argentinian president to have received the thumbs up from Jorge Luis Borges, Sarmiento is regarded by many as one of Latin America's all-time intellectual greats. Apart from presiding over Argentina between 1868 and 1874, during which time the nation made huge strides in the fields of education and communications, he's also the man who put the *rosada* (pink) into the Casa Rosada. Founder of various literary societies, schools and university faculties, he is best remembered as the author of one of the cornerstones of Latin American literature, *Facundo*, an attack on Juan Manuel de Rosas in the form of a biography of the latter's tyrannical gaucho sidekick, Quiroga.

100 pesos *General Julio Argentino Roca (1843-1914)*. Another controversial figure from Argentinian history, soldier-turned-statesman Julio Argentino Roca is best remembered for his controversial – some prefer the term 'genocidal'– Desert Campaign of 1879 in which he 'solved' the republic's 'Indian problem' by systematically killing them and driving them from their heriditary lands. This achievement earned him his first presidency in 1880 at the age of 37, and the Tucumán-born Roca was to dominate Argentinian politics for the following 30 years. He ruled over a time of great prosperity in Argentina, successfully oversaw the separation of church and state, and brokered peace with Chile during his second term. Roca remains a controversial figure to this day. His city centre statue is regularly defaced by graffiti comparing him with the despised military dictators of the 1970s.

Menem ruled largely by decree and with little regard for constitutional niceties. But he finally dominated the military, and the mutiny by army rebels in December 1990 was the last of its kind. Although he dismayed human rights campaigners by granting an amnesty to the jailed junta leaders, he also starved the armed forces of funds, leaving them operationally incapable of another coup. He negotiated a constitutional amendment allowing him to win re-election in 1995, although the opposition extracted some changes in return, including elected authorities for Buenos Aires city.

But Menem's second term could not sustain the impetus of his first. Local industry largely collapsed under foreign competition, turning the industrial belt around Buenos Aires into a wasteland, populated by an increasingly bitter and impoverished underclass. Real wages dropped and the gulf between the rich and poor steadily widened. Menem's flamboyant style and love of showbiz glitter – *la farándula*, as Argentinians call it – went hand in hand with numerous high-profile corruption scandals.

In the 1991 'Yomagate' or 'Narcogate' scandal, various Menem officials were accused of links to money laundering and the illegal drugs trade.

Menem's association with Alfredo Yabrán (a shadowy businessman implicated in the murder of journalist José Luis Cabezas in 1997), and allegations that his Middle Eastern connections (he is of Syrian descent) had hampered official investigations into the terrorist attacks on the city's Jewish communities in 1992 and again in 1994 were sufficient to give Argentinians the impression that every injustice led back to the presidential palace.

INTO THE ABYSS – AGAIN

Tired of such excesses, the population turned to Fernando de la Rúa, head of Buenos Aires' city council and self-styled antithesis of Menem. Running at the head of the Alliance, formed by the Radicals and Frepaso, a smaller left-wing party, de la Rúa was elected president in December 1999. For some, the rise of such an unexceptional man to the head of a coalition government marked the death of the *caudillo* and a new period in Argentinian politics. In retrospect, the de la Rúa years can be seen as little more than a period in which international financiers demanded payback for investing in Menem's chimerical new economy. Throughout his term, de la Rúa maintained an image of calm – soporific even – government, but the manner with which the Alliance led the country to economic meltdown was devastating.

The beginning of the end was a scandal over alleged vote-buying in the Senate, which dominated the media throughout the spring of 2000. The subsequent resignation of his popular vice president Carlos 'Chacho' Alvarez, left de la Rúa weak and isolated. By this time, Brazil's decision to devalue its currency by 30 per cent the year before had caused Argentinian exports, still pegged to the dollar, to plummet. The ensuing crisis was met by severe austerity measures, but recession worsened and the beleaguered president turned, in early 2001, to former Peronist financial guru Domingo Cavallo to turn the economy round. But this time Cavallo was unable to rescue the country, and eight billion dollars of emergency aid was sought from the International Monetary Fund.

It was not enough. The economic situation atrophied as unemployment rose to 20 per cent in Buenos Aires and far higher levels in many provinces. Argentina's credit rating fell to a historic low, its national bonds designated as junk stock, and the dithering, quiet-mannered president was ill-equipped to reverse the inevitable economic disaster. In October 2001, the Peronist opposition took control of both houses and began to lead a takeover.

On 19 December, protests segued into full-scale riots and looting, prompting heavy-handed police repression; de la Rúa declared a state of emergency. On 20 December, Cavallo resigned, followed the next day by de la Rúa after massive rallies took to the streets and more than 20 people were killed when riot police (and some shopkeepers) opened fire on looters, protesters and bystanders.

For Christmas 2001, Argentinians were gifted four presidents in just 11 days, the largest ever default in history – around US$150 billion – and the contempt of the IMF. When de la Rúa stood

Ex-president **Carlos Menem**. And a Ferrari.

down, Ramón Puerta took over as caretaker between 20 and 23 December; Adolfo Rodríguez Sáa ruled between 23 and 30 December but was ousted by fellow Peronists when he made it clear that he wanted more than an interim role; Puerta became caretaker again for 30 December and Eduardo Camano stood in between 31 December and 1 January.

The man then chosen by Congress to run Argentina until the next elections, Eduardo Duhalde, was a populist Peronist known for his opposition to neo-liberal ideology. A classic *caudillo* type, he had served as Menem's vice president. For 15 months, he managed, with the aid of his appointed finance minister, Roberto Lavagna, to contain the crisis, further exacerbated by the January 2003 devaluation of the peso, and, slowly, a semblance of calm and order was restored in BA and across the country.

BACK TO REALITY?

When Néstor Kirchner took office on 25 May 2003, his presidency was welcomed as a change of atmosphere and a break with the Duhalde-Menem-Cavallo dynasty. But his mandate was by no means strong. Menem opted out of presidential run-offs when he looked likely to lose, allowing Kirchner to come to power with just 22 per cent of the vote.

Since then Kirchner has built and broadened his power base, co-opting the opposition parties' best talents and leaving those that remain glowering ineffectually from the sidelines. With approval ratings consistently hitting the 70 per cent mark, the president (whose wife, Cristina, is a senator) is widely expected to cruise to re-election in 2007. But if any lesson can be divined from Argentina's past, it is perhaps that no one ever made money betting on her future.

Key events

1516 European settlers reach the River Plate and are killed by Querandí natives.
1536 First settlement of Buenos Aires.
1541 City abandoned.
1580 Juan de Garay resettles the city.
1620 Diocese of Buenos Aires created.
1776 Spain creates the Viceroyalty of the River Plate.
1806-07 British troops make two unsuccessful attempts to occupy Buenos Aires.
1810 Argentinian-born leaders replace the Spanish viceroy with an elected junta.
1816 Argentina formally declares independence in Tucumán on 9 July.
1826 Bernadino Rivadavia assumes the national presidency, declaring Buenos Aires the capital.
1853 Federal constitution drafted.
1862 Bartolomé Mitre elected first president of the new Republic of Argentina.
1871 Outbreak of yellow fever kills over 7,000 city residents, mostly in the south.
1880 Buenos Aires becomes federal capital.
1913 First South American underground railway – or Subte – is operated on Line A.
1919 During 'Tragic Week', gangs organised by employers help the government of Hipólito Yrigoyen brutally repress strikers.
1930 Yrigoyen government overthrown by an army coup.
1931 General Agustín Justo elected president, heralding period of 'patriotic fraud'.
1937 Official opening of Avenida 9 de Julio, at 140m (459ft) the widest avenue in the world.
1943 Army overthrows conservative regime.

1945 Workers mass on 17 October to force liberation of Juan Domingo Perón.
1946 Perón wins presidential elections by 1,487,886 votes to 1,207,080.
1951 Perón is re-elected.
1952 Perón's wife, Evita, dies aged 33.
1955 Perón is overthrown by a military coup.
1966 Military takes power.
1973 Perón elected president for a third term.
1974 Perón dies.
1976 General Jorge Rafael Videla leads military coup against Isabel Perón.
1982 The junta occupies the Falklands/Malvinas, but is defeated by the British.
1983 Radical leader Raúl Alfonsín democratically elected president.
1987 Rebel army leaders revolt. In response, the government halts trials of most officers.
1989 Peronist president Carlos Menem takes office five months early.
1994 Bomb attack on AMIA Jewish welfare centre kills 86 and wounds more than 250.
1995 Menem elected for second term.
1999 Fernando de la Rúa elected president for the Alliance.
2001 De la Rúa resigns when the economy collapses, prompting widespread rioting.
2002 Peronist Eduardo Duhalde is chosen as president by Congress on 1 January.
2003 Peronist Néstor Kirchner elected president in run-offs with 22 per cent of vote.
2006 Kirchner settles Argentina's outstanding debts to the International Monetary Fund.

BA Today

Buenos Aires is booming. What could possibly go wrong?

Diego Maradona's 'resurrection' was *the* news story of 2005. Thanks to a stomach-stapling operation, he lost around 50 kilos (110 pounds) and launched new careers as a chatshow host and vice-president of his beloved Boca Juniors football team. More unexpectedly, Argentina's favourite son became something of a poster child for the anti-Washington political movement currently sweeping Latin America; he upstaged George W Bush et al with a series of public appearances at the November 2005 Summit of the Americas, held in the Argentinian coastal city of Mar del Plata.

Pundits were quick to draw analogies between the dramatic turnaround of 'el Diego' and that of his nation. Five years ago the prognosis for both had been gloomy; a seriously overweight Maradona was stricken with health problems brought on by his alleged 'refuelling habits', while the country had just suffered its worst-ever economic crisis. Riots in Buenos Aires had been projected on television screens across the world and, as the currency crashed, it seemed everyone was crying for Argentina.

That was then. In the last few weeks of 2005, as Maradona was crowned 'Figure of the Year' at the *Clarín* (the nation's largest daily newspaper) entertainment awards, for his

ratings-topping TV programme *La Noche del 10* (The Night of the Number 10 – a glammed-up talkshow in which Diego basked in praise from famous guests such as Fidel Castro, Robbie Williams and Pelé), President Kirchner was preparing to pay off the country's US$9.8 billion debt to the International Monetary Fund. Cue amazement and some eating of crow from an international press that, just three years before, had written Argentina off as just another Third World basket case.

The recovery of the 'golden boy' was one thing. Quite another was the way this stricken nation (and its dynamic capital) had managed to pull itself out from the morass so quickly. And here's another teaser: Is it *really* out?

GOOD TIMES IN BUENOS AIRES?

When Argentina scrapped its rigid exchange rate in January 2002, after a decade's parity with the dollar, Buenos Aires went overnight from South America's most expensive capital, on a par with Paris or New York, to its cheapest. Imported goods became prohibitively expensive. As a result, local factories reopened and resumed manufacturing goods once judged too costly to compete. Over the past three years the Argentinian economy has grown by an impressive 25 per cent; it was the world's second fastest growing economy after China in the early months of 2005. More than a third of this economic output has been generated in and around Buenos Aires – notably in industries such as construction (still the strongest sector) and food-processing.

The most palpable transformation has been seen in the tourism sector. The old rap against Buenos Aires – that it's a great place to visit but too costly to hang around in– was instantly nullified by the currency devaluation of 2002. Tourists continue to stream into the city – four million of them in 2005, 15 per cent up on the previous year.

The improvements can be measured qualitatively as well as quantitively. As the city's tourist industry expands to meet demand, particularly in areas like Palermo Viejo and San Telmo, services have become more sophisticated. Instead of benignly ignoring tourists as before, enterprising *porteños*

Shock of the new Politics

May you live in interesting times, runs the old Chinese curse. Thanks, we usually do, is an imagined Argentinian response. But 500 years of 'interesting' history have created an appetite in BA for a few years of duller fare – jobs, good schools and hospitals, an end to endemic corruption, and so on.

The man bearing the weight of these expectations – indeed, the man largely responsible for creating them – is Néstor Kirchner, president of Argentina since May 2003. Kirchner talks passionately about a new kind of Argentinian politics, one in which the best old values are reinvigorated and the worst new ones jettisoned. So – how is he doing?

Pretty well, according to most Argentinians. Kirchner's approval rating has hovered around the 70 per cent mark since he came to office. His popularity is rooted in the blunt (some would say crude) style with which he confronts those who are, in his view, responsible for Argentina's decline. Regular recipients of Kirchner's ire include the International Monetary Fund, the Catholic Church, carpet-bagging corporations and most of his presidential predecessors.

Demagoguery? Of course. But Kirchner has also walked the walk. His popular early reforms included a purge of the Supreme Court (widely perceived during the Carlos Menem era of the 1990s as bootlicking stooges), the annulment of the Full Stop laws which gave amnesties to members of the 1970s military dictatorship, and a strategy of facing down international creditors over Argentina's whopping debt. And for every Argentinian who cringes at Kirchner's bull-in-a-china-shop approach to international diplomacy, there are three others who applaud his refusal to be bullied by the big guns.

But the most striking of Kirchner's innovations has been what he terms *'transversidad'*, or coalition politics. Kirchner is a political magpie who is happy to pinch ideas and personnel from opposition groups. In fact, like Winston Churchill before him, Kirchner seems to have an instinctive distaste for members of his own party.

It follows, then, that not everyone is enamoured of Kirchner. The *bien pensants* of Buenos Aires have proved particularly resistant to their president's 'charms'. Preferring statesmen of a philosophical bent, many *porteños* regard Kirchner's man-of-the-people act as, at best, pure schtick, and at worst, thuggishness. Kirchner, in turn, doesn't seem to give a hoot what the sophisticates of the capital think of him, which of course makes them madder still. Other opponents are more specific in their animadversions. Anti-corruption crusader Elisa Carrio and the *La Nación* newspaper are among those who believe Kirchner's modernising agenda is naked populism dressed up in the robes of reform.

Hogwash, says Kirchner – and most voters seem to agree. Even those wary of the president's blustering style are persuaded by his central argument: that something is rotten in the state of Argentina and that the *ancien régime* can't be trusted to put things right.

Wider issues come into play too. Kirchner has aligned himself with a new generation of Latin American leaders that includes Hugo Chávez of Venezuela and Evo Morales of Bolivia. All of them share the view that the region's ruling classes have consistently betrayed the interests of those they govern. Put simply, the New World needs new champions and new ideas.

These are interesting times, indeed.

are now competing like pumas in a sack for king dollar or euro. New services – short-term apartment rentals, English menus, football tour guides – now abound, and a news article from 2005 declared that bilingual books aimed at tourists now make up around ten per cent of bookshops' stock.

Attitudes have also improved. Though the sight of a grinning foreigner devouring an enormous US$3 tenderloin steak is jarring to some penniless *porteños*, grudges are rarely held. Instead, as soon they can cobble together a few bills, many will go out and do the same. As any affable local will tell you, hard times are no excuse for staying at home.

Nor has the huge variety of round-the-clock cultural offerings suffered, maintaining BA's prestige as one of the world's great cultural capitals. If anything, the arts flourished during the crisis as a shell-shocked middle class clung tightly to the one thing it had left – intellectual stimulation. Theatre and film attendance has increased in recent years, and the *electrónica* dance music scene has exploded; the 2005 Creamfields festival – the city's fifth – attracted a record 60,000 revellers (Creamfields Liverpool has never exceeded 42,000). Over the past couple of years, the city's refreshingly excitable music fans have also welcomed a plethora of international DJs, plus rock and pop legends such as the Rolling Stones, U2, Franz Ferdinand, Robbie Williams and, er, Iron Maiden.

'As any local will tell you, hard times are no excuse for staying at home.'

At the same time, the crisis inspired creative expression among the city's young artists, eager to talk, write and sing about their new reality, often on a shoestring budget and for little or no pay. If in the past, folk-rock and theatre were the most politicised artistic expressions, these days it's tango, *cumbia* music (the local answer to gangsta rap) and cinema.

CRACKS IN THE GILDING

Of course, not all that glitters is gold. Post-crisis Buenos Aires, like post-surgery Maradona, has scars that are invisible to the casual observer.

One of these is the ever widening gap between rich and poor. It is still the case that 40 per cent of the population of Greater Buenos Aires lives below the poverty line – a fact made all the more disturbing when you consider the country's export crops could feed the population many times over. Few salaries have kept pace with the country's recent economic growth and the threat of high inflation – the price of butter is a serious political issue here – is genuine and ever present.

And once you've mulled over the disturbing statistics, you're left with the images. *Cartoneros* (collectors of cardboard and glass for recycling) are still an everyday spectacle; street kids (of which there are around 3,000 in the metropolis) hand out astrology cards for *'una moneda'* (small change) on the subways and trains; and every evening families arrive by the truck-load from the city's many *villas miserias* (shantytowns) to sift through the day's refuse.

'Opposition to US foreign policy is one of only two issues with the potential to unite the country's fractured political scene.'

Although the government has pitched in with a series of urban improvement schemes to help the 700,000 people living in *villas miserias*, and local NGOs have also grown in size and number, much of the task of coping with the socio-economic emergency has been managed at street level. In the wake of the 2001-02 crisis, and as much out of desperation as political conviction, *porteños* banded together to form a host of grassroots collectives which became the toast of the worldwide anti-globalisation movement. The united front, which was achieved at this time between the newly impoverished middle classes and the more-impoverished-than-ever working classes, has mainly dissipated, leaving behind a few fringe leftist parties and alternative media collectives to assail the IMF, foreign debt, and indeed the entire capitalist system.

These groups had their finest hour in November 2005, when George W Bush (mistrusted even by Argentinian conservatives) flew in for the Summit of the Americas. It was the catalyst for massive demonstrations in the capital and across the country. But this bucked the trend. As the prospering middle classes become less and less inclined to take their grievances out on to the streets, opposition to US foreign policy is one of only two issues with the potential to unite the country's fractured political scene. (The other is crime.)

Furthermore, it would be lazy and wrong to characterise the *porteño* populace as some kind of monolithic anti-US and anti-globalisation claque. Not everyone in the capital is anti-capitalist; neo-conservative millionaire (and Boca Juniors president) Mauricio Macri is one of BA's key political players. And many of those who extol the benefits of direct democracy still hold nothing but scorn for the *'piqueteros'*, the picket groups that invade the centre on an

Another day, another demo.

end to official impunity. He's also bargained hard with the IMF, securing an agreement at the beginning of 2005 which saw the lifting of Argentina's default status. As an encore, Kirchner decided to pay off the country's entire IMF loan at the start of 2006. While this now means that the country is independent from the IMF and its neo-liberal policies, some economists have expressed concern that Kirchner's move (not to mention his sacking of popular economy minister Roberto Lavagna shortly afterwards) has increased, not lessened, the country's instability, since higher interest is now being paid on the nation's non-IMF loans. As one of Argentina's biggest creditors is now Venezuela's Hugo Chávez, Kirchner's decision could be derided as a populist move designed to buy into anti-Washington popular opinion. But so far it has worked to Kirchner's advantage. After the move his approval rating reached the giddy heights of 80 per cent. (For more on Kirchner, *see p23* **Shock of the new**.)

THE LEGACY OF TRAGEDY

Elected in 2003, and a close ally of Kirchner, Buenos Aires' urbane mayor Aníbal Ibarra used to be that rarest of Argentinian birds: a popular politician. In line with national trends, he spent lavishly on labour-intensive public works like the extension of subway lines (line H is due to open in late 2006) and the sprucing up of major thoroughfares in the capital.

Ibarra's honeymoon came to an abrupt and tragic end on 30 December 2004, when a fire sparked by a firework claimed the lives of 194 people in the overcrowded República Cromagnon nightclub. The responsibility for enforcing safety regulations in the city's music venues rests with Ibarra and his officials. The controls in place were found to be woefully inadequate and made worse by a culture in which bribery is commonplace. After repeated calls by relatives of the victims for him to resign, Ibarra was suspended by the city legislature in November 2005 and forced to face an impeachment trial. With the city polarised over the issue of his culpability, Ibarra defended himself vigorously at public rallies, arguing that opposition parties were using the Cromagnon tragedy for their own, purely political ends. But on 7 March 2006, Ibarra was found guilty by the impeachment committee and forced out of office. (For more on the Cromagnon tragedy, *see p182*.)

THE ROAD AHEAD

In a sense, the challenges facing Argentina are the same as they have always been – only now it has to meet them without the benefit of the free-spending foreign investment and international prestige that ex-president Carlos Menem flaunted in the booming 1990s. It's also

almost daily basis from the poor outer suburbs, blocking traffic and decamping in the city's plazas. Their demands – and tactics – vary considerably, ranging from desperate pleas by impoverished mothers for basic sanitation, to the blockading of government ministries by masked, crowbar-wielding gangs.

Although the majority of protests are peaceful, violence does sporadically take place. Despite controversial support from some leftist parties, many regard the *piqueteros* as little better than common thugs and berate the authorities for their softly-softly approach towards policing such groups and their protests. The government, weighing the relative demerits of being seen as soft on crime and generating news footage of riot cops beating up demonstrators, has stuck to its passive policing strategy with some success.

OUT WITH THE OLD

The man who makes these decisions is President Néstor Kirchner. A barely known governor from Patagonia when elected, he's so far surprised sceptics by adeptly handling an irate public's demand for social justice and an

hamstrung by the loss of many of its best and brightest professionals, part of an invisible but unprecedented brain drain. An estimated 280,000 Argentinians have emigrated since 2000. Although queues outside foreign embassies for visas and passports have disappeared, and enterprising *porteños* – along with bargain-hunting foreigners – have returned to open businesses they could scarcely afford in Europe or the US, polls indicate that 20 per cent still want to leave, fed up with vicissitudes such as double-digit inflation and the huge disparity that has been caused by recovering property values – still cheap for outsiders but unmanageably expensive for most locals. Property prices in Buenos Aires rose by 20 per cent in 2005 and were expected to increase by the same percentage again in 2006. As glitzy real estate projects in Palermo and the dockside Madero Este development, or in the 'countries' (private, gated communities) outside the city limits offer enviable lifestyles to the monied few, much of Buenos Aires' sizable middle class – once the envy of South America – has free-fallen into the ranks of the so-called 'new poor'. For an immigrant country built on the promise of upward mobility, that's a bitter pill.

But while many *porteños* view the socio-economic problems as symptomatic of a country still dominated by corruption, others are feeling tentatively optimistic. By some accounts the events surrounding the economic crisis of 2001-02 were burned into the collective consciousness in a way that was comparable – in the eyes of locals – with the disorienting impact the terrorist attacks of 9/11 had in the US. In the intense soul-searching that followed, a number of taboos have been confronted. Perhaps the most important is the once widely held view that Argentina's problems can be solved though magic or a quick bit of *viveza criolla* (native Creole wit). In a fundamental psychological shift, proud *porteños*, who long considered themselves a satellite European state, now accept that their future, for good or ill, is tied to Latin America's.

Argentina, and specifically Buenos Aires, has been down this road before, only to see its illusion of a better future go up in smoke and tear gas. For now, it's still too early to tell whether the current ethical and economic reawakening will flourish into real and permanent change. In the meantime, this proud city, with its beautiful and vivacious citizens, its renowned architectural beauty, its world-class nightlife and culture and its kamikaze taxi drivers, maintains the charm and chutzpah that have always been its greatest assets.

There's only one certainty: like Maradona, Buenos Aires' heart has yet to give up the fight.

BA by numbers

39 million Population of Argentina in 2005.

12.3 million Population of metropolitan BA in 2005 (2.9 million in the capital).

12th BA's ranking in list of world's biggest cities in 2005.

142nd BA's ranking (out of 144) in list of world's most expensive cities.

4th BA's ranking in list of world's noisiest cities (Corrientes and Madero is the loudest street corner).

1:30 Ratio of psychoanalysts to population in Argentina.

1:100 Same ratio in developed nations.

20 Percentage of *porteños* who define themselves as 'unhappy'.

1 in 30 Number of Argentinians who have undergone plastic surgery since 1970.

1 in 10 Number of adolescent girls in Argentina suffering from an eating disorder.

40 Percentage of Argentinian population living below the poverty line in 2005.

41 Percentage of young Argentinians who say they would accept a bribe.

3 Number of presidents since 1914 to complete a full term and hand power to elected successor.

6 Number of Argentinian presidents since the 2001 crisis.

20 Percentage of Argentinians who are practising Roman Catholics.

15 Age of sexual consent in Argentina.

1986 Year that divorce became legal in Argentina.

2003 Year that same-sex civil union was legalised in Buenos Aires.

14,000 Number of left-wing dissidents 'disappeared' under military rule from 1976 to 1983 according to official reports.

30,000 Number of left-wing dissidents 'disappeared' according to most human rights groups.

1st Argentina's world ranking for soy meal and soy oil exports.

4th Argentina's world ranking for beef exports in 2004.

60kg Amount of beef consumed per year per capita in Argentina.

7th Argentina's world ranking for wine consumption.

92 Percentage of Argentinian households in which *mate* is drunk.

50,000 Estimated number of tangos composed (and counting).

20 Percentage of city streets still cobbled.

A polite round of applause from the **Boca Juniors** faithful at La Bombonera.

Football

Goooooooooooooooooooooooooooooooooaaaaaaaal!

It's been said that the *porteño* love of football is tantamount to a religion. Actually, it's much more important than that. In this secular capital of this increasingly secular country, you'll encounter more blind devotion and passionate intensity at a match than at a mass.

Keeping the faith is a serious commitment. The average José no more chooses his football club than he chooses the orientation of his belly button. Born a supporter of the family team, he or she is expected to hold true from cradle to grave, for better or for worse. It's a brave teenage River Plate supporter who approaches his father and says, 'Dad, I've got something to tell you: I think I may be a Boca fan.' In free and easy Buenos Aires, switching gender may be less traumatic than switching teams.

And probably less common. Pariah status awaits the *hincha* (fan) who swaps his team of perennial losers for one that may actually win something during his lifetime. Such a decision would smack of good sense and reason – all very well for Voltaire but deplorable qualities in a true footie fan. Loyalty, tribalism and, above all, raw, full-throated *pasión* – these are the values that drive Argentinian football culture.

THE HISTORY

Like most of Argentina's culture and heritage, football came down the gangplank. It was British sailors in the 1860s who first introduced the game here, their shore leave kickabouts on the city's dusty plazas attracting first the attention and then the participation of locals. By the end of the 19th century amateur clubs had been founded in and around the city, and the game began its inexorable rise from fringe pastime to national pursuit.

So speedy was this process that, in 1930, Argentina reached the final of the first World Cup, losing to hosts Uruguay. The *selección* (as the Argentinian national team is known) gave an early demonstration of the two contrasting elements which always seem to define their play: brilliant skill and murky controversy. Unable to agree on which type of ball to use for the match, it was decided that an Argentinian brand would be used in the first half and a Uruguayan one in the second. At half-time Argentina were leading 2–1; by the end they had lost 4–2. Still muttering darkly about 'rigged balls', Argentinian footballers turned professional the following year.

Achievement and notoriety would continue to bless/dog Argentinian football. In the famously ill-tempered quarter-final between Argentina and England in the 1966 World Cup, Alf Ramsey's 'wingless wonders' beat the South Americans 1–0. After Argentinian captain Antonio Rattin had been sent off for dissent, the match degenerated into a scrappy, dirty affair, and a rivalry was born that endures to this day.

Argentina finally got their hands on the World Cup trophy in 1978 when, playing on home turf, they beat the Netherlands 3–1. For the ruling military junta, it was a public relations coup to go with their military one of two years before. There were rumours that the Peruvian team was bribed to throw their group match against Argentina, allowing the latter to reach the final ahead of Brazil.

But 1986 in Mexico was a different ball game. The record states that Argentina won the World Cup by edging out West Germany 3–2 in the final. Far more memorable, however, was the quarter-final against England, illuminated by the divine talent and devilish opportunism of Diego Maradona. 'El Diez' (after his shirt number) scored one goal through pure skill – often cited as the best ever – and another through sheer cheek, knocking the ball past a floundering Peter Shilton with his hand – the infamous 'Hand of God' goal. It was sweet revenge for 1966; some – Maradona included – have also referred to the now legendary moment as payback for the Falklands/Malvinas debacle of 1982.

As for the 2002 finals in Japan and Korea, Argentinians would rather not talk about that. After the trauma of the country's greatest ever economic crisis, with poverty and unemployment at record levels, savings wiped out and crime on the rise, few believed that things could get any worse. They hadn't reckoned on the *selección* losing to England in the tournament's group stages.

THE TEAMS

Even soccerphobes know that BA is the milieu for one of world football's greatest rivalries: Boca Juniors versus River Plate. The teams are alike in two ways: they both originated in the southern port barrio of La Boca and they both hate each other's guts. Everything else is about contrast. River, founded in 1901, are based in the smart northern neighbourhood of Nuñez and tend to be the team of choice for affluent *porteños*. Their stadium, Estadio Monumental, was the venue for the 1978 World Cup Final. River fans are 'officially' known as '*millionarios*', reflecting the supposed socio-economic status of their fanbase; off the record they are known as '*gallinas*' (chickens). (To remind them of this, Boca fans are fond of showering their rivals with feathers during derby matches, or *super clásicos*. If they're lucky, that's all they get showered with.)

If River Plate are the aristocrats of the *porteño* football world, Boca Juniors are its ragged-trousered proles – and proud of it. A magnet for the poor, the dispossessed and well-to-do celebs desperate for 'roots', the club was founded in 1905 by a group of friends living in La Boca. At the time, this barrio was dominated by Italian immigrants hence the team's 'official' nickname '*xeneizes*', meaning Genovese. Their less affectionate sobriquet is '*bosteros*', which roughly translates as 'scum' and alludes to the proximity of their stadium, La Bombonera, to the whiffy Riachuelo river. River fans like to

River Plate's '*millionarios*' see red at the club's Estadio Monumental.

ram this point home by donning surgical masks during games between the two sides. Both teams, it is fair to say, revel in these class warfare undercurrents.

These tensions are played out, and fleetingly resolved, when the two teams meet on the field (and sometimes when they meet off it). A *super clásico* is freighted with a rawness and intensity almost unmatched in the football world (both teams come with a set of hardcore fans known as *barra brava*). No other events on the BA calendar are so eagerly anticipated – it would take a direct hit on the Obelisco from an asteroid to shift the *super clásico* from the following day's front pages. For many tourists it's one of the highlights of their trip (the first River-Boca game of 2006 attracted a record 4,000 foreigners) but you'll need to go with your wits about you. Arriving at least an hour before the game is recommended, and although the fans are kept separate both before and after the game, police control can be alarmingly cavalier. But once safely inside, the spectacle is theatre at its most participative and visceral.

Although the blue and yellow of Boca and the red and white of River dominate the city's soccer spectrum, there are several other important and well-supported teams in and around the capital. These include San Lorenzo, the romantic's choice, whose profile is boosted by the support of Marcelo Tinelli, Argentina's top TV presenter; Argentinos Jnrs, Diego Maradona's first professional team; Racing Club and Independiente, both based in the poor southern neighbourhood of Avallaneda, and who share a mutual loathing to rival that of Boca and River; and Chacarita, whose *barra brava* is to other hooligan gangs what the SAS is to the Boy Scouts.

THE TOURNAMENTS

All professional football in Argentina comes under the aegis of the Argentinian Football Association (AFA). They don't believe in giving the players much of an off-season. The only significant hiatus in top-flight action comes during the summer months of December and January when the Torneo de Verano (Summer Tournament) is held. This is a chance for the bigger clubs to give their second-string players a run out; nonetheless, the matches, held in resort cities like Mar del Plata, still attract big crowds.

For teams in the Primera División (first division), the rest of the year is divided into two discrete seasons: the Clausura (Closing) tournament, from the end of January to May; and the Apertura (Opening), from August to December. If you're wondering why the Closing tournament comes at the beginning of the year, take a deep breath and then forget about it.

The system of relegation and promotion is an even harder nut to crack. Teams move between divisions in accordance with their average points score over a three-year period. Thus it's theoretically possible to win the Primera and be relegated from it on the same day. Cynics (that is to say, everyone bar AFA) believe this system was introduced to make it virtually impossible for the bigger teams to be relegated.

Argentina's top teams also qualify to play in the Libertadores Cup against championship winners from all over South America. It usually takes place towards the beginning of the year, while the same teams can also qualify for the Sudamericana Cup, played in various stages during the latter half of the year.

THE PLAYERS

Nothing whets the appetite of the Argentinian sports fan more than the emergence of a new football star. The current darling of the back pages is Lionel Messi, the lank-haired, twinkle-toed centre forward whose partnership with Ronaldhino at Barcelona has been shredding defences on a weekly basis. Another rising star is Carlos Tévez, formerly of Boca Juniors but now playing with Brazil's Corinthians

Tévez aside, all of Argentina's top players ply their trade in Europe. When a young footballer – or more likely his agent – says 'show me the money', it's more likely to be Real Madrid flashing the greenbacks than River Plate. Interestingly, Argentinians don't seem to resent the fact that their idols play so far away from home. On the contrary, it's a source of national pride. In the same way that 19th-century Irish emigrants would proudly post money back their families after making it good, the Argentinian soccer diaspora rewards its home following with goals and multimillion dollar transfer rumours.

THE CULTURE

There are hardcore football fans everywhere, of course. What sets BA apart is the sheer volume of soccer lore in the cultural mainstream and the way it impacts on *porteños*' everyday lives.

For example, think of your favourite newsreader. Do you know which football team he or she cheers for? *Porteños* do. They also know the soccer preferences of the weather reporter, the continuity announcer and, probably, the key grip. Critics of President Kirchner have been known to take the line: What do you expect from a Racing fan?

Even Argentinians who don't like football (they exist) aren't immune from the lure of tribalism. 'I hate football – but I'm Boca' is a common remark. In all likelihood this has never been said about Queen's Park Rangers.

Shock of the new
Diego Armando Maradona

'Inside every fat man, they say, there is a thin man trying to get out. In the case of Diego Maradona, it seems, there is an even fatter man trying to get in.' So wrote Martin Amis in 2004, in the UK's *Guardian* newspaper.

These are the words of an Englishman. But for most Argentinians, *El Diez es Dios* (Number Ten is God), and for decades now, they have worshipped at the Diego Maradona altar. Fanatic fervour has even spawned a Maradonian church, with the congregation celebrating their 'Christmas' on 30 October, Diego's birthday.

But even his legions of faithful followers couldn't have predicted Maradona's miraculous resurrection after his brush with death in 2004. While the famous hand that knocked in a goal during the 1986 World Cup may well be divine, the rest of the body was revealed as all too human. Weakened by chronic health problems, a bloated Maradona was rushed to a BA hospital in April 2004 where he was treated in intensive care for respiratory failure. His disciples, too, held their breath.

But El Diez was not ready to say die. A mere 18 months afterwards, a slimmed down, still smiling and ever beloved Diego launched his own talk show on Argentinian TV, *La Noche del Diez*. David Letterman won't have lost any sleep over it, but the programme was the biggest ratings success of the season.

Diego's legendary feet, which danced around so many English defenders in 1986 to score what has since been voted the goal of the century, were also seen that year tripping across a ballroom floor in the Italian TV show *Dancing with the Stars*. Added to all this showbiz glamour was Maradona's growing political agenda. He spoke at a mass Bush-baiting rally in the coastal town of Mar del Plata in 2005 to repudiate a visit by the US president.

He's also recently been the subject of a number of idealising documentaries, including *Amando a Maradona* (Loving Maradona), which received a cinema release in 2005. It told the familiar tale of a loveable, occasionally misunderstood genius conquering poverty and disease – and audiences loved it. The curly-haired icon also inspired a successful musical, and has appeared on advertising billboards across the city, proving that marketing execs are also aware of just how far the gospel according to Maradona can spread.

It seems, in the battle of the bulge, the thin man has vanquished his demons and the god of Argentinian football has emerged into the limelight once more. Looking at the slim, boundlessly energetic and gloriously omnipresent Diego Maradona, Amis must, if you'll forgive the pun, be eating his words.

For others, football is an addiction, and the media their daily fix. Such fans can't pass a news-stand without picking up a copy of daily sports paper *Olé*. They will sit on buses with an old radio clamped to their ear listening to match commentary. They will watch European league matches – the English Premiership is particularly popular – on the Fox and ESPN cable sports channels, and tune in to *La Última Palabra*, a nightly football talk show in which coiffured pundits chew over the day's gossip with a gravitas usually reserved for emergency sessions of the UN Security Council.

And every four years, BA's rival tribes call a temporary truce and cheer on the national side. In the two months prior to the 2006 tournament, high street stores reported a tenfold increase in sales of plasma TVs, which retail for upwards of AR\$6,0000. The average monthly wage in Buenos Aires is AR\$800. Work that one out.

Literary BA

Read all about it.

Books are everywhere in Buenos Aires: in the city's many bookshops, on market stalls, in the hands of the guy sitting beside you on the Subte. It's a city of printing presses and publishing houses, of literary circles and public readings, of poets scribbling over their *cortado* coffees, of mouldering editions of Kafka's *Collected Stories* on downtown news-stands next to this month's issue of *Horny Housewives*. An old adage has it that there are more writers than people in Buenos Aires, and in a city where everyone has something to say, it's no surprise that much of it has found its way into print.

There are just a handful of world-renowned authors working from the Argentinian capital these days; but then again, there is no Latin American literary boom like that of the 1960s. Yet new authors emerge all the time, penning novels, books on Argentinian identity, self-help manuals and short stories, the latter a genre Argentinian writers have all but made their own.

But you can get into the city's seminal texts, whatever your chosen genre. The earliest works were letters and travelogues. Ulderico Schmidt (1525-81), a sailor on Pedro de Mendoza's landmark 1536 voyage penned the first accounts of 'a new town… Bonas Aeres, that is, in German, Guter Wind'. Since then, travellers have been regular contributors to the foreign idea of what Buenos Aires and Argentina mean, with Charles Darwin, Graham Greene, VS Naipaul,

Bruce Chatwin and Paul Theroux passing through. But it is in the homespun poems, plays and narratives that a vividly colourful and far more complex story is to be found.

OLD MASTERS

Three authors in particular are considered to have laid Argentina's literary foundations. The first is José Hernández, who wrote *Martín Fierro* (1872), an epic poem about a persecuted *gaucho* which was the culmination of a 19th-century tradition of *gauchesco* writing. The second, Esteban Echeverría (1805-51), was the refined author of long Romantic poem *La Cautiva*, the blood-soaked short story, *The Slaughterhouse* – titles are given here in English where translations are widely available – and other books with rural settings that were strongly critical of authoritarian regimes. The third is Domingo Faustino Sarmiento (1811-88), writer, educationalist and Argentinian president. His wrote *Facundo*, widely considered to be the first Argentinian novel but more like a political treatise dressed up as fiction.

The 1880s are famous for producing a generation of authors who stressed the European texture of the capital. Miguel Cané's stories and Pedro Bonifacio Palacios aka Almafuerte's lyrical poetry respond to the first waves of immigration and the growth of Buenos Aires from a backwater into the 'Gran Aldea' (Grand Village). But it was Nicaraguan modernist Rubén Darío and Argentinian Leopoldo Lugones who introduced Symbolism and Spanish *modernismo* to *porteño* readers, preparing the way for the emergence of local movements such as *criollismo* and *simplismo*, both celebrations of the popular.

During the 1920s, a group of writers that included Jorge Luis Borges published a magazine called *Martín Fierro* which explored the poetic and critical potential of a native Argentinian cultural ideal. Borges was part of the so-called 'Florida Set' (named for the famous pedestrianised street in downtown BA) which defended the cultured and refined – in other words, the European – strain of Latin American literature against the purely folksy and parochial. The group also included Leopoldo Marechal, author of the vast, *Ulysses*-like novel, *Adán Buenosayres*, and poet Oliverio Girondo, author of *Veinte poemas para ser leídos en el tranvía*. More left-leaning writers, such as Leonidas Barletta and Elias Castelnuovo, took part in the Boedo gatherings – named after a humdrum street in southside Buenos Aires.

Standing apart was Roberto Arlt (1900-42), journalist and highly original author of *The Seven Madmen*, about the efforts of a marginal group of conspirators to organise an anarchist revolution. A *porteño* to his bones, Arlt – like his inspiration, Dostoevsky – was a tormented soul, whose complex and explosive style was considered clumsy by some critics. But his works have stood the test of time: they reveal a period marked by the downfall of a supposedly harmonious world and the birth of a chaotic and violent era.

MODERN MASTERS

Jorge Luis Borges (1899-1986) and Julio Cortázar (1914-84) are the two giants of Argentinian literature, known throughout the world for their complex portrayals of Buenos Aires and its inhabitants. The first went blind and the second exiled himself to Paris, yet both recounted the mysteries of the city better than any of their contemporaries. Utterly distinct in tone, vision and ideology, Borges and Cortázar are the two mainstream masters of prose (*see p33* **War of the words**).

Borges is considered one of the greatest writers of the 20th century, and despite his apparent nonchalance about the subject, most people are surprised to discover he was never awarded the Nobel Prize for Literature. (It is widely assumed that the Nobel committee's snub was based on political – Borges was a known reactionary – rather than critical grounds.) He was a prolific writer of poetry,

fiction and non-fiction. Not only have the vast majority of his writings been widely translated, but Borges himself was a professor of English literature in BA, and considered the best Spanish translator of works by Walt Whitman and Virginia Woolf.

Cortázar caused an upheaval in the literary world with his highly intelligent, imaginative style, known as *lo fantástico* (a precursor of what is now called magical realism), where the borders between the ordinary and the unreal are blurred. His most famous novel, *Hopscotch*, is a milestone in contemporary storytelling.

The pantheon of 20th-century *porteño* writers includes Adolfo Bioy Casares (1914-99), whose most celebrated work was *The Invention of Morel*. Bioy Casares was Borges' close friend and literary accomplice – they sometimes wrote under the joint pseudonym Bustos Domecq. His wife, the aristocratic Silvina Ocampo (1909-1993), wrote short stories and poems. Silvina's sister, Victoria Ocampo, a less accomplished writer than her sibling, was the founder of the magazine *Sur*, the most significant periodical in Argentinian letters; it was published regularly from 1931 until 1970.

Such were the range and ambition of their lyrics, major tango poets like Homero Manzi, Enrique Cadícamo and Enrique Santos Discépolo should also be included in a list of literary luminaries from Buenos Aires' belle époque. If the dance hall scene was a popular, low-brow affair at the beginning, both Borges and Cortázar would attempt to compose tangos during their careers – and neither could match the skilful economy of Manzi's 'Sur' or the sardonic bite of Discépolo's 'Cambalache'.

Manuel Puig (1932-90), along with Borges and Cortázar, is one of the Argentinian authors most widely translated into English. His 1976 novel, *The Kiss of the Spider Woman* – a dialogue between a Marxist and an apolitical homosexual in a South American prison – was turned into an Oscar-winning Hollywood movie in 1985, and is the reason most visitors will have heard of him, even if they don't realise he's Argentinian. Puig was born in a remote town in BA province, but his acclaimed detective novel, *The Buenos Aires Affair*, attests to the effect the city had on his work.

The surviving giant is Ernesto Sábato. The multi-prize-winning 92-year-old author of the ambitious novel *On Heroes and Tombs* is the best-known and respected living Argentinian writer. His publications range from dictionaries of philosophical aphorisms, through literary criticism, to *Never Again*, the definitive account of the tortures and murder perpetrated by the 1976-83 dictatorship. But it is an existentialist novella after the French school, *The Tunnel*,

War of the words

A national icon up there with Evita and Maradona, Jorge Luis Borges (1899-1986) is also the only Argentinian author to have found fame outside his own country. The American publication of *Labyrinths*, a collection of his short stories, in 1964, turned him almost overnight into a literary superstar.

Critics and, more particularly, fellow writers lavished praise on the sheer torrent of invention and playfulness that characterise his enigmatic '*ficciones*'. They also admired his championing of erudition and austerity in a land of populist demagogues and strutting sensualists.

Like all prophets, however, Borges is less popular in his home town. Many Argentinian critics regard his conundrum-ridden stories as pseudo-philosophical exercises in pedantry, and find his Anglophilia repellent. In 1999, to coincide with the centenary of the author's birth, a group of leading scholars published *Anti-Borges*, a collection of essays attacking Borges' life, politics, works and (in their view) exaggerated eminence in international letters.

At the other end of the political and fashion spectrum is a writer who, while barely known in Europe or anywhere else, enjoys runner-up status in Argentina's literary pantheon: Julio Cortázar (1914-1984). A left-wing, bearded, cigarette-smoking Francophone, he remains the idol of young university students of both sexes and the perfect cult hero for those who loathe Borges. Whereas the old gent was proudly apolitical, the young rebel openly supported the Cuban Revolution. Whereas Borges crafted short, elegant prose collections like *El Aleph*, Córtazar made his name with the hefty experimental novel *Hopscotch* and genre-busting books such as *Historias de cronopios y de famas*.

That Cortázar was born in Brussels and spent his last 30 years living in Paris matters little to the fans. He was a cool man of action in exile – far better than a lacklustre librarian at home.

Yet on the eve of the so-called Latin American literary boom of the 1960s, Borges was an inspiration to many of the writers who would go on to become world-famous. Cortázar was no different from Gabriel García Márquez, Carlos Fuentes and Mario Vargas Llosa in regarding Borges as a revolutionary role model – in literary terms at least.

In fact, Argentina's two literary giants had much in common. Both men hated Evita Perón. Both men were top-notch translators and internationalists. And, interestingly enough, it was Borges who first published one of Cortázar's stories in a magazine called *Los anales de Buenos Aires*.

So what exactly lies at the bottom of the Borges-Cortázar opposition? In fact it is just another of the many cultural dichotomies within BA. There are opposing camps who follow the Beatles and the Rolling Stones, Ford buyers who refuse even to be driven in a Chevrolet, hippies who beat up metalheads and punks, and *chetos* (middle-class snobs) who hate both *grasas* (wealthy slimeballs) and *cumbieros* (working-class slimeballs). Basically, *porteños* like factionalism; and the intellectuals are no different. It may simply come down to having no such rivalry in the political arena, and an empty, celebrity-obsessed mass media in which even pop stars and actors are all someone's nephew or boyfriend. It may also be that most people have never actually read Borges or Cortázar beyond the extracts they are compelled to decipher at school.

Everything else aside, the two writers have at least left their mark on BA's geography. The city now boasts a calle Jorge Luis Borges and a Plazoleta Cortázar – which just happen to intersect in the heart of ultra-fashionable Palermo Viejo.

published in 1948, which features on every school and college reading list – its spare prose unfurls into a dark, psychological thriller about jealousy, obsession and urban alienation.

Argentina's military dictatorship silenced some of the key voices during a time when many of the country's intellectuals were hunted down by a repressive regime. One of those whose defiant writings had him tracked down and killed was Rodolfo Walsh, an author of detective fiction, and the man who penned one of the country's most celebrated short stories, *That Woman*, a story about one of the military officers behind the disappearance of Eva Perón's body during Argentina's first military dictatorship.

CONTEMPORARY CONTENDERS

There is also a whole set of young and not-so-young writers, who together describe a very different city to that visualised and dreamed of by many of the above. Children of the military dictatorship, they reflect the authoritarian past and the ideological transformations of the city, not merely the physical changes. They harbour no nostalgia for the era of tango, and are more cynical, using acidic and corrosive humour. One such exponent is Ricardo Piglia (born 1940). His works include the critically acclaimed *Artificial Respiration* and, more recently, *Money to Burn*, which won the 1998 Premio Planeta – an important national literary prize. The film adaptation was a big hit in 2000.

Many of the outstanding writers of the 1970s have been greatly influenced by rock culture and postmodern cultural trends. Some remain faithful to the traditions of their predecessors, while others question the idea of literature as storytelling and lean more towards fragmentation and the combination of different styles. Exemplars of this school are writers/journalists Rodrigo Fresán, Juan Forn and Carlos Gamerro.

A bright new star is Federico Andahazi (born 1963), whose 1997 novel *The Anatomist*, about the discovery of the clitoris, was well received by critics and readers (although a prize awarded was then snatched away due to the book's erotic content). Since then he has published *Merciful Women* and *El secreto de los flamencos*, highly readable novels which, like *The Anatomist*, are set in the European past.

Other names to watch out for when browsing through the bookshops are José Luis Saer, Antonio Di Benedetto, and Tucumán-born Tomás Eloy Martínez, author of bestsellers *Santa Evita* and *The Perón Novel*. The same author has also produced a 'national identity' book, *Requiem para un país perdido* (Requiem for a lost country). This is part of a general boom in journalistic, political and philosophical essays

(as writers seek to rework a genre forged by Sarmiento in *Facundo*). For a long time, Argentina viewed itself critically as *un país sin memoria* (a country without memory), and the popularity of this genre reflects a desire to recover the country's lost political and social collective memory. Journalists like Jorge Lanata and José Pablo Feinmann are authoritative commentators on the excesses of the 1990s (the era of ex-president Carlos Menem) and Martín Caparrós is one of several left-leaning authors exploring the legacy of the military dictatorship.

If the novel has never quite attained the exalted status it enjoys in Europe and the US – and the 19th-century-style 'generational novel' is notably absent from the back catalogue – wonderful poems, essays and short prose works reflecting the frenzied, fragmentary character of contemporary life in Argentina enjoy wide appeal. Squeezed into these small spaces are an enthusiasm for experiment and edgy themes galore – whether exploring the Buenos Aires backstreets, bars, genteel mannerisms or genitalia, there's a text to take you through the multiple layers of meaning.

LITERARY EVENTS

Many visitors are struck by the number of bookshops in the city. The grander ones, especially Gandhi (*see p151*) and the Ateneo (*see p149*), also organise literary gatherings and are a good source of information on readings. For more details, check the 'Cultura' and 'Espectáculos' sections of daily newspapers. Admission to readings is usually free, although in bars you may have to buy at least one drink. Buenos Aires is also recognised as a great place to pick up antiquarian books at competitive prices. No self-respecting BA bookworm misses April's Feria del Libro (*see p171*); it regularly pulls a million visitors and, over the years, celebrated authors such as Isabel Allende, Paul Auster and Doris Lessing. There is a popular Children's Book Fair in July/August too.

Argentina is one of the strongest publishing markets in the Spanish-speaking world. But though book sales remain encouragingly high, many bookshops have been forced to close due to a drop in real income following the 2002 currency devaluation. The weak peso has also affected production costs, forcing up the retail price.

One new project to emerge from the post-2002 social and political crisis is the Eloisa Cartonera imprint (www.eloisacartonera. com.ar). A number of respected authors are participating in this venture, which publishes short works inside covers made from the waste cardboard collected by *cartoneros* (paper collectors) on the city streets.

Where to Stay

Features

KNOWING THAT YOU 'L
BE WILLING TO COME BAC
EVEN BEFORE YOU WAL
OUT THE DOOR

SOFITEL BUENOS AIRES

SOFITEL BUENOS AIRES Located on the elegant Arroyo Street, in
the neighbourhood of Retiro, The Bencihc Tower is surrounded by the most
exclusive art galleries and antique shops of the city. This neoclassical building
is the perfect match between contemporary design and traditional Art Decó. A
typical Café from the heart of Buenos Aires and Le Sud, a French restaurant with
authentic Mediterranean cuisine, complement themselves inside the building.

Arroyo 841 - Buenos Aires - Argentina - Tel.: 54 (11) 4131 0000
Fax: 54 (11) 4131 0001 - www.sofitel.com

SOFITEL
ACCOR HOTELS & RESORTS

The Leading Hotels of the World

Where to Stay

They've made your bed – now lie in it.

Invigorated by the recent tourist boom, hotel development is currently one of the key sectors driving the *porteño* economy. Foreign capital is pouring in and, for the most part, being invested wisely, uniting international savvy, local design creativity and the Argentinian genius for hospitality. Throw in the devalued peso and, most crucially of all, BA's allure as a holiday and conference destination, and you can see why that drab word 'accommodation' has a newly glamorous, not to say profitable, ring to it.

Every kind of lodging you can imagine – as well as some you'd probably never want to – is now available in BA, from converted convents (**1555 Malabia House**) and upmarket tango schools (**Mansion Dandi Royal**) to gay guesthouses (**Bayres B&B**; *see p195*). Mid-range hotels have been spruced up and, though dull four-star properties aimed at domestic business visitors remain, there are now some great value hotels in this sector. A hostel boom has also multiplied choices for budget travellers.

The most discernible trend is for recycling classic – and hitherto legally protected – structures, a process epitomised by French wunderkind designer Philippe Starck's **Faena Hotel + Universe**, whose postmodern opulence shelters coyly behind the austere red brickwork of the century-old 'El Porteño' grain silo. The latest stately pile from BA's golden age to receive the architectural kiss of life is the **Palacio Duhau** building on Avenida Alvear, soon to be a new Hyatt hotel thanks to a US$65 million investment. (It's expected to open in late 2006). Not to be outdone, the city's best-known and most exclusive crash pad, the **Hotel Alvear**, has treated itself to US$3 million worth of structural nip and tuck. As Argentinians are fond of saying when commenting on the construction boom: 'Buenos Aires will be beautiful when it's finished.'

The corporate Microcentro and leafy Recoleta are traditionally the most popular accommodation areas owing to their proximity to shops and monuments. The Microcentro has obvious advantages for business travellers, but noise and traffic may be a problem once the city rolls into gear at 8am. Outside of the five-star circuit many of the best options are to the north in hip Palermo Viejo, where a number of funky guesthouses and boutique hotels such as **Bo Bo** and **Home** are wowing fashion-conscious travellers. Far removed in terms of price and glamour, the *barrios* of Constitución and Barracas have dirt-cheap lodging, though most of it is aimed at poor immigrant families.

Geographically and demographically at the other end of the spectrum, BA's northern suburbs are starting to attract tourists keen to stay in the smart suburbs and commute in for sightseeing. The 19th-century **Hotel del Casco** (Avenida del Libertador 16170, 4723 3993, www.hoteldelcasco.com, double room US$135) in San Isidro offers modern comforts in a historic

The best Hotels

For rooms with a view
The **Sheraton** (*see p45*) and **Hotel Plaza Francia** (*see p51*) will take you higher.

For business as usual
The **NH Jousten** (*see p43*) and the **Intercontinental** (*see p43*) are classy corporate acts.

For rock stars and royalty
Just don't throw the telly through the window at the **Faena Hotel + Universe** (*see p57*) and the **Four Seasons** (*see p49*).

For taking a dip
The **Hilton Buenos Aires** (*see p57*) has the city's best hotel pool.

For a warm welcome
Make yourself at home at **1555 Malabia House** (*see p55*) and **La Otra Orilla** (*see p57*).

For a total tango immersion
Slap on the Brylcreem at the **Mansión Dandi Royal** (*see p47*).

For the cutting-edge crew
Hang with the in-crowd at **Home Hotel** (*see p55*) and **Bo Bo Hotel** (*see p53*).

For the old-school gang
Bring your pipe and slippers to the **Claridge** (*see p39*) and the **Marriott Plaza** (*see p39*).

house, while **Patio Inn** (Labardén 466, 4743 2981, www.patioinn.com.ar, double room US$50-$70) is a delightful three-bedroomed guest house close to Acasusso train station.

PRICES, BOOKINGS AND SERVICES

Our listings follow the following categories: **Luxury** (over US$250 – around AR$750 – for a double); **Expensive** (US$100-$250/AR$300-$750); **Moderate** (US$60-$100/AR$180-$300); **Budget** (under US$60/AR$180); and **Hostels**. To avoid confusion, we have listed all rates in US dollars – the rate of exchange is relatively stable at three Argentinian pesos to the dollar. Prices given in this chapter include VAT (here called IVA, a whopping 21 per cent) and breakfast – but always check what is included when booking. Youth hostels are listed together at the end of the chapter. For rental options, *see p41.*

> ❶ Green numbers given in this chapter correspond to the location of each hotel as marked on the street maps.
> *See pp276-285.*

The Centre

Luxury

Marriott Plaza Hotel

Florida 1005, Retiro (4318 3069/www.marriottplaza. com.ar). Subte C, San Martín/93, 130, 152 bus. **Rates** US$250-$300 single/double; US$340-$400 suite. **Credit** AmEx, DC, MC, V. **Map** p281 G11 ❶
For almost 100 years, this regal hotel (taken over by Marriott in 1994) overlooking the verdant Plaza San Martín has provided a white-gloved service fit for royalty. Guests have a choice of three sumptuous restaurants, including the Plaza Hotel Grill with its Dutch porcelain tiles and fabulous open grill. Cascading chandeliers light the ballrooms and corridors, and the rooms are, as you would expect, top-notch (ask for one with a view of the Plaza). The sophisticated and award-winning bar is open to the public, and a small pool overlooks the plaza.
Bar. Business centre. Concierge. Disabled-adapted rooms. Gym. Internet (high-speed, wireless). No-smoking rooms/floors. Parking. Pool (outdoor). Restaurants (3). Room service. TV (cable/DVD).

Panamericano Hotel & Resort

Carlos Pellegrini 551, Microcentro (4348 5000/ www.panamericanobuenosaires.com). Subte B, Carlos Pellegrini or D, 9 de Julio/24, 59, 67 bus. **Rates** US$260-$280 single/double; US$340-$400 suite. **Credit** AmEx, DC, MC, V. **Map** p281 G10 ❷
The two imposing towers of the large, deluxe Panamericano sit bang opposite the Obelisco. A recent renovation has brought the elder of the two towers up to standard. But it's the additional services that

give the hotel an edge: haute cuisine in Tomo I restaurant (*see p111*); and Nivel 23, the rooftop swimming pool and spa, with its tropical fruits buffet, sushi bar, sun loungers and mind-blowing views. Each of the rooms in the hotel is fitted with double glazing, so you can look at Avenida 9 de Julio without having to listen to it.
Bars (2). Business centre. Concierge. Disabled-adapted rooms. Gym. Internet (high-speed, wireless). No-smoking rooms/floors. Parking. Pool (indoor). Restaurants (2). Room service. Spa. TV (cable/DVD).

Sofitel Buenos Aires

Arroyo 841, Retiro (4131 0000/www.sofitelbuenos aires.com.ar). Bus 92, 93, 152. **Rates** US$250-$320 double; US$450-$550 suite. **Credit** AmEx, DC, MC, V. **Map** p281 H12 ❸
Housed in the flawlessly restored Torre Bencich (an art deco tower built in the 1920s), the Sofitel was opened in 2003 by French hotel group Accor. The impressive glass-roofed lobby with its black-and-white floor and huge chandelier sets the tone. Rooms are quite small, though the upper floors offer views of the river, and furnishings have a French twist. The district around the hotel has a similarly Parisian vibe, replete with smart cafés and hidden art galleries. But you may prefer to eat in: the hotel has a superb French restaurant called Le Sud.
Bar. Business centre. Concierge. Disabled-adapted rooms. Gym. Internet (high-speed, wireless). No-smoking rooms/floors. Parking. Restaurant. Room service. TV (cable/music/DVD).

Expensive

Claridge

Tucumán 535, Microcentro (4314 7700/www. claridge.com.ar). Subte B, Florida/93, 130, 152 bus. **Rates** US$150-$170 single/double. **Credit** AmEx, DC, MC, V. **Map** p281 F11 ❹

Sofitel Buenos Aires: art deco heaven.

A place to call home

If you're planning to stay in BA for a week or more, why not rent an apartment? The process is slightly more laborious than booking a hotel room, but world free of obsequious concierges, overpriced minibars and the palpitations caused from smuggling newly made friends into your room is worth its weight in paperwork.

Prices in the rental sector have increased since the bargain days of 2002, but there are still plenty of good deals out there. The best apartments are in the Palermo and Recoleta neighbourhoods, though San Telmo is snapping at their heels. Properties are available to tourists on a daily, weekly or monthly basis; many are equipped with terrace, barbecue, fully fitted kitchen and weekly maid service.

There are now a huge number of agencies offering short-term rentals. While some are well established, others are in the fly-by-night category, so be sure to shop around. **ByT Argentina** (www.bytargentina.com) has a strong reputation, offering budget and luxury apartments (expect to pay from US$150 to US$400 per week) in various neighbourhoods. **Rent Argentina** (www.rent-argentina.com) also offers premium accommodation all over Buenos Aires for stays of up to six months. **Alojargentina** (www.alojargentina.com.ar) has several hundred fully furnished apartments, also with a good geographical spread. They will relieve you of around US$400 per week for a two-bedroom loft in Palermo Viejo and slightly more for a similar property in upscale Recoleta. For a more immersive – and

considerably cheaper – experience, they can hook you up with host families; expect to pay from around US$350 per month.

The 'ethical traveller', or those simply looking for a good deal, should check out **Ojo** (www.ojopropiedades.com), an estate agency which claims to donate all its profits to the Red Cross and – somewhat ironically – the homeless. If you're looking for luxury, **Apartments BA** (www.apartmentsba.com) is a well-regarded company, offering clients the freedom of an apartment rental combined with the added-value services of a five-star hotel. All properties come with concierge service, high-speed internet access and designer furniture. Expect to pay from US$50 per night for a one-bedroom loft apartment, rising to around US$400 according to size and location. Also look out for **Ayres de Recoleta** (www.ayresderecoleta.com), a designer complex with outdoor swimming pool, barbecue area and fitness centre. You can rent one of 38 studios for around US$700 per month.

For those with spare cash or the urge to swap their bedsit in central London for a mansion in San Telmo, the temptation to buy is huge. But be on your guard: red tape is tangled, the jargon complicated and there are plenty of sharks around. **Maison Buenos Aires** (15 5753 0419, www.maison buenosaires.com), a new company with a growing reputation, offers an advisory and management service for would-be property buyers. They will help you close the deal and hook you up with a decent law firm and notary public. For a more traditional estate agent, try **JR Reynolds** (www.homes.com.ar).

Close to the business and banking district, and a few steps from some of the city's main tourist attractions, stands the Claridge Hotel. Decorated throughout in either mock-Tudor or classic-style design, the hotel offers 161 renovated rooms (though bear in mind that some are considerably smaller than they look on the hotel's website). The amenities shine: the health centre has an outdoor heated swimming pool, sauna, massage parlour and gym. Business travellers will enjoy the spacious meeting rooms, equipped with state-of-the-art technology – though most deals will be cut in the piano bar over cocktails and under the doleful gaze of the wall-mounted moose head. Check the website for special promotions.
Bar. Business centre. Concierge. Disabled-adapted rooms. Gym. No-smoking rooms/floors. Parking. Pool (outdoor). Restaurants (2). Room service. Spa. TV (cable/DVD).

Dazzler Tower

San Martín 920, Retiro (5256 7700/www.dazzlertower. com). Subte C, San Martín/93, 130, 152 bus.
Rates US$160-$175 single/double; US$210-$230 suite.
Credit AmEx, DC, MC, V. **Map** p281 G11 ⑤
Opened by Argentina's Fën Group in March 2005, the Dazzler Tower is in a superb location, just two blocks from Plaza San Martín. The sleekly designed, spacious but warm lobby leads to 11 floors of under-stated and stylishly furnished rooms, all of which are soundproofed and broadband connected – the ones on floors nine to 11 have views across the River Plate. Suites come with jacuzzi; but for a little extra pampering try a holistic massage at the hotel spa.
Bar. Business centre. Concierge. Disabled-adapted rooms. Gym. Internet (high-speed). No-smoking rooms/floors. Parking. Pool (indoor). Restaurant. Spa. TV (cable).

Home Hotel Buenos Aires. *See p55.*

Esplendor de Buenos Aires

*San Martín 780, Microcentro (5217 5710/
www.esplendorhotel.com.ar). Subte B, Florida/93,
130, 152 bus.* **Rates** US$145-$150 single/double;
US$210-$230 suite. **Credit** AmEx, DC, MC, V.
Map p281 G11 ❻
The resplendent Esplendor wears its glistening
Italianate façade on the intersection of Avenidas San
Martin and Córdoba. Built in the 1900s as Hotel
Phoenix, it was the first roof over the heads of many
hopeful immigrants in the days when boats moored
close to Avenida Córdoba. Monumental five-metre-
high (16-foot) ceilings, a total floor space of 4,000
square metres (13,100 square feet), and room doors
seemingly as tall as skyscrapers all give it a fairytale
aura, and every century-old window door has been
restored to its former rust-free glory. While the
downtown location is convenient, it means that
street noise can be a problem on weekdays.
*Bar. Business centre. Concierge. Disabled-adapted
rooms. Gym. Internet (high-speed). No-smoking
rooms/floors. Restaurant. Room service. TV (cable).*

Grand Boulevard Hotel

*Bernardo de Irigoyen 432, Monserrat (0800 444
2685/www.grandboulevardhotel.com). Subte C,
Moreno/67, 98, 195 bus.* **Rates** US$110-$160
single/double; US$185 suite. **Credit** AmEx, DC, MC,
V. **Map** p281 E9 ❼
The Grand Boulevard is a great value hotel, suited
to tourists and business travellers alike. A wide
range of rooms is offered, including standard rooms,
suites, executive suites with meeting room, and
three-room family apartments. The hotel's amenities
include conference rooms, fitness centre and a travel
agency. The ironically named Petite Rue restaurant
has bay windows looking out on to Avenida 9 de
Julio, the world's widest boulevard. Perhaps the
best feature of the hotel, however, is the service,
which is friendly, personalised and attentive.
*Bar. Business centre. Concierge. Gym. Internet
(high-speed, wireless). No-smoking rooms. Parking.
Restaurant. Room service. TV (cable/music).*

Hotel Emperador

*Avenida del Libertador 420, Retiro (4131 4000/
www.hotelemperador.com.ar). Subte C, San Martín/
93, 152 bus.* **Rates** US$190-$210 single/double;
US$220-$300 suite. **Credit** AmEx, DC, MC, V.
Map p281 H12 ❽
At the heart of Retiro's art gallery district, and
minutes from Avenida 9 de Julio, the Emperador,
like its Madrid namesake, fuses classic design with
state-of-the-art technology. All rooms are king sized
– room size starts at 45 square metres (145 square
feet) – and come with either panoramic vistas of the
River Plate or intimate views of the hotel's private
garden. All rooms boast handcrafted furnishings,
including superbly equipped work stations hand-
made in Valencia from African hardwoods.
*Bar. Business centre. Concierge. Disabled-adapted
rooms. Gym. Internet (high-speed). No-smoking
rooms/floors. Parking. Pool (indoor). Restaurant.
Room service. TV (cable/DVD).*

Intercontinental

*Moreno 809, Monserrat (4340 7100/www.inter
continental.com). Subte C, Moreno/45, 86, 100 bus.*
Rates US$200-$230 single/double; US$400 suite.
Credit AmEx, DC, MC, V. **Map** p281 E10 ❾
The Intercontinental goes further than most to
justify its five-star rating. The lavish interior design,
with leather, wood and marble predominating, is
accompanied by outstanding service and facilities.
The hotel is ideal for the business traveller, with
three meeting rooms, bilingual assistance and top-
notch audio-visual equipment. The only problem for
workers could be the irresistible pull of the indoor
heated pool, sun deck and health club. Football fans
should note that the Boca Juniors team stay here
when preparing for a match.
*Bar. Business centre. Concierge. Disabled-adapted
rooms. Gym. Internet (high-speed, wireless). No-
smoking rooms/floors. Parking. Pool (indoor).
Restaurant. Room service. TV (cable/DVD).*

NH Jousten

*Avenida Corrientes 280, Microcentro (4321
6750/www.nh-hoteles.com). Subte B, LN Alem/26,
93, 99, 152 bus.* **Rates** US$120-$150 single/double;
US$170-$260 suite. **Credit** AmEx, DC, MC, V.
Map p281 F11 ❿
Built in 1928, the Jousten oozes style, its stunning
façade sheltering a neo-Hispanic interior. During its
illustrious years, Argentinian icons like boxer Carlos
Monzón, President Hipólito Yrigoyen and Juan and
Evita Perón slipped through its imposing doors. It
then lost its lustre, shutting for over 20 years before
NH invested US$10 million in a revamp. The results
are magnificent – the Jousten has become *the*
boutique business hotel of downtown Buenos Aires.
Long wooden corridors lead to stylish rooms furnished with king-size beds and minimalist furniture;
each of the suites benefits from a large, airy terrace.
The staff is extremely warm and helpful and the
buffet breakfast is one of the best in town.
*Bar. Concierge. Internet (high-speed, wireless). No-
smoking rooms. Restaurant. Room service. TV (cable).*
Other locations: NH City, Bolivar 160, Monserrat
(4121 6464).

Pestana Buenos Aires

*Carlos Pellegrini 877, Retiro (5239 1000/www.
pestana.com). Subte B, Carlos Pellegrini/146, 152
bus.* **Rates** US$150-$190 single/double; US$250-
$300 suite. **Credit** AmEx, DC, MC, V.
Map p281 G11 ⓫
Towering over Avenida 9 de Julio, the tinted glass
exterior of Portuguese chain Pestana's Argentinian
outpost houses 133 spacious rooms. Close to the
transportation hub of Retiro and a host of tourist
sites (the Teatro Colón is opposite), Pestana provides
comfort on prime real estate. Recreational facilities
include a pool, spa, sauna and gym. The best
executive suites have balconies providing dramatic
views of the northern end of 9 de Julio.
*Bar. Business centre. Concierge. Gym. Internet (high-
speed). No-smoking rooms/floors. Restaurant. Spa.
Room service. TV (cable/DVD).*

Where to Stay

THE PLEASURE OF ENJOYING A FIVE STAR HOTEL.

IN THE HEART OF RECOLETA. BUENOS AIRES.

IN LOISUITES RECOLETA HOTEL YOU WILL FEEL AS WARM AS AT HOME COMBINED WITH THE UNIQUE DISTINCTION OF OUR FIVE - STAR SERVICE. ACCOMMODATE WITH US AND ENJOY AN UNFORGETTABLE STAY IN THE CENTER OF THE HISTORIC AND CULTURAL AREA OF BUENOS AIRES.

LoiSuiteS
RECOLETA HOTEL
★ ★ ★ ★

• WWW.LOISUITES.COM.AR

VICENTE LÓPEZ 1955 C1128ACC | BUENOS AIRES, ARGENTINA |
PHONE [+5411] 5777.8950 FAX [+5411] 5777.8999 | RECOLETA@LOISUITES.COM.AR

Sheraton Buenos Aires Hotel & Convention Centre

San Martín 1225, Retiro (4318 9000/www. sheraton.com). Subte C, Retiro/93, 130, 152 bus. **Rates** US$150-$200 single/double; US$250-$280 suite. **Credit** AmEx, DC, MC, V. **Map** p281 G12 ⑫

Towering high over Retiro, the Sheraton's top floors afford an awe-inspiring view of the River Plate. Newer and bigger than its sibling on Avenida Córdoba, the Retiro Sheraton has vast convention facilities and very little individual charm. Still, the 742 rooms are sizable and the staff welcoming and efficient. Decent recreational facilities include a gym, tennis court and two pools, indoor and outdoor. Popular with members of struggling boy bands and International Monetary Fund bureaucrats.
Bar. Business centre. Concierge. Gym. Internet (high-speed, wireless). No-smoking rooms/floors. Parking. Pools (indoor & outdoor). Restaurants (2). Room service. TV (cable/DVD).

Moderate

Cambremon

Suipacha 30, Microcentro (4345 0118/www. cambremonhotel.com.ar). Subte A, Piedras/10, 17, 64, 86 bus. **Rates** US$95 single/double; US$115 suite. **Credit** AmEx, DC, MC, V. **Map** p281 F10 ⑭

Welcoming, well equipped and centrally located, the Cambremon offers great value for money. The large, stylish lobby is completely Wi-Fi connected, making it an ideal spot to surf the net, hold an impromptu meeting or simply hang out over a cocktail. The room rate includes a very good breakfast and use of the hotel's small fitness centre, which includes a sauna.
Bar. Business centre. Concierge. Gym. Internet (high-speed, wireless). No-smoking rooms. Parking. Room service. TV (cable/music).

Castelar Hotel & Spa

Avenida de Mayo 1152, Congreso (4383 5000/www. castelarhotel.com.ar). Subte A, Lima/39, 64, 86 bus. **Rates** US$70-$80 single/double; US$120-$140 suite. **Credit** AmEx, DC, MC, V. **Map** p281 F9 ⑬

Halfway along Avenida de Mayo, this history-laden hotel was home to Spanish poet and playwright Federico García Lorca for over a year; his room has been restored and is now open to the public. Interior rooms have limited light and are a tad melancholic – perfect for a self-exiled poet, but those of a less rarified sensibility may prefer one of the 44 rooms overlooking the tree-lined Avenida. But if you prefer a sense of history over mod cons, you'll enjoy the Castelar – the tangible sense of pride in the place displayed by the staff is infectious. In the lobby, there's an attractive cocktail bar, while an elegant Turkish spa is hidden in the basement, with steam rooms, sauna and massage facilities for men and women (it's open to the general public too). An evocative leftover from BA's golden past.
Bar. Concierge. Gym. Internet (high-speed). No-smoking rooms/floors Parking. Restaurant. Room service. Spa. TV (cable).

Lancaster Hotel

Avenida Córdoba 405, Retiro (4311 3021). Subte B, LN Alem/26, 93, 152 bus. **Rates** US$80-$90 single/double; US$125 suite. **Credit** AmEx, DC, MC, V. **Map** p281 G11 ⑮

Opened in 1945, the red-brick Lancaster Hotel – a sensible mid-range downtown option – is as British-looking as its name suggests. The reception area is fairly discreet, but take the lift upstairs and you'll be greeted by wooden corridors bathed in a soothing creamy hue. Several dainty antique touches adorn the slightly small but properly equipped rooms. Avoid the rooms that overlook noisy Avenida Córdoba; instead, reserve on the higher floors above quiet Tres Sargentos street.
Bar. Internet (high-speed). Restaurant. Room service. TV (cable).

Budget

Gran Hotel Hispano

Avenida de Mayo 861, Monserrat (4345 2020/www. hhispano.com.ar). Subte A, Piedras or C, Avenida de Mayo/10, 17, 64 bus. **Rates** US$35 single; US$40 double; US$65 suite. **Credit** AmEx, DC, MC, V. **Map** p281 F10 ⑯

Since the 1950s, Gran Hotel Hispano has offered good value in the heart of BA's old Spanish *barrio*. Just three blocks from Plaza de Mayo, the hotel shares the block with the legendary Café Tortoni and its adjoining Academia Nacional de Tango. Those seeking silence should ask for an interior room away from the frequent, clamorous protests staged on Avenida de Mayo.
Bar. Internet (high-speed, wireless). No-smoking rooms/floors. Restaurant. Room service.

Gran Hotel Orly

Paraguay 474, Retiro (4312 5344/www.orly. com.ar). Subte C, San Martin/93, 130, 152 bus. **Rates** US$49 single; US$52 double; US$63 triple. **Credit** AmEx, DC, MC. **Map** p281 G11 ⑰

Just a few blocks from Florida street (the only pedestrianised thoroughfare in the city) this is the perfect base for those wanting close access to shops and central sights – and value for money. The rooms are clean and quiet, if a little worse for wear in places, and the helpful English-speaking desk staff are always on hand.
Bar. Internet (high-speed). Parking. Room service.

Hotel Bauen

Avenida Callao 360, Congreso (4372 1932). Subte B, Callao/12, 37, 124 bus. **Rates** US$40-$50 single/double; US$60 suite. **Credit** MC, V. **Map** p281 G9 ⑱

Originally built for the 1978 World Cup finals, the Bauen's rollercoaster history mirrors the trials and tribulations of modern Argentina. The hotel closed in 2001 under crushing debt. But the story has an interesting twist. Buoyed up by popular support, 30 or so former employees took matters into their own hands and broke back into the hotel. Ridding the

Grand Boulevard Hotel
BUENOS AIRES
★ ★ ★ ★

Enjoy Buenos Aires!

Tel (54-11) 5222-9000
Bernardo de Irigoyen 432
Buenos Aires, Argentina
info@grandboulevardhotel.com
www.grandboulevardhotel.com

hotel of rats and several years of dust has taken time, but well over half of the original 224 rooms are available, and the conference halls, ballrooms and even the theatre are up and running. So if you're looking for a shrine to classic 1970s architecture, or want to raise a stiff two fingers at corporate arrogance, this could be the lodging for you.
Bar. Business centre. Gym. Internet (high-speed). Parking. Restaurant. Room service.

Hotel Facón Grande

Reconquista 645, Microcentro (4312 6360/ www.hotelfacongrande.com). Subte B, Florida/61, 92, 132 bus. **Rates** US$40-$60 single/double. **Credit** AmEx, DC, MC, V. **Map** p281 F11 ⑮
Dolled up in 2002, the decor of this decent mid-range hotel leans heavily on a folkloric theme, inspired by the heroic gaucho José Font (aka Facón Grande or Big Dagger). Downstairs, the lounge area is scattered with indigenous weavings, wooden sofas and poncho-covered armchairs, while the 97 dimly lit bedrooms are enlivened with gaucho photos and have farming tools tacked on to the walls. Most guests gather in the hotel's restaurant, which, aptly enough, serves up a fine steak.
Bar. Business centre. Internet (high-speed). No-smoking rooms/floors. Parking. Restaurant. Room service. TV (cable).

San Telmo & south of the centre

Moderate

1890 B&B

Humberto 1º 843, San Telmo (4312 2532/www. buenosaires1890byb.com.ar). Bus 59, 98, 195. **Rates** US$80-$120 double. **Credit** Amex, DC, MC, V. **Map** p281 D9 ⑳
Just a few blocks from San Telmo's epicentre, this family-run B&B is perfect for the sedate and sophisticated European couple. All rooms are elegantly designed and comfortably furnished, with king-size beds, Egyptian-cotton bed linen and plush private bathrooms. The spacious suite is easily worth the extra cost. A skilful fusion of the classic and modern in an atmospheric neighbourhood, 1890's big selling point is the personalised assistance offered to guests interested in purchasing art.
Bar. Internet (high-speed). TV (cable).

Mansión Dandi Royal

Piedras 922, San Telmo (4361 3537/www. dandiroyal.com.ar). Bus 10, 24, 29. **Rates** US$85-$125 single/double; US$180 suite. **Credit** AmEx, DC, MC, V. **Map** p280 E9 ㉑
Tango is synonymous with San Telmo and this self-styled 'Residential Tango Academy' – created by Héctor Villalba, globetrotting entrepreneur and tango teacher – fuses attentive service with the spirit of the sensual dance. The 15 rooms of this converted mansion are sumptuously appointed, with lush

bedspreads and stately wooden furnishings. Round-the-clock butler service is standard and facilities include a small heated rooftop pool, exercise machines and two pretty tiled patios. But it's all about the dancing: two-hour classes in the hotel's adjoining salon are available daily, and a week's package incorporates extra excursions including *milongas* and tango tours.
Bars (2). Business centre. Concierge. Internet (high-speed). No-smoking floors/rooms. Parking. Pool (outdoor). Room service. TV (cable/DVD).

Budget

Posada Histórica Gotan

Sánchez de Loria 1618, entre Pavón y Juan de Garay, Boedo (4912 3807/www.posadagotan.com). Subte E, Boedo/75, 126, 160 bus. **Rates** US$50-$60 double; US$80 family suite. **No credit cards.**
Owner Gabriella rescued her 1890s ancestral home from near abandon when she opened this gorgeous guesthouse in December 2004 with French husband Thibaud. Tucked away on a quiet street in one of BA's most historic tango neighbourhoods, Gotan (*porteño* slang for tango) has ten rooms, two of which are family-sized. All rooms are stylishly contemporary and look out across a shaded passageway to the posada's spacious Italianate patio. Inside, the hotel's lounge and dining areas are equally pleasant, while topping the lot is a sun-trapping roof terrace. *Une très belle* – as Thibaud might say – addition to BA's hotel scene.
Bar. Internet (high-speed). Restaurant. TV (cable).

Posada de la Luna

Perú 565, San Telmo (4343 0911/www.posada luna.com. Bus 26, 28, 86. **Rates** US$55-$65 single/double; US$75 triple. **No credit cards.** **Map** p281 E10 ㉒
This charming, old colonial house sits on the cusp of San Telmo, just a ten-minute walk from Plaza Dorrego. Wooden furniture and tropical plants have been scattered throughout to give the *posada* a relaxed and homely feel. The four rooms vary in size – one can sleep up to four – but they all showcase the creative, bohemian touch of the owner, Franco-Argentinian Nelida Reugger. Breakfast can be taken in the bright salon or on the fabulous roof terrace.
Bar. Internet (high-speed). Room service. TV (cable).

Youkali Kultur-Hotel

Estados Unidos 1393, Constitución (4381 6064/ www.youkali.com.ar). Subte E, San José/39, 53, 60, 102, 168 bus. **Rates** US$38-$70 single; US$45-$85 double. **Credit cards** AmEx, DC, MC, V. **Map** p281 F8. ㉓
According to its German owner, Youkali Kultur-Hotel (formerly colourful and kitsch 'pop' hotel Boquitas Pintadas) is selling itself as the weirdest hotel in town. It's named after a song by composer Kurt Weill, a melancholy tango about a paradise found at the end of the world. The five glacier-themed rooms, with bright whites and cool blues, play effectively

with this end-of-the-world motif. The small pool on the sun-trapping roof terrace ensures meltdowns are avoided during the sweaty summer months.
Bar. Internet (high-speed). No-smoking rooms/floors. Pool (outdoor). Restaurant. TV (cable).

Recoleta & Barrio Norte

Luxury

Alvear Palace Hotel
Avenida Alvear 1891, Recoleta (4808 2100/www. alvearpalace.com). Bus 67, 93, 130. **Rates** US$440-$500 single/double; US$630-$3,700 suite.
Credit AmEx, DC, MC, V. **Map** p282 I11 ㉙
The clue is in the word 'palace' – not, in this case, pretentious hyperbole. For the Alvear is more than a hotel. It's also a source of civic pride, a symbol of grandeur and an enduring reminder of BA's golden, affluent era (it was built in 1932). Filling half a block of the lavish Avenida Alvear, it shares a pavement with the likes of Armani, Ralph Lauren and Cartier. The 210 rooms – 100 of which are suites and among the largest in the city – are an ocean of opulence: rich burgundies, antique French furniture and Hermès bathroom goodies scattered around the jacuzzis. They also come with butler service – perfect for wannabe Bertie Woosters or those simply too lazy to lift a finger for themselves. Such resplendence is not withheld completely from hoi polloi, however; the bar and restaurants are open to the public. The jewel in the crown is La Bourgogne, overseen by French chef Jean-Paul Bondoux. L'Orangerie bar and terrace is the most exclusive brunch and buffet venue in the city and the best way for non-guests to soak up the hotel's ambience.
Bars (2). Business centre. Concierge. Disabled-adapted rooms. Gym. Internet (high-speed, wireless). No-smoking rooms/floors. Parking. Pool (indoor). Restaurants (2). Room service. TV (cable/DVD).

Caesar Park
Posadas 1232, Recoleta (4819 1100/www.caesarpark.com). Bus 67, 93, 130. **Rates** US$360-$440 single/double; US$500-$3,025 suite. **Credit** AmEx, DC, MC, V. **Map** p282 I11 ㉕
Directly behind the exclusive Patio Bullrich shopping centre, the 148 rooms (18 of which are suites) of this sumptuous Recoleta hotel make ideal closets for your latest acquisitions. Step inside the reception and survey the marble floors, towering pillars and gleaming stairways. Tapestries and paintings by local artists line the corridors that lead to the suites, which are decadently furnished with lavish gold trimmings and dark wood. A communal lounge for waltzing and schmaltzing has a resident classical pianist tickling the ivories. Shops, the acclaimed Agraz restaurant and a small swimming pool area add to the experience.
Bar. Business centre. Concierge. Disabled-adapted rooms. Gym. Internet (high-speed, wireless). No-smoking rooms/floors. Parking. Pool (indoor). Restaurant. Room service. TV (cable/DVD).

1555 Malabia House. *See p55.*

Four Seasons Hotel
Posadas 1086, Recoleta (4321 1200/www.four seasons.com). Bus 67, 93. 130. **Rates** US$420-$450 single/double; US$480 Club Floor; US$570 suite; US$6,500 mansion suite. **Credit** AmEx, DC, MC, V. **Map** p282 I11 ㉘
A quartet of elderly gentlemen travelling under the names of Mick, Keith, Ronnie and Charlie stayed here in early 2006 (they were in town for a concert or something) – proof, if any were needed, that the Four Seasons is suited to luxury seekers of all ages. Frequently cited as the best hotel in Buenos Aires, it's also the lodging of choice for top executives and the occasional communist icon (Fidel Castro has hung his fatigues here). Towering over Posadas and Libertad streets, it's a 13-floor, 138-room masterpiece, with marble walls, capacious rooms and well-chosen artworks in the lobby and lining the corridors. Behind the tower lies an attractive, if quite small, outdoor pool and a seven-suite mansion with 24-hour butler service; it's styled like a mini French chateau and is frequently booked by visiting celebs (U2 also stayed here in 2006). All guests, illustrious or otherwise, are privileged with a personalised check-in and allotted a service tailored to their specific needs. It's rare to find an establishment that orchestrates such a classy blend of modern facilities and old-fashioned values.
Bar. Business centre. Concierge. Disabled-adapted rooms. Gym. Internet (high-speed, wireless). No-smoking rooms/floors. Parking. Pool (outdoor). Restaurant. Room service. Spa. TV (cable/DVD).

Expensive

Design Suites & Towers

Marcelo T de Alvear 1683, Recoleta (4814 8700/ www.designsuites.com). Subte D, Callao/39, 132, 152 bus. **Rates** US$125-$180 double. **Credit** AmEx, DC, MC, V. **Map** p282 I10 ㉗

The lobby sets the tone for hip Design Suites: around an elongated decorative pool fashionable travellers and stylish staff relax while electronic music thumps away in the background. It has the communal and relaxed feel of a backpackers' hostel – only one for wealthy young hipsters. The well-lit, large and minimalist suites – some of which, it must be said, could do with a lick of paint and the attention of a joiner – come in two sizes: 'junior' for one or two people and larger suites for up to four (five if agreed in advance). If you are in a couple, ask for one of the smaller suites with a view of neighbouring Plaza Rodriguez Peña. With your room comes access to a pool and fitness centre around the corner, where sweaty shoulders can be rubbed with the locals. The location is also a bonus – it lies on a relatively quiet street with quick access to shopping on Avenida Santa Fe and sightseeing in Recoleta.

Bar. Internet (high-speed, wireless). No-smoking rooms/floors. Parking. Restaurant. Room service. TV (cable).

Hotel Plaza Francia

Eduardo Schiaffino 2189, Recoleta (4804 9631/ www.hotelplazafrancia.com). **Bus** 61, 67, 93, 130. **Rates** US$100-$120 single/double; US$150-$180 suite. **Credit** AmEx, DC, MC, V. **Map** p282 J11 ㉘

In the heart of Recoleta, Hotel Plaza Francia offers upper-class refinement and elegance at middle-class rates. The 50 cosy rooms mix contemporary comforts with old-fashioned touches, but the most attractive feature of the front-facing rooms (some with balcony) is the park views afforded by the bay windows. Even better are the top-floor suites with postcard-perfect panoramas of the River Plate and the seemingly endless northern suburbs. Popular with Europeans, Hotel Plaza Francia's singular, intimate atmosphere is a far cry from the cold efficiency of some of the area's other luxury hotels. For fitness fanatics, free access is provided to a nearby gym.

Bar. Business centre. Concierge. Internet (high-speed). Room service. TV (cable).

LoiSuites Recoleta Hotel

Vicente López 1955, Recoleta (5777 8950/www. loisuites.com.ar). Bus 37, 59, 102. **Rates** US$240-$250 single/double; US$360 suite. **Credit** AmEx, DC, MC, V. **Map** p282 J11 ㉙

Part of a small chain of well-run local hotels, this LoiSuites – in the bosom of Recoleta, close to the cemetery and Village Recoleta complex – is the flagship. The 112 decent-sized suites in the 13-floor building are chic and contemporary in style with double glazing and soundproofed walls to muffle snuffles and grunts. Below in the spacious white lobby, large pastel sofas and potted plants sit in front of the *jardín de invierno* (winter garden), a two-tiered patio with a retractable roof and a Roman-style pool. It's extremely popular, so book early or settle for one of the other LoiSuites downtown.

Bar. Business centre. Concierge. Gym. Internet (high-speed). No-smoking rooms/floors. Parking. Pool (indoor). Restaurant. Room service. Spa. TV (cable).

Other locations: LoiSuites Arenales, Arenales 855, Retiro (4324 9400); **LoiSuites Esmeralda**, Marcelo T de Alvear 842, Retiro (4131 6800).

Meliá Recoleta Plaza

Posadas 1557/59, Recoleta (5353 4000/www. meliabuenosaires.solmelia.com). Bus 61, 67, 93. **Rates** US$160 single/double; US$290 suite. **Credit** AmEx, DC, MC, V. **Map** p282 J11 ㉚

Opened in December 2005, this stylish addition to the Spanish hotel chain has been getting rave reviews. Comprising 57 rooms, it's smaller than its Retiro sister (*see below*) and succeeds in creating a personal, non-corporate atmosphere. Classic decor (Louis XV furniture) blends artfully with the latest mod cons (plasma TVs in every bedroom), and while the hotel is too small to have a pool, the rooftop terrace is a fantastic place to relax and sunbathe. For more pampering, pop over the road to the hotel's health club which has a sauna, solarium and spa. Or treat yourself to an aperitif in the piano bar before dining in the excellent Bistro restaurant. With its great location and super-friendly staff, the Meliá already looks like a classic.

Bar. Business centre. Concierge. Gym. Internet (high-speed). No-smoking rooms/floors. Parking. Restaurant. Room service. Spa TV (cable/DVD).

Other locations: Meliá Buenos Aires Boutique Hotel, Reconquista 945, Retiro (4891 3800).

Moderate

Art Hotel

Azcuénaga 1268, Recoleta (4821 4744/www.arthotel. com.ar). Subte D, Pueyrredón/39, 61, 152 bus. **Rates** US$75-$115 double. **Credit** AmEx, MC, V. **Map** p282 J10 ㉛

With an art gallery covering the entire ground floor and 36 tasteful rooms blending neo-industrial modernity with classic designer chic, this stylish Recoleta hotel has no trouble living up to its name. Brainchild of Gallic businessmen Vincent Chevalier and Yannick Loop, its palpably French aura makes it a favourite with European visitors. Some of the rooms are small and cosy, while others feel more spacious; all are well equipped and have comfortable beds. The exhibits change each month – soak up the culture in the lounge and become an artful lodger.

Bar. Business centre. Concierge. Internet (high-speed). Room service. TV (cable).

Hotel Bel Air

Arenales 1462, Recoleta (4021 4070/www.hotel belair.com.ar). Bus 39, 67, 152. **Rates** US$80-$120 single/double; US$125-$150 suite. **Credit** AmEx, DC, MC, V. **Map** p282 I11 ㉜

With an attractive 1920s decorative façade, a hip bar and restaurant off the lobby, and a location just steps from leafy Plaza Vicente López, the Bel Air is a great place to pass a few days in a pretty part of town. The service is poised and helpful and rooms are pale and fresh – a tasteful blend of avant-garde furnishings and stripped pine. Double glazing insulates late risers from car horns and barking dogs. There are two banquet rooms for meetings, and comprehensive facilities for business travellers, but the overall feel is more hip than corporate. It's not as cheap as it used to be, but the Bel Air is still great value for money.

Bar. Business centre. Concierge. Gym. Internet (high-speed). No-smoking rooms/floors. Restaurant. Room service. TV (cable).

Budget

Guido Palace Hotel

Guido 1780, Recoleta (4812 0674/www.guidopalace. com.ar). Bus 102, 124. **Rates** US$30-$50 single/ double. **Credit** AmEx, MC, V. **Map** p282 I11 ⓷

Tucked deep in Recoleta, the quiet, spacious Guido Palace is a pleasant homely option in an upscale district. Rooms are simple but clean, well lit and large; most of them are equipped with surprisingly spacious balconies. On the fourth floor there's a patio with seating – a perfect spot for a chilled beer.

Bar. Internet (high-speed). Room service. TV (cable).

Palermo & Palermo Viejo

Expensive

Bo Bo Hotel

Guatemala 4882, y Thames, Palermo Viejo (4774 0505/www.bobohotel.com). Subte D, Plaza Italia/36, 55, 60, 64, 93, 152 bus. **Rates** US$120-$135 single/ double; US$160 suite. **Credit** AmEx, DC, MC, V. **Map** p279 M6 ⓸

Bo Bo stands for 'bohemian bourgeois' – a shrewd choice of name for an establishment whose target market is the sophisticated modern traveller who wants style and comfort without vulgarity. This popular, high-concept boutique hotel had an entry in *Condé Nast Traveler*'s 'Hot List' of 2005, and each of the seven rooms represents a 20th-century art or design movement. While some of these themes inevitably work better than others, a sense of affordable luxury runs throughout. The cool, friendly and efficient staff brings international experience from five-star hotel chains, and with a top-notch contemporary restaurant downstairs and the perfect location from which to explore Palermo Viejo's bar and boutiques scene, this is a smart choice. All of the bathrooms were refitted in 2005, with the top-priced 'Argentinian' deluxe suite benefiting from a lagoon-sized jacuzzi. Book well in advance.

Bar. Internet (high-speed). Parking. Restaurant. Room service. TV (cable/DVD).

The swish **Faena Hotel + Universe** where life becomes a fantasy. *See p57.*

Five (Cool Rooms Buenos Aires)

Honduras 4742, Palermo Viejo (5235 5555/www.
fivebuenosaires.com). Bus 39, 93, 111.
Rates US$110-$130 double; US$170 suite.
Credit AmEx, MC, V. **Map** p279 M5 ③⑤

The owners and architects had this superb new 16-room venue up and running in a mere six months. Minimalist bare pine flooring, stainless steel furniture, a Zen-like gravel and bamboo-shoots decor scheme and 24-hour wireless internet access help make this the perfect Palermo Viejo base for trendy thirtysomethings. The warm and efficient staff puts its local knowledge at the guest's disposal, helping organise excursions, tango lessons, Spanish courses, and so on. Three of the rooms have balconies overlooking the street, and jacuzzi baths to ensure you reach your own personal nirvana.
Internet (high-speed, wireless). Parking. Room service. TV (cable).

Home Hotel Buenos Aires

Honduras 5860, entre Carranza y Ravignani, Palermo Viejo (4778 1008/www.homebuenos aires.com). Bus 39, 93, 111. **Rates** US$145 double; US$240 suite; US$340 garden suite. **Credit** AmEx, MC, V. **Map** p279 O5 ③⑥

Aptly named, Home delivers an unforgettable accommodation experience. Opened in 2005 as the brainchild of ex-record producer Tom and his wife Patricia, this 17-room boutique hotel has become an instant classic, offering outstanding service and impressive added-value facilities. Each of the rooms has its own distinctive look, with vintage French wallpaper catching the eye. The attention to detail stretches to the handmade soaps and staff uniforms designed by Burberry of London. But the real show stopper is the gorgeous secluded patio and garden, where guests and visitors can dip their feet in the infinity pool over drinks mixed by cocktail-king Norman Barone. Add on the Ayurvedic spa and Friday night DJ events and you'll see why so many are saying there's no place like Home. **Photo** *p42.*
Bar. Internet (high-speed). Room service. TV (cable/DVD). Pool (outdoor). Spa.

1555 Malabia House

Malabia 1555, Palermo Viejo (4833 2410/www.malabiahouse.com.ar). Bus 39, 55, 168. **Rates** US$95-$110 single; US$125 double; US$145-$170 suite. **Credit** AmEx, DC, MC, V. (20% discount if paying in cash). **Map** p279 M5 ③⑦

The interior design savvy of owner Maria is apparent throughout this converted convent, formerly the home of the San Vicente Ferrer ladies. The use of simple colours, natural light and three mini gardens come together to create a relaxed oasis. The quality and warmth of the welcome are unsurpassed in the area, and invite you to spend your days lounging on the comfy living room sofas. Eleven of the 15 rooms are categorised as 'superior', but all have queen-size beds and private bathrooms. **Photo** *p49.*
Business Centre. Concierge. Internet (high-speed). Parking. Room service. TV (cable).

Moderate

Casa Bloody Mary

Volta 1867, Las Cañitas, Palermo (4777 7106/ www.casabloodymary.com). Bus 29, 59, 60. **Rates** US$60 single; US$85-$95 double. **Credit** AmEx, MC, V. **Map** p283 P9 ③⑧

The name alludes to England's Protestant-burning queen rather than the cocktail; the *casa* in question is a mock-Tudor residence down a pretty Las Cañitas side street. Recently opened as a B&B, this gay-owned lodging boasts spacious, air-conditioned rooms in a great location – it's within walking distance of Báez street, the popular Las Cañitas bar and restaurant strip.
Bar. Internet (high-speed). Restaurant.

Posada Palermo

Salguero 1655, Palermo (4826 8792/www.posada palermo.com.ar). Subte D, Bulnes/39 bus.
Rates US$60 single; US$75 double. **No credit cards. Map** p278 L6 ③⑨

After a visit to this B&B you won't be surprised to learn that it's owned and managed by an architect. The tasteful Italian-influenced design scheme preserves the aura of the building's former life as a lodging for Italian immigrants in the early 20th century. The four bedrooms, all with bathrooms en suite, boast careful attention to detail. Wind down in the hammock on the terrace or relax in the homely living room where Chungi, Marie and Laila, the three purring house cats, set the pace. A solid choice for those seeking a cosy retreat in the heart of Palermo.
Internet (high-speed, wireless).

Budget

Che Lulu Trendy Hotel

Pasaje Emilio Zola 5185, Palermo Viejo (4772 0289/ www.luluguesthouse.com). Subte D, Palermo/39, 55, 111 bus. **Rates** US$35-$50 single/double. **No credit cards. Map** p279 N6 ④⓪

Hidden down an inconspicuous side street, Che Lulu is a pioneer of the Palermo Viejo guesthouse scene. All areas, including the eight bedrooms, are air-conditioned and benefit from abundant light. They are given extra colour by local artists and plentiful plant life. The dining area with TV is a good spot to plan the day's activities; nearby excursions include Palermo parks, zoo, golf course and race track.
Internet (high speed). TV room (cable).

Como en Casa B&B

Gurruchaga 2155, Palermo Viejo (4831 0517/ www.bandb.com.ar). Subte D, Plaza Italia/29, 39 bus. **Rates** US$35-$55 single/double; US$65-$85 suite. **Credit** AmEx, MC, V. **Map** p279 M6 ④①

Como en Casa was one of the first guesthouses established in Palermo Viejo. Long and narrow, most of the 11 rooms sit on the ground floor along a corridor. They're a little samey, but the rest of the building is dressed up in a warm, colonial style, with

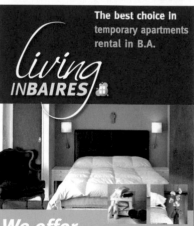

lots of rugs and heavy wood – perfect for winter. Most of the socialising takes place in the kitchen and lounge or, in summer, in the delightful little garden. *Internet (high speed). TV room (cable).*

Cypress In

Costa Rica 4828, Palermo Viejo (4833 5834/ www.cypressin.com). Bus 34, 36, 55, 93, 161. **Rates** $US54 double. **Credit** AmEx, MC, V. **Map** p279 M5 ⓐ
The cypress trees that tower in the back garden inspired the name for this highly recommendable B&B. Located on an atmospheric cobbled street in the middle of Palermo Viejo, Cypress In boasts eight slickly designed rooms at bargain rates, especially considering its prime location just minutes from Plazoleta Cortázar. Book in as quick as you can – with an upgrade in progress, the rates are set to rise.

Garufa

Fitz Roy 1925, Palermo Viejo (47716431/www. garufabuenosaires.com). Bus 39, 93, 166. **Rates** US$30-$60 single/double. **No credit cards.** **Map** p279 N5 ⓑ
The tangerine walls of this charming B&B surround antique furniture and traditional Argentinian decor. There are two double and two single rooms, all facing the inner glass-roofed courtyard. Best of all is the large roof terrace for *asados* (barbecues). *Internet (high-speed). No smoking rooms. Parking. TV room (cable).*

La Otra Orilla

Julián Alvarez 1779, Palermo Viejo (4867 4070/ www.otraorilla.com.ar). Subte D, Plaza Italia/39, 60, 152 bus. **Rates** US$35-US$65 single/double; US$85 suite. **No credit cards. Map** p278 L5 ⓒ
During the 2001 banking restrictions, Cecilia and Agustina decided to put their money in a more secure financial institution: their own home. They went out and bought some stylish furniture and reopened it as a comely, five-bedroom bed and breakfast. Two of the top rooms have small balconies which overlook a typical Palermo cobbled street. It's the suite, however, with a view of the garden and a lovely en suite bathroom that, for just a fistful of dollars more, is the real catch. *Internet (high-speed). TV room (cable).*

Puerto Madero

Luxury

Faena Hotel + Universe

Martha Salotti 445, Dique 2, Madero Este, Puerto Madero (1010 9000/www.faenahotelanduniverse. com). Subte B, LN Alem/2, 130, 152 bus. **Rates** US$350-$423 double; US$545 studio; US$605-$1,452 suite; US$2,500 Presidential Suite. **Credit** AmEx, DC, MC, V. **Map** p280 D11 ⓓ
Designed by French master Philippe Starck, this swish Buenos Aires landmark was built from the shell of an English-style red-brick silo – previously

known as 'El Porteño' – in the heart of Puerto Madero Este. Project mastermind Alan Faena modestly christened the venture 'Faena Hotel + Universe', the 'Universe' being the value added amenities included within the spacious hotel complex: a bistro, beauty corner, outdoor pool bar, slick cabaret, spa, boutique shops, business centre, gourmet market and – most intriguingly – a 'School of Good Living'. Faena's self-consciously *au courant* vision is to create for his guests an immersive lifestyle experience where 'dreams are transformed into reality.' After all that it feels a little lame to talk about accommodation, but it should be noted that the complex includes 105 gorgeous hotel rooms and 83 privately owned apartments. **Photo** *p53.* *Bar. Business centre. Concierge. Disabled-adapted rooms. Gym. Internet (high-speed, wireless). No-smoking rooms/floors. Parking. Pool (outdoor). Restaurants (2). Room service. Spa. TV (cable/DVD).*

Hotel Madero

Rosario Vera Peñaloza 360, Dique 2, Madero Este, Puerto Madero (5776 7777/www.hotelmadero.com). Subte B, LN Alem/2, 130, 152 bus. **Rates** US$240-$390 single/double; US$400-$420 suite. **Credit** AmEx, DC, MC, V. **Map** p280 D11 ⓔ
Inconspicuously tagged on to the far end of Puerto Madero Este, Sofitel's latest BA venture breaks their traditional mould with this chic 193-room hotel. It is aimed at the discerning business traveller, although couples and families will be equally happy with the attractive features which include a rooftop pool and the sensational open-plan Rëd Resto & Lounge restaurant. The inside wooden terrace is soothingly Zen-like and the upper floors afford stunning views of downtown BA. Rooms are fresh and tastefully decorated. Be sure to indulge in a cocktail or two in the stunning White Bar. *Bar. Business centre. Concierge. Disabled-adapted rooms. Gym. Internet (high-speed, wireless). No-smoking rooms/floors. Parking. Pool (outdoor). Restaurant. Room service. TV (cable/DVD).*

Expensive

Hilton Buenos Aires

Avenida Macacha Güemes 351, Dique 3, Madero Este, Puerto Madero (4891 0000/www.hilton.com). Bus 130, 152. **Rates** US$150-$260 single/double; US$484 suite. **Credit** AmEx, DC, MC, V. **Map** p281 E12 ⓕ
The Hilton was designed with prominent executives and affluent couples in mind. The vast glass-roofed atrium/lobby is embellished with chrome sofas, a marble reception and a pair of glass elevators at the back. The 418 modern rooms have deluxe amenities and king-size bathrooms. This is a fine hotel in a cool location, and boasts the killer advantage of having the best hotel pool in town. *Bar. Business centre. Concierge. Disabled-adapted rooms. Gym. Internet (high-speed, wireless). No-smoking rooms/floors. Parking. Pool (outdoor). Restaurants (2). Room service. TV (cable/DVD).*

Youth hostels

El Cachafaz

*Viamonte 982, Microcentro (4328 1445/www.
elcachafaz.com.ar). Subte C, Lavalle/10, 99, 111 bus.*
Rates US$8 per person dorm; US$22 double.
No credit cards. Map p281 G11 **48**
El Cachafaz is regarded as one of the friendliest
backpacker joints in the city. Well decorated, it has
four dorms and one double, and an airy living room.

Casa Esmeralda

*Honduras 5765, Palermo Viejo (4772 2446/www.
casaesmeralda.com.ar). Bus 39, 93, 111.*
Rates US$9 per person dorm; US$20-$25 double.
No credit cards. Map p279 N5 **49**
An unpretentious and comfy hostel run by amiable
Franco-Argentinian Sebas. It has four doubles, two
dormitories and a beautiful back garden.

La Casa Fitzroy

*Fitz Roy 2461, Palermo Viejo (4777 3454/www.casa
fitzroy.com.ar). Bus 39, 93.* **Rates** US$8 per person
dorm; US$25-$30 single. **No credit cards.**
Map p279 N6 **50**
This big backpacker joint has a relaxed vibe – but
it's also a slick operation. It's got 60 beds, a cosy
TV room, a terrace and a large courtyard.

Casa Jardín

*Charcas 4422, Palermo Viejo (4774 8783/
www.casajardinba.com.ar). Subte D, Plaza Italia/
39, 41, 60, 93 bus.* **Rates** US$10 per person dorm;
US$15 single; US$30 double. **No credit cards.**
Map p279 M6 **51**
This converted townhouse is packed with well-
stocked bookcases and hosts art exhibitions. It also
boasts a roof terrace for barbecues.

Casa Única

*Jean Jaures 715, Almagro (4962 5406/www.
casaunica.com.ar). Subte B, Carlos Gardel/29, 68,
188 bus.* **Rates** US$7 per person dorm; US$12-$15
single/double. **No credit cards. Map** p278 J6 **52**
Cosy rooms, kitsch furnishings and a big courtyard
are Casa Única's standout features. Located in a
colonial-style house, it's run by backpackers.

Che Lagarto

*Venezuela 857, Monserrat (4343 4845/www.
chelagarto.com). Subte E, Belgrano/59, 67, 98 bus.*
Rates US$8 per person dorm; US$15 single; US$20
double; US$25 triple. **Credit** AmEx, DC, MC, V.
Map p281 E9 R **53**
With some 30-odd beds, in dormitories, triple, double
and single rooms, Che Lagarto offers clean, cheap
accommodation in a spacious, spruced up building.
It also has one of the best hostel bars in town.

Garden House

*Avenida San Juan 1271, Constitución (4304
1824/www.gardenhouseba.com.ar). Subte C, San
Juan/29, 39, 59, 60, 102 bus.* **Rates** US$7-$8 per
person dorm; US$20-$25 double. **No credit cards.**
Map p281 E8 S **54**

Despite its proximity to one of BA's less reputable
barrios, this hostel comes recommended. There's a
book-stacked library, and a large terrace above with
hammocks and a chill-out room.

Hostel Inn – Tango City

*Piedras 680, San Telmo (4300 5764/www.hostel-
inn.com). Subte E or C, Independencia/2, 17, 59 bus.*
Rates US$7-$9 per person dorm; US$15 double.
Credit MC, V. **Map** p281 E9 **55**
Hand-carved furnishings and diverse artwork are
standout features of this boisterous joint, with
capacity for 100 backpackers.

Milhouse

*Hipólito Yrigoyen 959, Monserrat (4345 9604/4343
5038/www.milhousehostel.com). Subte A, Piedras or
C, Avenida de Mayo/39, 64, 86 bus.* **Rates** US$7-$8
per person dorm; US$30 double. **No credit cards.**
Map p281 F10 **56**
This three-tiered turn-of-the-century house is the
city's liveliest hostel. Always buzzing, it also offers
tango sessions, tours and barbecues.

Ostinatto Hostel

*Chile 680, San Telmo (4362 9639). Bus 2, 9, 10, 28,
29, 86.* **Rates** US$8 per person dorm; US$25 double.
No credit cards. Map p281 E9 **57**
The most impressive feature of this BA hostel is the
modern design, evident in the six interweaving
staircases that tower above you upon walking in.
There's a bar with leather couches, a piano for late-
night knees-ups and an in-house art gallery.

Portal del Sur

*Hipólito Yrigoyen 855, Monserrat (4342 8788/
www.portaldelsurba.com.ar). Subte A, Piedras or C,
Avenida de Mayo/45, 56, 86 bus.* **Rates** US$7-$9 per
person dorm; US$20 single; US$30 double.
Credit MC. V. **Map** p281 F10 **58**
This hostel challenges travellers to name better
backpacker digs in South America. Clean dormitories come with air-conditioning and telephone,
while private rooms include cable TV.

SoHostel

*4416 Charcas, Palermo Viejo (4779 2949/www.
sohostel.com.ar). Bus 34, 55, 93.* **Rates** US$7 per
person dorm; US$30 double. **No credit cards. Map**
p279 M6 **59**
Cut your lodging budget by staying at this cheap
and trendy hostel, and blow what you've saved in
the restaurants, boutiques and bars nearby.

V&S

*Viamonte 887, Microcentro (4322 0994/
www.hostelclub.com). Subte C, Lavalle/10, 99, 111
bus.* **Rates** US$9 per person dorm; US$25-$30 single/
double. **No credit cards. Map** p281 G11 **60**
An upmarket hostel for the bourgeois backpacker,
what V&S lacks in party atmosphere it makes up
for with a raft of added-value facilities. With advice
on activities as diverse as polo and paragliding, and
with tango, salsa and Spanish classes, a mini gym
and a giant TV, it fills up fast.

Sightseeing

Features

Introduction

Find your feet and then start using them.

Plazas, palaces and pizzerias, parks and picket lines, belle époque landmarks and pestiforous landfills, some European elegance here, some South American exuberance there, dog poop everywhere – welcome to the Ciudad Autónoma de Buenos Aires. There's a lot to see.

There's a lot, period. BA is a big city, covering some 200 square kilometres (77 square miles) of what was once featureless pampas. Luckily for the visitor, however, most of BA's points of interest can be found on the eastern side of the city, in a corridor that runs from La Boca in the south through the centre and in a north-westerly direction up the coast along the River Plate.

One general point. Buenos Aires doesn't have the instant 'wow factor' of (say) New York, London or Paris. You have to be prepared to fall in love with BA; having a quick fling just won't do. So be patient. Talk to the locals. Walk in a random direction. Hop on a bus. Find a special place that isn't in the guidebooks.

GETTING AROUND

The city is largely laid out on the standard Spanish colonial-style grid pattern of wide *avenidas* and narrower *calles* in regular blocks – called *cuadras* or *manzanas* – with a regular numbering system that makes navigation relatively easy. Maps (ours included) are rarely oriented north, instead flipping the city to show the river to the south. In fact, Avenida 9 de Julio, the city's main thoroughfare runs north–south. Traffic is one-way; to orient yourself, remember that on Avenidas Santa Fe and Corrientes traffic heads towards downtown, and away from it on Avenida Córdoba. The names of the north–south streets change at Avenida Rivadavia.

We've provided detailed street maps covering the barrios you'll spend most time in. Maps start on page 274 and the street index on page 286.

If you want a quick overall view of the city, take a *colectivo* (public bus), or if you're in a hurry, one of the guided air-con buses serving the hotels (ask your hotel concierge for details). Taxis are also affordable, and it's enjoyable to roll down the window and watch the city pass by. The Subte (subway) is ideal for central areas, but Buenos Aires only truly lays bare its soul to those prepared to go overground and on foot. In recognition of this, the local government (Gobierno de la Ciudad de Buenos Aires) has launched a free 'guided walks' service. For further details, go to the 'Recorridos' section

on their website (www.bue.gov.ar). For more detailed information on all methods of transport, *see pp250-252*.

Note that many museums and government-run sights are closed on Monday. A lot of museums close for a break in the Austral summer (January and February) too, though market demand from the ever-increasing influx of tourists is shortening closed periods. Take cash when visiting museums: those that aren't free charge at most a few pesos, and rarely accept credit cards. You may be asked for some form of photo ID (a photocopy is sometimes acceptable) in certain public buildings. Most museums and historical sites offer scheduled guided tours in Spanish. If you phone ahead, many larger museums will try to arrange a guided visit with an English-speaker – alternatively talk to a tour specialist (*see p63*).

Barrio guide

Not all *porteños* use the city government's *barrio* denominations, although you'll see them on many maps. For instance, Once (pronounced *on*-say, meaning 11) is not, technically, a barrio, but everyone uses the term for the commercial zone around 11 de Septiembre train station. Hardly anyone uses the barrio names Balvanera or San Nicolás, preferring to highlight major buildings in those zones, such as the Abasto shopping mall and Congreso. In this chapter, and in our maps, we have tried to delineate the city in a way that acknowledges and incorporates both officialdom and common usage.

The Centre's focal point is Plaza de Mayo – the city's original main square and site of many important public buildings. Elegant Avenida de Mayo runs from the plaza across gaping Avenida 9 de Julio to the Plaza del Congreso, in the barrio of Congreso. Next door is Tribunales, the legal quarter, and to the north the railway terminal of Retiro. The Microcentro is the capital's downtown, a busy commercial and financial hub. East of *calle* Florida – one of only three pedestrianised streets – is the Bajo, with its banks, bars and skyscrapers.

The **South of the Centre** chapter includes Monserrat, the historical district south of the Plaza de Mayo. San Telmo follows, drawing visitors to its antiques, tango and bustling Plaza Dorrego. Lying on the Riachuelo – the

MAISON BUENOS AIRES

ADVISORY
SERVICE

REAL ESTATE
MANAGEMENT

TEMPORARY
RENTALS

Peter Haller   T. 15 5388 3993
Teresa Sanchez Terrero   T. 15 5752 0419
info@maisonbuenosaires.com   www.maisonbuenosaires.com

little river that empties into the River Plate – is La Boca, a working-class barrio famous for its football team and colourful street, Caminito. Run-down Constitución contains the railway terminal for the south. Barracas, historically a factory zone, is starting to enjoy the fruits of long overdue redevelopment.

North of the Centre, beyond Retiro, is Recoleta, where the rich live and the famous are buried. Its cemetery, plazas, shops and museums make it a tourist magnet. Barrio Norte is a neighbouring residential district. Further north is Palermo. It has three distinct sub-areas around the huge Parque Tres de Febrero: expansive Palermo proper, a middle-class residential area with gardens, the zoo and well-kept plazas; opulent, tranquil Palermo Chico; and trendy Palermo Viejo (unofficially divided into sub-barrios Palermo Soho and Palermo Hollywood), full of hip restaurants and boutiques. The dining quarter of Las Cañitas is in Palermo too.

Just to the **West of the Centre** are Once and Abasto, rich in immigration, history, tango and commerce. Other western barrios for visitors willing to wander are Caballito, Villa Crespo and, slightly north, Chacarita, home to a vast proletarian necropolis.

Along the River is the Costanera Norte, north of the city airport, a popular place for weekend promenades. Next to the southern bank of the river is Puerto Madero – BA's yuppie dockland complex – and Costanera Sur, skirting the coastal eco-reserve.

Heading **Further Afield** to the north is Belgrano, with its plazas, museums and shops; nearby are Nuñez and Saavedra. Further still, beyond the limits of the capital, are the wealthier suburbs of Zona Norte: Olivos, Martínez and San Isidro. On the city's western edge are Liniers and Mataderos, both associated with cowboys, cattle-dealing and meatpacking.

See the sights

On a bus

There are any number of bog standard BA bus tour outfits and several very good ones. **Eternautas** (4384 7874, www.eternautas.com) has a team of university teachers and historians who lead visits to different barrios, exploring tango, politics and history. **Opcion sur** (4777 9029, www.opcionsur.com.ar) is a new and highly professional company whose tour buses are fitted with video screens that play archive footage of historical events related to whatever neighbourhood the bus is passing through. Other operators include **Travel Line** (4393 3557, www.travelline.com.ar), **Buenos Aires Tours** (4785 2753, www.buenosaires-tours.com.ar) and **QN Guias Argentinos** (4833 6525, www.guiasargentinos.com.ar).

On a bike

If you're willing to risk BA's infamous traffic, then pedal power may be the way to see the sights. **Bike Tours** (4311 5199, www.biketours.com.ar, US$30-$40) offers trips around the city and the suburbs (helmets included). **Urban Biking** (4568 4321, www.urbanbiking.com, AR$70-$100) tours the city's southern and northern barrios and can arrange night-time rides. It also offers a rental service.

From the air

For the ultimate panoramic view of BA, you can see it from the sky. **Argentina Travel Services** (4326 2854/www.ats-travel.com.ar) offers tours by helicopter and hot air balloon. **Tangol** (4312 7276, www.tangol.com) has 15-minute helicopter rides over the city (from US$70).

On foot

Cicerones is an organisation offering free, tailor-made tours. Fill in the online form detailing your topic of interest, allow 72 hours, and a guide will be chosen from among 50 multilingual volunteers. Two other good companies offering walking tours are **Urban Explorer** (4813 0385, www.urbex.com.ar) and **PlanBA** (4776 8267, www.planba.com). Both are run by native English speakers.

With the specialists

To understand the history of Argentina's immigrant communities, join a walking tour with an architecture specialist (4374 2222, www.espacioverde.com.ar, AR$25). Explore Jewish Buenos Aires on a private tour with Deb Miller of **Travel Jewish** (4257 5977, www.traveljewish.com, US$35 per hour).

The best Sights

Brilliant buildings

El Abasto shopping centre (see p98); **Edificio Kavanagh** (see p73); **Palacio Barolo** (see p67); **Palacio Duhau** (see p89).

Dramatic deathvilles

Chacarita (see p99) and **Recoleta** cemeteries (see p89).

Sensational sculptures

Canto al Trabajo (see p79); **Floralis Genérica** (see p90)

Gorgeous greenery

Jardín Japonés (see p95); **Parque Lezama** (see p80); **Plaza San Martín** (see p73); **Parque Tres de Febrero** (see p92).

Soccer shrines

La Bombonera (see p81); **Estadio Monumental** (see p104).

Sightseeing

The Centre

Symbols of power, politics and protest in BA's historic heart.

French-style palaces, wide avenues and green plazas meet choking traffic and clamorous protestors: the city's historic and commercial nerve-centre is where reminders of an erstwhile splendour and utopian urban dream compete with the grittier, more cynical realities of today.

Spread over several barrios, the centre is the daytime home to millions. Renowned landmarks lend their names to some of its sectors, but otherwise the zones that compose it converge under the '*el Centro*' label. On weekdays, the combination of modern life and pre-independence town planning makes the central business district a sometimes claustrophobic experience. Commuter traffic pours into the narrow roads, shoppers throng pedestrianised Florida and Lavalle streets and workers head for offices in the *bajo* (low place). A mass evacuation takes place between 6-8pm, after which the show is stolen by the entertainment venues, late-opening bookstores and pizzerias along Corrientes.

The centre has also become the main stage for picketers' protests and, after dusk, hordes of *cartoneros* (cardboard collectors) descend, hauling their carts around before heading back to Retiro station or shanty town Villa 31. Just a stone's throw from such poverty is the affluence of surrounding lush, stunning Plaza San Martín. Startling to outsiders, such contrasts are taken for granted by *porteños* accustomed to the centre's contending visions of past and present.

Plaza de Mayo

The **Plaza de Mayo**, the original *plaza mayor* (main square), was laid out by Juan de Garay in the 1580s, shortly after the successful foundation of Buenos Aires. Garay still stands as a bronze statue in a tiny square just metres north-east of the plaza, beside an oak tree from his Basque motherland.

The colonial plaza became Plaza de Mayo to commemorate 25 May 1810, when the masses assembled there to celebrate the deposition of the Spanish viceroy and the swearing in of the Primera Junta (First Council). Ever since, the plaza has been centre stage in the dramatic political life of the nation. Famously, it was the site of the great gatherings of the *descamisados* or 'shirtless ones' under Perón and was bombed by the military in 1955 (to oust Perón); bullet holes are still visible in the **Ministerio de Economía** building on Hipólito Yrigoyen next to Avenida Paseo Colón. Today, the Madres de Plaza de Mayo still march here every Thursday at 3.30pm to protest the 'disappearance' of their loved ones during the last military government. *See also p66* **Mothers of reinvention?**

At the plaza's centre is the **Pirámide de Mayo**, an obelisk raised in 1811 for the anniversary of the May revolution. The Madres' famous symbol – a headscarf that alludes to motherhood and to the nappies of their lost children – is painted on the tiles circling the pyramid. To the east is a statue of independence patriot Manuel Belgrano – the only national hero to be honoured with a statue in the plaza.

Glowing like a psychedelic vermilion fantasy, especially at sunset, the **Casa Rosada** (Pink House) is the presidential palace (not the residence, which is out in the sticks in Olivos). Built between 1862 and 1885, it stands where Buenos Aires' 17th-century fort, later the viceroy's palace, used to be. The splendour of its European Renaissance-style façade came together in several stages. The emblematic rosy hue originated during Sarmiento's 1868-74 presidency, when it was traditional to add ox blood to whitewash to provide colour and thicken the mix. Today the front is pinker than the rest because a project to doll it up during the Menem years ran out of funds when only one side had been finished.

The central balcony has been the soapbox of diverse demagogues and dictators, although the Peróns used the lower balcony, to be 'closer to the people'. This was also used by Madonna in the filming of Alan Parker's *Evita*, despite protests by Perónists who felt the material girl was tarnishing the memory of Saint Evita.

The **Museo de la Casa Rosada** (*see below*) displays portraits, hats, *mate* gourds, cigar boxes, military decorations and carriages that once belonged to Argentinian presidents. There are more curious items, including a black doll given to poor kids by Evita's charity.

Surrounding the Plaza de Mayo are several important buildings. On the corner of Avenida Rivadavia and 25 de Mayo is the **Banco de la Nación**, the country's state bank. The present building, constructed between 1940 and 1955, is topped by an enormous, neo-classical dome.

Heading west on Avenida Rivadavia is the neo-classical **Catedral Metropolitana** (*see below*). The plan for the present cream-coloured building, the sixth cathedral on this site, was hatched in 1753; the first façade was blessed in 1791 and the final touches were added in 1910. The high baroque interior arches create a sombre atmosphere and one of the side chapels contains a popular statue of Christ donated in 1981 by two local football players. The rococo main altar stands out, as does a life-sized Christ to its left made from the wood of the native *algarrobo* (carob) tree in 1671. The right-hand nave houses the mausoleum containing – since 1880 – the repatriated remains of the Liberator José de San Martín (who died in France in 1850).

The Plaza's other main building, the **Cabildo**, was HQ of the city council from 1580 to 1821, and the place where revolutionaries took the first steps towards independence. Seemingly the oldest building on the plaza, it recovered its colonial style only in the 1940s, a few decades after six of the original 11 arches on the façade were lopped off to make room for Avenida de Mayo and Avenida Julio A Roca (known as Diagonal Sur). Today it houses the **Museo Histórico Nacional del Cabildo y de la Revolución de Mayo** (*see below*). Austere rooms preserve valuable items such as a magnificent gold and silver piece from Oruro (Bolivia), one of the country's first printing presses, and items relating to the English Invasions. Behind the Cabildo is a shaded colonial patio. Accessible from Avenida de Mayo and Hipolito Yrigoyen, it hosts a handicrafts fair on Thursdays and Fridays.

Behind the Casa Rosada is a green space called **Parque Colón**, where a monument of Columbus looks out to sea. A massive Argentinian flag – which Graham Greene likened to the steam from a ship cutting into the blue of the heavens – waves against the sky.

Catedral Metropolitana

Avenida Rivadavia, y San Martín (4331 2845). Subte A, Plaza de Mayo or D, Catedral or E, Bolívar/24, 64, 130 bus. **Open** 8am-7pm Mon-Fri; 9am-7.30pm Sat, Sun. **Guided tours** (Spanish) *Temple* 11.30am, 4pm Mon-Fri. *Crypt* 1.15pm Mon-Fri. **Admission** free. **Map** p281 E11.

Museo de la Casa Rosada

Hipólito Yrigoyen 219, entre Balcarce y Paseo Colón (4344 3802/www.museo.gov.ar). Subte A, Plaza de Mayo or D, Catedral or E, Bolívar/24, 64, 130 bus. **Open** 10am-6pm Mon-Fri; 2-6pm Sun. **Guided tours** *Museum* (Spanish) 11am, 4pm Mon-Fri; 3pm, 4.30pm Sun. *Casa Rosada* (Spanish) 4pm Mon-Thur; (Spanish & English) 4pm Fri. **Admission** free. **Map** p281 E11.

Museo Histórico Nacional del Cabildo y de la Revolución de Mayo

Bolívar 65, entre Avenida de Mayo y Hipólito Yrigoyen (4334 1782/4342 6729). Subte A, Plaza de Mayo or D, Catedral or E, Bolívar/24, 64, 130 bus. **Open** 12.30pm-7pm Tue-Fri; 3-7pm Sun. **Guided tours** (Spanish) 3pm, 4.30pm Sun. **Admission** *Museum* contribution AR$1. *Tours* AR$3. **No credit cards. Map** p281 E10.

Plaza de Mayo. *See p64.*

Mothers of reinvention?

Every Thursday afternoon for almost 30 years they have been gathering in Plaza de Mayo for a weekly walk that has become a global symbol for resistance to oppression. With their trademark white headscarves and photos of their lost children hanging round their necks, the Mothers of Plaza de Mayo march on.

But Argentina has seen many changes in the three decades since the first group of 14 mothers convened outside Government House to demand an audience with then dictator Rafael Videla. Then, as now, they were demanding answers about the whereabouts of their children, who were 'disappearing' under the military regime.

Now, with the amnesty laws passed in 1990 by the Carlos Menem administration repealed by Nestor Kirchner's government, some of those responsible for the tens of thousands of disappearances during the so-called 'dirty war' are finally facing justice.

Encouraged by this, the Mothers announced that their annual 'March of Resistance' would be held in January 2006 for the last time (pictured), with leader Hebe de Bonafini admitting that her organisation no longer had an enemy in Government House. 'It's not that we have changed,' she said at a rally. 'It's that there is a new political movement in the country and in Latin America.'

And the Mothers of Plaza de Mayo are in the vanguard of this movement. Long-time promoters of human rights, these women's weekly walks have come to embrace broader political issues; these days they circle the plaza behind a banner repudiating the Free Trade Agreement of the Americas and demanding an end to US interference in the region. In November 2005, Bonafini strode side by side with Bolivian president Evo Morales through the streets of Mar del Plata protesting the arrival of US president George W Bush in Argentina for the Summit of the Americas. Days later, the Mothers were a visible presence at a huge anti-Bush rally addressed by firebrand Venezuelan president Hugo Chávez. For De Bonafini and many of her followers, the enemy now resides in the White rather than the Pink House.

But De Bonafini's leadership has at times been divisive, and not all of the Mothers have followed her lead. Her bellicose style and uncomprising leftwing politics were blamed for a split in the group as far back as 1986, when a number of members broke away to form the Mothers of Plaza de Mayo Founder Line.

It wasn't the only time that this vocal woman has raised hackles. Her ill-judged reaction to the 9/11 terrorist attacks caused an instant kerfuffle in the media – she had labelled the destruction of the World Trade Centre 'revenge' for what she believes is the blood spilt as a consequence of an aggressive US foreign policy.

De Bonafini's anti-imperialist stance may be leading the Mothers of Plaza de Mayo in a new direction, but for many of the headscarved women who still march at Plaza de Mayo, it will always be about their lost children.

Avenida de Mayo

Opened in 1894, the grand **Avenida de Mayo**, its spacious pavements dotted with plane trees, is the most obvious example of Buenos Aires trying to emulate the wide boulevards of Paris. In reality, though, it's more closely associated with Spain, due to the large numbers of Spanish immigrants who settled in – and still live in – the neighbourhood and its resemblance to Madrid's Gran Via and La Rambla in Barcelona.

Newly elected presidents make their way down this avenue to the Casa Rosada after being sworn in at the Palacio del Congreso. Common folk travel below, on Latin America's oldest underground railway, opened in 1913, just nine years after New York's subway started rolling. Although the Subte's *linea* A has lost much of its old lustre to modernisation, the retro posters and fittings at Perú station (Avenida de Mayo between Bolivar and Perú) recall the Argentina that used to be.

Despite run-down sections, modern towers and some of the more faded-looking Spanish restaurants along and around its ten blocks, fine European-style buildings with exquisite architectural details still abound. The best example of art nouveau, richly decorated with elements from the natural world, is the **Hotel Chile**, on the corner of Santiago del Estero.

Heading west from Plaza de Mayo, the first highlight is the Gallic *La Prensa* newspaper building, from 1896, crowned by a Pallas Athena statue and now the city government's **Casa de la Cultura** (*see below*). The French feel goes beyond the façades – the impressive Salón Dorado, inspired by the Palace of Versailles, hosts regular classical concerts; ask inside for the programme. A siren on top, sounded during crucial moments in the city's history, was last heard in 1983 when democracy was restored.

The avenue's outstanding edifice and one of the city's notable buildings is the **Palacio Barolo**. It was built as, and remains, office space, but you can enter its ground floor passageway with gargoyles, Latin inscriptions and several kiosks that look like they were stolen from the set of *Brief Encounter*. Erected in 1923, and the tallest building in the city until the construction of the Edificio Kavanagh (*see p74*) in 1935, Italian architect Mario Palanti designed it to be a neo-gothic shrine to Dante's *Divine Comedy*. Mirroring the medieval epic's 100 cantos, the 22-floor building, with its Gaudiesque curves and lumps, reaches a height of 100 metres (328 feet). Hell is on the ground floor, Purgatory comprises the first 14 floors and the building tapers into Paradise in the upper reaches.

Another stunning building marks the avenue's west end. With its two slender domes the **Edificio de la Inmobiliaria**, built in 1910 for an insurance company, is a nattily eclectic celebration of several styles including Italianate balconies and Eastern motifs. From here it's a few steps to the Plaza del Congreso.

Casa de la Cultura

Avenida de Mayo 575, entre Perú y Bolívar (4323 9669). Subte A, Perú or D, Catedral or E, Bolívar/ 24, 29, 64, 86, 111, 130 bus. **Open** *Feb-Dec* 8am-8pm Mon-Fri; by tour Sat, Sun. Closed Jan. **Guided tours** (Spanish & English) 4pm, 5pm Sat; hourly 11am-4pm Sun. **Admission** free. **Map** p281 F10.

Congreso & Tribunales

Plaza del Congreso is the popular name for the three squares filling the three blocks east of the Palacio del Congreso. Run down in recent years by protestors, vagrants and metal thieves who hijack commemorative plaques, all that's left of its once stately elegance are the shady jacarandas, *tipa* and *ceibo* trees (whose red

blossom is the national flower) that colour the plaza in spring. It contains a version of Rodin's *Thinker* and a statue of Mariano Moreno, one of the May revolutionaries. There's a small flea market on the Hipólito Yrigoyen side.

The western section of the plaza is dominated by the **Monumento a los Dos Congresos**, in remembrance of the first constitutional assembly held in 1813 and the Declaration of Independence three years later in Tucumán. The monument's centrepiece is the statue of the republic, propped up by a plough and waving a victorious laurel branch.

Like Argentina's federal constitution, which was inspired by the US model, the Greco-Roman **Palacio del Congreso** (*see p70*) is a dome-and-column affair resembling Washington's bicameral legislature. Finished in 1906, its extravagant interior can be visited with a guided tour (no access when in session).

On the corner to the right of the palace is a historical *confitería* (closed since 1996) where politicians used to sip their espressos between sessions. It's called **El Molino**, a reference to the windmill above its entrance. Currently under refurbishment, the small **Teatro Liceo**, on the corner of Rivadavia and Paraná, is one of the

The Dante-esque drama of **Palacio Barolo**.

bue

destination **buenos aires**

✉ infobue@buenosaires.gov.ar

PHOTO GALLERY: **LOOK AT BUENOS AIRES AND SEND YOUR POSTCARD**
AUDIO MOBILE GUIDE: **VOICES AND MUSIC OF THE CITY / TANGO OF CENTURY 21° / THE CITY AND THE RIVER**
AGENDAS **OF CULTURE AND EXPOS / FESTIVALS**
BUENOS AIRES GUIDES **IN SPANISH, ENGLISH, PORTUGUESE, GERMAN, FRENCH, ITALIAN, RUSSIAN, JAPANESE, MANDARIN CHINES**

www.
bue.
gov.ar

SUBSECRETARIA DE TURISMO DEL GOBIERNO DE LA CIUDAD

Wing your way through **Plaza del Congreso**. *See p67.*

oldest playhouses in BA. It opened in 1876 and has been the stage for many of the country's greatest thespians. It's also where a struggling young actress named Eva Perón once performed.

To visit the rest of civic Buenos Aires, a good starting point is **Diagonal Norte**, running north-west from Plaza de Mayo. The avenue is a masterpiece of urban harmony; every building is ten storeys tall with a second-floor balcony, though a rigidly monumental style dominates many of its edifices. Empty on weekends, the Diagonal's finest architecture is on the corner of Florida where Bank Boston shows off its decorative façade and the heavily decorated gilt ceiling of its inner hall (visible during bank opening hours only).

Diagonal Norte links the Plaza de Mayo with the barrio of Tribunales, where the law courts are surrounded by solicitors' offices, law firms and kiosks selling legal pamphlets. At the end of 2003 the block between Cerrito and Libertad was pedestrianised. The avenue's disappointing dead-end is the grubby-looking **Palacio de Justicia**, seat of the Supreme Court and another popular venue for public protest. Stretching out in front as far as Avenida Córdoba is the **Plaza Lavalle**, an attractive green spot rich in history and sprawling *ceibo* trees. Its focal point is a monument to Juan

Lavalle, one of the military heroes who crossed the Andes with San Martín. Also look out for **La Fuente de los Bailarines** (Dancers' Fountain), a simple and touching memorial to two dancers from the Teatro Colón killed in a plane accident in 1971. Across the Plaza, and filling a whole block, is the **Teatro Colón** itself. With its regular lines and tempered classicism, it's a key landmark and an internationally renowned venue for opera and classical music. A one-hour tour, available in English, visits the Colón's elegant salons (*see p202* **Theatre of dreams**).

On the corner of Avenida Córdoba and Libertad, is the **Teatro Cervantes** (*see p225*), the capital's grand old lyric theatre. Unveiled in 1921, its façade is a near replica of the university at Alcalá de Henares in Spain, where Don Quixote's creator was born. Equally impressive inside, the building also houses the **Museo de Teatro** (*see p70*), a comprehensive tribute to Argentina's thespian history.

It's just a short walk from here to the wide asphalt canyon of Avenida 9 de Julio and its iconic central monument, the **Obelisco**. As soon as work on the 68-metre (223-foot) obelisk was completed in 1936, the critics went to town, describing it as an undignified phallic cement spike. Radical feminist groups suggested lopping

Walk on History and caffeine

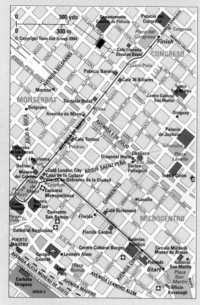

Start: Plaza San Martín
Finish: Plaza del Congreso
Length: Two kilometres (1.2 miles)
What kind of walking tour leaves you as full of beans when you end it as when you began it? Answer: a café crawl. This walk takes you past some of BA's most famous buildings, streets and squares, and inside many of the city's historic coffee shops.

Start early, under the hooves of the equestrian statue to General José de San Martín in the plaza that bears his name. You can take your starting time from the clocktower of the **Torre de los Ingleses** (English Tower) to the east of the square.

Walk south along Florida, BA's main pedestrian thoroughfare. You'll pass two emblems of *porteño* commerce, one defunct (the old **Harrods** store at No.887), the other thriving (**Galerías Pacífico** at No.737, with its stunning ceiling frescos; see p148).

Take your first coffee in **Florida Garden** (*see p140*) at No.111. This was once the gathering place for the artists of the influential Di Tella group in the 1960s. Now its customers are mainly businessfolk and tourists. Munch on a *medialuna* (croissant) and brood awhile over the commercialisation of art.

Start burning off the calories by continuing up Florida towards Avenida Corrientes. Have another *cortado* at **Confitería Richmond**, a café with a clubbish vibe, full of Brylcreemed and blazered gents reading the papers.

Carry on along Florida, crossing Avenida Corrientes, BA's mythical 'street that never sleeps'. The next stretch of Florida has several points of interest. Look out for **Galería Güemes** at No.165, the city's first shopping arcade (*see p218*). The bookish can have a browse in **El Ateneo** bookshop at No.340.

it in half, and three years after its inauguration the city's parliament voted for its demolition. The decision was ignored, however, and the Obelisco became, over time, the city's postcard emblem and a symbol of its tendency towards self-conscious monumentalism.

Museo del Instituto Nacional de Estudios de Teatro

Avenida Córdoba 1199, y Libertad (4816 7212). Subte D, Tribunales/29, 39, 109,111, 115, 140 bus. **Open** 10am-6pm Mon-Fri. **Admission** free. **Map** p281 G10.

Palacio del Congreso

Hipólito Yrigoyen 1849, entre Entre Ríos y Combate de los Pozos (4370 7100). Subte A, Congreso/12, 37, 64, 86 bus. Closed sometimes Jan. **Guided tours** *Spanish & English* 11am Mon-Wed. *Spanish only* 5pm, 7pm Mon, Tue, Fri. *English only* 4pm Mon, Tue, Fri. **Admission** free. **Map** p281 G9/G8.

Microcentro

It's every claustrophobe's worst nightmare: weekdays during business hours the whole downtown district is a maelstrom of *porteños* shopping, working, running, shouting, flouting traffic laws and generally fulfilling their big-city stereotype.

The district is nicknamed La City – and was once known as 'the 20 blocks that rule the country' – for its early association with British commerce. It has the largest concentration of financial institutions in the country, extending almost the entire length of Florida, San Martín and Reconquista (named after the reconquest, when Buenos Aires repelled the English in 1806-07). Many of the banks were built during the first half of the 20th century, at a time when affluent Argentinians had money to deposit, and stand

Turning left on Roque Sáenz Peña (better known as **Diagonal Norte**) you'll hit **Plaza de Mayo**. Orbit the square in a clockwise direction, passing by the **Catedral Metropolitana**, the **Banco de la Nación** and the **Casa Rosada** (Pink House).

Exit the square on **Avenida de Mayo** and grab a *café con leche* at **London City** at No.599. Famed author Julio Cortázar made this lively coffeehouse the setting for the opening chapter of his novel *Los Premios*. Another three blocks along the Avenida is **Café Tortoni** (*see p139*), BA's most famous beanhouse. It's been serving coffee to the city's literati since 1858. Continue up Avenida de Mayo, crossing the grand asphalt canyon of **9 de Julio**. Passing the statue of Don Quixote you'll reach the **Castelar Hotel** at No.1152 (*see p45*), where Federico García Lorca lived between 1933 and 1934. You can mimic Lorca's old routine by dropping in at **Café Los 36 Billares** at No.1317.

It's now just three blocks to Plaza del Congreso. Admire, as you pass, the Gaudí-esque lumps and bumps of **Palacio Barolo**, and then settle in for your final cup of java at **Café Literario Osvaldo Bayer** on the southern edge of the plaza. It's run by the Mothers of Plaza de Mayo.

Complete your odyssey in front of the **Palacio del Congreso**. It may interest you to know that the 72 Senate desks all have a button for direct calls to the cafeteria.

out for their architectural refinement. A good example is the former **Banco Tornquist**, at Bartolomé Mitre 559, on the first section of street to be paved in BA. Scale models of what the district looked like during the 19th century and how it is now are on display in the **Museo del Banco de la Provincia** (Sarmiento 362, 4331 1775). Another financially-themed museum, the excellent **Museo Numismático** (First Floor, San Martín 216, 4348 3882) exhibits exotic early bank notes featuring dogs, goats, sheep, cows and even a kangaroo, plus rare coins minted in Tierra del Fuego.

To see how affluent *porteños* lived during the economic boom of the late 19th century, step into the **Museo Mitre** (*see below*) – home of former president and founder of *La Nación* newspaper, Bartolomé Mitre. It contains his rich library specialising in American history.

At the corner of Reconquista and Perón, protected by wonderful wrought iron gates is the 18th-century **Basílica Nuestra Señora de la Merced**, the richly decorative façade of which was restored in 1905. Next door, the **Convento de San Ramón**'s patio contains small attractive shops and a hidden lunchtime eaterie overlooking an attractive garden.

Along the west side of Avenida Leandro N Alem, more commonly called *el bajo* – meaning the low place – runs an almost uninterrupted arcade packed with banks, cafés, the stock exchange and, on its east side, the colossal **Correo Central**, located at Sarmiento 151. Inaugurated after 41 years of construction in 1928, the Central Post Office is one of BA's best examples of French-inspired classical architecture. Philatelists will want to check out the little museum inside. Diagonally opposite the post office's northeast corner is **Luna Park**, where Carlos Gardel's funeral was held in 1935 and where in 1944 Perón met Eva. It's now a music venue (*see p204*).

Though once an elegant thoroughfare, Florida, the only completely pedestrianised street in BA, is now unashamedly commercial. However, amid the cybercafé promo girls and money changers, you can find still find traces of its refined past (*see left* **Walk on**).

As Florida's old glamour wanes, more modern variations on retail sophistication spring up. **Galerías Pacífico** (*see p148*) is the city's most aesthetically inspired mall. In its south-east corner (with an entrance at the corner of Viamonte and San Martín) is the **Centro Cultural Borges** (*see p191*), built in memory of Argentina's greatest writer, and a thriving venue for the arts. Behind it on the corner of San Martín and Viamonte is the 18th-century church of **Santa Catalina**.

Lavalle, for pedestrians only between San Martín and Carlos Pellegrini, is even brasher than Florida, packed with blockbuster and B-movie cinemas, fast-food outlets, advertising boards and neon lights, plus a Bible-bashing, liberal-lashing evangelical church.

Close by, but extending beyond the Microcentro, is Corrientes. Though it's been an *avenida* since 1936, people still fondly call it a *calle*. Until the 1970s it was the mecca for tango artists, BA's Broadway and a coffee-drinking, literature-loving nocturnal scene, where *bohos* would meet to talk revolution and rock 'n' roll.

Museo Mitre

San Martín 336, entre Corrientes y Sarmiento (4394 8240/7659/www.museomitre.gov.ar). Subte B, Florida/93, 99, 109, 132 bus. **Open** *Museum* 1-6.30pm Mon-Fri. *Library* 12.30-6pm Mon-Fri. **Admission** AR$1 suggested contribution; free under-12s, concessions. **No credit cards. Map** p281 F11.

The **Edificio Kavanagh** (*top left*), the **Monumento al Libertador General San Martín** (*top right*) and **Plaza San Martín**. For all, *see p73*.

Retiro

For centuries this area – a natural point on the river – was the northern edge of the town, and was once the refuge of a hermit known as '*la ermita de San Sebastián*'. When a late-17th-century Spanish governor built a country house in the area for his retirement, and called it El Retiro – *retiro* means 'retreat' – the district took its name. Today the area's main attraction is its open space – the well-shaded green swath that is the lovely **Plaza San Martín**, the city's second most important plaza.

This natural bluff stretches down to three railway terminals, beyond which lie a jumble of official buildings and the docks. It's named after José de San Martín, who trained his troops here. The Liberator is still revered. According to protocol, all visiting dignitaries must lay a wreath at the **Monumento al Libertador General San Martín**, the city's most important monument. It's a heroic marble and bronze equestrian affair created in 1862 by French sculptor Louis Joseph Daumas.

Sun-worshipping office workers lunch in the plaza, while an inordinate number of couples locked in marathon kissing sessions loll underneath overhanging branches or lie exposed to the sun on the windy vantage point of the green slopes.

The first block of Florida leading off the plaza was called '*la manzana loca*' (the crazy block) in the 1960s for the avant-garde art experiments held at the Instituto di Tella at Florida 940 (now a multi-brand shop with a small art space). The district is still arty – with numerous galleries and regular gatherings among the creative set at trad cafés such as **Florida Garden** (*see p140*) and funky bars like **Dadá** (*see p139*).

Several impressive buildings surround Plaza San Martín. South-west is the gargantuan **Palacio Paz**, the largest private residence in the country and formerly the home of José C Paz, founder of the once important (but now derided) *La Prensa* newspaper. Since 1938, by which time the Paz empire had shrunk to insignificance, military officers have luxuriated in part of the palace renamed the **Círculo Militar** (to see inside, you have to join a 90-minute Spanish guided tour; 4311 1071, www.circulomilitar.org). One wing now houses the **Museo de Armas de la Nación** (*see p74*), a sizable collection of arms and military uniforms, some dating from medieval times, plus a room of ancient Oriental weapons.

At the edge of the plaza, the **Palacio San Martín** (Arenales 761, 4819 8092) – until recently home of the Argentinian foreign ministry – was built between 1909 and 1912

for the mega-rich Anchorena family. Nowadays, it's mostly used for official galas, although it opens for guided tours in Spanish most Thursdays and Fridays, which include a view of the garden containing a section of the Berlin Wall and an excellent collection of pre-Columbian Argentinian art.

On the opposite side of the plaza, the **Basílica del Santísimo Sacramento**, at San Martín 1039, regularly plays host to society weddings. Also built with Anchorena money (before they lost it all in the Depression) and consecrated in 1916, the French exterior hides an inner sanctum combining Flemish and Italian handiwork with French and North African raw materials. Mercedes Castellanos de Anchorena, the woman who used some of her savings to build the church and lived at the Palacio San Martín, rests in expensive peace in an ornate marble vault in the crypt. The **Edificio Kavanagh** next door also points heavenward – at 120 metres (394 feet) it was South America's tallest building when completed in 1935, the project bankrolled by Irishwoman Corina Kavanagh. At the time of its construction, this apartment block was admired by rationalist architects all over the world and is still considered an art deco landmark. Next door the luxurious **Plaza Hotel** (now part of the Marriott chain; *see p39*) was built, in 1908, by Alfred Zucker, architect of Saint Patrick's Cathedral in New York.

At the very foot of the plaza is a black marble cenotaph to those who fell in the Falklands/Malvinas War, watched over by two soldiers in traditional uniforms who perform a stiff changing of the guard several times a day.

Across the road from this sombre memorial, in an ironic twists of history, stands a Big Ben lookalike. The British-designed and built clock tower used to be known as the **Torre de los Ingleses** – it was presented as a gift to Argentina by local Anglo-Argentinians for the 1910 centennial celebrations. Since war with the UK in 1982, though, the authorities have insisted on using its official name, Torre Monumental, though most locals are too stubborn to hop on the patriotic bandwagon. Likewise, the land around it, formerly called the Plaza Británica, was renamed **Plaza Fuerza Aérea Argentina**. For a panoramic view of the plaza and the English-built railway stations, you can take a lift to the sixth floor – 35 metres (115 feet) up (though opening hours are irregular). There are occasional exhibits in the small photo gallery inside.

Shattering the peace is the endless din from horn-honking lorries on Avenida del Libertador leading to the railway stations. Though everyone says they are going 'to Retiro' to get

Sightseeing

a train or bus, there are, in fact, three separate train terminals plus a bus station along Avenida JM Ramos Mejia. The largest, English-built terminal, the Mitre, dates from 1915, and stands out as one of South America's best examples of Crystal Palace-inspired architecture. A plaque on an arch of its iron structure reads 'Francis Morton & Co Ltd – Liverpool'. Although recently renovated it still retains a hue of the golden age of railways in objects such as a tobacco-stained map of Argentina's once 45,000-kilometre (27,000-mile) network, by far the largest in South America.

Surrounding the terminals, food stands and market stalls add to the general noise and chaos, making for a colourful though stressful walk, especially in rush hours. The **Paseo del Retiro** handicrafts fair, created to give some life to the uninviting wasteland opposite the bus station, runs every weekend.

Just north of the bus terminal is Villa 31, the capital's best-known shanty town. The reason for the slum's notoriety is the community's refusal to move from this potentially prime real estate until the city offers them something better. The adjacent badlands consist of run-down military and other buildings. Avoid this area, especially after dusk.

A couple of blocks up Libertador in an old railway building is the **Museo Nacional Ferroviario** (*see below*). The two floors

are an intriguing hotchpotch from a railway era that puts recent car-obsessed governments to shame. Beside the museum is the workshop of Carlos Regazzoni, an internationally respected sculptor whose creations are made from the scrap he finds in the railway yards.

Just a hop across the road and up the incline at Suipacha 1422 is one of BA's cultural gems, the **Museo de Arte Hispanoamericano Isaac Fernández Blanco** (*see below*) in a beautiful Peruvian-style mansion The white baroque building – also known as the Palacio Noel, for its architect – houses Spanish American paintings, religious objects and silverware. The ghost of a lady in white is said to inhabit the house. Classical and folk music fans can catch concerts on Friday, Saturday and Sunday evenings at 7pm, often featuring the museum's own baroque chamber orchestra. If time permits, take a stroll in the mansion's peaceful, ivy-lined Andalucian courtyard. Tours of the museum for groups of ten or more are available in English by appointment only.

The **Plaza Embajada de Israel** lies on the corner of Suipacha and Arroyo streets. A bomb destroyed a previous Israeli embassy on this site in 1992. Each of the 29 trees represents a victim of the blast. The surrounding area has recovered from this atrocity and the secluded *calle* Arroyo is now the heart of an art gallery circuit.

At Suipacha 1333, Argentina's main English-language teaching organisation runs the **British Arts Centre** (BAC; *see below*). It puts on loads of free events such as plays and films in English as well as jazz, Celtic and classical concerts, and photo and art exhibits and workshops.

British Arts Centre

Suipacha 1333, entre Juncal y Arroyo, Retiro (4393 6941). Bus 59, 61, 93, 130, 152. **Open** *Feb* 12.30pm-6.30pm Mon-Fri. *Mar-Dec* 3-9pm Mon-Fri. Closed Jan. **Admission** free. **Map** p281 H11/H12.

Museo de Armas de la Nación

Avenida Santa Fe 702, y Maipú (4311 1071). Subte C, San Martín/10, 17, 70, 152 bus. **Open** *Mar-Dec* 1-7pm Mon-Fri. Closed Jan, Feb. **Admission** AR$2; free under-5s, concessions. **No credit cards**. **Map** p281 G11.

Museo de Arte Hispanoamericano Isaac Fernández Blanco

Suipacha 1422, entre Arroyo y Libertador (4327 0272). Bus 93, 130, 152. **Open** 2-7pm Tue-Sun. **Guided tours** (Spanish) 4pm Sat, 3pm Sun. **Admission** AR$3. Free Thur. **No credit cards**. **Map** p281 H12.

Museo Nacional Ferroviario

Avenida del Libertador 405, y Suipacha (4318 3343/3538). Subte C, Retiro/59, 61, 93, 130, 152 bus. **Open** *Feb-Dec* 10am-4pm Mon-Fri. Closed Jan. **Admission** free. **Map** p281 H12.

Círculo Militar. *See p73*.

South of the Centre

Crumbling colonial mansions and gleaming internet cafés – welcome to *el Sur*.

BUENOS AIRES PROVINCE

Liniers

BUENOS AIRES CITY

South of the Centre

RÍO DE LA PLATA

The ghosts of BA's romantic, bohemian past are stubborn spirits indeed. Harangued by commercialism, the construction boom and the endless drive for progress, they continue to haunt the low-lying barrios south of Plaza de Mayo – Monserrat, San Telmo, La Boca and Barracas. With his trademark blend of nostalgia and irony, the young Borges wrote that 'the Sur is the original substance from which Buenos Aires is made.'

Although spruced up for tourists in recent years (particularly the San Telmo barrio), its crumbling façades, narrow passageways and sepia-toned cafés still breathe history and the south has shed little of its lyrical melancholy. At least for a while longer, el Sur remains a magnet for nighthawks, romantics and anyone searching for the city's primordial soul.

Monserrat

A recent influx of money and youthful residents hasn't yet transformed moody Monserrat into a competitor for its tourist-friendly neighbour San Telmo, but when it comes to history, Monserrat is in a class of its own.

At the time of independence, when Buenos Aires was still a *gran aldea* ('big village'), the sector known as Catedral al Sur was an affluent area of patrician families and merchants. A rivulet running down Chile street was the city limit and artisans from the suburb of San Telmo had to cross a bridge to sell their goods. Over time, a building spree would make the dividing line all but illusory. Indeed, today the two barrios share a common identity as an enclave of tranquillity just a few steps from the downtown bedlam.

What distinguishes them from each other is Monserrat's pivotal role in the country's independence struggle, still apparent in the district's colonial-era churches. Bounded by Alsina, Bolívar, Moreno and Perú streets is a complex of historical buildings filling the whole city block and known as the **Manzana de las Luces** (Block of Enlightenment; *see p79*). The illumination moniker was coined in the early 19th century in allusion to the wisdom garnered by the leading lights who were educated here. A church and school have their own entrances, the former open for Mass, the latter only for those going to classes. The main attractions are the Jesuit and early political institutions, now a museum which can be accessed at Perú 272.

Top five | Churches

Basílica de Santo Domingo
Shelled by the English invaders, and later a hospital for the defeated. *See p79*.

Catedral de San Isidro
Neo-Gothic glory in the upscale suburbia of Zona Norte. *See p105*.

Catedral Metropolitana
Worship central, where the Liberator rests in peace. *See p65*.

Nuestra Señora del Pilar
Simple, elegant church on Spanish colonial lines for the Recoleta gentry. *See p87*.

Iglesia Ortodoxa Rusa
Gloriously, garishly incongruous onion domes at Parque Lezama. *See p80*.

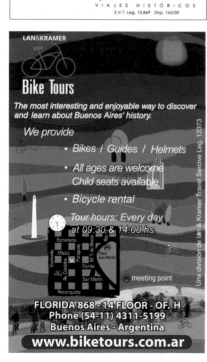

The courtyard is sometimes used in the evenings for cultural events and by day a small café serves drinks and sandwiches. From the museum you can peek into the subterranean passageways that once connected the complex with neighbouring buildings.

The block's **Iglesia de San Ignacio**, on the corner of Alsina and Bolívar, dates from 1734 and is the oldest church in the city. Despite its importance, it almost collapsed in 2003 when the gaping fissures caused by neglect started to rupture. After frocked priests took to the streets in protest, the city closed the block and erected scaffolding to prop up the edifice. The priests have retreated to their cloisters but the scaffolding remains.

Hidden behind the church is the brick-walled patio of the **Procuraduría de las Misiones**, accessed on Avenida Julio A Roca (also known as Diagonal Sur), which cuts into the block, via a small handicrafts market. This was the HQ of the Jesuits who ran the New World conversion programme in the 18th century.

Next door, at Perú 272, is the **Sala de Representantes** (Representatives' Chamber), from which BA province was governed until 1880, when the federal district was created and provincial capital moved to La Plata. You can take a guided tour of the semicircular chamber, the patios and a series of 18th-century tunnels – whose purpose remains a mystery – which once linked the building to the coast behind what is now Plaza de Mayo, several hundred metres away. Another law-makers' edifice, the belle époque **Legislatura de la Ciudad**, is at Perú 130 (www.legislatura.gov.ar).

On the opposite corner of Alsina and Bolívar from the church is the **Librería de Ávila** (4331 8989), the city's oldest bookshop, dating from 1785. There's another bookish haunt a few blocks south; the old Biblioteca Nacional building on Mexico 564, now a research centre for musicologists, is where Jorge Luis Borges served as library director for 17 years. It's now a research centre for musicologists.

On the corner of Alsina and Defensa is the charming 1894 chemist La Estrella, whose mahogany interior has barely been touched. At lunchtime office workers file in to test its two-metre (seven-foot) Toledo, Ohio-made iron weighing scale, reputed to be the most accurate in the city. Directly above is the **Museo de la Ciudad** (*see p79*), created as a labour of love in 1968 by José María Peña, a leading authority on Buenos Aires' architecture. In addition to displays of antiques, photos and junk collected by Peña, there's a re-creation of the living quarters of a well-heeled 19th-century family. Around the corner on Alsina a row of crumbling houses saved from the wrecking ball

gives testament to Monserrat's successive facelifts. In an attempt to link Monserrat with more vibrant San Telmo, free walking tours of this historic area, in Spanish, set out from the museum on Sundays at 3pm.

Opposite the chemist's is the **Iglesia de San Francisco**, begun in 1730 by Jesuit architect Andrés Blanqui, who also worked on the Pilar church in Recoleta and the Cabildo. Inside, there is a startlingly gaudy 20th-century tapestry of St Francis by Argentinian artist Horacio Butler, evidently a fan of psychedelic flowers and cartoon animals.

Adjacent to this church is the smaller **Parroquia San Roque** (Roque parish church), built in the 1750s. Opposite, the **Plazoleta San Francisco** contains four statues, moved here from Plaza de Mayo in 1972. They depict geography, sailing, astronomy and industry – in short, all of the disciplines that have tested belief in the God worshipped across the road.

In the middle of all these Roman Catholic ramparts and monuments to post-colonial ambition, the **Museo Etnográfico** (*see p79*) delivers a salutary reminder that before the arrival of the Europeans, Argentina had such a thing as an indigenous population. The small collection contains headdresses, masks, cooking implements and panels describing the

Shopping at **Manzana de las Luces**. See p79.

The other side of the tracks

There are two kinds of gated community in Argentina, sharing nothing in common save or the fences. One is the rural residential estate – known simply as 'countrys' – where wealthy families reside in comfort and tranquillity. The other is the *villa miseria, or* shanty town, where poor families reside in squalor and insecurity. Both types of community have proliferated in Argentina over the last decade.

There are more than 30 *villas* in the Federal Capital and many more in Greater Buenos Aires. Each can house – or rather shack – up to 25,000 people, the majority living in conditions not seen in the First World since the early days of the Industrial Revolution.

In a typical *villa* dwelling the roof is a rusty sheet of corrugated iron slung over tottering walls. Where the brickwork is particularly bad, well, there's your window. Improvised bunk beds might allow six children to share a single, sunless room, and anything resembling plumbing and sanitation raises the householder to nouveau riche status.

There's no gloss to be put on this kind of poverty: it's simple, raw and, for many, unrelenting. But if you assumed destitution and dignity to be mutually exclusive you'd be wrong. Many *villa* dwellers do their best to keep their places tidy and ordered; to break the visual monotony, interior and exterior walls are splashed in primary colours.

This isn't something you'll hear often in the local media. Press reports on shanty town life tend to cleave to one of two extremes. Either the *villa* is a kind of sprawling vice den harbouring criminals, delinquents and the terminally hopeless; or else it is a symbol of social injustice, a concentration camp in all but name for the misfits capitalist society has deemed surplus to requirement.

Both these portrayals tend to duck an important point. Which is that along with the familiar spectres of the modern slum (hard drug use, chronic unemployment, malnutrition, teenage pregnancy and so on) *villas* have a lot in common with conventional communities. For every glue-sniffing cop killer, there are countless ordinary people trying to live ordinary lives. They go shopping, they get their hair cut, they watch soaps – all within the *villa*.

BA shanty towns also have a surprisingly formal structure of self-governance. Every *villa* has a president, elected once every four years. It's hardly Jeffersonian democracy in action – but then this could equally be said about the country at large.

There are obvious reasons why *villas* aren't usually included in BA sightseeing guides. But a new tour – the first in Argentina – gives visitors the opportunity to witness at first hand everyday life in a BA *villa*. The tour has attracted a lot of local press, not all of it favourable. Some argue that it makes a fetish out of poverty and is hardly the face Argentina should be showing to the world. You might agree. But tour or no tour, keep the *villa* in mind for the next time you see a 'Buenos Aires is booming' headline.

Villa Tour

Tour Experience (4833 0717 ext 36/ www.tourexperience.com.ar). US$70.

different tribes region by region. However, a wood-carved Japanese Buddhist altar is the museum's most valuable object.

The **Basílica de Santo Domingo** and the adjoining **Basílica Nuestra Señora del Rosario**, at Defensa and Belgrano, are two other important 18th-century centres of worship. One of the towers of the former was punctured by bullets during the English Invasions of 1806-07. The flags seized from the vanquished invaders are on display in the far corner left of the altar and even the street name Defensa pays homage to this first popular local resistance against foreign forces.

Manzana de las Luces
Perú 272, entre Moreno y Alsina (4342 9930). Subte A, Plaza de Mayo or D, Catedral or E, Bolívar/24, 29, 86, 126 bus. **Open** 3-8pm daily. *Tours* (Spanish) 3pm Mon-Fri. **Admission** *Manzana* free. *Guided tours* AR$4; free for under-6s. **No credit cards.** Map p281 E10. *Photo p77.*

Museo de la Ciudad
Defensa 219, entre Alsina y Moreno (4331 9855/ 4343 2123). Subte A, Plaza de Mayo or D, Catedral or E, Bolívar/24, 29, 64, 86, 130 bus. **Open** *Museum* 11am-7pm Mon-Fri; 3-7pm Sun. *Library* 1-6pm Mon-Fri. **Admission** AR$3, free under-12s. Free Wed. **No credit cards.** Map p281 E10.

Museo Etnográfico
Moreno 350, entre Balcarce y Defensa (4331 7788/www.museoetnografico.filo.uba.ar). Subte A, Plaza de Mayo or D, Catedral or E, Bolívar/24, 29, 64, 152 bus. **Open** Feb-Dec 3-7pm Wed-Sun. *Tours* (Spanish) 4pm Sat, Sun. **Admission** AR$2. **No credit cards.** Map p281 E10.

San Telmo

Tourists love San Telmo; *porteños*, as a rule, do not. This perception gap is easy to explain. While visitors to Buenos Aires are entranced by the barrio's cobbled streets and crumbling stucco, and thrill to its echoes of European old quarters long since sanitised by municipal clean-ups and Olympic-bid investments, many locals view the barrio as dirty, run-down and unsafe.

But San Telmo is changing. It is becoming more glamorous and less faded. A regeneration spurred by the arrival of antique dealers and restaurateurs – and more recently hostel owners and a thriving gay scene – has brought the area into the 20th century, if not yet the 21st.

Heading to San Telmo from the Plaza de Mayo, Defensa and Balcarce are the most pleasant streets to walk along. The former is full of antique shops and considered the main vein running through the barrio, while the latter is a quieter, cobblestoned street lined with tango venues (even though San Telmo is not historically linked to the dance) and tiny cafés.

While walking you will pass by several of the tattered mansions and drooping balconies that give San Telmo its unmistakable appearance. Most were occupied by grand families until a mass exodus from cholera and yellow fever took place over a century ago.

Subsequently the old houses were turned into tenements – called *conventillos* – with poor immigrant families occupying what were formerly single rooms round the main patio. As these humble abodes are still very much lived in, no matter how open the doors look, the general public are not welcome. To see the inside of an 1880 house, visit the lovely **Pasaje de la Defensa** (at Defensa 1179), a refurbished two-storey building originally owned by the Ezeiza family, and now hectic with souvenir and bric-a-brac shops.

The adjacent streets are also of interest, with a myriad of bars and restaurants punctuating the houses. The quaint Pasaje San Lorenzo and Pasaje Giuffra – their cobbles harking back to a more attractive city from the 1930s and '40s – were formerly streams running down to the river where Avenida Paseo Colón now pullulates. San Lorenzo 380 is the location of the strikingly ultra-thin colonial house **Casa Mínima**, the narrowest house in the city at just two metres (six feet) wide – but 50 metres (165 feet) long. According to local legend, the house was built by freed slaves in 1800 on a sliver of land bestowed by their master next door.

Casa Minima is part of the same conservation initiative that rescued **El Zanjón**, a beautifully restored colonial mansion capturing three centuries of urban living, situated round the corner where San Lorenzo butts against Defensa. While the façade dates from 1830, traces from an early patrician home – an open-air cistern, a lookout tower and a 1740 wall comprised of seashell mortaring – magically transport you to the era of Spanish settlement.

Down on Avenida Paseo Colón is Rogelio Trutia's intriguing bronze monument **Canto al Trabajo** (Song to Work) on the plaza of the same name (at Avenida Independencia). Another five blocks south there's a different, less exalting monument. Beneath the motorway flyover, a grim sculpture of climbing bodies stands guard over an unearthed pit where Argentina's long-buried, 'Dirty War' past is literally being resurrected. In 2002, a team of archaeologists discovered intact the basement torture centre of the former Club Atlético, where some 1,800 prisoners 'disappeared' before the military government demolished the building to build the highway in 1978.

The rest of Avenida Paseo Colón is dominated by a series of serious-looking public buildings, three of them – the army's **Edificio** del Libertador, the **Aduana** (headquarters of the customs service) and the **Secretaría de Agricultura** (Ministry of Agriculture) – built along French Academic lines. The Libertador is fronted by tanks, cannons and a Soviet-looking statue of an Unknown Soldier. The soldier has a hole in his chest, a symbol of those who died in the Falklands/Malvinas, but, while not buried on the islands, left their hearts there.

The fourth public building is the University of Buenos Aires' **Facultad de Ingeniería** (Faculty of Engineering), a harsh classical building that originally housed the Fundación Eva Perón, the charity created by Evita. Far more attractive is the tall, slim red-brick **Iglesia Dinamarquesa** at Carlos Calvo 257. A Lutheran church built in 1931, its modern gothic style is jovially at odds with everything else in San Telmo.

On Sundays, **Plaza Dorrego**, one of the few Spanish-style plazas in the city where you can drink beer and coffee in the open air, is taken over by traders, tango and tourists. Although it's a genuine, fully functional and ever-expanding antiques market, it also provides one of BA's most popular days out for visitors and locals alike, especially when the sun is shining. The fun of the feria now spreads all the way down Defense, spilling over to Avenida Independencia where some arts and crafts stalls have made it their Sunday destination. Buskers of all types and talents throng to the area on market day, and once the stalls close down in the evening, an open air *milonga* kicks off. Arrive early if you want to avoid the often overwhelming crowds.

Half a block from the square's busy **Bar Plaza Dorrego** (*see p140*) at Humberto I° 378 is the **Museo Penitenciario Nacional** (open Sundays only; 4362 0099) tracing penal life from the city's foundation to the present. On the same block, at Humberto I° 340, stands the **Iglesia Nuestra Señora de Belén**, an architecturally eclectic church crowned by blue and white Andalucian-style tiled towers. Nine altars and assorted virgins and saints adorn the busy interior, among them San Pedro Telmo, the patron saint of the barrio and guardian of sailors. The church's role as a place of asylum for those injured in the so-called English Invasions is recorded in a thank-you message from the 71st Regiment of the Scottish Rifles.

For fashion victims only, there's an enjoyable small museum – **Museo del Traje** (Museum of Suits – Chile 832, 4343 8427, www.funmuseo deltraje.com.ar) – tracing Argentinian fads and fashions from 1850 to the present. Art lovers should head for the under-appreciated **Museo de Arte Moderno** (*see below*). It's no Tate Modern or MOMA, but it serves as a vital proving ground for contemporary Argentinian artists working in a variety of media. The museum, housed in a recycled tobacco warehouse, has no permanent exhibits. Instead it hosts excellent temporary shows, as well as various music and video events.

Next door, with an entrance on Defensa, the compact **Museo del Cine** (*see p81*) contains relics and movie posters from almost a century's worth of Argentinian filmmaking.

At the southern end of San Telmo, **Parque Lezama** is a dramatic patch of greenery on the bluff of the old city, which, for many historians, is the location of the initial settlement of Buenos Aires. A monument at the Brasil and Defensa corner commemorates Pedro de Mendoza's hypothetical landfall at this spot in 1536 and on the south side is the **Monumento a la Confraternidad** (Monument to Brotherhood), expressed as a neo-industrial boat.

A beautiful terracotta-coloured colonial mansion houses the **Museo Histórico Nacional** (*see p81*), a useful introduction to the city's history. Outside the museum, the park is a dramatic cliff, covered in majestic palms and yellow-flowered *tipa* trees. Musicians and second-rate market stalls populate the park at weekends and a wonderfully out-of-place **Iglesia Ortodoxa Rusa**, topped with blue onions in the Muscovite style, adds further colour to the Lezama scene.

Until not so long ago San Telmo was busiest during the day, but new bars, restaurants and a high concentration of new hostels are putting it on the BA after-hours circuit. Some touristy eateries around Plaza Dorrego are richer in history than in food and service, and thus better for a drink than meal. Tango supper shows at the venues on Balcarce are another option. New cafés and eateries are springing up along Bolívar and Defensa streets, with an impressive concentration along Chile between Bolívar and Balcarce. A scattering of underground nightclubs, and the justly famed Gibraltar pub (*see p143*) are where much of the late-night action is concentrated.

El Zanjón

Defensa 755, entre Chile y Independencia (4361 3002). Bus 24, 29, 93, 130, 152. **Open** 11am-5pm Mon-Fri; noon-5.30pm Sun. **Tours** (English) Mon-Fri on the hr 11am-5pm. **Admission** AR$20; AR$13 Mon; AR$8 under-12s. **No credit cards.** **Map** p281 E10.

Museo de Arte Moderno

Avenida San Juan 350, entre Defensa y Balcarce (4361 1121). Bus 29, 64, 86, 130, 152. **Open** Mar-Jan 10am-8pm Tue-Fri; 11am-8pm Sat, Sun. **Closed** Feb. **Guided tours** (Spanish) 5pm Tue, Wed, Fri, Sun. **Admission** AR$3. **No credit cards.** **Map** p280 D9.

19th-century bricks and mortar in **San Telmo**. *See p79.*

Museo del Cine

Defensa 1220, entre San Juan y Cochabamba (4361 2462/www.museos.buenosaires.gov.ar). Bus 29, 64, 86, 130, 152. **Open** 10am-7pm Tue-Fri; 11.30am-6.30pm Sat, Sun. **Admission** free. **Map** p280 D9.

Museo Histórico Nacional

Defensa 1600, y Caseros (4307 1182/4457). Bus 10, 24, 29, 39, 64, 130, 152. **Open** *Feb-Dec* 11am-5pm Tue-Fri; 3-6pm Sat; 2-6pm Sun. **Closed** Jan. **Guided tours** (Spanish) 3pm Sat, Sun. **Admission** AR$2. **No credit cards. Map** p280 C9.

La Boca

With its down-on-their-luck *cantinas* and crowded tenements, the waterfront quarter of La Boca still feels like the melting pot where tango was first cooked up a century ago. The working-class barrio derives its name from its location at the mouth of the Riachuelo, until the late 19th century the obligatory entry point to the city. But when the docks moved north to Puerto Madero, decline set in. Today, all that's left of the once bustling port are a few abandoned hulks and rusting warehouses. But the barrio's waterfront is enjoying its own renaissance, partly thanks to a booming tourist trade that has more and more people making the long trek down to the tiny, multicoloured Caminito.

The barrio stretches from the river right up to the roundabout where Avenida Paseo Colón becomes Avenida Martín García, and where a mast and a 3-D frieze announce that you are entering the 'República de la Boca'. The lively artwork, made from the scrap left behind when one of the tin tenements was torn down, is a collage of all the barrio's best-loved icons and sights. Buses enter the neighbourhood here, heading down Avenida Almirante Brown, named after the Irishman who founded the Argentinian navy.

Set back from the river, on Brandsen, is the reason why people who have never been to Buenos Aires have heard of La Boca. The port a thing of the past, the communal heart now beats at the Estadio Alberto J Armando, aka **La Bombonera**, where top-flight football team Club Atlético Boca Juniors have held court for nearly a century. The blue and yellow of the team strip is ubiquitous on walls and balconies throughout the neighbourhood. Boca's most famous ex-player and fan, Diego Armando Maradona, is still idolised by the club's ardent and multitudinous supporters (*see also p205*).

You can't miss the stadium from Avenida Almirante Brown, as the sheer walls rise high above the wasteland where community events take place. Murals on the stadium walls by

Colourful characters at the **Centro Cultural de los Artistas**. *See p83.*

Argentinian painter Pérez Celis and others tell the story of the port. Football motifs record how the workers embraced the beautiful game as an escape from hardship. It's best to avoid the area surrounding the stadium on game days.

The team's exploits have spurned an empire controlled by its politically ambitious president Mauricio Macri, who finished a close second in Buenos Aires' 2003 mayoral race and was elected to Congress in 2005. In addition to a Boca theme bar and cable TV channel, Macri is responsible for what's become a mecca for football-worshipping tourists: the **Museo de la Pasión Boquense**, located at the stadium's entrance. Much of the museum and gift shop consists of ephemera appealing to the already devout Boca fan, such as an exhibit of a century's worth of shirts or Boca Juniors deodorant. But tourists will appreciate the exhibit that puts the club's successes in their larger, national context. Football-as-opiate conspiracy theorists will note that Boca's on-field performance seems to improve the more Argentina unravels. The entrance fee to the museum includes a tour of the stadium, the only way to see inside if not attending a game.

From the Museo's entrance a disused railway track runs down Garibaldi (where Nazi Adolf Eichmann once lived), which comes out two blocks later at the back end of **Caminito**, a short, banana-shaped pedestrianised theme street recognised as Argentina's only open-air museum. The better way to arrive is via the riverside promenade. Its name – which means 'little walkway' – comes from a 1926 tango by legendary composers Gabino Coria Peñaloza and Juan de Dios Filiberto, the melancholic lyrics of which are inscribed on a wall plaque.

One of several barrios claiming to be the birthplace of tango, La Boca is the kind of place where you can imagine sailors, hustlers, drinkers and wide-boys from all over Europe rubbing shoulders and flashing blades in the early 1900s. The corrugated zinc shacks on Caminito owe their vivid colours to the imaginative but impoverished locals, who begged incoming ships for excess tins of paint so that they could doll up their houses. At Magallanes 861, a former *conventillo* slum dwelling has been transformed into crafts studios and souvenir shops, called **Centro Cultural de los Artistas**. There's not much to see, but it's interesting to peek into an old slum dwelling. Papier-mâché models of famous Boca figures lean from the balconies. At Del Valle Iberlucea 1261 is the tiny **Museo Histórico de Cera de La Boca** (4301 1497, www.museodecera.com.ar), an old-fashioned museum housing a waxwork collection of mummies, national figures and native fauna.

La Vuelta de Rocha, the road that follows the bend in the river at the opening to Caminito, is marked by a mast and rigging. A painting at the Museo Nacional de Bellas Artes in Recoleta bears the same name, and its stylised portrayal of this corner is an acknowledgement of the near-mythical status the area has for *porteños*.

However, it's not all nostalgia in La Boca. **Fundación Proa** (*see p193*), in a recycled waterfront mansion just south of Caminito, is one of the city's premier spaces for contemporary art and a great reason to visit the area. The area's other outstanding gallery is housed in the buildings donated to La Boca by painter Benito Quinquela Martín (1890-1977), close friend of tango composer Juan de Dios Filiberto. It was Quinquela Martín who suggested that the main street be named Caminito when the musician fell ill. The **Museo de Bellas Artes de La Boca** (*see below*) contains works by Quinquela Martín and other Argentinian artists, as well as a large collection of bowsprits, relics of the neighbourhood's nautical past.

There is a real sense of being on the edge of a city in La Boca. Three bridges at the northern end of Avenida Pedro de Mendoza connect the capital with the province and symbolise the changes that have taken place as La Boca has dwindled as a maritime and commercial centre. The oldest is the **Puente Trasbordador** (transporter bridge), a massive iron contraption that ferried trains, livestock and people across to Isla Maciel in the industrial suburb of Avellaneda from 1914 to 1940.

The Riachuelo, which for over a century was a repository of cattle carcasses, oil, oxidised metals and assorted toxins, is nearer black than brown – you'll smell it before you see it. Some progress has been made in cleaning it up but the only real change has been to remove most of the beached oxidised barges and wrecked ships that gave La Boca some character. A complete emptying of the river would strip the area of some of its most important ghosts.

Museo de Bellas Artes de La Boca Benito Quinquela Martín

Avenida Pedro de Mendoza 1835, entre Palos y Del Valle Iberlucea (4301 1080). Bus 29, 53, 64, 130, 152, 159. **Open** Feb-Dec 10am-5pm Tue-Fri; 11am-5.30pm Sat, Sun. **Closed** Jan. **Admission** suggested contribution AR$1. **No credit cards. Map** p280 A9.

Museo de la Pasión Boquense

Brandsen 805, y la Vía (4362 1100/www.museo boquense.com). Bus 10, 24, 29, 53, 64,. **Open** 10am-7pm daily (closed on match days). **Guided tours** (of stadium) hourly 11am-5pm. **Admission** *Museum or tour only* AR$7.90; AR$4 under-12s. *Museum & tour* AR$12.90; AR$8 under-12s. **Credit** AmEx, DC, MC, V. **Map** p280 B8.

Sightseeing

Constitución & Barracas

Sightseeing

Constitución and Barracas are run-down barrios that most *porteños* prefer to avoid. But without the former's railway station and the latter's warehouses, Buenos Aires would never have reached its late-19th-century economic splendour. Although close to the centre, these areas are rarely explored due to their desolate streets and dodgy after-dark reputation. A mini-renaissance, however, is under way in Barracas, and with so many pyramids to the golden age of industry for the taking, it's possible that the area could yet regain some of its former glory.

Dominating Plaza Constitución, the **Estación Constitución** is an imposing 1880s construction that has recently been restored. Built to shuttle the rich to the Atlantic resort of Mar del Plata, it now shuttles weary commuters southwards. The forecourt is a mad whirl of vagrants, vendors and commuters, with numerous bus lines terminating here too, just to add to the chaos.

The name Barracas refers to the warehouses that clustered here from the late 18th century onwards; cheap housing and brothels completed the picture by the early 1900s. The barrio was once BA's ground zero for worker uprisings and their subsequent repression, but with its anarchist bent long faded, a fledgling gentrification effort is converting many of the crumbling warehouses and grand relics of capitalism into affordable housing and offices for young artists and professionals. Indeed, with its quiet streets and panoramic views, Barracas feels like a post-industrial urban oasis. An early anchor of the renewal is the **Centro Metropolitano de Diseño** (*see below*), a city-run incubator for young designers that set up shop in 2001 in a remodelled facility that long ago housed the city's fish market. One block away along Villarino, underneath the elevated, art deco Yrigoyen train station, the recently restored **Arcos de Barracas** are a fine example of English-built, exposed brick arches.

Among the artists breathing new life into Barracas is Marino Santa María. Since 2001, on the dead-end *calle* Lanín, Santa María has been spearheading an imaginative public art project he calls the post-modern version of La Boca's Caminito. Every house on the curved two-block street is painted with colourful, abstract streaks resembling psychedelic tiger stripes. Santa María's studio can be visited at Lanín 33.

Centro Metropolitano de Diseño

Villarino 2498, y Santa María del Buen Ayre (4126 2950/www.cmd.org.ar). Train to Hipólito Yrigoyen/12, 37, 45 bus. **Open** 10am-6pm Mon-Fri. **Admission** free.

La Boca's **Fundación Proa**. *See p193.*

North of the Centre

Palaces and park life in BA's greenest, most affluent neighbourhoods.

The greenest and most pleasant land in Buenos Aires is concentrated in the neighbourhoods of Recoleta, Barrio Norte and Palermo, north of the city centre. It was to here that the *porteño* elite gravitated in 1871, fleeing the yellow fever epidemic then sweeping the city's southern zones. It was BA's first real estate boom. Now, with the exception of Puerto Madero, the northern neighbourhoods are the most exclusive and expensive of all BA's districts.

The area is bordered by Avenida Córdoba and a string of plazas and parks along busy Avenidas del Libertador and Figueroa Alcorta. The city is monumental and notably French in style in these parts, the wide boulevards and open spaces exploited as sites for statues honouring national heroes, immigrant communities and assorted international bigwigs. Many of Argentina's late greats are buried in the Cementerio de la Recoleta.

The greenery is in no small part due to the vision of French landscaper Charles Thays (1849-1934), who travelled to Argentina in the 1880s to study trees and ended up staying and designing the zoo, the Jardín Botánico, Parque Tres de Febrero and numerous private gardens.

Recoleta

In & around the Cementerio

It's BA's most exclusive patch of real estate – but nobody lives there. We refer, of course, to the **Cementerio de la Recoleta**, one of the world's great necropolises. Originally conceived by Bernardino Rivadavia and designed by Frenchman Próspero Catelin, the cemetery was opened in 1822. The narrow passages and high walls make comparisons with the real city outside inevitable. Entrance to the cemetery is through a Doric-columned portico designed in 1886 by Juan Buschiazzo, one of Argentina's most important architects.

The cemetery is home to hundreds of illustrious corpses, laid out in a compact maze of granite, marble and bronze mausoleums – most of the materials came from Paris and Milan – and a slow walk down its avenues and alleyways is one of BA's undisputed delights. Originally a public cemetery on the fringes of the city – nearby Avenida Callao marked the limit of Buenos Aires until the 1880s – it is now even harder to get into than the posh flats that surround it. Seafarers and freed slaves were once given their final berths in Recoleta, but now ordinary folk can only get in alive. Many Argentinian presidents are entombed here, though most visitors come to see the resting place of María Eva Duarte de Perón, aka Evita.

There are also impressive collective tombs (housing fallen soldiers), great pantheons and cenotaphs, inches away from one another. Assorted architectural styles are arranged side by side, from distinguished chemist Dr Pedro Arata's diminutive Egyptian pyramid to aristocrat Dorrego Ortiz Basualdo's monumental sepulchre, decorated with 'prudent virgins' and topped by a great candelabra. Among the patrician families here, residing in a style befitting one-time mansion dwellers, are the Alvears, the Estradas, the Balcarces and the Alzagas, together with members of the Paz clan.

The plazas outside the cemetery walls were once on the banks of the river, like the cliffs in *el bajo* (downtown). Though barely a bump in its present landscaped form, the mount was of sufficient size to serve as a hiding place for bandits and other undesirables in the 17th century. Between 1716 and 1730, a French chapter of the Franciscans, known as the Padres Recoletos, chose the area to build a chapel and convent as a place of retreat. At the same time, the Jesuits, already established as missionaries and merchants in northern Argentina, Paraguay and Brazil, settled in the Recoleta. Building of their **Basílica Nuestra Señora del Pilar** (Junín 1904, 4803 6793) began in 1716 and the church site was consecrated in 1732.

The plain-looking façade, the whiteness barely interrupted but for the sky-blue Pas-de-Calais ceramic tiles that decorate its upper reaches, is reminiscent of many colonial churches found in remote northern provinces. Inside is a superlative baroque altar, featuring Incan and other pre-Hispanic motifs. The altar was brought along the mule trails from Peru, the heart of colonial South America, and given a wrought-silver frontal in Jujuy in north-west Argentina. You can visit the cloisters, with a mini-museum of religious art, the crypt beneath the church and adjoining tunnels, thought to connect with tunnels in Monserrat, on regular guided tours.

To the north of the Pilar church, on the site of the Franciscan convent, is the **Centro Cultural Recoleta** (*see p191*). It promotes contemporary visual arts and contains several performance rooms. There is also a film projection room and an interactive science museum for kids (*see p180*). From the roof terrace, you can view the surrounding plazas and other sights.

It's not all high culture and high church though: a specialised mall, **Buenos Aires Design** (*see p151*) has two floors showcasing the latest in designer furniture and interiors. The mall's terraces are lined with cafés and restaurants, while south-west of the cemetery on Vicente López, is the **Village Recoleta** shopping centre (*see p188*), completing the incongruous picture of a city of the dead encircled by outer suburbs of fun and frivolity.

In the attractive grassy spaces in front of the Centro Cultural stretching down to Avenida Libertador are three giant *gomero* trees that provide shade for strollers, loungers and dog walkers. **Plaza Francia**, directly north-east of the cultural centre is commandeered on weekends and most public holidays by a handicraft fair, which draws tourists, stragglers and neo-hippies (*see p168*).

Across Posadas is the belle époque **Palais de Glace** (*see p89*), which was an ice-rink, a ballroom and an important tango salon in the 1920s, run by aristocrat Baron de Marchi. It was in this circular building that tango was officially embraced by the bourgeoisie. More recently it has been adopted by the city for trade expos, high-profile art exhibitions and fashion displays.

In front of the Palais de Glace stands a monument to Carlos María de Alvear, an officer who founded the horseguards regiment in 1812 with San Martín, and was the first in a line of

Take tea on the terrace at **Buenos Aires Design**.

Sightseeing

Walk on Mind your manors

Start: French Embassy, Recoleta.
Finish: British Embassy, Recoleta.
Length: 1.5 kilometres.

Recoleta boasts some of the city's most beautiful buildings. This walk through the barrio will get you up close to many of them.

Begin at the **French Embassy** on the corner of Cerrito and Arroyo (Cerrito 1399). This beautiful belle époque building, built in 1912, regally encroaches on multi-laned Avenida 9 de Julio. It's rumoured that the city government wanted it demolished when the avenue was being expanded, but the French put up a *résistance* and the building remains.

Walk to where Arroyo street becomes Avenida Alvear, and you'll find another entrancing embassy on your left, at Arroyo 1133. The Brazilian diplomatic headquarters in **Palacio Pereda** incorporates elaborate Corinthian columns and has a more lavish exterior than its French equivalent.

Further down the impeccably clean Avenida Alvear, **Banco Alvear** on your right is another example of the French neo-classicism that characterises the area. On the same street, the **Nunciatura Apostolica** (No.1637) dates from 1907 and was once the residence of then president Marcelo T de Alvear. It's also housed several popes over the years.

Just next door, the stunning curved lines of the **Palacio Duhau** (No.1661) now front the Park Hyatt Hotel. The yellow-tinged Doric columns and imposing courtyard dominate the street, but the French façade is all that remains of the original building, which was built in 1934 by French architect Leon Dourge. In stark contrast to the rest of the street, the neo-gothic **Residencia Maguire**

(No.1683) looks more like the Addams Family home than its neighbouring French palaces. Its gloomy aspect has all sorts of weird and wonderful features, including some maritime touches like the boat pro over the door and a strangely incongruous art deco shell, all part of this multi-brick mix that dates from 1890. Across the road, the **Casa Naciónal de Cultura** boasts similar brickwork but is infinitely less sombre.

Further up the street, the **Emporio Armani** shop (No. 1750) is a spruced up mansion, with huge windows and complete glass panes lending a modern spin to the otherwise old-style façade. Two doors down, the much more ornate Ralph Lauren store's best feature is the delightful baroque terrace.

Stroll on past the **Alvear Palace Hotel** (No.1891; *see p49*) and peep into its lush, chandeliered interior. Built in 1932, numerous visiting dignitaries have lodged within its neo-classical walls.

At the corner of Alvear and Schiaffino, turn left up Pte Eduardo Victor Haedo and take the small path to the corner of Quintana and Ortíz where you'll pass the legendary **La Biela** café (*see p143*). Turn right and head across the green, using the white steeple of the **Basílica Nuestra Señora del Pila**r (*see p87*) as your compass. For a moment of calm, step inside the ornate interior and breathe deep inside one of the oldest churches in the city.

Outside again, turn right as you leave and, keeping the cemetery on your right, follow the old wall around past Village Recoleta Centre. Hang a left on Azcuenaga, where the ominous-looking **Facultad de Ingeniería** building looms large on Las Heras. This huge neo-gothic structure, now housing a science and technology museum, was built in 1912.

Turning right on Las Heras, it's just a few steps to General Gelly y Obes street, a pleasant cobblestoned, tree-lined path that takes you up a slight incline to a tiny square. With the **National Library** peeping through the narrow streets that fan out on your left, you'll find yourself facing your final diplomatic port of call, the **British Embassy** (No.2333) at the crest of the slope. As you're unlikely to be invited in to inspect the spectacular gardens within this plush diplomatic hideaway, you'll have to content yourself with the expansive views of Recoleta's sweeping green parks afforded from this hilltop location.

Sightseeing

Alvears to become key figures in the city's history. Opposite are the monument and plaza dedicated to Carlos María's son, Torcuato de Alvear, the first governor of the city of Buenos Aires and an important urban planner.

The pedestrian walkway **RM Ortíz**, which runs from the corner of Junín and Vicente López to Avenida Quintana, is one of BA's most popular strips for the time-honoured evening stroll known as *el paseo* – though the new trend of restaurant staff hustling passers-by to come and eat is annoying. At the corner of Avenida Quintana is traditional, classy café **La Biela** (*see p143*). Opposite the café, its tentacle-like bowers casting a great shadow over the outdoor terrace, is a magnificent tree known as the Gran Gomero (*see p98* **Bloom town**).

Of all the streets in the area, **Avenida Alvear** is the most palatial and rents here can hit New York levels. It's all super smart, but walking south-east from the Recoleta plazas towards downtown, the first really grand building is the **Alvear Palace Hotel** (*see p49*), at No.1891, a 1932 French-style construction. Further along are some early 20th-century palaces, once the homes of the *porteño* gentry, including the art nouveau **Palacio Duhau** (No.1661 – about to reopen as a luxury Hyatt hotel) and several mansions, among them the neo-gothic **Residencia Maguire** (No.1683)

and the neo-classical **Nunciatura Apostólica** (No.1637). The latter once belonged to the mega-rich Anchorena family and was used in the 1920s by president Marcelo T de Alvear; the last big name to sleep there was Pope John Paul II on visits in 1982 and 1987. The palaces are not open to the general public, but you can visit the restaurants and shops off the lobby of the Alvear Palace Hotel.

Cementerio de la Recoleta

Junín 1760, entre Guido y Vicente López (4803 1594). Bus 10, 17, 60, 67, 92, 110. **Open** 7am-5.45pm daily. **Guided tours** (English) 11am Tue, Thur. **Admission** free. **Map** p282 J11.

Palais de Glace

Posadas 1725, y Schiaffino (4804 1163). Bus 17, 61, 67, 92, 93. **Open** 2-8pm Tue-Sun. **Admission** suggested contribution AR$1. **Map** p282 J11.

Avenida del Libertador

Beyond the cluster of life, leisure and style that has sprung up around the necropolis, Recoleta has other public spaces and venues along Avenida del Libertador. At the centre of Plaza Francia, at Libertador and Pueyrredón, is a baroque marble monument to Liberty, which was presented to Argentina by France as part of the 1910 centenary celebrations.

Basílica Nuestra Señora del Pilar (*below; see p87*) and the **Cementerio de la Recoleta** (*right; see p86*).

Across the avenue from the Palais de Glace is the newest patch of urban landscaping, **Parque Carlos Thays**, boasting a heroic bronze *Torso Masculino* by Colombian sculptor Fernando Botero. At Libertador and Callao is the **Museo de Arquitectura** (4800 1888), located in a former railway water tower dating from 1915. Exhibitions trace the evolution of Buenos Aires and more general issues of design and architecture. It's open afternoons only from March to December; phone for more details.

A few blocks north-west stands the dusty orange-coloured, quietly neo-classical **Museo Nacional de Bellas Artes** (*see p91*). Not vast by international standards, the MNBA is nonetheless home to 32 rooms, sculpture patios, an architecture display, studios, library and an auditorium. It houses the country's most extensive collection (11,000 pieces) of 19th- and 20th-century Argentinian works, which were put on permanent display after extensive refurbishment in 2004/5. It includes outstanding works from Ernesto de la Corcova and Condido Lopez. Twentieth-century pieces feature all the major names in Argentinian art, including Eduardo Sivori, Antonio Berni and Xul Solar. The museum added its first permanent display of indigenous art in November 2005.

The international collection on the ground floor contains works by El Greco, Rubens, Rembrandt, Goya, Van Gogh, Monet, Chagall, Picasso and Pollock among other big names. The MBNA is compact enough to visit in a few hours. It also has an excellent bookshop, free guided tours, audio tours (AR$15 English, AR$10 Spanish) and makes imaginative use of its space to hold other cultural events.

Behind the museum, on Avenida Figueroa Alcorta, is the **Facultad de Derecho** (Law Faculty), thronged all year round by students. Plazas Urquiza, Uruguay and Naciones Unidas are plain public spaces. *Floralis Genérica* by Eduardo Catalano is a popular steel and aluminium sculpture, its six petals opening each day as the sun rises and closing at dusk.

Occasionally, a building or two gets in the way of the greenery – such as the Bauhaus-style, state-owned ATC Channel 7 TV studios, built in 1978 to broadcast the World Cup – but there are open spaces all the way to Palermo and beyond on the river side of Libertador.

Back across the road, the plazas don't last as long but they are more dramatic. At the top of **Plaza Mitre** a great red granite pedestal is adorned with lively allegorical and lyrical figures in marble, above which rides a stern bronze of Bartolomé Mitre, president from 1862-88 and founder of *La Nación* newspaper.

The next patch of grass, the **Plaza Rubén Darío** – named after the Nicaraguan poet and philosopher – is brooded over by the jutting upper half of the functional-looking **Biblioteca Nacional** (*see p91*), designed in the 1960s by three prominent architects, Clorindo Testa, Alicia Cazzaniga de Bullrich and Francisco Bullrich. Building dragged on for years and

Museo Nacional de Arte Decorativo. *See p91.*

the library only opened to the public in 1992. Most of the two million books and manuscripts are kept in the underground vaults, so there's not much to see except for occasional exhibits catering to history buffs. Current and back issues of periodicals and newspapers are available, however – go to the Hemeroteca in the basement, with photo ID.

Before the concrete block of the library was conceived, this was the land of the Unzué family and for a time the site of the presidential residence, where the Peróns lived and Evita died at 8.25pm on 26 July 1952. The military tore down the mansion to erase the memory of Peronism, unswayed by the fact that Juan Domingo had risen from its very own ranks.

A monolithic monument of a stylised, skinny, athletic-looking Evita was erected on the plaza in 1999 after years of wrangling about shifting the existing statue of Darío, who now sits across the road. There's also a statue of the late Pope John Paul II in front of the library. To the rear of the library is the attractive **Plaza del Lector**, with benches for reading. It is also home to a fountain, art gallery and restaurant.

At the Palermo end of Recoleta, at Avenida del Libertador 1902, is the beautiful French-style mansion Palacio Errázuriz, which houses the **Museo Nacional de Arte Decorativo** (*see below*). French architect René Sergent, who built the mansion in 1911, gave the building a complex façade containing French, Corinithian and Tuscan elements. The building was converted into a museum in 1937 and its stunning ballrooms, sumptuous bedrooms and hallways today display over 4,000 pieces of decorative art – plus works by El Greco and Manet – collected by Chilean aristocrat-diplomat Matías Errázuriz and his wife, Josefina de Alvear. The museum has a good bookstore located in the basement. Guided tours in English can be organised by prior arrangement.

Biblioteca Nacional

Agüero 2502, entre Libertador y Las Heras (4806 4721 ext 1140/www.bibnal.edu.ar). Bus 59, 60, 93, 102. **Open** 9am-9pm Mon-Fri; noon-8pm Sat, Sun. **Admission** free. **Map** p282 K11.

Museo Nacional de Arte Decorativo

Avenida del Libertador 1902, y Pereyra Lucena (4806 8306/4802 6606/www.mnad.org). Bus 10, 59, 60, 67, 130. **Open** 2-7pm daily. Closed 1st 2wks Jan. **Admission** AR$2 Mon, Wed-Sun; AR$1 concessions. Free Tue. **No credit cards**. **Map** p282 K11.

Museo Nacional de Bellas Artes

Avenida del Libertador 1473, y Pueyrredón (4803 8814/4691/www.mnba.org.ar). Bus 17, 62, 67, 93, 130. **Open** 12.30-7.30pm Tue-Fri; 9.30am-7.30pm Sat, Sun. **Guided tours** (Spanish) 5pm Tue-Sun. **Admission** free. **Map** p282 J11.

Barrio Norte

When alluding to the overcrowded, middle-class residential area between Avenida Las Heras and Avenida Córdoba, though still officially Recoleta, most *porteños* – and estate agents – use the term Barrio Norte. The nickname is often associated with the *chetos* (social-climbing, nouveau riche poseurs) and *paquetes* (also poseurs, but with the confidence of older money) who live here. Evita, in one of her many fiery speeches to seduce the working classes, declared her ambition to 'bomb Barrio Norte'. The neighbourhood's main consumer corridor and a Barrio Norte symbol par excellence is **Avenida Santa Fe**, a gauntlet of big-name brand shops and boutiques.

If you take a stroll down this commercial thoroughfare, slip into the converted cinema at No.1860 that now houses the **Ateneo** bookshop (*see p149*). Though the movie theatre closed, the bookshop is at least a nod to a continuing cultural presence in the area. Just a few blocks from here (between Callao and Pueyrredón), is one of BA's most openly gay scenes, especially on weekend evenings.

The rest of the area is taken up by the **Universidad de Buenos Aires**, including the dental and medical faculties with their respective state hospitals, and lots of private clinics. Barrio Norte is also littered with language schools, where *mamá* and *papá* send their little ones to learn fluent *inglés*.

Literary pilgrims should check out the **Museo Casa de Ricardo Rojas** (*see p93*). Rojas (1882-1957) was an influential writer and one of Argentina's most important educators, teaching Argentinian literature at the state university before becoming its rector in 1926. His ascetic house, with its original furnishings and household objects and Rojas' personal library of 20,000 volumes, is the quintessential writer's refuge – a guide will escort you through the rooms. It's also of note for the mixture of Spanish and Incaic styles in the patio, tiles and ornamental motifs.

Another cultural highlight is the **Museo Xul Solar** (*see p93*), two blocks from Santa Fe. This museum – installed in an award-winning modern space – contains a wondrous collection of esoteric objects, weird instruments and artworks by the city's most eccentric visionary: sailor turned painter, astrologer, musician, inventor, mathematician, writer and philologist Oscar Agustín Alejandro Schulz Solari (1887-1963) – Xul Solar, as he chose to be called. Rightly acclaimed by friend Borges as 'one of the most singular occurrences of his time', Solar invented his own language (Pan) and lived in his own personal time zone.

Sightseeing

Walk on Step on the grass

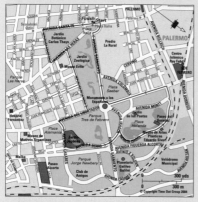

Start and finish: Plaza Italia, Palermo.
Length: 3.5 kilometres.
Spend enough time in Buenos Aires' traffic-choked city centre and you'll begin to wonder if the city shouldn't be rechristened. To really breathe 'good airs', you need to head north, to the parks and gardens of Palermo.

This walk takes you around and through some of the most attractive spaces in this bucolic patch of the city. Digress as often as time allows; smell the roses along the way.

Start in **Plaza Italia**. You won't want to linger long here: it's one of the noisiest junctions in the city and a far cry from the lawned idylls that punctuate most of the area.

Head east along Avenida Santa Fe, in a downtown direction. Turning left on to República Arabe Siria, and then left again on to Avenida Las Heras, you'll skirt around the **Jardín Botánico Carlos Thays**. Fountains, orchids, cacti, ferns and spectacular trees and bushes make this a paradise for anyone who likes to potter around the garden. Monuments include a Venus, a Saturnalia and a Romulus and Remus, and there's a botanical library, but the main attraction is the calm offered by this small hedged-in triangle.

As you head north-east along República de la India, the calm is broken by the howls and yelps emanating from the **Jardín Zoológico** on your right. On your right is the exclusive sub-barrio of **Palermo Chico**, home to diplomats, TV stars and corporate ex-pats. It's a tranquil if largely soulless neighbourhood.

Turning left on to busy Avenida del Libertador you'll begin to pass through and around

Parque Tres de Febrero. The park (sometimes known as Palermo Woods) is named after the date in 1852 when the forces of General Urquiza defeated the despotic General Rosas at the Battle of Monte Caseros. Using land formerly owned by Rosas, President Sarmiento – who razed Rosas' mansion – envisioned the park as a way for BA to resemble more closely the capitals of Europe. Statues of a dashing Rosas and a saturnine Sarmiento face off at the Libertador–Sarmiento crossroads, the latter's monument (by Auguste Rodin) on the site of the flattened house.

Continuing along Avenida Casares and then Avenida Berro, you'll pass another glorious spot for greenfingered visitors: the **Jardín Japonés** (see p95). The garden is awash with artificial lakes brimming with weirdly anthropomorphic giant koi carp, ornate bridges and – in the pagoda – an attractive all-day tearoom serving green teas and cakes, and a fine Japanese restaurant open in the evenings. Botanic species include black pines, sakura and ginkgo, and there are regular bonsai exhibitions.

Your Zen moment over, continue through the park on Avenida Berro and then Infanta Isabel. Highlights on this stretch include the delightfully pretty **Rosedal** (Rose Garden – entered at Avenidas Iraola and Puerto Montt), the **Jardín de los Poetas** with its peaceful fountains surrounded by busts of literary giants, a lovely, tiled **Patio Andaluz** and a shaded pergola by the lake. In these well-planted spaces, look out for native bird life, such as the *hornero* (oven bird – it has an oven-shaped nest) and the yellow and black *cabecita negra*, not to mention the common-or-garden sparrow, introduced from Europe by Sarmiento as yet another 'civilising' presence. Non-birders and kids may prefer to float on the lake (pedalos and boats are for hire opposite the excellent **Museo Sívori** – see p95).

Turning back on to Avenida del Libertador, walk along the southern fringe of the park until you reach the striking **Monumento de los Españoles** (see p95). You'll have Plaza Italia back in your sights, at the southern end of the broad, Parisian Avenida Sarmiento. On your right is BA's largest exhibition complex, the **Predio La Rural**. It hosts two of BA's most important annual events: the **Feria del Libro** (Book Fair) in June (see p175) and the **La Rural** agricultural fair in August (see p176).

Sightseeing

Museo Casa de Ricardo Rojas

*Charcas 2837, entre Anchorena y Laprida
(4824 4039). Subte D, Agüero/12, 39, 152 bus.*
Open 10am-6pm Mon-Fri. **Admission** suggested
contribution AR$1. **Map** p282 K9.

Museo Xul Solar

*Laprida 1212, entre Mansilla y Charcas (4824 3302/
www.xulsolar.org.ar). Subte D, Agüero/12, 39, 64,
152 bus.* **Open** *Mar-Dec* noon-8pm Tue-Fri. Closed
Jan, Feb. **Admission** AR$3; AR$1 concessions. **No
credit cards.** Map p282 J9.

Palermo

Palermo has pretty much everything on the
neighbourhood wish list, including museums,
parks, lakes, a zoo, polo and cricket clubs, an
airport, botanic and Japanese gardens, and a
planetarium. Confusingly, it contains a number
of sub-divisions, but everyone accepts three
basic areas: tiny Palermo Chico (bordering
Recoleta) for embassies and the filthy rich;
atmospheric Palermo Viejo (comprising
Palermo Hollywood and Palermo Soho) for
global cuisine and funky boutiques; and plain
Palermo for the rest, including all the greenery.

From the little street called Cavia to Monroe
in Belgrano (the next barrio along), there is a
patchwork of plazas and parks congregating
round the **Parque Tres de Febrero**,
formerly a flood plain drained in the late
16th century by the barrio's namesake, Italian
farmer Giovanni Domenico Palermo. At the
northern limit of the park is the **Hipódromo
Argentino** racecourse (*see p207*), but keen
walkers and cyclists (there's a bike path all
the way) can skirt this by heading towards the
river and continue on to Nuñez and the River
Plate football stadium.

Although you may stroll into Palermo as
a continuation of your wanderings through
Recoleta, the point of access with the most public
transport options is **Plaza Italia**. Here, Buses
and the Subte empty out shoppers, visitors to
the exhibition centre – which commercial events
and, most famously, the Exposición Agrícola,
Ganadera e Industrial, usually known simply as
La Rural (*see p176*), in mid winter – and anyone
heading for the parks. The monument to Italian
hero Giuseppe Garibaldi at the centre of the plaza
is the only static figure in this hectic scene.

The **Jardín Botánico Carlos Thays**,
created in 1902 in between Avenida Santa Fe,
Las Heras and Gurruchaga, is quieter and more
attractive. Thousands of species (and feral cats)
flourish here, and there is a sizeable greenhouse
brought back from the Argentinian pavilion at
the 1900 Paris Exhibition.

Sightseeing

Stucco meets the swoosh at **Nike Soho** in Palermo Viejo. *See p96.*

Monumento de los Españoles.
See p95.

The **Jardín Zoológico** (*see p179*) across the road is one of those interesting but somewhat discomfiting attractions many animal lovers will shun, although serious zoological work takes place here. This small city zoo houses big cats, a polar bear and various native species. Of more general interest are the buildings, designed mainly by Eduardo Holmberg (the zoo's first director) between 1888 and 1904, and finished off by Charles Thays in 1905. Holmberg's idea was to house each animal in a building that aped the architecture of its native country, resulting in a hotchpotch of scaled-down monumental follies where the animals live.

The **Museo Evita** (*see p96*) is located on one of Palermo's quieter back streets in a neo-Gothic residence that Perón expropriated to convert into a women's shelter for his wife's quasi-statal welfare agency. It's worth a visit to see the range of myths her person has inspired. Paintings and propaganda posters are displayed alongside clothes she wore on her regal tours of Europe.

South of the zoo, at the busy junction of Avenidas Sarmiento and del Libertador is the bleached-white **Monumento de los Españoles**. A centenary gift from the Spanish, the four bronzes represent Argentina's four main geographical regions: the Pampas, the Andes, the Chaco and the River Plate.

Designed and overseen by Thays, the **Parque Tres de Febrero** – which locals call Parque Palermo or Los Bosques de Palermo (the Palermo Woods) – boasts well-kept lawns, beautiful jacarandas and palms and a lake, as well as cafés and a good art gallery, the **Museo de Artes Plásticas Eduardo Sívori** (*see below*). Once a restaurant, it now houses a major collection of Argentinian paintings and sculpture, with a café that looks out over the green inner patio. (For more on Parque Tres de Febrero and its attractions, *see p92* **Walk on**.)

Along Avenida Figueroa Alcorta are a number of facilities, including **Paseo Alcorta** shopping centre (*see p148*). But the area's most important addition is a cultural space, paid for and stocked by art collector Eduardo Costantini, the Museo Latinoamericano de Buenos Aires (**Malba** – *see below*). It's an impressive contemporary gallery containing works by some of the very best Latin American artists of the past century. Frida Kahlo and Diego Rivera, Tarsila do Amaral and other groundbreaking painters share the walls with wonderful Argentinian modern masters such as Antonio Berni and Jorge de la Vega. There are also a café and a cinema specialising in cult and art-house retrospectives. It's an essential visit for anyone interested in the arts.

Back on Libertador, heading towards the centre, is the refurbished **Museo de Motivos Argentinos José Hernández** (*see p96*), so-named because of the gaucho motifs and other decorative elements of Argentina's rural past that constitute the main collection. It's named after the author of Argentina's national epic, *Martín Fierro* (1873). Two buildings off a patio are hung with *mate* gourds, spurs, weapons (especially knives) and other gaucho paraphernalia. There's also a reconstruction of a *pulpería*, the inn-cum-grocer's shop that was the focal point of 19th-century country life. The museum also features temporary exhibits of modern arts and crafts inspired by issues of identity and Argentinian history.

Heading back to Recoleta from the park, or vice versa, you can detour off Avenida del Libertador into **Palermo Chico** (aka Barrio Parque). This tiny, upscale patch of suburbia is where TV stars like Susana Gimenez and diplomats park their bullet-proof jeeps. There are no shops or even *kioscos* to spoil the views, just plenty of grand architecture to admire. One exception: at the roundabout where Bustamante hits Rufino de Elizalde is the **Monumento San Martín Abuelo**, a rare effigy of the general without his horse. *Abuelo* means 'grandfather' and this likeable likeness of the Liberator shows him in his later years, dispensing advice to his granddaughters (how to garden, how to walk along the Seine, how to clean guns). Arranged south of the monument are statues of those who aided San Martín in his independence campaign. The **Instituto Sanmartiniano** research centre nearby is an over scale replica of Grand Bourg, the house where he lived in exile in France.

Jardín Japonés

Avenida Casares y Berro (4804 4922/9141/www. jardinjapones.com.ar). Bus 37, 67, 102, 130. **Open** 10am-6pm daily. **Guided tours** (Spanish) 3pm Sat. **Admission** AR$4; AR$1 6-10s, concessions; free under-6s. **No credit cards**. **Map** p283 M11.

Malba: Colección Costantini

Avenida Figueroa Alcorta 3415, entre Salguero y San Martín de Tours (4808 6500/www.malba. org.ar). Bus 67, 102, 130. **Open** 9am-9pm Sun-Wed; 9am-1pm Thur-Sat. **Guided tours** (Spanish). **Admission** AR$5; AR$2.50 concessions. Free Wed. **Credit** AmEx (AR$20 minimum). **Map** p282 L11. Tours in English by prearrangement for groups of 15 or more (AR$12 per person, including entry).

Museo de Artes Plásticas Eduardo Sívori

Avenida Infanta Isabel 555, y Libertador (4774 9452/4778 3899). Bus 10, 34, 37, 67, 130. **Open** *Dec-Apr* noon-8pm Tue-Fri; 10am-8pm Sat, Sun. *May-Nov* noon-6pm Tue-Fri; 10am-6pm Sat, Sun. **Guided tours** *Mar-Dec* twice daily Sat, Sun; call for times. *Jan, Feb* 4pm Sat, Sun. **Admission** AR$3; AR$1 residents Tue, Thur Sun; free students, under-12s. Free Wed. **No credit cards**. **Map** p283 N10.

Museo Evita

Lafinur 2988, entre Gutiérrez y Las Heras (4807 9433/0306). Subte D, Plaza Italia/37, 59, 60, 102 bus. **Open** 2-7.30pm Tue-Sun. **Admission** AR$10; AR$5 residents. **No credit cards. Map** p283 M9.

Museo de Motivos Argentinos José Hernández

Avenida del Libertador 2373, entre San Martín de Tours y Coronel Díaz (4802 9967/4803 2384/www. museohernandez.org.ar). Bus 10, 37, 59, 60, 92, 102. **Open** 1-7pm Wed-Sun. **Admission** AR$4; AR$2 residents; free under-12s, concessions. Free Sun. **No credit cards. Map** p278 I7.

Palermo Viejo

Away from the high rises, open spaces and views of the river, Old Palermo clusters. Run-down and romantic until the early 1990s, it's since been thoroughly brightened up by restaurants, fashion and design outlets. Most of the homes here are just one or two storeys high, and the town houses, many of them revamped into urban lofts, come with terraces or trees and long, crepuscular entrance ways. There's a literary/boho past here as evidenced by the street called Borges and the Plazoleta Cortázar (at the junction of Borges and Honduras – sometimes referred to by its former name,

Palermo Viejo – a blossoming barrio.

Plaza Serrano), but thanks to the recent influx of nightclub and cocktail bars, these days there's more emphasis on high jinks than high culture.

East European and Armenian communities made Palermo Viejo their home in the early 20th century and cuisines from all over the world are served in its many restaurants. For open air drinks, Plazoleta Cortázar is popular, and those who find the pseudo-bohemian bars too expensive lounge beneath the trees with a beer.

Such has been the impact of new money on Old Palermo that the food and lifestyle boom has expanded across the barrio's limit at Avenida Juan B Justo, and now the sub-barrio once known as Pacífico is being give a face-lift too. It's been renamed Palermo Hollywood, a nickname happily adopted by eager estate agents and residents.

In the southern corner of Palermo Viejo, inside restaurant-theatre-wineshop **Club del Vino** (*see p204*) is a small wine museum. It falls short of a complete history of Argentinian wine, but a series of maps, labels and presses tell part of the story and when you've finished you can pop upstairs for a tasting session in the bar.

Elsewhere in Palermo

Fringed by the polo ground and racecourse is a buzzing residential and dining district known as **Las Cañitas** (there were once sugar canes growing wild here). A popular focal point for the monied socialites of Palermo and Belgrano, there is little historical interest by day, though the **Cañitas Creativa** street fair on Fridays and Saturdays at 6pm brings in visitors. The area made the news big time when former president Carlos Menem gave the Saudis land to build BA's mega-mosque and religious centre, the **Centro Islámico Ray Fahd** at Avenidas Bullrich and del Libertador. For information on Spanish guided tours call 4899 1144.

One of Palermo's most curious unofficial sub-barrios just south of Plaza Italia, is called **Villa Freud**, in reference to the number of psychoanalysts working there. Sharing the area with the shrinks are several spiritual centres, including a Buddhist cemetery, a mosque and the **Basílica del Espíritu Santo** on Plaza Güemes (at the corner of Mansilla and Medrano). This sturdy church, built between 1901 and 1907, is known by locals as Guadalupe – after the local parish, which was named in honour of the saint that Pope Pius X appointed as Empress of the Americas in 1945. A church run by the monastic Order of the Divine Word and a chapel complete the religious nucleus: Jesus, Guadalupe and gang vying with the secular scripts of the Lacanian analysts for the souls of the locals.

West of the Centre

Cemeteries, synagogues, diners and dinosaurs – welcome to BA's wild west.

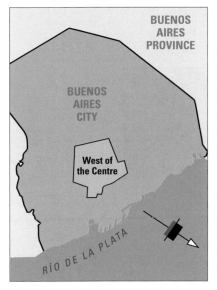

If you're looking for something that feels a little more like the genuine article, Buenos Aires' western districts provide something closer to the general *porteño* reality than the chi-chi northern *barrios* or the south's old-world charm. This is where ordinary folk live, work and die, and yet it still has its own distinctive vibe. Once is a riotous commercial hub, while neighbouring Abasto has undergone a recent makeover to give it back some of its tango heritage. Chacarita's cemetery is a built-up, brick and mortar version of Recoleta's glamorous deathville, and Caballito and Villa Crespo both offer something decidedly different for the fringe-friendly tourist.

Once & Abasto

Once (pronounced '*on*-say'), about 20 blocks west along Avenida Corrientes, is the city's most hectic commercial district – a warren of wholesale and retail outlets. Visitors who find BA a touch too European should take a detour here – Once is as loud, bustling and brash as a Guatemalan bus station. Historically associated with the city's large Jewish population, it now has sizable Korean and Peruvian communities.

The barrio is named after the ugly 11 (Once) de Septiembre railway station – which in turn commemorates an 1852 battle between the provinces and the capital – on **Plaza Miserere** (usually called Plaza Once). The plaza, for years a rubbish-strewn hub for transport, sex trade and preachers proclaiming apocalypse, is now also home to the monument for the dead from the Cromagnon nightclub fire (*see p182*). On the corner of Bartolomé Mitre and Ecuador there is a blazing mural in their honour, while in the north-east corner, Mitre is cut off and tents now stand where survivors have taken up residence among makeshift shrines to their lost friends.

Avenidas Rivadavia and Pueyrredón are Once's main arteries, but the neighbourhood's pulse is found in the blocks to the south and west of their intersection.

Here, Latin dance beats blast out from every other store and the selling of tack and trash spills on to the streets as visual pollution is taken to extremes. If you like sterile shopping malls, forget Once, although it certainly deserves a quick jaunt just to experience what local author Alvaro Abós calls a 'branch of hell'.

As for Jewish Once, the **Congregación Sefardi**, a Moorish-style Sephardic synagogue at Lavalle 2400, is worth a visit. Two blocks away, at Paso 400, is the elegant **Ashkenazi Templo de Paso**. The synagogues are best visited with a tour, as access has been restricted since the 1990s Jewish-targeted terrorist attacks. Victims of the 1994 car bomb attack on Once's AMIA Jewish Welfare Centre are remembered by the moving **Monumento de Homenaje y Recordación a las Víctimas del Atentado a la AMIA**, situated in the courtyard of the reconstructed building, at Pasteur 633. Tour agencies require 48 hours' notice to arrange visits here.

Once is, in fact, part of a barrio officially known as Balvanera, with its northern limit at Avenida Córdoba. At Córdoba 1950 is the striking **Palacio de Aguas Corrientes** (Palace of Running Water) occupying a whole block. It's home to the capital's water works, which were run by private company Aguas Argentinas, until the government stepped in in 2006. Constructed between 1887 and 1895, this flamboyantly decorated building, with its vivid colours and jigsaw of architectural styles, is a real one-off among the city's civic piles.

The map labels:
BUENOS AIRES PROVINCE
BUENOS AIRES CITY
West of the Centre
RÍO DE LA PLATA

Bloom town

Among all its asphalt black and cement grey, Buenos Aires sports an impressive array of trees. One of the most prevalent is the *palo borracho* (drunken branch). Like something from a Dr Seussian savannah, a thorny pot-bellied trunk gives way to fantastical twisting branches often laden with fat pink blossoms. *Palos borrachos* can be found in most major plazas (Plaza San Martín has an especially nice line-up), but for an exclusive display of this expressive tree, check out Plaza Roberto Arlt (Esmeralda between Rivadavia and Mitre).

The *ombú* (pictured) is not really a tree, technically speaking, but don't try to argue this one, as most locals consider it to be the godfather of the city's trees. Comprised of huge limbs that extend high above but also grow parallel and close to the ground, *ombús* form an otherworldly canopy of respite from the glare and noise of the city. Perhaps the city's most spectacular example is the unmissable, enormous *ombú* on the upper tier of Plaza San Martín. With its staked limbs

casting a broad pall, it feels like a set from *The Lord of the Rings*, worlds apart from the surrounding high-decibel bustle of Retiro.

Similar to the *ombú*, the *gomero* (rubber tree) is generally smaller and distinguished by fatter leaves. Its limbs supported by an impressive 24 stakes, the best-known *gomero* in Buenos Aires, which grows in Plaza Francia next to La Biela, is 20 metres (65 feet) high and a staggering 50 metres (164 feet) wide. From the comfortable benches in its great shadow you can observe street performers at the markets and watch people stroll into the surrounding cafés.

Another spectacular native species is the ubiquitous *jacaranda*. Fast-growing and hearty, *jacarandas* grace plazas and sidewalks all over town, packing the city with an effusive display of violet flowers. Avenida 9 de Julio is lined from one end to the other, and on a spring day, when thousands of violet flowers push against a clear blue sky, it's one of the city's most breathtaking, colourful vistas.

Just up from Once, at Avenida Corrientes and Anchorena, is the beautiful **Mercado de Abasto** building, an art deco masterpiece built between 1930 and 1934 as a central wholesale market for the city. It was neglected for decades and the building's powerful, but empty, decaying presence became symbolic of the Abasto neighbourhood's own downward spiral into a seedy scene of blues, booze and cocaine.

In 1998 the market building was the first in the barrio to see rejuvenation, converted into a shopping mall known simply as **El Abasto** (*see p148*). Inside the mall is the **Museo de los Niños Abasto** (Abasto's Children's Museum – *see p180*), three floors of educationally minded displays about the commercial and industrial activities of Buenos Aires.

Completion of the ambitious 'Cultura Abasto' initiative, currently under way, will see El Abasto's surrounding ten blocks benefit from a full, 1930s-style make-over, transporting the curious back to the barrio's heyday. Tango

will be a central theme, and the small but neat **Museo Casa Carlos Gardel**, offering a peep into the house of the legendary crooner, has already opened (*see below*).

Centre stage in Abasto's redevelopment plan, is the multipurpose **Ciudad Cultural Konex** (*see p225*), a vast arts complex at the intersection of Sarmiento and Jean Jaurès, which opened in 2005. The building's exterior echoes the geometric design of the Abasto's art deco style, and inside there's an opera house and a number of theatre spaces. Inspired by Paris's Pompidou Centre, it's the nervecentre of the Fundación Konex .

Museo Casa Carlos Gardel

Jean Jaurès 735, entre Zelaya y Tucumán (4964 2071). Subte B, Pueyrredón or Carlos Gardel/ 19, 92, 124 bus. **Open** 11am-6pm Mon, Wed-Fri; 10am-7pm Sat, Sun. **Guided tours** (Spanish) 3pm Mon, Wed-Fri; 1pm, 3pm, 5pm Sat, Sun. **Admission** AR$3; free under-10s. Free Wed. **No credit cards.** **Map** p282 J8.

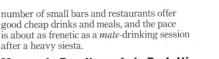

Palacio de Aguas Corrientes. *See p97.*

Almagro, Caballito & Villa Crespo

West of Abasto, Almagro, Caballito and Villa Crespo are districts with particularly proud residents and a real neighbourhood air. **Parque Centenario**, in Caballito, serves as the sole public park for these densely populated barrios and is as local and mundane as you'd expect.

The main crowd-puller, and great for kids, is the **Museo Argentino de Ciencias Naturales Bernadino Rivadavia** (*see p180*), a sizable collection of stuffed fauna, with plenty of fossils and botanical exhibits, as well as several enormous Patagonian dinosaurs.

Another museum, the **Museo de Esculturas Luis Perlotti** (*see below*), brings together some 900 wooden, bronze and stone sculptures by one of Argentina's foremost artists.

Caballito is also a reminder of a gentler era in Buenos Aires, when the tram was king. Now, this is the only barrio that keeps the soothing clankety-clank alive, with a 25-minute service departing from Emilio Mitre and José Bonifacio every 15 minutes on Saturday afternoons and Sunday mornings and afternoons. For times, check the website of the **Asociación Amigos del Tranvía** (www.tranvia.org.ar).

Almagro and Villa Crespo are tranquil, traditional neighbourhoods, although the latter is becoming increasingly gentrified, in large part due to its proximity to hip Palermo Viejo. Life in both revolves around the main Avenidas Corrientes and Rivadavia; off the avenues, a number of small bars and restaurants offer good cheap drinks and meals, and the pace is about as frenetic as a *mate*-drinking session after a heavy siesta.

Museo de Esculturas Luis Perlotti

Pujol 644, entre Felipe Vallese y Méndez de Andes (4431 2825/4433 3396). Subte A, Primera Junta/ 92, 99, 106 bus. **Open** 11am-7pm Tue-Fri; 10am-1pm, 2-8pm Sat, Sun. **Admission** AR$1. Free Wed. **No credit cards. Map** p278 L1.

Chacarita

Like many one-time outlying barrios, Chacarita developed around a railway station, Federico Lacroze. The terminus, opened in 1880, is now little more than a run-down shed for suburban trains. Equally gloomy but far more interesting is the **Cementerio de la Chacarita** on the other side of Avenida Guzmán. The cemetery was conceived as a home for the staggering numbers of dead from the yellow fever outbreak of 1871. A funeral train was set up that year, with an Englishman, Mr Allen, piloting the steam engine (until he too caught the plague and died).

Now far more expansive than Recoleta's exclusive necropolis, with numbered streets and car access to its thousands of vaults, it's largely for ordinary folk. Still, a number of popular heroes have also made Chacarita their choice of charnel-house, including Carlos Gardel, Juan Domingo Perón and aviation pioneer Jorge Newbery.

Until 1939, Chacarita also held the cemeteries of the Jewish, British and German communities. With Hitler affecting relations even in far-off Argentina, the Jews left for a new site west of the city, and the Brits and Germans built walls to separate their dead.

Cementerio de la Chacarita

Guzmán 630, y Federico Lacroze (4553 9034/9038/ tours 4553 0041). Subte B, Federico Lacroze/42, 93, 111 bus. **Open** 7am-6pm daily. **Admission** free. **Map** p279 O2/P2.

Museo Casa Carlos Gardel. *See p98.*

Sightseeing

Along the River

It's big, it's brown, and little by little, it's becoming beautiful.

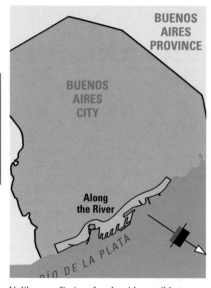

Unlike, say, Paris or London, it's possible to spend weeks in Buenos Aires without seeing its river. For decades the city turned its back on the muddy estuary that was once its lifeblood – the River Plate – but the tide, as it were, has turned, and a slew of ambitious development programmes around the old port and along the coastline has helped reinvigorate the zone.

Puerto Madero & Costanera Sur

The appearance of **Puerto Madero** – the dockland area to the east of Plaza de Mayo – is the embodiment of BA's self-image as a grand European-style city. The red-brick port buildings and grain warehouses, built between 1889 and 1898, were the first view of BA seen by incoming immigrants and the city fathers wanted to impress with a modern skyline.

Yet as early as 1911 a new harbour was being built, the narrow rectangular wharves having proved hopelessly inadequate. Puerto Nuevo, as it is known, is still loading up container ships north of Retiro. Meanwhile, Puerto

Madero went into decline and the dream docks became rat-infested husks. It was only in the late 1980s that the area was upgraded, along the lines of London and Baltimore. When the new-look Puerto Madero was opened in 1996, many locals would have liked to see a more civic, cultural slant. Instead, they got exclusive restaurants with high-rent offices on top.

Puerto Madero, however, is nothing if not open to change, and new projects with history and the arts are springing up. Aware that BA needed a monument to its early-20th-century settlers, the **Museo de la Inmigración** (*see p101*) was inaugurated by the city government in 2001. The museum is housed in the former Hotel de Inmigrantes, the first entry point for thousands of Europeans arriving in Argentina. The museum's collection of film, photos and objects – with information panels in Spanish – shows how it all started for many *porteños*.

Just south of here is **Dársena Norte** (North Harbour), where naval vessels are stationed. They can sometimes be visited for free at weekends, but admission is at the discretion of on-duty officers. When not at sea the impressive training ship, the **Fragata *Libertad***, and the towering icebreaker *Irízar*, used for Antarctic expeditions, also dock here intermittently.

A short distance south are the promenades of Puerto Madero's ever expanding dockland complex, a world created for the rich and beautiful. While unabashed in celebrating the finer things in life, much of Puerto Madero is, curiously, also dedicated to struggle, as all its streets are named after women who fought for female emancipation within Argentina. Encarnación Ezcurra, wife of 19th-century *caudillo* Juan Manuel de Rosas, and Azucena Villaflor, founder of the Mothers of Plaza de Mayo, are among those honoured.

At the entrance to the quays, on the eastern side of Dique (Dock) 4, is a building modelled on the Sydney Opera House, but in fact home to **Opera Bay**, a glitzy if pretty cheesy night club aimed squarely at the after-office crowd.

For evidence of the area's maritime history visit the impeccable **Corbeta *Uruguay***, moored further down on Dique 4 at Alicia Moreau de Justo and Corrientes. A museum vessel of Argentina's Naval Academy dating back to 1874, regular warfare would appear to have been beneath the 'glorious' *Uruguay*

Sightseeing

which distinguished itself in revolutions, expeditions and search-and-rescue missions. At Dique 3 is the even more impressive **Fragata *Presidente Sarmiento*** (Alicia Moreau de Justo y Belgrano). This frigate, built in Birkenhead, was used as a training ship from 1899 to 1961 and is now a walk-on museum full of photos, maps and domestic objects, with cabins of original oak and teak.

Stretching in front of the Sarmiento is the elegant **Puente de la Mujer**, a pedestrian bridge, designed by the renowned Spanish engineer Santiago Calatrava. Opened to acclaim in December 2001, the bridge's US$6 million construction costs were covered by Alberto R González, late owner of much of Madero Este and its **Hilton** hotel (*see p57*). The Hilton now faces competition from the **Faena Hotel + Universe**, a Philippe Starck-designed hotel which opened in early 2005 (*see p57*).

Beyond Madero Este is an altogether earthier experience, the River Plate's other urban jungle: the **Reserva Ecológica Costanera Sur** (*see below*), BA's biggest – free – wilderness on the edge of the city. Within its boundaries, four lakes, giant *cortaderas* (foxtail pampas grass), willows and shrubs provide natural habitats for more than 200 bird species and 50 varieties of butterfly. Moonlight tours are arranged one night per month closest to the full moon; phone ahead to book your place.

The long esplanade skirting the reserve is one of the city's most pleasant spaces for walking, sunbathing and inhaling something other than sulphur dioxide. A lavish 1927 beer cellar, the **Cervecería Munich** houses the Centro de Museos, from where all the city's museums are administered. A guided tour of the picturesque pub gives an insight into how good life used to be for wealthy weekenders.

Slightly south, at the centre of a roundabout near the reserve's entrance (Avenida Tristán Achaval Rodríguez and Padre ML Migone), is an eye-catching fountain, executed in 1902 by Tucumán-born artist Lola Mora. The **Fuente de las Nereidas** is a marble allegory set in a clam shell, depicting fishily erotic (if mermaids are your thing) female forms.

One block south is the **Museo de Calcos y Escultura Comparada**, an outpost of the city's main public art college, with a collection of sculpted and moulded replicas of ancient and Renaissance masterpieces. Around the museum, the land is occupied by cheap *parrillas* making this a popular weekend lunch spot.

Museo de la Inmigración

Antiguo Hotel de Inmigrantes, Avenida Antártida Argentina 1355, y Avenida de los Inmigrantes (4317 0285). Bus 6, 20. **Open** 10am-5pm Mon-Fri; 11am-6pm Sat, Sun. **Admission** free; suggested contribution AR$1. **Map** p281 G12.

Reserva Ecológica Costanera Sur

Avenida Tristán Achaval Rodríguez 1550, entre Brasil y Estados Unidos (4893 1588/0800 444 5343 freephone). Bus 2,4. **Open** *April-Sept* 8am-6pm Tue-Sun; *Oct-March* 8am-7pm Tue-Sun. **Guided tours** (Spanish) 10.30am, 3.30pm Sat, Sun. **Admission** free. **Map** p280 C12/D12.

Puerto Madero Este. *See p102.*

Shock of the new
Puerto Madero Este

Everybody loves a good dockside regeneration. Local politicians get to strut around in yellow hard hats, yuppies make downpayments on their fantasy penthouses, and demolition workers are allowed to blow up huge disused warehouses in the name of urban renewal.

This global yen for urban makeovers may explain why BA's own port project has proved such a hit with both foreign tourists and locals. The west side of the old docks (Puerto Madero Oeste), with its six converted red-brick warehouses, has been an established part of the city's commercial and social scene since 1996. The east side (Puerto Madero Este), however, was largely a wasteground up until 2002, when the devaluation of the Argentinian peso made the city an attractive target for international property developers.

Look at it now. Puerto Madero Este currently boasts the most valuable residential real estate in Latin America, with prices averaging US$1,800 per square metre in early 2006. The target market is wealthy foreigners and corporate expats; the watchword is exclusivity. For Buenos Aires this blend of modernity and luxury is something new, but thanks to the area's proximity to the city centre, demand is high.

If you had to put a face to the Madero Este renaissance it would belong to Alan Faena, owner of the Phillipe Starck-designed Faena Hotel + Universe (*see p57*). An urban idealist with a keen business brain, Faena's goal is to create a new kind of barrio in BA, one that is both prosperous and accessible and that reflects a city comfortable with its past and confident about its future. On a practical level, his vision involves the restoration of structures associated with the docks' halcyon days. (The Faena Hotel is a recycled grain silo previously known as El Porteño.) More fundamentally, it means persuading *porteños* that tradition is about more than crumbling stucco mansions, and that modernity doesn't have to be soulless. Faena has called his dream-in-progress the 'Art District', a name that neatly captures his bourgeois-bohemian disposition.

Will it work? Is Puerto Madero Este the shape of things to come in Buenos Aires? We would say watch this space – if only the property developers had left any.

Costanera Norte

North of town, skirting the Aeroparque Jorge Newbery – the city airport that runs the length of Palermo – is a traditional promenade. One of the few places where the mud-coloured river laps close to the land, the paved thoroughfare contains numerous restaurants and is thronged on Sundays with anglers, walkers and *mate*-supping, picnic-eating day-trippers. The city's beach clubs, where thousands go to melt during the hot months, dot the avenue.

North of the airport is religious theme park **Tierra Santa**. Heralded by its proud creators as a chance 'to visit Jerusalem all year round', it's the kind of project that might have been realised had Billy Graham and Walt Disney put their heads together. For the devout only.

On the final northern curve of the Costanera Norte, near the Ciudad Universitaria, the **Parque de la Memoria** is being developed in remembrance of Argentinian victims of human rights violations. Due for completion in late 2006, the park's central work will be a monument bearing the names of Argentina's 'disappeared', many of whom were thrown to their deaths in the adjacent river. Check the website at www.parquedelamemoria.org.ar.

Tierra Santa

Avenida Costanera Rafael Obligado 5790 (4784 9551/www.tierrasanta-bsas.com.ar). Bus 33, 37, 42, 160. **Open** *May-Nov* 9am-9pm Fri; 11am-10.30pm Sat, Sun. *Dec-Apr* 5.30-11.30pm Fri; 3-11.30pm Sat, Sun. **Guided tours** (Spanish) every 20mins. **Admission** AR$10; AR$4 under-11s. **Credit** MC, V. **Map** p285 R11.

Further Afield

Beat a path to the 'burbs.

Tigre ■

BUENOS AIRES PROVINCE

San Isidro ■

Olivos ■
Vicente López ■

Saavedra
■ Nuñez
Liniers
BUENOS AIRES CITY

RÍO DE LA PLATA

0   10 km
0   10 miles

Buenos Aires is a city of extremes. And if you think this sounds glib, take a trip out to the suburbs. Here you'll find mansions and shanty towns within yards of one another, thriving commuter neighbourhoods and shabby slums, gated communities reminiscent of Beverly Hills and warren-like *barrios* reminiscent of Mumbai. All life is here – even the bits we usually prefer not to think about.

A number of attractions tempt visitors off the beaten track. The northern neighbourhood of Belgrano hides historical and art museums, while Zona Norte offers you the chance to rub shoulders with Buenos Aires high society while enjoying a spot of aquatic diversion; and out in the west by the cattle market, an urban rodeo draws in the tourists every Sunday.

Belgrano & Núñez

From the north–south downtown axis, all roads initially lead west, but Avenidas Santa Fe, Córdoba and Corrientes eventually fan out to the smarter north-western neighbourhoods in the conurbation of **Belgrano**. Those who live there rave about it, but it's essentially a

residential and commercial district. Named after independence hero General Manuel Belgrano, it was originally a city in its own right, but its incorporation into the capital in 1887 turned the area into a des res option for affluent *porteños*. Though the Subte from town gets you there in a matter of minutes, it still feels like a separate town and its main thoroughfare, Avenida Cabildo, is as important and as horribly busy as any downtown.

The most attractive parts of Belgrano are a block from the commercial epicentre; the two museums on Plaza General Belgrano are definitely worth a visit. The **Museo de Arte Español** (*see p104*) is housed in a neo-colonial mansion that once belonged to wealthy Uruguayan exile Enrique Larreta. His varied collection, which includes Renaissance and modern Spanish art, is displayed among stunning furniture, tapestries and silverware. Equally eye-catching are the gardens, a riot of flowering and climbing plants skirting a large native *ombú* tree.

Across the road is the **Museo Histórico Sarmiento** (*see p104*), dedicated to one of America's greatest educators, Domingo Sarmiento, Argentinian president from 1868 to 1874. He was also a writer; his major work, *Facundo*, was a treatise on the need for Argentinians to stop being gauchos. The museum, housed in a neo-classical building that once served as Belgrano's city hall, contains documents, old books and household objects gathered by the liberal thinker in his travels.

Juramento Street runs north to the *barrancas* (cliffs) bordering the Belgrano C railway station (on the Mitre line from Retiro). On and around Arribeños, running parallel to the northbound railway line, is BA's diminutive **Chinatown**, populated by mainland Chinese and especially Taiwanese immigrants, who arrived in several waves after World War II and own most of the restaurants and supermarkets in the area. At Chinese New Year (*see p174*), the community takes its celebrations on to the streets in style.

Nearby, at O'Higgins 2390, is the **Museo Casa de Yrurtia** (*see p104*), the home of sculptor Rogelio Yrurtia (1879-1950) and a joy to visit as much for the beautiful white house and lush garden as for the small sculptures and casts of major works. You'll see many of his notable creations dotted around the city.

Avenida Cabildo runs on into **Núñez**, which borders BA province. Again, this is largely a residential district, with the smartest houses encircling the huge 100,000-spectator **Estadio Monumental** (*see p210*), home to River Plate Football Club and the venue for the 1978 World Cup final – which Argentina won amid rumours of bribery and protests about atrocities being committed under military dictator Videla. Nearby, at Avenida del Libertador 8000-8500, is the Escuela Mecánica de la Armada, the country's most notorious torture centre and death camp of the 1970s. ESMA, as it is known, is being transformed into a museum and is expected to open in 2007.

Flanking Nuñez is Saavedra, where Parque Saavedra and Parque Sarmiento provide urban dwellers with cleaner air and greenery. The **Museo Histórico Cornelio de Saavedra** (*see below*) is located in the former residence of Luis María Saavedra (descendant of the museum's namesake who was one of the heroes of Argentinian independence). In addition to 18th- and 19th-century furniture, silverware and arms, the museum records daily life and highlights the fashions used in the old city, including the oversized *peinetones* (decorative combs) worn by well-to-do ladies in the early 19th century to remind admirers, including a young Darwin, that they were every bit as voguish as their Spanish peers.

Museo de Arte Español Enrique Larreta

Juramento 2291, y Vuelta de Obligado (4783 2640/ 4784 4040). Subte D, Juramento/60, 152 bus. **Open** 2-8pm Wed-Sun. *Feb-Dec* 2-8pm Mon, Wed-Sun. **Guided tours** (Spanish) 4pm, 5.30pm Sun. **Admission** AR$1. **No credit cards. Map** p285 S8.

Museo Casa de Yrurtia

O'Higgins 2390, y Blanco Encalada (4781 0385). Bus 29, 59, 60, 152. **Open** 1-7pm Tue-Fri; 3-7pm Sun. **Admission** AR$1; free concessions. Free Tue. **No credit cards. Map** p281 O5.

Museo Histórico Cornelio de Saavedra

Crisólogo Larralde 6309, y Constituyentes (4572 0746). Train to Villa Urquiza, then bus 176/28, 110, 111, 176 bus. **Open** *Mar-Jan* 9am-6pm Tue-Fri; 4-8pm Sat, Sun. Closed Feb. **Guided tours** (Spanish & English) by arrangement Sat, Sun. **Admission** AR$1; free under-12s. Free Wed. **No credit cards.**

Museo Histórico Sarmiento

Juramento 2180, entre Cuba y Arcos (4782 2354/http://museosarmiento.gov.ar/). Subte D, Juramento/60, 68, 152 bus. **Open** *Museum* Apr-Dec 2-7pm Tue-Fri; 3-7pm Sun. Jan-Mar 2-7pm Mon-Fri. *Library* Feb-Dec 2-6pm Mon-Fri. **Guided tours** (Spanish) *Apr-Dec* 4pm Sun. **Admission** AR$1. Free Thur. **No credit cards. Map** p285 R8.

Mataderos & Liniers

In the far west, the barrios get noticeably poorer, with occasional shanty towns dotting the gloomscape of high-rise 'mono-blocks'. People tend to be friendlier and calmer in the outer reaches, but some streets are dodgy and night strolls are not recommended. This is definitely the case at the outer city limits in the barrio of **Mataderos**, named after its slaughterhouses and formerly known as Nueva Chicago for the cattle carnage theme it shares with the Windy City.

On Sundays (Saturday evenings in summer), the place is brightened up by a rural-style fête, the **Feria de Mataderos** (*see below*). Restaurants lay out tables under the arcade of the 100-year-old administration building of the **Mercado Nacional de Hacienda**, a massive livestock market where cows and sheep are corralled for auction. Folk bands perform on a small central stage and locals join in the *chacareras* country dance. On the southern spoke of Lisandro de la Torre, brilliant horsemen take one another on at spearing the *sortija* – a small ring dangling on a ribbon – while standing high on *criollo*-breed horses.

The excellent **Museo Criollo de los Corrales** (*see below*) – the entrance is beneath the same arcade as the market – exhibits farming implements and country artefacts, along with cartoons by Argentina's most famous painter of gaucho life, Florencio Molina Campos and a reconstruction of a *pulpería* (rural bar/grocer's store). It's only open on Sundays.

In nearby **Liniers**, another barrio linked closely with the meatpacking business, the country's second most important saint (after the Virgin of Luján) has his shrine. San Cayetano, a 15th-century Venetian priest, is the patron of bread and work, to whom proletarian pilgrims flock each month.

Feria de Mataderos

Lisandro de la Torre y Avenida de Los Corrales (information Mon-Fri 4374 9664/Sun 4687 5602). Bus 55, 80, 92, 126. **Open** *Jan-Mar* 6pm-1am Sat. *Apr-Dec* 1-7pm Sun. **Admission** free.

Museo Criollo de los Corrales

Avenida de los Corrales 6436, y Lisandro de la Torre (4687 1949). Bus 55, 80, 92, 126. **Open** *Mar-Dec* noon-6.30pm Sun. Closed Jan, Feb. **Guided tours** (Spanish) by arrangement. **Admission** AR$1; free concessions. **No credit cards.**

Zona Norte

Originally home to the grand *quintas* (or summer houses) of BA's 19th-century aristocracy, the riverside neighbourhoods

Sightseeing

of Zona Norte, stretching from Olivos to San Isidro, still exude exclusivity – elegant abodes, private country clubs and a wealthy minority renowned for its love of the 'upper class' sports of rugby, windsurfing and yachting.

To lord it with the privileged or simply to enjoy the river life, take the **Tren de la Costa** (*see p180*), which skirts the River Plate all the way up to Tigre. The train departs from Olivos' Maipú station, and three blocks from here is **La Quinta Presidencial**, the presidential residence. The *quinta*'s main entrance is at the intersection of Maipú and Libertador, but its grounds cover nine blocks; it's so big that ex-President Carlos Menem kept a private zoo here. Views of the residence are obscured by tall perimeter walls.

For dramatic vistas head towards the river, to **Puerto Olivos**, situated between Corrientes and Alberdi streets. This private yacht club's 200-metre-long (656-foot) public pier offers a stunning panorama spanning the River Plate and BA's city skyline to the south.

Windsurfers and kiteboarders should hop off at Barrancas Station – serving the barrios of both Martínez and Acassuso – five minutes up the line from Olivos. The **Perú Beach** complex opposite the station (*see p212*) has numerous wet and dry sports activities and, along with Club Social bar and restaurant next door, is a popular place to hang out. These areas are favourites with kite-flyers and rollerbladers too. For a swampy alternative to the trendy vibe, try Acassuso's **Reserva Ecológica** (*see p106*), habitat to over 200 animal species – including snakes and iguanas.

Far removed from nature, but perfect for shopaholics, is Martínez's **Unicenter** shopping mall (Paraná y Panamericana, Martínez, 4733 1130, www.unicenter.com.ar), Argentina's biggest. For dining, check out the riverside bars or Acassuso's strip on Avenida del Libertador, between Roque Saénz Peña and Almafuerte.

Another eating strip is developing on Dardo Rocha, which runs inland alongside the grassy expanses of the **Hipódromo de San Isidro** racetrack (*see p211*) and the Jockey Club. Funky menswear boutique **Etiqueta Negra** (*see p158*) is also upping this strip's hip factor.

Sticking to the coastal train, the next stop is San Isidro, the most exclusive, and enchanting, of all the riverside neighbourhoods. Highlights are dotted around the main square, Plaza Mitre, located in front of the station and home to an artisans' fair every Sunday. At the square's far end is the towering, neo-Gothic **Catedral de San Isidro**, home to excellent programmes of classical music (*see p200*). Situated opposite are the area's tourist office and the **Museo del Rugby** (*see p106*), where the toothless and cauliflower-eared, but wonderfully humorous,

Feria de Mataderos. *See p104.*

Sightseeing

Horacio Cufre shows visitors around. Located on the same corner is the **Museo Biblioteca y Archivo Histórico Municipal** (*see below*), a colonial-era building that houses exhibits relating the area's rich history.

Beccar Varela, one of several cobbled streets wending from Plaza Mitre, leads visitors to the **Mirador de los Tres Ombúes**, which offers breathtaking views across the River Plate to the lush islands of Tigre's delta. This hidden lookout point is surrounded by some of the most sumptuous summer abodes of Argentina's upper class. Hummingbirds, flowering jasmine and fragrant orange groves complete an idyllic scene.

Three blocks east is the **Museo Histórico Municipal Juan Martín de Pueyrredón** (*see below*), the Spanish-colonial style *quinta* of one of the heroes of Argentinian independence. Its glorious gardens include the carob tree under which Generals Pueyrredón and San Martín sat and compared battle scars while they plotted the defeat of the Spanish.

Another mansion where ghosts of the past linger is the masterfully eclectic **Villa Ocampo** (Elortondo 1811, y Uriburu, 4732 4988), former residence of literary luminary and arts patron Victoria Ocampo. The guest list at Ocampo's parties here reads like a Who's Who of 20th-century literature and included the likes of Borges, Albert Camus, Aldous Huxley and Graham Greene. Almost destroyed by fire in 2003, after three decades of neglect this national monument and UNESCO-protected site has

been fully restored and opened to visitors, though you'll need to phone in advance to arrange a guided tour (AR$10).

Museo Biblioteca y Archivo Histórico Municipal

Avenida del Libertador 16362, San Isidro (4512 3282). Train Mitre or de la Costa to San Isidro/ 60, 168 bus. **Open** *Museum* Feb 8am-2.30pm Tue, Thur; 2-5pm Sat, Sun. Mar-Dec 8am-noon, 2-6pm Tue, Thur; 2-5.30pm Sat, Sun. *Library* Feb 10am-3pm Mon-Fri. Mar-Dec 10am-6pm Mon-Fri. Closed Jan. **Admission** free.

Museo Histórico Municipal Juan Martín de Pueyrredón

Rivera Indarte 45, y Roque Saéz Peña, San Isidro (4512 3131). Train Mitre or de la Costa to San Isidro/60, 168 bus. **Open** 2-6pm Tue, Thur, Sat, Sun. **Guided tours** (Spanish) *Garden* 3pm 2nd Sun of mth. *Museum* 4pm Sat, Sun. **Admission** free.

Museo del Rugby

Ituzaigó 608, y Libertador, San Isidro (information 4732 2547/www.museodelrugby.com). Train Mitre or de la Costa to San Isidro/60, 168 bus. **Open** 10am-6pm Tue-Sat; 10am-8pm Sun. **Admission** free.

Reserva Ecológica Municipal

Camino de la Ribera, entre López y Planes y Almafuerte, Acassuso (4747 6179/www.geo cities.com/riberan). Train Mitre or de la Costa to Acassuso/168 bus. **Open** *Jan-Mar, Nov* 9am-7pm daily. *Apr-Oct* 9am-6pm daily. **Guided tours** (Spanish) *Jan-Mar, Nov* 5pm Sat, Sun. *Mar-Oct* 4pm Sat, Sun. **Admission** free.

Reach for the sky at **Perú Beach**. *See p105.*

Eat, Drink, Shop

Restaurants

The thrills and grills of BA's increasingly eclectic dining scene.

It wasn't too long ago that deciding what you wanted for supper in Buenos Aires meant choosing between *jugoso* (rare) and *bien cocido* (well done). But while meat still rules, the capital's culinary repertoire has expanded in recent times to cater to an increasingly discerning *porteño* palate.

Grilled meat aside, BA's foodscape has long been dominated by those twin classics of Italian comfort food, pizza and pasta, popularised by homesick immigrants and never likely to be supplanted. But these days trendy *porteños* are as likely to order sushi or smörgåsbord as a tortilla or plate of cannelloni. The newest and most diverse gastrozone is concentrated in and around the Palermo Viejo neighbourhood, but the tendency towards ethnic and global cuisine is increasingly making its presence felt in barrios such as San Telmo and Villa Crespo.

For faithfully rendered haute cuisine look no further than top hotel restaurants like **La Bourgogne** (Alvear Palace) and **Agraz** (Caesar Park). The culinary buzz, however, is centred around 'modern Argentinian', a term

loosely applied to the efforts of a younger generation of chefs to do more to the high quality local produce than simply grill it. This ethos is epitomised in restaurants such as **Casa Cruz** (*see p124*), **Central** (*see p124*) and **Gran Bar Danzón** (*see p119*).

Service can be slow in this unrushed capital, although it usually compensates with warmth and character for what it lacks in speed and efficiency. A ten per cent *propina* (tip) will be greatly appreciated by underpaid staff.

Argentinians eat late. Many kitchens stay open till two in the morning, and restaurants don't get full until after 10pm. This means that early bird tourists and canny locals are usually guaranteed a table if they roll up a little earlier.

The Centre

Argentinian (Traditional)

El Establo
Paraguay 489, Retiro (4311 1639). Subte C, San Martín/93, 132, 152 bus. **Open** 7am-2am daily. **Main courses** AR$20-$32. **Credit** AmEx, DC, MC, V. **Map** p281 G11 ❶
Happy diners throng this central, brightly lit Ibero-Argentinian classic: locals come back again and again, mixing with tables of tourists from nearby hotels. Vast steaks come off the *parrilla* perfectly, and there's a wide range of pizzas, salads, fish and pasta too, not to mention classic Spanish tapas of *jamón* (ham), peppers and tortilla.

Sabot
25 de Mayo 756, Microcentro (4313 6587). Subte B, LN Alem/93, 152 bus. **Open** noon-4pm Mon-Fri. **Main courses** AR$17-$27. **Credit** AmEx, MC, V. **Map** p281 F12 ❷
For an authentic *porteño* cuisine that doesn't simply follow the tried-and-tested neighbourhood steakhouse formula, Sabot can't be bettered. The congenial welcome comes from Spanish-born owner Ramón Couñago, while the menu of delicately prepared meat and fish classics is the work of Italian partner Francesco de Nicola. Look out for the caramelised apple pancake dessert, which is ambrosial.

❶ Purple numbers given in this chapter correspond to the location of each restaurant as marked on the street maps. See pp276-285.

The best Restaurants

For a fashionable feast
Casa Cruz (see *p124*); Gran Bar Danzón (see *p119*); Olsen (see *p125*).

For a romantic rendezvous
Abril (*see p117*); Tomo I (*see p111*).

For home cooking
Café San Juan (see *p115*); Cumaná (*see p119*); La Cupertina (see *p121*).

For bargain bites
Club Eros (*see p123*); El Cuartito (*see p121*); La Reina Kunti (see *p133*).

For global grub
Azema Exotic Bistró (*see p127*); Osaka (see *p129*); Sudestada (*see p130*).

For haute cow
Cabaña Las Lilas (*see p136*); La Cabrera (*see p121*); Miranda (*see p123*).

Get the scoop

Warning: the following article is not for the lactose intolerant. In fact, the next 500 words or so will be dedicated to things delightfully, deliciously dairy – specifically, BA's most undervalued food resource, ice-cream.

Ice-cream is to Buenos Aires what chocolate is to Switzerland: the dieter's nightmare but hedonistic heaven for those in need of a post-prandial sugar rush or simply looking to put on another clothes size overnight.

One of the few traditions inherited from the Italian immigrants that *porteños* arguably improved upon, Buenos Aires' *helado artesanal* (home-made ice-cream) is everything that ice-cream should have been had it not sadly lost its way somewhere between Mr Whippy's and Wall's. Free from the chemical-induced rush that those reared on square-blocked, tri-colour Neapolitan will remember all too painfully, the ice-cream here is so faithful to its raw ingredients that you can actually taste, and sometimes even see, real strawberries in the strawberry cream, and crunch on chopped nuts in the pistachio.

There is a myriad of other enticing flavour options, from sorbet to sinfully creamy with all manner of variations in between. For some specifically Argentinian delights, there are a thousand different *dulce de leche* options, each more decadent than the last and with all sorts of strange hidden delights running through, like chocolate balls, nuts, huge chunks of brownies and even extra swirls of pure *dulce de leche*. Then there's the alcohol-soaked enchantment of *sambayón*, or the numerous takes on chocolate, cream, mascarpone, fruit... the calorific list goes on.

And the choices don't end there. Never mind selecting your flavours – many a brave heart has been paralysed from the word go when faced with the selection of cups and cones and other vessels inside which their ice-cream choice will be as carefully constructed as the Obelisco itself. And that's before toppings are considered (true chocolate fanatics drool over the legendary *baño de chocolate*, which involves dipping your sweetly leaning ice-cream tower into melted chocolate for a crunchy coat of cocoa bliss).

It's no wonder that ice-cream parlours have become the preferred late-night haunt of the young and trendy. In fact, should you be dining out on a balmy Buenos Aires evening, we recommend you skip dessert entirely and head for your nearest *heladeria*, where you'll find a scene going late into the night that rivals any downtown bar.

It's worth noting, however, that standards vary, but while you often get just what you pay for, even the average chains are a cut above their Western counterparts.

Vying for top position are two ice-cream shops so revered that their names illicit swoons and sighs whenever they are mentioned in polite conversation. While it's hard to pick a favourite in terms of quality – both serve exquisite (a word we don't use lightly) ice-cream – **Persicco** (on the corner of Salguero and Cabello, Palermo, 4808 0888) boasts a younger and trendier clientele, and as such can be a more inviting spot for those looking to meet their match over mint-choc-chip. **Un Altra Volta** (Avenida del Libertador 3060, Palermo, 4805 1818), owned by a branch of the same family that created Persicco, serves a slightly more traditional crowd and tends to change its menu less often, but packs the same punch in terms of taste and quality. **Saverio**, the alleged favourite of tango crooner Carlos Gardel (Avenida San Juan 2816, 0800 222 1909) offers old-style excellence and delivers all over town. More prevalent chains include the perennially popular **Freddo**, a cut above the average ice-cream emporium, and **Munchi's**, whose famously creamy concoctions are churned from the milk of the company's own herd of Jersey cows.

Eat, Drink, Shop

Bar Uriarte

Restaurant - Bar
Lunch, Afternoon Tea & Dinner

Happy hour from 7pm to 10:30pm
Brunch Saturdays, Sundays and Public Holidays
Open 7 days a week from 12 pm till late

Uriarte 1572 - Reservations 4834 6004

uriarte@baruriarte.com.ar - www.baruriarte.com.ar

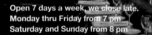

Argentinian (Modern)

Azzurra

Avenida Corrientes 222, Microcentro (4315 8381).
Subte B, LN Alem/6, 23, 130, 143 152 bus. **Open**
noon-5pm, 8pm-2am Mon-Fri; from 8pm Sat. **Main**
courses AR$26-$36. **Credit** AmEx, DC, MC, V.
Map p281 F11 ❸
Forget the food – modern Argentinian cuisine with
a strong Italian influence, served with panache by
stylish waiters. The truly breathtaking thing about
Azzurra is the incredible view its wide bay windows
afford of the twinkling city. Not for the vertiginous.

Crizia

Lavalle 345, Microcentro (4312 2803/www.crizia.
com.ar). Subte B, LN Alem/6, 22, 28, 93, 152 bus.
Open noon-4.30pm Mon; noon-2am Tue-Fri; 8pm-
2am Sat. **Main courses** AR$18-$30. **Credit** AmEx,
MC, V. **Map** p281 F11 ❹
Located on the first floor of the same belle époque
building that houses the Bahrein nightclub (*see*
p183), this new, upmarket eaterie is just as plush
inside as out. The old-style oak floors and crystal
chandeliers are tastefully incorporated into a modern look, characterised by low banquettes, cream
walls, clean lines and a large rectangular bar.
Specialising in Patagonian lamb dishes, Crizia also
boasts a sushi bar and a well-stocked wine cellar.

Restó

Montevideo 938, Tribunales (4816 6711). Subte D,
Callao/39, 152 bus. **Open** noon-3pm Mon-Fri; 8-
11pm Thur, Fri. **Main courses** AR$8-$12 lunch.
Set menu (dinner only) AR$35-$58. **No credit**
cards. Map p281 H10 ❺
A disciple of the great Michel Bras, Francophile
chef María Barrutia prepares reasonably priced but
exquisite cuisine in this petite restaurant on the
ground floor of the Central Architect's Society. The
lunch menu offers two fish options and a choice of
beef and chicken, though their preparation is altered
daily. On Thursday and Friday nights, by reservation only, a choice of three thoughtfully combined
set menus awaits. You can bring your own wine.

Tomo I

Hotel Panamericano, Carlos Pellegrini 521, Microcentro
(4326 6695/www.tomo1.com.ar). Subte B, Carlos
Pellegrini/10, 17, 29 bus. **Open** noon-3pm, 7.30pm-
1am Mon-Fri; 8pm-midnight Sat. **Main courses**
AR$25-$68. **Set menu** AR$72. **Credit** AmEx, DC,
MC, V. **Map** p281 G10 ❻
Regularly cited as BA's best restaurant, Tomo I
derives its fame from the care sisters Ada and Eve
Concaro take in preparing every single dish, dip
and detail. Pastas are extraordinary, the fish and
seafood are so fresh they should come with a death
certificate, and you'll also find seasonal Patagonian
game on the menu. It's expensive by BA standards
but if you have something to celebrate – a lottery
win, perhaps, or a successful bank heist – you can
be assured of VIP treatment.

French

Le Sud

Sofitel Hotel, Arroyo 841, Retiro (4131 0131/www.
sofitelbuenosaires.com.ar). Subte C, Retiro/62, 92, 93
bus. **Open** 6.30-11am, 12.30-3pm, 7.30pm-midnight
daily. **Main courses** AR$25-$45. **Set menu**
(lunch only) AR$38-$45. **Credit** AmEx, DC,
MC, V. **Map** p281 H11 ❼
Inside the art deco tower of the Sofitel Hotel hides
Le Sud, one of the city's most hallowed temples
to French haute cuisine. Using the best ingredients
and techniques from his native Provence along with
carefully selected local produce, virtuoso chef
Thierry Pszonka conjures up dishes such as duck
foie gras terrine with cognac, date mousse and warm
brioche – mouthwatering to read about, let alone eat.

Italian

Filo

San Martín 975, Retiro (4311 0312/www.filo-
ristorante.com). Subte C, San Martín/10, 93,
130, 152 bus. **Open** from noon daily. **Main**
courses AR$12-$18. **Credit** AmEx, DC, MC,
V. **Map** p281 G12 ❽
Madonna, Schumacher, Coppola... This 1960s-style
pop art pizzeria attracts a steady stream of A-list
superstars. There are more than 100 delicious flat-
base pizzas to choose from, plus a healthy selection
of salads, sandwiches and meat dishes. Gnocchi,

Green Bamboo. *See p130.*

Eat, Drink, Shop

Central. *See p124.*

Shock of the new Wine

Right now Argentinian wine is exactly where it should be: on everybody's lips. After decades of underachievement, the sleeping giant of the global wine industry is waking up and beginning to deliver on its vast potential.

About time too. Argentina has long been the world's fifth biggest producer of wine, but in the bad old days its role was to churn out crude booze like Saudi Arabia churns out crude oil. Virtually all of it was reserved for undemanding local drinkers who were largely content to wash down the world's best beef with some of the world's worst plonk. The issue of whether the wine came in a bottle, a box or a sweat sock was rendered largely irrelevant by the custom of decanting it into an aluminium jug before serving it in the kind of chunky-bottomed glasses usually found holding toothbrushes in motel bathrooms.

While cheapskates and dedicated anthro-oenologists will be relieved to find this ritual still performed in many of Buenos Aires' neighbourhood restaurants, both the quality and cultural status of Argentinian wine are changing. The adjectively challenged ravings of influential wine critics like Robert Parker and Jancis Robinson have made malbec, Argentina's most popular varietal, the grape *du jour*. Wineries from Catena Zapata, Alta Vista and Terrazas have put Mendoza, the country's main grape growing province, firmly on the wine tour trail. What was once just an industry is now a phenomenon.

As importantly, Argentinians, always glad to hear good things said about their country but often slow to believe them, are falling in love

with fine wine. In a restaurant where once the waiter would simply ask, 'Red or white?', you're now likely to find a sommelier stroking his chin while proferring the dilemma, '2001 or 2002?' Restaurants reviewed in this chapter with outstanding wine lists include **Casa Cruz** (*see p124*), **Oviedo** (*see p121*) and **Gran Bar Danzón** (*see p119*).

Another recent noticeable trend is the rise of '*bodegas boutiques*': independent microwineries that sell directly though small outlets and participating restaurants. Quality is never assured, of course, but therein lies the joy. You might just discover a great malbec that Robert Parker has never heard of.

Five to slurp

Santa Ana malbec Ubiquitous, utilitarian, bereft of bouquet. Think diluted cherryade without sugar. Acceptable with a shot of soda as a steak sluicer on hot days.
San Telmo cabernet sauvignon Medium-bodied, workmanlike *tinto* that delivers frank flavours of berries, cocoa and spices. A mid-price classic.
Humberto Canale semillón Smooth floral varietal from a Patagonian wine pioneer.
Nicolás Catena Zapata Pricey, posh malbec-cabernet sauvignon blend not overloaded with oakiness. Look out for the 1999 vintage.
San Pedro de Yacochuya Torrontés Crisp, dry, lasting lemon-and-honey tongue-teaser, reared on the Etchart family's boutique vineyard near Cafayate in Salta province. Explore the malbecs too.

---

focaccia, antipasti, pickled calamesotti and Cavani sponge cake remind you this is an authentic Italian joint. Between courses, grab a cocktail at the cowhide bar and take a gander around the 180° art gallery in the basement (*see p190*).

Latin American

Status

Virrey Cevallos 178, Congreso (4382 8531/www. *restaurantstatus.com.ar). Subte A, Sáenz Peña/* *37, 60, 168 bus.* **Open** noon-5pm, 8pm-1am Mon-Thur; noon-1am Fri-Sun. **Main courses** AR$7-$20. **Credit** AmEx, MC, V. **Map** p281 G9 **❾**
Although Argentinians tend to shun most things indigenous to their own continent, one day soon they're going to wake up to the potential of Peruvian cuisine, which is tasty, cheap and different from

criollo beef and wine culture. This canteen owned by the friendly Valenzuela family from Trujillo serves abundant platters of *ceviche* and lamb, as well as spicy starters such as the must-order *papas a la huancaína*, spuds cooked with cheese and chilli.

South-east Asian

Empire Thai

Tres Sargentos 427, Retiro (4312 5706). Subte C, *San Martín/26, 93, 152 bus.* **Open** noon-midnight Mon-Fri; 7pm-1am Sat. **Main courses** AR$17-$32. **Set menu** (lunch only) AR$16-$18. **Credit** AmEx, MC, V. **Map** p281 G11 **❿**
This groovy, dimly lit grotto of a restaurant offers the gamut of heat from tongue-frazzling red and green curries to milder, Argentinian-friendly noodle and vegetable dishes. Coconut and tropical fruits

sweeten much of the menu and there are chilli-free seafood options for the puritanical palate. The mixed satays make for mean starters, especially with a cocktail – the bar stocks a superb range of vodkas.

Constitución

Argentinian (Traditional)

Miramar
Avenida San Juan 1999 (4304 4261). Subte E, Entre Ríos/37, 53, 126 bus. **Open** 11am-4pm, from 8pm Wed-Mon. **Main courses** AR$8-$62. **Credit** AmEx, MC, V. **Map** p281 E7 ⓬
Beloved by its barrio, Miramar boasts a well-stocked wine store and an unpretentious eaterie with super-amiable waiters. For lunch, try a Spanish tortilla or shrimps in garlic while listening to the crackly tangos. The justly famed *rabo del toro* (oxtail stew) has a limb-warming quality that's nigh on narcotic. *Bandoneón* master Julio Pane plays live on Sundays.

French

Les Anciens Combattants
Santiago del Estero 1435 (4305 1701). Subte C, Constitución/12, 39, 96, 102, 151, 168 bus. **Open** from 9pm Tue-Sat. **Main courses** AR$30-$50. **No credit cards. Map** p281 E8 ⓭
Not an old soldier in sight – just some of the most authentic French food in the city, from *soupe à l'oignon* to coq au vin, not to mention the chef's own speciality, sweet tomato pudding. Obelix wannabes can also scrunch on Patagonian wild boar. With only five tables, booking is a must. The neighbourhood's less savoury than the food, so it's best to go by taxi.

Japanese

Yuki
Pasco 740 (4942 7510). Bus 95, 98, 105, 168. **Open** 7.30-11.30pm Mon-Sat. **Main courses** AR$25-$30. **Credit** AmEx, MC, V. **Map** p281 F8 ⓮
The crème de la crème of BA's Japanese community eat at Yuki, a true oriental paradise tucked discreetly behind a bland façade on a gloomy street. Choose between the Zen-style dining room, private side rooms with tatami floors or the sushi bar. Ask the friendly sushi man to create your own customised sushi/sashimi combo. Reservations are essential.

San Telmo

Argentinian (Traditional)

La Brigada
Estados Unidos 465 (4361 4685). Bus 9, 10, 20, 22, 24, 29, 126, 195. **Open** noon-3pm, 8pm-midnight Mon-Thur; noon-4pm, 8pm-1am Fri-Sun. **Main courses** AR$18-$32. **Credit** AmEx, DC, MC, V. **Map** p280 D10 ⓮

La Brigada: perfect for a meat overload.

Parrillas of the cheap and cheerless variety are a plague in San Telmo, but this one is a cut above most for steak, wine and genteel ambience. For around AR$50 per person they'll bring you grilled cheese and a rump to share, loads of salad, some *chorizos* (spicy sausages) and *morcilla* (black pudding), and an excellent bottle of red. If you're up for a game of guess-the-gland, try the offal – the *chinchulines de chivito* (kid tripe) are as good as entrails get.
Other locations: Peña 2475, Recoleta (4800 1110); Demaria 4701, Palermo (4777 1414).

El Desnivel
Defensa 855 (4300 9081). Subte C, Independencia/ 24, 29 bus. **Open** noon-4pm, from 7.30pm daily. **Main courses** AR$6-$14. **No credit cards. Map** p280 D10 ⓯
This classic steakhouse on the main antiques shop drag staffs the grill with bloody-apron-wearing, knife-wielding cooks (think Sweeney Todd meets Joe Pesci) and cheeky waiters. The mix of expatriates, tourists and locals makes for a boisterous and very friendly scene. If you want to feel part of the action, make sure you get a table in the main restaurant rather than the new annex out the back.

Lezama
Brasil 359 (4361 0114). Bus 33, 62, 74, 64, 143. **Open** noon-4pm, from 7.30pm Tue-Sat; noon-4pm Sun. **Main courses** AR$5-$30. **Credit** AmEx, MC, V. **Map** p280 C9 ⓰

Eat, Drink, Shop

Beef for beginners

When hunger strikes in Argentina, one and all worship the sacred cow. Peckish local construction workers convert their wheelbarrows into pavement *parrillas*; visiting vegetarians wonder if, just this once, they could get away with murder; and the sounds of the suburbs are sizzling *chorizos*, fat hissing on hot coals and popping corks. So just this once you can believe the hype: the best beef in the world *is* Argentinian.

Just as crucially, they know how to cook it. While the British boil it down and the French sauce it up, Argentinians prefer their meat to arrive on the plate pretty much as it left the cow. Only the intervention of direct heat is required, using either the *al carbon* (charcoal) or *a la leña* (wood) methods. Most commonly, the cuts are laid out on a grill (*a la parrilla*)

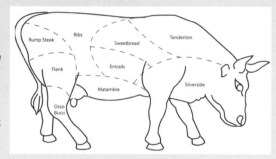

and cooked slowly to retain the natural juices. More exotically, the eviscerated carcass can be hung on cross-poles over a pit of glowing embers, a style known as *al asador*. This latter method (still seen in several of the city's traditional steakhouses and on country *estancias*) is a throwback to the gaucho era: a survival technique that has morphed into a gourmand's fantasy.

Once you've made friends with a local (a process that can take anything up to ten minutes) there's a fair chance he or she will invite you to attend an *asado* (barbecue), a supremely important ritual in which the whole canon of Argentinian social habits is played out. Look for the person who is attending the *parrilla*, cranking the height-adjustment handle like he is fine tuning an Aston Martin. This person will, of course, be a man – the complexities of putting meat on a grill and turning it over once in a while are thought by the locals to be too profound for the female mind to fathom. In reality the women of the house end up doing most of

the real work, including the shopping, preparing the meat, making the side dishes and entertaining the guests. And probably washing the dishes.

Never offer advice to the *asador*. Should he set fire to the shed, it is only because he meant to do so. But lend an ear and he will tell you everything you need to know about the art of *asado* and plenty besides. Spices and marinades are regarded as effete fripperies, but occasionally your new best friend will throw some salt in the general direction of the meat or perhaps douse it in a little lemon juice. Auguste Escoffier this ain't.

As the wine starts to flow, you'll probably be handed a *choripan* (spicy sausage sandwich), which is often served along with *chimichurri* (a tasty chilli and herb sauce). Make sure you don't fill up as this is just the prologue. A dizzying procession of offal and prime cuts will follow. Very little food is wasted; one could almost reassemble the cow at the table as if it were a jigsaw puzzle.

Extras will include green salads, plenty of bread and gallons of wine. Like a python, you should put enough away to last you several days, while keeping in mind Miss Piggy's advice to never eat more than you can lift.

All of the above, plus the famous Argentinian steaks can, of course, be enjoyed in a parrilla restaurant. Many tourists will head for the more sophisticated and pricey joints in the Puerto Madero and Recoleta districts. Most of these restaurants will bring the meat-eating experience to the table and you can try out what you like the look of when you see it cooked. Don't get hooked on these establishments though, since the local-frequented eateries found in every neighbourhood, while a little more intimidating for the novice, are a lot cheaper, often tastier and much more fun. (For what's on the menu, *see p120* **Crack the carta**.)

Attracting everybody from neighbourhood families and arty couples to the odd well-informed tourist and even Latin heart-throb Ricky Martin, this handsome San Telmo *bodegón* (traditional restaurant) is superb value and has the added boon of a view over Parque Lezama. Ask the waiter for his preferred wines and dishes, since going pot luck can be hit and miss.

Argentinian (Modern)

Abril

Balcarce 722 (4342 8000). Bus 29, 86, 93, 130, 152. **Open** noon-4pm, 8.30pm-midnight Mon-Fri; 8pm-2am Sat. **Main courses** AR$15-$26. **Credit** AmEx, DC, MC, V. **Map** p280 D10 ⑰

If you're in the mood for love, Abril is San Telmo's best bet for a candlelit rendezvous. Serving Asian and Argentinian crossover cuisine, the daily set menu is one of the city's gourmet bargains, though the dishes can fall short of the à la carte options.

Nacional

Estados Unidos 302 (4361 5539). Bus 22, 24, 29, 93, 152. **Open** 9am-6pm Mon; 9am-2am Tue-Fri; from 6pm Sat; from 10am Sun. **Main courses** AR$9-$18. **Credit** AmEx, MC, V. **Map** p280 D10 ⑱

Though lacking the pzazz of its trendier Palermo competitors, Nacional is an understated San Telmo gem. Quietly going about the business of doing what it does best, this modern Argentinian restaurant serves up a short menu of tasteful dishes alongside a well-stocked art deco bar. It also boasts a secret door – well, it used to be a secret door – behind the bookcase, leading to whereabouts unknown, adding an element of surprise missing from the menu.

Basque

Burzako

México 345 (4334 0721). Bus 29, 93, 130, 152. **Open** noon-4pm Sun-Wed; noon-4pm, 8pm-1am Thur-Sat. **Main courses** AR$10-$20. **Credit** AmEx, MC, V. **Map** p281 E10 ⑲

A lively bar-restaurant with touches of a traditional Spanish tavern, but which also tries to show that Basque cuisine can be young and cool. The fish specialities and tasty tapas are highlights, and a fine bottle of La Rural Cepa Trad 97 at AR$16 makes this a classy yet wallet-friendly meal.

Taberna Baska

Chile 980 (4334 0903). Subte C, Independencia/ 59, 60, 126, 143 bus. **Open** noon-3.30pm, from 8pm Tue-Sat; noon-3.30pm Sun. **Main courses** AR$14-$80. **Credit** AmEx, DC, MC, V. **Map** p281 E9 ⑳

Open for over 30 years, Taberna Baska has found little reason to alter its approach to dining – there's something about this old-style restaurant with its bright lights and brighter tablecloths that keeps regulars coming back for seconds. The menu is of Proustian proportions, so try to narrow it down to the fine seafood dishes, Basque stews and soups that

arrive at your table in earthenware bowls. Or just close your eyes, point at something at random and let the surly waiters (no tourist trap this) do the rest.

French

Brasserie Petanque

Defensa 596 (4342 7930/www.brasseriepetanque. com). Bus 29, 93, 130, 152. **Open** 12.30-3.30pm Mon; 12.30pm-1am Tue-Fri; from 8pm Sat; 12.30pm-1am Sun. **Main courses** AR$17-$23. **Credit** AmEx, DC, MC, V. **Map** p281 E10 ㉑

A quintessential Parisian brasserie in the middle of Buenos Aires, come here to reacquaint yourself with old friends like boeuf bourguignon, cassoulet and garlic-drenched snails, all served in a roomy, informal space. A perfect Sunday brunch spot, the crêpes and salad deal is a steal, allowing you to blow the rest of your budget on kir royales.

Japanese

Comedor Nikkai

Avenida Independencia 732 (4300 5248). Bus 22, 24, 29, 86. **Open** noon-3pm, 7.30-11pm Mon-Thur; 8pm-midnight Fri, Sat. **Main courses** AR$10-$27. **Credit** AmEx, MC, V. **Map** p281 E9 ㉒

This informal yet traditional diner inside San Telmo's Asociación Japonesa centre is a real gem – the sushi is up there with the best of Buenos Aires, and the beamed-in Japanese TV for local clients adds an element of uncontrived authenticity.

Spanish

Café San Juan

San Juan 450 (4300 1112). Subte C, San Juan/ 10, 24, 28, 29, 86 bus. **Open** noon-4pm, from 7.30pm Tue-Sun. **Main courses** AR$13-$22. **No credit cards. Map** p280 D9 ㉓

Neither the location nor the façade inspire – and that's what makes this family-run restaurant such a rewarding find. Vegetables are hand picked from the local markets and the meats deboned in front of your eyes. Best to choose a combination of tapas – the cured ham with tomatoes and the smoked salmon are the best – and one of the seasonal mains which are easily big enough for two. **Photo** *p135*.

La Boca

Argentinian (Traditional)

El Obrero

Agustín Caffarena 64 (4362 9912). Bus 25, 29, 68, 130. **Open** noon-4pm, from 8pm Mon-Sat. **Main courses** AR$6-$14. **No credit cards. Map** p280 B10 ㉔

Everyone from U2's Bono to film director Wim Wenders – has discovered this museum piece in the heart of the old port (best to come by taxi and with

Eat, Drink, Shop

company). The decor is busy with boxing and soccer legends, the paint is peeling and the toilet is a glorified outhouse, but it's still a classic spot for long lunches or dinners with a gang of friends.

Italian

Il Matterello

Martín Rodríguez 517 (4307 0529). Bus 29, 64, 86, 152. **Open** 12.30-3pm, 8.30pm-midnight Tue-Sat; 12.30-3pm Sun. **Closed** Jan. **Main courses** AR$14-$25. **Credit** AmEx, DC, MC, V. **Map** p280 B9 **②**
This attractive, family-owned-and-run restaurant in a poor quarter is still faithful to the barrio's Italian roots. Fantastic dishes include a *cima rellena* (cold pork roll with peas, cheese, carrot and egg) and a rocket tagliatelle with sundried tomatoes and onion. Desserts include *postre de la nonna* ('grandma's sweet'), a trifle-like calorie bomb.

Recoleta & Barrio Norte

Argentinian (Traditional)

Cumaná

Rodríguez Peña 1149 (4813 9207). Bus 10, 37, 39, 101, 124, 152. **Open** noon-1am daily. **Main courses** AR$5-$13. **No credit cards.** **Map** p282 I10 **②**
Cumaná is the kind of restaurant that makes you hungry as soon as you walk in the door, even if you only did so to use the washroom. Make sure you surrender to the onslaught of tantalising aromas and settle at one of the rustic tables and order some *locro* (a thick Argentinian stew) and home-made empanadas. With food served piping hot from the *horno al barro*, which is a domed adobe oven used in the north of Argentina, this country kitchen is hard to beat.

El Mirasol de la Recova

Posadas 1032 (4326 7322). Bus 17, 59, 61, 93, 152. **Open** noon-2am daily. **Main courses** AR$15-$29. **Credit** AmEx, DC, MC, V. **Map** p281 H11 **②**
El Mirasol's Recoleta branch was established in the early 1990s to serve up king-size cuts of beef to visiting executives and upmarket tourists who wander in from the nearby luxury hotels. Despite its location under the motorway flyover, there's been no dearth of human traffic through the doors of this upscale *parrilla*. Dependable rather than daring, El Mirasol embodies the kind of no-nonsense excellence that confirmed carnivores delight in.

Rodi Bar

Vicente López 1900 (4801 5230). Bus 60, 101, 102, 110. **Open** 6am-2am Mon-Sat. **Main courses** AR$8-$20. **Credit** AmEx, DC, MC, V. **Map** p282 J11 **②**
Rodi's is a great spot for a Recoleta lunch. The restaurant's roots are Galician; here you'll find old-time waiters, bright lighting and a menu of Spanish-sounding dishes such as *merluza a la catalana* (hake in seafood sauce) and *pulpo a la gallega* (octopus in

tomato and pepper sauce). From the Argentinian side of the kitchen comes one of the tastiest *bifes de lomo* in Buenos Aires.

Argentinian (Modern)

Bond

Posadas 1011 (4326 4499). Bus 17, 59, 67, 102. **Open** noon-2am daily. **Main courses** AR$16-$28. **Credit** AmEx, MC, V. **Map** p281 H11 **②**
Tucked on to the end of a string of eateries known as La Recova, and embodying everything slick and debonair about its namesake, Bond is likely to leave you more stirred than shaken. Though it serves a peerless Martini (as well as the other cocktails), most of the wannabe starlets are frequenting Bond for quality sushi and a varied menu that includes tacos, teriyakis and tapas. And, of course, to be seen.

Gran Bar Danzón

Libertad 1161 (4811 1108/www.granbardanzon. com.ar). Subte D, Tribunales/17, 39, 102, 152 bus. **Open** from 8pm daily. **Main courses** AR$20-$27. **Credit** AmEx, DC, MC, V. **Map** p281 H11 **③**
The '*gran*' is fully merited – this is a great wine bar and restaurant, and a banquet for the senses from the moment you enter via the candlelit and incense-scented stairwell. The main menu roams between Europe and Latin America, offering flawlessly executed fusion dishes like confit of duck served with a *ceviche* taco, and rack of Patagonian lamb in a brioche crust. Or if you think east is best, try the superb sushi (quite properly not served on Mondays). A wine list of over 400 bottles (many available by the glass), happy-hour promotions, guest chef weeks and live jazz on Wednesdays and Fridays keep the constant crowds happy. If you want to dine in peace, dine early. **Photo** *p131.*

Lola

Ortíz 1805, Recoleta (4804 5959/www.lola restaurant.com). Bus 59, 60, 110. **Open** noon-4pm, from 7.30pm daily. **Main courses** AR$20-$35. **Credit** AmEx, DC, MC, V. **Map** p282 J11 **③**
A far cry from the 'roll 'em in, roll 'em out' eateries that litter this restaurant strip on Ortíz street, Lola represents a classic of elegant Buenos Aires dining. Sober and sophisticated, it's the place to take your parents-in-law if you're out to impress. The European-style menu deserves its reputation as one of the best in town; a welcome blend of creativity and first-class consistency. The battered salmon in champagne sauce and the melt-in-your-mouth braised duck are equally divine.

French

Granda Bistró

Junín 1281 (4826 2317). Bus 39, 59, 60. **Open** noon-3pm, 8pm-midnight Mon-Sat. **Main courses** AR$18-$25. **Credit** AmEx, DC, MC, V. **Map** p282 I10 **③**

Eat, Drink, Shop

Crack the *carta*

Basics

Menú/carta menu; **desayuno** breakfast; **almuerzo** lunch; **merienda** afternoon tea/snack (often *mate* and *medialunas*); **cena** dinner; **entrada** entrée; **minutas** short orders; **plato principal** main course; **postre** dessert; **aceite y vinagre** oil and vinegar; **ajo** garlic; **casero** home-made; **pan** bread; **sopa** soup; **agua** water (**con gas** fizzy, **sin gas** still); **mate/yerba** local herb tea; **te** tea; **vino** wine (**tinto** red, **blanco** white, **de la casa** house).

Cooking styles & techniques

A la parrilla grilled; **al horno** baked; **al vapor** steamed; **asado** grilled; **frito** fried; **hervido** boiled; **picante** spicy/hot; **salteado** sautéed; **jugoso** rare; **a punto** medium rare; **bien cocido** medium to well done; **muy bien cocido** between well done and shoe leather.

Carne y aves (meat & poultry)

Albóndigas meatballs; **asado** barbecue(d); **asado de tira** or **tira de asado** rack of ribs; **bife de chorizo** rump/sirloin; **bife de costilla** rib; **bife de lomo** tenderloin; **cerdo** pork; **chimi churri** spicy sauce for meat; **chivito** kid; **choripan** spicy sausage sandwich; **chorizo** sausage; **chinchulín** chitterling/intestine; **chuleta** chop; **conejo** rabbit; **cordero** lamb; **entraña** entrail; **hígado** liver; **jamón** ham (**cocido** boiled, **crudo** Parma-style); **lechón** suckling pig; **lengua** tongue; **lomo** tenderloin; **milanesa** breaded cutlet; **mondongo** tripe; **morcilla** blood sausage/black pudding; **molleja** sweetbread; **pancho** hotdog; **parrillada** small table grill; **pato** duck; **pollo** chicken; **riñones** kidneys; **ternera** veal; **vacio** flank.

Pescados & mariscos (fish & seafood)

Anchoa anchovy; **almeja** clam; **atún** tuna; **calamar** squid; **camarón** prawn; **cangrejo** crab; **centolla** king crab; **langosta** lobster; **langostino** king prawn; **lenguado** sole; **mejillón** mussel; **merluza** hake; **ostra** oyster; **pulpo** octopus; **rabas** squid rings; **trucha** trout.

Verduras, arroz y legumbres (vegetables, rice & pulses)

Apio celery; **arroz** rice; **arveja** green pea; **batata** sweet potato; **berenjena** aubergine/ egg plant; **berro** watercress; **calabaza** pumpkin/squash; **cebolla** onion; **chaucha** green beans; **choclo** corn; **espinaca** spinach;

This small French bistro is dedicated to the memory of the owner's grandmother, Maria de las Mercedes Granda. And her spirit lives on in the antique glass cabinets, stained menus and elderly clientele. With age, of course, comes experience, and the food is good and anything but run-of-the-mill. One waiter attends all tables and copes remarkably well.

Nectarine

Vicente López 1661 (4813 6993). Bus 10, 37, 59, 110, 124. **Open** noon-3pm, from 8pm-midnight Mon-Sat. **Main courses** AR$46-$56. **Credit** AmEx, MC, V. **Map** p282 I11 ⓭

Nectarine is a peach of a destination for a special Buenos Aires evening. Hidden up a small pedestrian alley in the centre of the upmarket Recoleta neighbourhood, the small interior is sophisticated without being formal, providing the ideal setting for a romantic tryst. Both the wine list and the menu are rich in options and flavours, and the well-trained staff will help you match the one with the other.

Italian

Sottovoce

Avenida del Libertador 1098 (4807 6691). Bus 61, 93, 130. **Open** noon-3.30pm, 8pm-midnight Sun-Thur; noon-4pm, 8pm-1am Fri, Sat. **Main courses** AR$17-$30. **Credit** AmEx, DC, MC, V. **Map** p282 I12 ⓮

Simple but exquisitely prepared cuisine from the Veneto-Emilia Romagna region means the tables go quickly at Sottovoce. The wild rocket starters are

garbanzo chickpea; **humita** grated, cooked sweetcorn; **lechuga** lettuce; **lenteja** lentil; **palmito** palm heart; **palta** avocado; **papa** potato; **pepino** cucumber; **puerro** leek; **remolacha** beetroot; **repollo** cabbage; **soja** soya; **zanahoria** carrot; **zapallito** courgette/zucchini.

Fruta (fruit)
Ananá pineapple; **cereza** cherry; **ciruela** plum; **durazno** peach; **frambuesa** raspberry; **frutilla** strawberry; **manzana** apple; **naranja** orange; **pera** pear; **pomelo** grapefruit.

Postres (desserts)
Budín de pan bread pudding; **flan** crème caramel; **helado** ice-cream; **miel** honey; **queso** cheese.

Local specialities
Alfajor cornflower biscuits, often coated in chocolate and filled with *dulce de leche*; **carbonada** thick local stew of corn, meat, rice and veg; **dulce de leche** milk jam (tastes like caramel); **locro** stew of pork, beans, spices; **medialunas** croissants (**de manteca** sweet and buttery, **de grasa** saltier, made with oil).

delicious – try the peppery prosciutto with rocket and parmesan – while the home-made pastas, often described in the breathy undertones the name implies, are full of earthy, aromatic flavours. A softly lit, oak wood interior adds a cabin-like warmth.

Pizza

El Cuartito
Talcahuano 937 (4816 1758). Subte D, Tribunales/Bus 152, 111. **Open** from noon daily. **Main courses** ARS$16-$40; portions from AR$2. **No credit cards. Map** p281 H10 🗷
A national institution if the flags in every window are anything to go by, this pizza joint dates from 1934 and is still one of the best in town. The walls

are covered with ancient framed photos of everyone from the ubiquitous Diego Maradona to a host of local boxing greats. Grab a table under Bruno versus Tyson or stand at the pizza bar and sprinkle your slice with the sundry dried toppings to hand. A must for lovers of all things unchanging.

Piola Pizzerie Italiane
Libertad 1078 (4812 0690). Bus 39, 67, 102, 152. **Open** noon-2am Mon-Fri; noon-3am Thur, Sat; 6pm-2am Sun. **Main courses** AR$9-$25. **Credit** AmEx, DC, MC, V. **Map** p281 H11 🗷
This successful, gay-friendly pizzeria is part of a chain started in Treviso, Italy. It's taken up the challenge of rolling the base down to wafer thinness – perhaps to match the waists of the hip Barrio Norte diners who regularly fill it. There are about 50 toppings, as well as a dozen pasta dishes and salads.

Spanish

Oviedo
Beruti 2602 (4822 5415). Subte D, Pueyrredón/ 12, 64, 152 bus. **Open** noon-4pm, 8pm-1am daily. **Main courses** AR$25-$65. **Set menu** AR$59-$75. **Credit** AmEx, DC, MC, V. **Map** p282 J10 🗷
Outstanding *alta cocina* from the motherland, taking the standards of the Iberian kitchen – sole, sea bass, cod – and a netful of freshly caught seafood to forge good-looking, tantalising dishes. Beef, rabbit and lamb appear too, the latter dressed in traditional *setas* (wild mushrooms). The wine list is regarded by connoisseurs as one of the best in the city.

Palermo & Palermo Viejo

Argentinian (Traditional)

La Cabrera
Cabrera 5099 (4831 7002). Bus 39, 55. **Open** 8pm-1am Mon; 12.30-4pm, from 8pm Tue-Sun. **Main courses** AR$22-$28. **Credit** AmEx, DC, MC, V. **Map** p279 M5 🗷
Although located in Palermo Viejo, this modern take on the traditional *parrilla* hasn't completely succumbed to the barrio's Soho-style pretensions. In an attractive corner site which used to be a general store, professional staff serve extra-large portions of expertly prepared beef, grilled with a dash of rosemary or sage. Unconventional but completely natural items like goat's cheese and roasted almonds make great accompaniments. Outside tables are a plus, and a recently opened sister restaurant a block away, La Cabrera Norte, has helped cut wait times.

La Cupertina
Cabrera 5296 (4777 3711). Bus 39, 55. **Open** 8.30pm-2am Mon; 12.30-3.30pm, 7.30pm-midnight Tue-Sun. **Main courses** AR$6-$12. **No credit cards. Map** p279 M5 🗷

Eat, Drink, Shop

When it comes to making empanadas and *locro*, most Argentinians will tell you that grandma is in a class of her own. Battling for second place is Tucumán-born Cecilian Hermann, owner and cook at La Cupertina, a corner restaurant with the look and feel of a snug farmhouse kitchen. The menu is familiar in the truest sense of the word but also includes dishes like *guiso de lentejas con chocolate* (lentil stew with chocolate) and *chivitos*, the Uruguayan take on the transport caff sandwich.

Club Eros

Uriarte 1609 (4832 1313). Bus 39, 55, 111. **Open** from noon daily. **Main courses** AR$6-$10. **No credit cards. Map** p279 M5 ③
Unless you get sexually aroused by laconic waiters in shabby tuxedos serving up fried food in a setting redolent of a 1970s union soup kitchen, Club Eros only half lives up to its name (the dining room is an adjunct to various indoor sports facilities). So why is this *cantina* crammed full of greedy punters at lunch and supper? It's the economy, stupid. For around AR$6 they'll bring you steak, chips and a brimming tumbler (cork fragments and all) of Vasco Viejo, Argentina's most popular plonk.

Don Julio

Gurruchaga 2100 (4831 9564). Bus 35, 55, 93 111, 161. **Open** noon-4pm, from 7.30pm daily. **Main courses** AR$12-$18. **Credit** AmEx, DC, MC, V. **Map** p279 M6 ④
It's very reassuring to know that certain bastions of familiarity remain in this fast-changing barrio; trends come and go, but Don Julio remains standing on the corner of a cobbled street, doing what it's always done and doing it well. The owner, Pablo, is a stickler for good meat and service: the beef is carefully selected and waiters are put through their paces at local wine schools. The menu doesn't veer far from the usual *parrilla* staples, but the quality is a cut above the average. Add to that an exemplary wine list and you understand why regulars swear it's the best value in town.

La Dorita

Humboldt 1911 (4773 0070). Bus 39, 93. **Open** noon-4pm, 8pm-1am daily. **Main courses** AR$12-$24. **No credit cards. Map** p279 N5 ④
'Little Dora' had a growth spurt recently: this crowd-pleasing *parrilla* was expanded to occupy two corners of the intersection. The original, La Dorita, is snug and intimate, while its sister, La Dorita Enfrente, is roomier and less restrained, with junk chandeliers and pop art mixed media setting the mood. In both, families rub elbows with local celebs but the A-list star here is the meat. A *tablas de carnes* (three beef cuts of your choice) arrives sizzling in its own juices. Grilled *provoleta* cheese – crisp on the outside, oozing within – and *papas fritas con cebolla* (fried potatoes with onions) make perfect side dishes. The wine list is short but knowing, with many of the quality mid-range malbecs available in half-litre, penguin-shaped jugs.

Miranda

Costa Rica 5602 (4771 4255). Bus 39, 111. **Open** from 9am daily. **Main courses** AR$12-$20. **Credit** AmEx, MC, V. **Map** p279 N5 ④
One of the few downsides to eating in a traditional BA *parrilla* is that you'll invariably emerge smelling like a coal scuttle – hardly ideal if you're en route to a classy nightspot. Miranda, with its high ceiling and chic-but-functional ventilation ducts, is here to help. The steaks still come fat and smoky, however, and at a very competitive price for the neighbourhood. The set lunch deal is particularly good.

El Preferido de Palermo

Guatemala 4801 (4774 6585). Bus 39, 55, 111. **Open** 8am-11.30pm Mon-Sat. **Main courses** AR$8-$80. **Credit** AmEx, DC, MC, V. **Map** p279 M6 ④
A century-old former *almacén* (general store) that seems straight out of a Borges story occupies the corner of the block where the writer grew up. Family-owned since 1952 and converted into an excellent Spanish restaurant, its dusty bar decorated with regional crests of Spain, El Preferido is one of the last and best of a dying breed. Try traditional Asturian dishes like paella, and on Saturdays a soul-warming *fabada* (stew of black pudding, chorizo, bacon, beans and Parma ham).

El Trapiche

Paraguay 5099 (4772 7343). Subte D, Palermo/ 29, 60, 111, 152 bus. **Open** noon-4pm, 8pm-1.30am daily. **Main courses** AR$7-$20. **Credit** AmEx, DC, MC, V. **Map** p279 N6 ④
Surrounded on all sides by fashionable foreign food haunts, El Trapiche is unstintingly Argentinian and always full. The grilled meat is magnificent, from the fillet steaks to what is probably the best pork flank (*matambrito de cerdo*) in town. Mountainous desserts include the classic Don Pedro (whisky and ice-cream) and hot *sambayón*.

Argentinian (Modern)

Bar 6

Armenia 1676 (4833 6807). Bus 15, 39, 151, 168. **Open** from 8am Mon-Sat. **Main courses** AR$15-$29. **Set menu** (lunch only) AR$18. **Credit** AmEx, MC, V. **Map** p279 M5 ④
A curved Scandinavian ceiling, cement and brick walls, velvet couches and a minuscule patio create a modern coffee house feel for one of Palermo Viejo's best loved hangouts. It's brimming most hours of the day and night, and the menu of vegetable wok dishes, fusion *bifes* and daily chalkboard specials is solid and slightly less expensive than nearby bistros of half the quality or funkiness..

Bar Uriarte

Uriarte 1572 (4834 6004/www.baruriarte.com.ar). Bus 39, 55, 111, 166. **Open** noon-2.30am daily. **Main courses** AR$18-$25. **Set menu** (lunch only) AR$14 Mon-Fri. **Credit** AmEx, DC, MC, V. **Map** p279 M5 ④

Eat, Drink, Shop

From part of the clever team behind Sucre (*see p135*) comes this less pretentious but still visually and gastronomically impacting eaterie. As you walk into the superbly designed interior, by the open kitchen, you'll catch a whiff of the Med-inspired creations. Grab a sofa upfront or a table past the long bar towards the back patio, and start with some stuffed mushrooms or the rocket, tomato and tapenade pizza cooked in an adobe oven. Sophisticated main dishes include delicious home-made pastas.

Casa Cruz

Uriarte 1658 (4833 1112/www.casa-cruz.com). Bus 33, 55, 111. **Open** from 8.30pm Mon-Sat. **Main courses** AR$26-$45. **Credit** AmEx, MC, V. **Map** p279 M5 ❸

Forget Narnia and Turkish delight. For BA's most otherworldly dining experience, pass through a pair of 16-foot brass doors and enter the magical land of Casa Cruz, the most daring and imaginative restaurant venture to hit the city since…well, ever. Loiter by the sleek oval bar in the lobby on the oversized Chesterfield sofa and sip on a sublime Martini. Then glide (no walking – this is a classy joint) through to the spot-lit, redwood-panelled dining area, a large space dominated by a ceiling-high wine rack showcasing most of Argentina's top wineries. Then, with the help of the attentive sommelier and gorgeous staff, get stuck in to what head chef and co-owner Germán Martitegui has dubbed 'modern urban Argentinian' cuisine. For those not hungry, or arriving late, the bar is a lively nexus of local celebs and tourists. **Photo** *p132*.

Central

Costa Rica 5644 (4776 7374). Bus 39, 93, 111. **Open** 12.30pm-2am Mon-Fri; 10.30am-3am Sat, Sun. **Main courses** $18-$23. **Set menu** (lunch only) AR$12-$16 Mon-Fri; AR$25 Sat, Sun. **Credit** AmEx, DC, MC, V. **Map** p279 N5 ❹

Even the bathrooms are slick and sophisticated at Central, a pioneering Palermo lounge/restaurant/ deli. Bustling with beautiful people, this marble and concrete hangar offers superb crossover cuisine. Relax on a low, hide-covered couch and sample head chef Guillermo Teston's supple handling of local ingredients – the raviolis are always good. Then there's the Monday to Friday happy hour, which from 6-8pm includes two-for-one deals on long drinks in dangerously full pint glasses. **Photo** *p112*.

Cluny

El Salvador 4618/22 (4831 7176/www.cluny.com.ar). Bus 15, 39, 55. **Open** 11am-2am Mon-Sat. **Main courses** AR$25-$35. **Credit** AmEx, DC, MC, V. **Map** p279 M5 ❺

With its sofas, long bar and permanently twilit ambience, Cluny is stylish – albeit in a safe way. A strong French influence (think simple aperitifs and complex sauces) means that as well as *lomo* and Patagonian lamb you might also find duck, wild partridge and a frogs' leg starter on the menu. With its extensive wine list, efficient service and tasty

desserts, Cluny keeps its high maintenance regulars happy, achieving a balance of coolness and reliability to which many of its neighbours merely aspire.

Desde el Alma

Honduras 5296 (4831 5812). Bus 39, 111. **Open** 8.30pm-1am Mon-Sat. **Main courses** AR$21-$28. **No credit cards.** **Map** p279 N5 ❺

Amiable owner Alberto Verdi converted his own Palermo Viejo house into Desde el Alma (From the Soul), keeping the intimacy and adding a romantic feel. In the kitchen, head chef Lucio Cantini brings flair and imagination to bear on classic Argentinian ingredients; the slow-braised lamb served in a pepper sauce with potato boulettes and smoked Patagonian girgola mushrooms is outstanding. Desserts such as the chocolate tart with ginger, orange and mascarpone are more sinful than soulful.

Dominga

Honduras 5618 (4771 4443/www.dominga restaurant.com). Bus 39, 93, 111. **Open** 12.30-3.30pm, 8.30pm-1am Mon-Sat. **Main courses** AR$17-$24. **Set menu** AR$15-$17. **Credit** AmEx, MC, V. **Map** p279 N5 ❺

Adorned with the now standard feng shui style of the district, Dominga is also graced with an ivy-clad patio for intimate late evening chitchat. Half the menu consists of expertly rolled sushi, the other a hotchpotch of tasty modern Argentinian cuisine.

Freud y Fahler

Gurruchaga 1750 (4833 2153). Bus 39, 55. **Open** 12.30-3.30pm, 8.30pm-midnight Mon-Thur; 12.30-3.30pm, 8.30pm-1am Fri, Sat. **Main courses** AR$22-$30. **Credit** AmEx, V. **Map** p279 N5 ❺

Portion sizes can be a tad 'nouvelle', and in some dishes originality outstrips execution, but both the traditional fare – fish, chicken, meat, pastas – and the occasional excursions into exotica such as Patagonian pheasant and quail are prepared with care. Mediterranean ideas abound, especially in the soups and pâtés, and there's even a special Japanese oven for smoking shrimps.

Kómodo

República de la India 2899 (4802 8064/www. komodo-restaurant.com). Bus 10, 37, 67. **Open** 8pm-12.30am Mon-Sat. **Main courses** AR$28-$40. **Credit** AmEx, MC, V. **Map** p283 M10 ❺

Clearly pursuing the well-heeled residents of Palermo Chico and the discerning tourist, Kómodo does its best to play the part of a classy local. A huge window dominates the façade, while inside the dark wooden furnishings, soft sofas and delicate illumination create a stylish and sophisticated ambience. The menu is both bold and creative; starters include a miso soup and grilled scallops with black pudding, while among the main courses you'll encounter such rarities (for Buenos Aires at least) as beef tataki salad, slow-braised lamb with mint, and outstanding smoked salmon. Beautiful presentation and a downstairs wine cellar make this slightly off-the-beaten-track location well worth the visit.

Lomo

Costa Rica 4661 (4833 3200/www.lomorestaurant. com.ar). Bus 15, 39, 55. **Open** 12.30-3.30pm Tue-Sun; 8.30pm-12.30am daily. **Main courses** AR$15-$45. **Credit** AmEx, DC, MC, V. **Map** p279 M5 **❺**

Lomo is Argentina's prime cut, but it's also slang to describe a great bod. At this hip *multiespacio*, beauty and *bife* co-exist, with an art gallery and record store tacked on for good measure. The meaty menu goes beyond beef – try the *jabali entre vegetales* (wild boar and glazed vegetables) – and showcases the best regional flavours integrated with finesse. The Zen-like roof terrace is gorgeous for a drink even if you're not staying for dinner.

Olsen

Gorriti 5870 (4776 7677). Bus 39, 93, 111. **Open** noon-1.30am Tue-Sat; from 10am Sun. **Main courses** AR$16-$28. *Sunday brunch* AR$20-$30 **Credit** AmEx, MC, V. **Map** p279 O5 **❺**

Some quandaries are more enjoyable than others. For example, how do you choose between 50 brands of vodka? Tackle this and other conundra at Olsen, German Martigui's hugely popular Scandinavian bar-restaurant where the atmosphere is as chilled as the drinks. It's hard to say which stands out more – the wooden sculptures and verdant garden or the fried oysters and wooden platters of exotic starter combos, which go down great with a sampler of ice cold vodka and aquavit shots. Sunday brunch is the perfect way to wind down from an extended Saturday night.

Social Paraiso

Honduras 5182 (4831 4556). Bus 39, 55. **Open** 12.30-3.30pm, 8.30pm-midnight Tue-Sat; 12.30-4pm Sun. **Main courses** AR$21-$30. **Set menu** (lunch only) AR$14 Mon-Fri; AR$16-$18 Sat, Sun. **Credit** AmEx, V. **Map** p279 N5 **❺**

Youngsters and seniors, new world and old, mix freely in this sober, high-ceilinged bistro that helped to pioneer the Palermo Viejo gourmet explosion. Chef-owner Federico Simoes was raised on Syrian-Lebanese cuisine and his constantly changing menu reflects his polyglot roots. One refreshing item his regular clients won't let him change is the *maracuyá* (passion fruit) mousse and Szechwan pepper ice-cream wedged between caramelised apple slices.

Brazilian

Me Leva Brasil

Costa Rica 4488 (4832 4290/www.melevabrasil. com.ar). Bus 15, 39, 55. **Open** 8am-3am daily. **Main courses** AR$14-$42. **No credit cards**. **Map** p279 L5 **❺**

One for the Caipirinha connoisseur, this laid-back, authentic ode to Brazil is also a great spot for those craving a break from meat mania. You can nibble on delicious *empadinhas* and *risoles* before settling down to a seafood bonanza. If you're lucky, you'll catch one of their legendary samba nights, usually held on Brazilian public holidays.

Eat, Drink, Shop

Even the fence is cool at **Olsen**.

Eastern European

La Casa Polaca

Jorge Luis Borges 2076 (4899 0514). Subte D,
Plaza Italia/15, 39 bus. **Open** 8pm-12.30am
Tue-Sat. **Closed** Jan. **Main courses** AR$12-$21.
Credit AmEx, DC, MC, V. **Map** p279 M6 ⑲
This basement restaurant in the Dom Polski cultural centre for Polish immigrants is poles apart from anything else in Palermo Viejo, but don't let the crusty decor put you off. Ultra-friendly, wildly camp chef Antos Yaskowiak and his trusty staff serve delicious rollmops, stews and goulash, each course punctuated by a sharp vodka and informative chat.

Fish

Coyar de Buitres

Honduras 5702 (4774 5154). Bus 39, 93,
111. **Open** from 6pm Mon-Sat. **Main courses**
AR$21-$26. **Credit** AmEx, MC, V. **Map** p279 N5 ⑳
Succulent oysters are the signature of this young, happening spot, with its small pavement terrace and pub-style wooden tables. There's also tasty clam, mussel, octopus and squid dishes. The menu is divided into main courses and tapas, so you can drop in for a bite, or make a night of it.

French

Christophe

Fitz Roy 1994 (4771 1155). Bus 93, 111.
Open 12.30-3.30pm, 8.30pm-midnight Mon-Thur,
Sun; 12.30-4pm, 8.30pm-1am Fri, Sat. **Main courses**
AR$15-$30. **Credit** AmEx, V. **Map** p279 N5 ㉑

Proprietor and chef Christophe Krywonis serves up creative French-based cuisine in this charming chalkboard bistro. Starters are numerous, including an array of salads that steer away from France all the way to Thailand, an outstanding beet gazpacho, and the house-speciality camembert. Main courses run the gamut from flavourful French renditions of typical Argentinian meat dishes to daily vegetarian specials cooked up with seasonal vegetables. The lunch menu – a starter, main course, dessert and beverage for AR$18 – is a steal, and the wine list is vast. The interior design leaves a little to be desired, but a lively kitchen within view of the small dining room combines with quick, friendly service to create a warm, typically Gallic atmosphere.

French Creole

Azema Exotic Bistró

Angel Carranza 1875 (4774 4191). Bus 39,
93, 111, 161. **Open** from 8pm Mon-Sat. **Main**
courses AR$18-$30. **Credit** AmEx, DC, MC, V.
Map p279 O5 ㉒
Paul Jean Azema spent 15 years wandering around the far east, and another ten saving up the cash, but once he opened his own restaurant it was an overnight success. His presence stretches from the name all the way back to the men's toilet where his picture hangs, but it's in the kitchen where he is most appreciated, dressing up and dishing out delicious Thai platters, pastas and an outstanding fish curry. The wines have been thoughtfully picked with plenty of good whites to complement the spices. Sophisticated and colorfully decorated, Azema is effortlessly fashionable and highly recommendable.

Azema Exotic Bistró.

IT USUALLY TAKES TEMPTATION ABOUT SEVEN OR EIGHT SECONDS
TO ACCOMPLISH ITS GOAL.

WELL, SOMETIMES EVEN LESS.

piedrasfischer

Italian

Guido's Bar

República de la India 2843 (4802 2391). Subte D, Plaza Italia/29, 39, 152 bus. **Open** noon-4pm Mon-Sat; from 8pm Mon-Fri. **Main courses** AR$15-$25. **No credit cards. Map** p283 M10 ❸

This pea-sized trattoria is the kind of place one always looks for but rarely finds in Italy. With every inch of the letterbox-red walls plastered in movie poster kitsch, featuring real Italians (Mastroanni and Caruso) alongside honorary ones (John Lennon and Sammy Davis Jr), Guido's is as much an evocation of an era as it is a culture. But there's nothing tongue-in-cheek about owner Carlos's passion for Italian food. For around AR$30, smirking waiters will forcefeed you a parade of colourful appetisers followed by home-made pasta and dessert. A kitchen radio turned deliberately too loud is the epitome of the Italian nonchalance this neighbourhood landmark is after.

Lucky Luciano

Cerviño 3943 (4802 1262). Subte D, Plaza Italia/29, 39, 152, 188 bus. **Open** from 8pm Mon-Sat. **Main courses** AR$18-$35. **Credit** AmEx, MC, V. **Map** p283 M10 ❹

One of the reasons the Sosto brothers originally opened Lucky Luciano was to pick up the overflow from dad Carlos's place (Guido's; *see above*) around the corner, but they have since managed to stamp this colourful, busily decorated place with its own distinctive identity. Apart from an abundance of starters and plenty of richly sauced and perfectly cooked pasta dishes, there's never a dull moment for meat eaters with lamb, pork and even buffalo on the menu. Linger over the *lingote de chocolate hesperidina* (laced with a liqueur made from bitter orange skins) and, with the help of a bottle from the excellent wine list, you should find yourself lying horizontal by coffee time.

Japanese

Dashi

Fitz Roy 1613 (4776 3500/www.dashi.com.ar). Bus 93, 111. **Open** 12.30-3pm, 8pm-12.30am Mon-Fri; 8pm-1am Sat. **Main courses** AR$16-$44. **Set menu** (lunch only) AR$20. **Credit** AmEx, DC, MC, V. **Map** p279 N5 ❺

Vast windows on a prime corner site reveal the elegant nature of Buenos Aires' classiest sushi restaurant, artfully designed by Jorge, its gregarious, globetrotting gourmet owner. The chic, dusky rose and grey interior and zero-calorie salad court the Palermo crowd, but sushi man Gabriel Takakura's creative rolls and superb sashimi slivers are second to none. Those who prefer the cooked to the raw should try the hot seafood platter or a stir-fry of langoustines, squid and shiitake mushrooms. **Other locations:** Salguero 2643, Palermo (4805 5575); Aguilar 2395, Palermo (4782 2666/3666); Arribeños 2308, Belgrano (4783 1070).

Middle Eastern

El Manto

Costa Rica 5801 (4774 2409). Bus 34, 55, 93, 111. **Open** noon-3.30pm, 8.30pm-1am Mon-Sat. **Main courses** AR$15-$26. **Credit** AmEx, DC, MC, V. **Map** p279 O5 ❻

Putting the chic into sheek kebabs, El Manto is easily the smartest and arguably the best Armenian restaurant in Buenos Aires. The interior is modelled on a typical Armenian convent from the year AD 301, which apparently means candles throwing shadows on terracotta walls and mock-Byzantine arches – all very Umberto Eco. For all that, the best place to take your mezze and *kebab de cordero* (lamb) is without doubt the terrace.

Bereber

Armenia 1880 (4833 5662). Bus 39, 55. **Open** 8.30pm-1am daily. **Main courses** AR$21-$26. **Credit** AmEx, MC, V. **Map** p279 M6 ❼

The restaurant's location bang on Plaza Palermo Viejo and its modern North African cuisine make Bereber an ideal spot to line your stomach before hitting the bars. Besides a full range of fluffy couscous options and rich tagines, Bereber douses Argentina's tender meats in a slew of marinades to make exquisite, delicious dishes. Even vegetarians have something to tickle their taste buds here, and the cocktails are heavenly. Staff are charming and there's an attractive rooftop terrace above.

Mexican

Cielito Lindo

El Salvador 4999 (4832 8054). Bus 39, 55. **Open** 8pm-midnight Mon-Thur, Sun; 8pm-1am Fri, Sat. **Main courses** AR$6-$16. **No credit cards.** **Map** p279 M5 ❽

Rightly priced and colourfully decorated with Mayan textiles, sombreros and Day-of-the-Dead skeletons, this cheerful little box of a Mexican restaurant is so popular on weekends that lengthy queues snake around the outdoor tables.

Peruvian-Japanese

Osaka

Soler 5608, Palermo Viejo (4775 6964/www.osaka fusion.com). Bus 21, 111, 161. **Open** noon-4pm, 7.30pm-1am Mon-Sat. **Main courses** AR$25-$40. **No credit cards. Map** p279 N5 ❾

Long on fresh flavours and inventiveness, short on gimmickry and experiment for experiment's sake, Osaka is what every fusion restaurant should be but rarely is. A hit in its hometown of Lima, Peru, the chain's adroit synthesis of Peruvian and Japanese cuisine has been wowing *porteños* since it opened in 2005. They're coming for the shellfish tapas (the crunchy Scallop Philly is as addictive as a legal substance can be), *ceviche*-sashimi crossover dishes, and genre-defying instant classics like the unctuous

Eat, Drink, Shop

Caramel Lamb. The design scheme is as tastefully eclectic as the cuisine, with Peruvian rain sticks sharing wall space with Japanese wood block art. If you don't want a full meal, nibble at the bar over a peerless Pisco Sour, or go *mano a mano* with the sushiman (who, it almost goes without saying, is Dutch) next to the open kitchen. The wine list includes some great mid-range whites from Bodegas Terrazas and Catena Zapata.

North American

Kansas

Avenida del Libertador 4625 (4776 4100).
Bus 64. **Open** 11am-2am daily. **Main courses** AR$14-$22. **Credit** AmEx, MC, V. **Map** p283 P9 **70**
With its neon lighting, numerous gas torches and commercial architecture, Kansas feels like it could be in a wealthy suburb of, you guessed it, Kansas. Big, but consistently busy, there are no reservations, so if you don't feel like waiting, get there before 9pm. The menu is varied but the speciality is American-style barbecue, the huge kitchen cranking out large portions of beef and pork ribs and nearly every kind of steak imaginable. Although at times it feels like a strange machine, the barbecue sauce alone will make you want to click your heels three times.

Pizza

Angelín

Avenida Córdoba 5270 (4774 3836). Bus 34, 55, 140, 142, 151, 188. **Open** 8pm-midnight daily. **Main courses** AR$9-$30. **No credit cards.** **Map** p279 M4 **71**
A tiny pizza joint with a big reputation, in part thanks to the endorsement of actor and occasional BA resident Robert Duvall. Hollywood connections aside, this has been a barrio favourite since 1938, and the locals propping up the L-shaped counter look like they wouldn't bat an eyelid if Elvis dropped in. For the true pizza *al paso* (pizza on the go) experience, order a slice of *fugazzeta con queso* (cheese and onion stuffed crust pizza) with a shot of *cidra* (cider) and slouch around the front parlour, getting in the way as much as possible.

South-east Asian

Green Bamboo

Costa Rica 5802 (4775 7050). Bus 93, 111. **Open** 8.30pm-2.30am daily. **Main courses** AR$17-$25. **Credit** AmEx, DC, MC, V. **Map** p279 O5 **72**
Busily but charmingly decked out to convincing oriental effect, Green Bamboo is a touch of class on a picturesque Palermo street corner. The look is elegant, green and moody, with candlelit floor-level or regular tables, a long L-shaped bar and a red, Warhol-esque Ho Chi Minh peering down sternly from above. The menu, too, is spot on: try their pork in minty sauce, perfectly complemented by a

refreshing fruit gazpacho. The lengthy cocktail list isn't just for show – they shake and stir some of the best drinks in Palermo here. **Photo** *p111.*

Sudestada

Guatemala 5602 (4776 3777). Bus 15, 55, 111. **Open** noon-3.30pm, 8pm-midnight Mon-Sat. **Main courses** AR$8-$20. **Set menu** (lunch only) AR$12. **Credit** AmEx, V. **Map** p279 N6 **73**
Don't be fooled by the cool and minimalist decor – Sudestada's dishes are hot enough to set your palate dancing. The food is packed with ingredients and flavours Vietnamese chef Tien Duic has drawn from Laos, Thailand, Burma and his homeland, like the unmissable Nem Cua (spicy minced crab and pork wrapped in lettuce) and the yellow curry of fish and mussels. The uninitiated can douse the exquisite taste sensations with a glass of freshly squeezed lemonade, while spicephobes can choose from some of the milder menu options. For afters, fruit crumble and coconut ice-cream are excellent complements to a classic Vietnamese coffee.

Spanish

Al Andaluz

Godoy Cruz 1823 (4832 9286). Bus 39, 55, 111. **Open** 8.30pm-midnight Tue-Sat. **Main courses** AR$14-$20. **Set menu** AR$15. **Credit** AmEx, DC, MC, V. **Map** p279 N5 **74**
Dizzying tapestries and Muslim spice scales are just some of the exotic delights decorating Al Andaluz's *Arabian Nights*-style dining room. Just as intriguing are the medieval recipes personable chef-owner Ricardo Araujo has culled from his frequent gastronomic pilgrimages to southern Spain. Don't miss the decadent *cordero de konga*, a lamb meatball cooked for seven hours and served with spicy yoghurt and pilaf, and start with salmon marinated in Jerez vinegar, honey and herbs. One of a kind.

Sinclair

Sinclair 3096 (4899 0283). Bus 12, 37, 152. **Open** noon-4pm Mon-Fri; 8pm-1am Mon-Sat. **Closed** Sun **Main courses** AR$18-$72. **Credit** AmEX, MC, V. **Map** p283 N9 **75**
A celebrity chef, a chic locale, muted tones and fresh ingredients – what more can a restaurant require except perhaps mirrors on the ceilings? Oh, wait, Sinclair has got that covered too. Ramiro Rodriguez Pardo's newest venture specialises in lovingly prepared and impeccably presented modern Spanish cuisine, with the country's traditional fish and seafood options dominating. One of the few eateries in BA where the paella lives up to expectations.

Vegetarian

Artemisia

Cabrera 3877 (4863 4242). Bus 36, 92, 106. **Open** from 8.30pm Tue-Sat. **Main courses** AR$10-$20. **Credit** AmEx, MC, V. **Map** p282 K7 **76**

Treat all your senses to a great night out at **Gran Bar Danzón**. *See p119*.

Artemisia is the kind of restaurant that restores one's faith in healthy eating. Its thoughtfully constructed dishes, which include home-made pastas, polenta and grilled salmon, are a far cry from the usual lentils-laden wholefood fare. The wine list will disappoint those who like to temper the salutary effects of too much clean living.

Bio
Humboldt 2199 (4774 3880). Train or Subte D to Palermo/93, 111 bus. **Open** 10am-3pm Mon; 10am-1am Tue-Sun. **Main courses** AR$13-$16. **Set menu** (lunch only) AR$12-$15. **Credit** AmEx, MC, V. **Map** p279 N6 ⑦
Even hardened carnivores will consider going green after vegging out at this utterly organic gourmet corner bistro. The fish- and meat-free menu reflects what is seasonally available – in summer there's gazpacho, or aubergine *milanesa*, while in winter pumpkins are carved open and filled with sweetcorn stew. Veg juices and refreshing ginger lemonade are available throughout the year. Great salads too.

Krishna
Malabia 1833 (4833 4618). Bus 39, 55. **Open** noon-5pm Tue; noon-midnight Wed Sun. **Main courses** AR$10-$14. **No credit cards. Map** p279 M5 ⑦
In an ideal Palermo Viejo location, in a purplish haze of esoteric Gaias, Vishnus and an out-of-place Jimi Hendrix, an all-Krishna kitchen staff says a mantra before offering its protector – and New Age hippie guests – Indian delights like kofta dumplings and a

thali platter with pakoras, raita, and other spicy vegetarian meals. Ideal for a quick, cheap and divinely nutritious lunch.

Las Cañitas

Argentinian (Traditional)

El Portugués
Báez 499 (4771 8699). Bus 15, 29, 60, 64. **Open** 11am-4pm, from 7.30pm daily. **Main courses** AR$8-$18. **No credit cards. Map** p283 O9 ⑦
Before the new cuisines hit Las Cañitas, Señor Merinho and family were well established as hosts of the barrio beefery. It might seem a bit rich that the Portuguese should take on Argentina in the steak stakes, but this is a very popular *parrilla*, with two floors jammed with a noisy mix of local families, television divas and the just plain hungry. Whoever's in charge of portion control is clearly incompetent, so prepare to share. Perfect for groups.

Argentinian (Modern)

Novecento
Báez 199 (4778 1900). Bus 5, 29, 59, 60, 64. **Open** 10am-12.30am Mon-Fri; 12.30-4pm, 8pm-1.30am Sat, Sun. **Main courses** AR$16-$28 lunch. **Set menu** (lunch only) AR$13-$20 Mon-Fri. **Credit** AmEx, DC, MC, V. **Map** p283 O9 ⑧

Eat, Drink, Shop

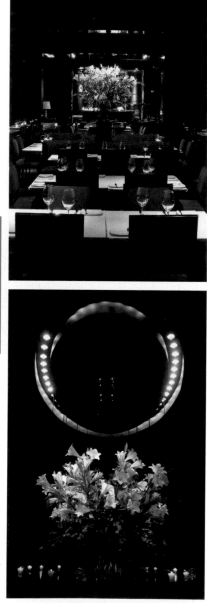

Casa Cruz: the place to be seen. *See p124.*

A thriving, self-styled North American bistro which manages to be bustling and intimate at the same time. The outdoor tables are often full too. It has branches in Manhattan, Miami and Punta del Este, but here at the flagship, the menu is classic mod Argentinian, with great meat dishes like the pepper steak or booze-soaked sweetbreads. Its strength is in the simplicity of its menu, which transcends typical *parrilla* fare without being too exotic.

Japanese

Bokoto
Huergo 261 (4776 6505). Bus 41, 60, 92, 118. **Open** noon-3pm Mon-Sat; 8.30pm-1am daily. **Main courses** AR$15-$22. **Set menu** (unlimited sushi) AR$44. **Credit** AmEx, MC, V. **Map** p283 O9 ⑤
Located in a long, narrow house, with a red-and-black colour scheme that extends from the tableware to the uniforms, Bokoto has over five years in the business and is a safe bet to outlast further pruning of the area's many sushi options. A lengthy menu includes everything you'd expect, raw and cooked, as well as special items such as the Crazy Roll with shrimp, avocado, cream cheese and salmon. Cooked options include the Yaki Guy – a speared *lomo* kebab with white rice and teriyaki sauce.

Moshi Moshi
Ortega y Gasset 1707 (4772 2005). Bus 29, 60, 64. **Open** from 8pm Tue-Sun. **Main courses** AR$11-$24. **Credit** AmEx, MC, V. **Map** p283 O9 ⑥
Buenos Aires sushi queen Suzana Morizohno's latest culinary adventure is on a picturesque street corner. Stylish presentation is the hallmark of Morizohno restaurants and Moshi Moshi is no exception: the black uniformed staff look just as good as the sushi platters. While the nigiris and makis are decent rather than outstanding, steaming Asian dishes like the tepanyaki ooze Asian expertise (a Ruca Mayer Chardonnay complements it perfectly). Flashes from the open kitchen complement the moody decor and for summer evenings there's a large roof terrace.

Abasto & Caballito

Argentinian (Modern)

Tipo Casa
Bulnes 843, Abasto (4866-2854). Subte B, Medrano/ 26, 92, 128, 151 bus. **Open** 9pm-1am Tue-Sat. **Main courses** AR$14-$18. **No credit cards**. **Map** p282 J7 ⑥
Small, friendly and intimate, Abasto's Tipo Casa is an underground delight. Ring the bell to be ushered down a long hallway to two vibrantly painted rooms. Shy chef Marcelo Licari goes table to table explaining the evening's four or five specials, which usually include *lomo* in various tasty incarnations and a number of home-made pasta dishes. Make reservations as space is limited.

Indian

La Reina Kunti

*Humahuaca 3461, Abasto (4863 3071). Subte B,
Carlos Gardel/26, 124, 146 bus.* **Open** 5pm-midnight
Mon; 10am-midnight Tue-Sat. **Main courses** AR$6-
$12. **No credit cards**. Map p282 J7 ❽

How you feel about Reina Kunti will depend in part
on how you feel about cats roaming freely in
restaurants. If you don't mind the moggies, you'll
love this cult Indian veggie restaurant which does a
pretty authentic – for Buenos Aires – rendition of
sub-continental street food: kachoris, pakoras, kof-
tas, and so on. The design aesthetic is beach-after-
a-shipwreck, with pirate chests, wine barrels and
antique sewing machines doubling as tables.
Puddings are more old deli than New Delhi; round
off your feast with a Simply Marvellous truffle and
a sharp, strong coffee.

Italian

Cantina Pierino

*Lavalle 3499, Abasto (4864 5715). Subte B,
Carlos Gardel/24, 26, 168 bus.* **Open** 8pm-2am
daily. **Main courses** AR$8-$16. **Credit** AmEx, V.
Map p282 J8 ❽

Way off the tourist track, Pierino has been
serving authentic Italian food since 1907. Tango legends Astor Piazzolla and Anibal Troilo were regulars in the 1960s. Pedro, grandson of the original
owners, is liable to suggest what he regards as best
for you, but the tasty starters – *fritata* (mozzarella
tortillas) and *chiambotta* (baked aubergine with
onion, courgettes and mushrooms) – and home-made
pasta dishes lend credence to his telepathic skills
and it's all excellent value for money.

Almagro, Once & Villa Crespo

Argentinian (Traditional)

Cantina los Amigos

*Loyola 701, Villa Crespo (4777 0422). Bus 55,
106, 109.* **Open** from 7.30pm Mon; 12.30-3.30pm,
from 7.30pm Tue-Sat; 12.30pm-4pm Sun. **Main
courses** AR$10-$22. **Credit** V. Map p279 M4 ❽

Thrumming with that late-night good-time vibe for
which Buenos Aires is famed, Cantina los Amigos
is a crackerjack of a traditional *porteño* eaterie.
Packed every night with local families, TV stars,
footballers and indeed anyone on the run from the
healthy-eating gestapo, the dining area is decked out
with football posters, tango bits and bobs and the
occasional impact stain from a stray meatball. Let
the cocky waiters bring you a selection of starters
and then loosen your belt for an assault on one of
the pasta specials or whatever's sizzling most tempt-
ingly on the grill. Everything's fresh, homemade and

served in asteroid-sized portions. Smile sweetly
enough at the owner, Hugo, and he may bring you
some complimentary champagne. If ever a restaurant could kick out the blues, it's this one.

Argentinian (Modern)

Thymus

*Lerma 525, Villa Crespo (4772 1936). Bus 55,
106, 110.* **Open** 8.30pm-12.30am Mon-Fri; noon-
3pm, from 8.30pm Sat, Sun. **Main courses** AR$22-
$38. **Credit** AmEx, MC, V. Map p279 M4 ❼

As romantic as it is aromatic, Thymus deserves all
the rave reviews it gets from discriminating local
gourmets. Sculptor Martin Vegara's skilful copies of
classical antiquities decorate his former house and
studio, converted into a restaurant made for all five
senses. Chef Fernando Mayoral, who trained with
Michel Bras, uses fresh garnishes of rosemary,
thyme and pineapple mint from a rooftop garden to
flavour fusion dishes like grilled loin of pork in
an orange mustard glaze served with spicy pan-
cakes and pakchoi. The discerning hangover victim
should note that the weekend brunch (served from
noon) is one of the best in the city.

Middle Eastern

Sarkis

*Thames 1101, Villa Crespo (4772 4911). Bus 34,
55, 106, 109, 168.* **Open** noon-3pm, from 8pm daily.
Main courses AR$10-$20. **No credit cards**.
Map p279 M4 ❽

The fluorescent-lit atmosphere is wanting and the
Monday night belly rippler could be your grandma,
but Sarkis's authentic Levantine cuisine means it's
packed at weekends (be prepared to wait unless you
turn up early). Choose tasty dips, snacks, soufflés,
raw mince and kebabs, or ask for a miscellany of
biggish starters, which will have you jumping
straight to dessert. You can then have your coffee
grains read by a local fortune teller.
Other locations: 9 de Julio 1465, Recoleta
(4394 4888).

South-east Asian

Bi Won

*Junin 548, Once (4372 1146). Subte B, Pasteur or D,
Facultad de Medicina/24, 26, 60, 124 bus.* **Open**
noon-3pm, 7pm-midnight Mon-Sat. **Main courses**
AR$17-$25. **No credit cards**. Map p281 H9 ❽

Ignore the Korean tourist board posters and hammy
backing track at this authentic community res-tau-
rant down a dark Once street, because the food is
delightful and inexpensive. Two should share, since
meals come with eight tasty side dishes including
turnip, anchovies, corn, seaweed, spinach, kimchi
(the Korean national dish of marinaded, slightly fer-
mented vegetables), cucumber and beans, most of
them doused in chilli and garlic.

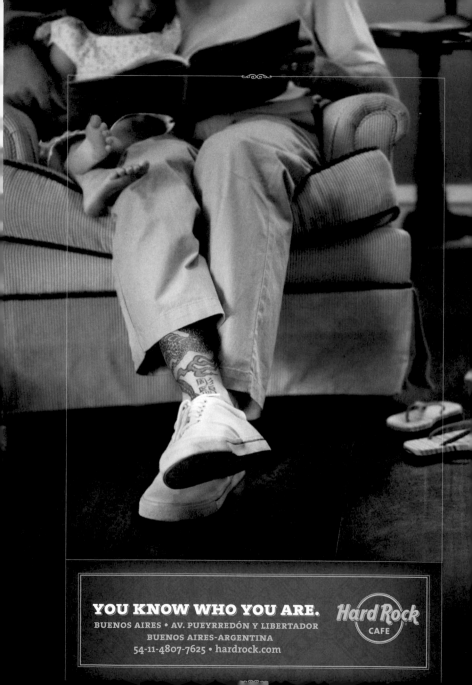

Belgrano & Colegiales

Argentinian (Traditional)

El Pobre Luis
*Arribeños 2393, Belgrano (4780 5847). Bus
29, 60, 64, 113, 130.* **Open** from 8pm Mon-Sat.
Main courses AR$16-$24. **Credit** AmEx, MC, V.
Map p285 S9
Football and dining legend Diego Maradona cites this
as one of his favourite BA restaurants; the shirt of 'El
Diez' hangs on one of the walls. But its meat, not memorabilia, that maketh the *parrilla* and the steaks here
are in the premier league. Charismatic, ever-present
owner Luis Acuña is Uruguayan, so you'll find nov-
elties from over the River Plate like *pamplona de cerdo*
(pork flank stuffed with cheese and peppers) on the
menu. Offal lovers will rhapsodise over the *mollejas*
(sweetbreads), charred on the outside, meltingly tender within. No reservations taken, so get there early
or be prepared to queue.

Argentinian (Modern)

Sifones y Dragones
*Ciudad de la Paz 174, Belgrano (15 4413 9871/
www.sifonesydragones.com.ar). Bus 68, 152.*
Open 9pm-2am Tue-Sat. **Main courses**
AR$18-$26. **No credit cards. Map** p283 O8

Argentinian couple Mariana and Favio are quick to
point out that 'this is not a restaurant, but a kitchen
with tables.' And so it is; just 16 covers, dotted
around a flame-throwing hob, where the pair drum
up made-on-the-spot wonders like *lomo* in a Syrah
reduction and potato gnocchis with shellfish. French
designer Philippe Starck named this as his favourite
restaurant in Buenos Aires – quite an endorsement.
Reservations are a must.

Sucre
*Sucre 676, Belgrano (4782 9082). Train to Scalabrini
Ortiz/37, 130 bus.* **Open** noon-4pm, 8pm-2am daily.
Main courses AR$18-$25. **Credit** AmEx, DC, MC,
V. **Map** p285 R10
The stunning interior of Sucre is the last word in
neo-industrial design, its centrepiece a bunker wine
cellar and kaleidoscopically coloured ceiling-high
bar. Celebrity chef Fernando Trocca jazzes up local
classics with pan-Latin flavours like diced mango,
papaya dressings and jalapeños. The 18-page wine
list has few rivals in the city.

Chinese

Palitos
*Arribeños 2243, Belgrano (4786 8566). Bus 60,
130.* **Open** noon-4pm, 8pm-2am Tue-Sun. **Main
courses** AR$8-$25 *Set lunch* AR$10. **No credit
cards. Map** p285 S9

Eat, Drink, Shop

Have a taste of what the season brings at **Café San Juan**. *See p117.*

Muted red paper lanterns mean that everything is rosy in this stand-out Taiwanese restaurant in BA's Liliputian Barrio Chino. Eager punters are prepared to queue for the sizzling *langostinos enteros fritos* (fried whole shrimps) and the sticky, more-ish *pollo agridulce* (sweet and sour chicken). And so long as you can wrench your mind away from a flash-fried Bambi, you'll find house speciality *ciervo salteado con verdeo* (sautéed venison with spring onions and ginger) a surprisingly successful fusion dish.

Japanese

Maiko Sushi & Wok

Maure 1643, Belgrano (4777 6816). Bus 29, 55, 60, 64, 118. **Open** 8pm-midnight Thur-Sat. **Main courses** AR$18-$25. **Credit** AmEx, DC, MC, V. **Map** p283 P9 **94**

This smart Belgrano newcomer has ditched sushi's reputation for cold modernism in favour of a warm, sophisticated vibe. The salmon is the best southern Chile has to offer, and there are enough quality nigiris, makis and sashimi to keep serious sushi aficionados content. There's also a generous hot menu for those not into eating in the raw and a secluded garden that's almost as pretty as the food. Wash your meal down with a glass of sweet plum 'Hoya' wine, an authentic taste of Japan.

Latin American

Contigo Perú

Echeverría 1627, y Montañeses, Belgrano (4780 3960). Bus 64, 118. **Open** 11am-midnight Tue-Sun. **Main courses** AR$5-$15. **No credit cards. Map** p285 R9 **95**

Enough steak already? Then let the technicolour-waistcoated waiters at this cool *cantina* bring you a short, sharp, citric shock in the shape of a plate of *ceviche* and a brace of Pisco Sours. Crowded with backpackers looking to relive Cuzco nights and Peruvian expats more interested in the taped soap operas on the telly than in actually ordering anything, Contigo Perú represents global cuisine at its most splendidly parochial. Great fun – and cheap.

Puerto Madero

Argentinian (Traditional)

Cabaña las Lilas

Alicia Moreau de Justo 516, Dique 4 (4313 1336/ www.laslilas.com.ar). Subte B, LN Alem/62, 93, 130, 152 bus. **Open** noon-3.30pm, 7.30pm-midnight daily. **Main courses** AR$35-$55. **Credit** AmEx, V. **Map** p281 E11 **96**

Eating steak at Cabaña las Lilas is a little like taking tea at the Ritz. You know it's a tourist trap, you know you're being overcharged, but somehow you're still glad you came. The atmospheric dockside location helps, as do the exemplary service and jumbo wine

list. But what really matters is the meat. Every chop, chump and *chorizo* is sourced from the company's own *estancias* and the award-winning thoroughbred cattle that graze there. And whatever ends up on the plate, from whatever part of the cow, will be cooked as requested and unforgettably tender. The bill is memorable too, reflecting the restaurant's status as a haven for tourists and executives. Fifty pesos for a *bife de chorizo*, while extortionate by local standards, is small change on an expense account or foreign credit card statement.

Argentinian (Modern)

El Bistro

Faena Hotel + Universe, Martha Salotti 445, Dique 2 (4010 9200/www.faenahotelanduniverse.com). Subte B, LN Alem/2, 130, 152 bus. **Open** noon-3.30pm, 8.30pm Mon-Sat. **Main courses** AR$35-$50. **Credit** AmEx, DC, MC, V. **Map** p280 D11 **Ú**

From chandeliers and showgirls to unicorns and universal excess, the Bistro at the Faena Hotel + Universe promises an evening far removed from the usual BA dining experience. Step down from the regally inspired rouge vestibule into the whiter-than-white dining room and be instantly transported to an *Alice in Wonderland*-esque world. The menu is more colourful than the decor, featuring goodies like grilled octopus in a vanilla vinaigrette, and venison carpaccio. If this sounds too rich, try the hotel's El Mercado brasserie which serves simpler fare.

Hondo

Olga Cossettini 230, Dique 4 (4312 7762). Subte B, LN Alem/2, 130, 152 bus. **Open** noon-1am daily. **Main courses** AR$30-$40. **Credit** AmEx, DC, MC, V. **Map** p281 F12 **98**

With views of the striking Telecóm and Microsoft buildings and a menu specializing in cheese and meat platters and fish dishes, Hondo is perfect for a sunset-watching romantic tryst. The walls made of Mendozan volcanic pumice stone, rustic country house tables and black and brown decor scheme make it easy to see why this *vinoteca* has featured in numerous glossy magazines since it opened in 2003. For those who enjoy a wine-cigar combo the top Cuban brands are on sale.

Italian

Bice

Alicia Moreau de Justo 192, Dique 4 (4315 6216). Subte B, LN Alem/ 20, 26, 99, 109, 126, 140 bus. **Open** noon-4pm, from 7.30pm daily. **Main courses** AR$20-$35. **Credit** AmEX, DC, MC, V. **Map** p281 F12 **99**

For upscale Italian with a waterside view, Bice, part of the Italian restaurant chain of the same name, offers the standard Mediterranean pasta and fish dishes while incorporating into the extensive menu a few local ingredients like Patagonian lamb. It's decent European fare, at European prices.

Cafés, Bars & Pubs

Drink and be merry. (You can worry about eating later.)

If your idea of a good night out is eight pints by midnight rounded off with a prawn vindaloo, you might find boozing in BA a bit of a let-down. For everyone else the *porteño* drinking scene is spot on. It's cheap, it's fun and it boasts the world's most licentious licensing laws – that is to say, none.

Argentinians aren't born inebriates, but this doesn't stop them propping up the bar until past dawn. Non-drinkers can choose from soft drinks, fruit smoothies (*licuados*) and juices – and you won't get called a sissy. Or you may just fancy a cold *cerveza* (beer). Quilmes – decorated in the national colours – is the most ubiquitous, but the slightly pricier Isenbeck is tastier and less chemical. Beer is generally consumed in a small bottle, called a *porrón*; for draught, ask for a *chopp*.

Some of the best bars are concealed within the city's hotels. Try the bar and garden at **Home Hotel** (Bono and the boys spent a few happy hours here during U2's 2006 visit; *see p55*), the ultra-stylish pool bar at the **Faena Hotel + Universe** (*see p57*) and the minimalist **White Bar** at the Hotel Madero (*see p57*). Many restaurants also make fine spots for a drink, especially early evening or after the main dinner rush. For a cocktail, stop by Italian eaterie **Filo** (*see p111*); for the best choice of wines by the glass, try **Gran Bar Danzón** (*see p119*); and for a peerless late-night Martini, go slump on the designer Chesterfield at **Casa Cruz** (*see p124*).

CAFE CULTURE

Buenos Aires runs on caffeine. Very little gets accomplished in advance of the morning's first *cortado*. Every block has a café and most cafés have a standard menu, a bleary-eyed waiter in a dicky bow and a selection of daily papers and weekly mags strewn on the tables. But don't be fooled by this apparent uniformity; whether it's down to history, atmosphere or just damn fine coffee, many of the city's cafés are true classics, integral to the capital's cultural and social life.

Little wonder, given BA's strong Italian heritage, that coffee is so popular here. And even if it sometimes fails to meet Italian flavour standards, there are plenty of ways to drink it. The most common caffeine kicks are a *café* (a single espresso) and a *cortado* (a single espresso with a 'cut' of hot milk). Other options include café con leche, cappuccino and the *lágrima* (warm milk with a 'teardrop' of coffee). A sweet speciality for winter is a *submarino*, a frothy glass of hot milk with a bar of chocolate submerged in it. For an early morning sugar rush, try one accompanied with *churros* (sticky, cucumber-shaped doughnuts).

The best **Drinking holes**

For a classy cocktail
Home Hotel (*see p55*); Casa Cruz (*see p124*); Faena Hotel + Universe Bar (*see p57*).

For a happy hour (or four)
Shamrock (*see p145*); Gran Bar Danzón (*see p119*).

For a cultured cup of coffee
Café Tortoni (*see p139*); La Biela (*see p143*); Clásica y Moderna (*see p139*).

For a superior snack
Mark's Deli (*see p147*); Bangalore Pub & Curry House (*see p145*).

For a downtown drink
Dadá (*see p139*); La Cigale (*see p139*).

For a hot date
Milión (*see p145*); Lelé de Troya (*see p147*); Olsen (*see p125*).

For a skinful of real ale
Gibraltar (*see p143*); Rubia y Negra (*see p145*).

For a fashionable fiesta
Unico Bar Bistro (*see p147*); Supersoul (*see p147*).

For a breath of fresh air
Congo (*see p146*); Omm (*see p147*).

For a late, late night
878 (*see p147*); Kim y Novak (*see p146*); Mundo Bizarro (*see p147*).

The Centre

Café Tortoni

*Avenida de Mayo 829 (4342 4328). Subte A, Piedras/
17, 64, 86 bus.* **Open** 8am-3am Mon-Sat; 9am-1am
Sun. **Credit** AmEx, MC, V. **Map** p281 F10 ❶
Since it opened in 1858, the splendid Tortoni –
Argentina's oldest and most venerated traditional
café – has played host to a stellar cast, from the
depths of bohemia to the heights of the literati and
across the political spectrum. Today its reputation
attracts bus loads of camera-swinging tourists, but
don't be put off – the Tortoni is one of a kind.

La Cigale

*25 de Mayo 722 (4312 8275). Subte B, LN Alem/
93, 130, 152 bus.* **Open** from 6pm Mon-Fri; from
8pm Sat. **Credit** AmEx, MC, V. **Map** p281 F11 ❷
A huge bar counter, booth seating, fairy lights and
big moon lamps – this is not your classic French café.
Nevertheless, La Cigale, a forerunner among late-
night drinking dens, does very well, with a crowd that
leans towards music mag readers and French expats.
Big nights include Tuesday's Soirée Française, when
Cardinal and Pastis drop to three pesos and DJs spin
electronica, while in the wee small hours of the weekend a party atmosphere prevails.

Clásica y Moderna

*Avenida Callao 892 (4812 8707). Subte D, Callao/
12, 29, 37, 124 bus.* **Open** 8am-2am Mon-Thur;
8am-4am Fri, Sat; 5pm-2am Sun. **Admission**
(shows) AR$15-$25 plus minimum spend AR$10.
Credit AmEx, DC, MC, V. **Map** p281 H10 ❸

Bookstore, café, restaurant, bar, art gallery, tango
venue… it would probably be easier to enumerate
the things Clásica y Moderna *doesn't* do. The live
tango events (Tuesday to Sunday nights) are a good
alternative to the showier offerings elsewhere.

Dadá

*San Martín 941 (4314 4787). Subte C, San Martín/
61, 93, 130, 152 bus.* **Open** noon-3am Mon-Sat.
Credit AmEx, MC, V. **Map** p281 F11 ❹
Drenched in colour with Mondrian glass, pop art
walls and a mosaic bar, Dadá is a bar-restaurant
with serious sex appeal. It draws an engaging mix
of intellectuals, artists and tourists, there to indulge
in Paolo and Julián's classy cocktails and the bistro
cuisine featuring classics like the Lomo Dadá steak
alongside more adventurous options. **Photo** *p140*.

Deep Blue

*Reconquista 920 (4312 3377). Subte C, San Martín/
93, 152 bus.* **Open** 11am-4am Mon-Fri; 8pm-4am
Sat, Sun. **Credit** AmEx, MC, V. **Map** p281 G12 ❺
Deep Blue is where fashion-conscious poolheads
come to cross cues (AR$5 per game). Although the
place is awash with helpful staff, some tables are
equipped with their own self-service beer tap.
Other locations: Ayacucho 1204, Recoleta
(4827 4415).

---

❶ Pink numbers given in this chapter
correspond to the location of each café,
bar and pub as marked on the street
maps. *See pp276-285.*

Time passes slowly at **Bar Plaza Dorrego**. *See p140.*

Eat, Drink, Shop

Surreal and sexy **Dadá**. *See p139.*

Florida Garden

Florida 899, y Paraguay, Microcentro (4312 7902).
Subte C, San Martín/93, 130, 152 bus. **Open**
6.30am-midnight Mon-Fri; 8am-11pm Sat, Sun.
Credit AmEx, V. **Map** p281 G11 **❻**
Many of the clients of this exalted two-tier establishment – a leader in literary café culture – are
the same people who were frequenting the place
when it came to eminence in the 1960s. Prominent
local artists have been gathering here on Saturday
mornings for decades. These days they are joined
by business people and tourists, sitting between the
handsome copper columns or leaning nonchalantly
on the glass- and marble-topped bars.

La Giralda

Avenida Corrientes 1453 (4371 3846). Subte B,
Uruguay/24, 26, 102 bus. **Open** 8am Mon-Sat; 4pm-
midnight Sun. **No credit cards**. **Map** p281 G10 **❼**
The pre- and post-theatre crowds flock to La Giralda
for its famous *chocolate y churros* (hot chocolate with
a doughnut for dipping), while wise night owls drop
in for a last drink before bedtime. Brightly lit, with
white-tiled walls and ashen-faced waiters, this
quirky little café remains a Corrientes classic.

The Kilkenny

Reconquista 1000 (4312 7291). Subte C, San
Martín/26, 93, 152 bus. **Open** from 5.30pm Mon-Fri;
from 8pm Sat, Sun. **Credit** AmEx, DC, MC, V.
Map p281 G12 **❽**

BA's Irish pubs have long been prime movers of the
city's drinking scene, yet the staggering popularity
of Kilkenny is still something of a phenomenon. The
ultimate after-office hang out, droves of thirsty
thirtysomethings stream in from the surrounding
towers for some light drinking and heavy flirting.
By Saturday it's all-out mayhem as the tourist set
joins in with the alcohol-fuelled game of sardines.

San Telmo

Bar Plaza Dorrego

Defensa 1098 (4361 0141). Bus 9, 10, 20, 126,
195. **Open** 8am-3am daily. **No credit cards**.
Map p280 D12 **❾**
With outdoor seating on Plaza Dorrego, this century-
old watering hole embodies the *tanguero* spirit of
San Telmo. Inside, a pale lemon hue is cast over the
dusty bottles and etched walls, while tango crackles
over black-and-white images of Carlos Gardel. It's
an ideal spot from which to watch the Sunday
market goings-on; or on a warm evening to drain a
frosty *chopp* (glass of draught beer) and dismember
a few complimentary monkey nuts. **Photo** *p139.*

Bar Seddón

Defensa 695 (4342 3700). Bus 24, 29, 126, 130,
152. **Open** from 5pm Tue-Sun. **No credit cards**.
Map p281 E10 **❿**
When a local government rescue package failed to
materialise and the Seddón was forced to change
location – the original was perhaps the most
handsome bar in Buenos Aires – many feared the
worst. Thankfully, the owners found themselves an
attractive San Telmo corner site and brought over
much of the spirit from the original. Weekdays are
tranquil verging on dead, but then the space packs
out on weekends when live bands play.

El Británico

Avenida Brasil 399 (4300 6894). Bus 10, 29, 39,
93, 152. **Open** 24hrs daily. **No credit cards**.
Map p280 C9 ⓫
There's something of a Jim Jarmusch feel to this
creaking relic. During the Falklands/Malvinas War,
the bar diplomatically changed its name but the
decor remained – and the waiters too, it seems. El
Británico is open round the clock – very handy for
that final 'one for the road'.

Cha Cha Cha Club

Defensa 683 (4343 8342). Bus 28, 29, 86.
Open from 8.30pm Tue-Sun. **Credit** AmEx, V.
Map p281 E10 ⓬
Disco kitsch pervades this popular two-storey hangout, with surrealistic motifs such as dogs chasing
saints. Upstairs, reruns of 1950s cartoons and classic
TV shows are projected on to a white curtain, while
down in the basement it's all disco balls and funked-
out tunes taking you back a decade or three to the
days of flares and roller skates. Cocktails are
imaginative, if not outstanding; house special El
Trago Pop mixes coke, rum, ginger and meringue.

Bluffer's guide to BA boozing

'Vamos a tomar algo?' It's loosely translated as let's go for a drink, but don't be fooled by this ubiquitous Argentinian phrase. Whereas back home it would most certainly imply a beer or 12, in this part of the world it can mean anything from a painstakingly constructed basil Daiquiri to a slowly sipped soft drink. In Argentina, the point of the exercise is not the inebriating effects of alcohol but the social interaction it fosters. Suffice to say that Argentinian drinking habits can be soberingly different for those more familiar with the down-the-hatch method. To prepare yourself for the culture shock of boozing in BA, read on.

The first issue is getting served. Barmen in Argentina are more likely to be concerned with the perfection of the carefully crafted cocktail than with slaking your thirst. But be patient. The drink will come in its own good time. And thanks to the ludicrously liberal licensing laws, there's no last orders, so the rush to stockpile the alcohol before closing time is entirely unnecessary.

It's also worth noting that, as a rule, Argentinians are not big boozers. Entire groups of people have been known to occupy privileged bar space for hours on end while sharing a Diet Coke, and no one even bats an eyelid. Blind drunkenness is not considered the objective of a night on the town, with the focus more on pulling members of the opposite sex than pulling pints. Even the beer

festivals are less about the brew itself and more about the talent in attendance.

Still, Argentinians can enjoy a tipple as much as the next *hombre*, although their taste in alcohol is a whole other issue. In a country boasting some of the continent's best wine, you'll be shocked to find the locals adding a sacrilegious dash of soda to their *vino tinto*, not to mention ice to their champagne. And then there are the bizarrely popular alcoholic concoctions: Fernet Branca, for example, a herbal brew usually mixed with Coke that tastes like frothy mouthwash; or the sweet and sickly Gancia Batido, made from Gancia vermouth, and mixed with lemon and sugar until it resembles the bathwater you probably just got out of.

It's also worth pausing before shelling out for a 14-pint round as the night kicks off. Your gift will be gratefully accepted, but don't expect a return on your lavish investment – besides, you'll be on your own from pint three onwards so the whole 'round' system makes little sense. And because alcohol has been relegated in terms of importance, few Argentinians will think twice about sipping away at your drink, so guard the glass jealously if you are hell bent on oblivion.

Just be warned: the night is long and the party may last till dawn, so pacing is key. Finally, be aware that blindingly bright, bustling BA is no place in which to negotiate a hangover, least of all on a *colectivo* (city bus): the combination of dodgy suspension, cobbled streets and a queasy stomach makes Jack the all-night party lad a very ill boy.

La Farmacia

Bolívar 898 (4300 6151). Bus 10, 24, 29.
Open 9am-1.30am Tue-Thur, Sun; 9am-2.30am Sat.
Credit AmEx, MC, V. **Map** p280 D10 ⓭
This former pharmacy (hence the name and array of old medicine bottles) is a charmingly skewed amalgam of lots of little spaces spread around a three-tiered corner spot. As well as serving fairly priced food from a lengthy and imaginative menu, this gay-friendly joint also boasts an attractive roof terrace – something of a rarity in San Telmo.

El Federal

Carlos Calvo 599 (4300 4313). Bus 10, 22, 24, 29, 86. **Open** 7.30am-2am Mon-Thur, Sun; 7.30am-4am Fri, Sat. **Credit** MC, V. **Map** p280 D9 ⓮
Built in 1864, El Federal is officially listed as one of BA's most historic bars. It's also one of the best kept – check out the magnificent cash registers. It's pretty original too; bar staff work from a lowered floor while the bar itself is thigh high. There's a standard offering of beers and spirits and a long menu of sandwiches and other snacks. With the faded yellow

lamps hanging overhead and the old advertising posters, it captures that elusive spirit of a bygone era.

Fin del Mundo

Defensa 700 (15 5314 4729 mobile). Bus 24, 29, 126, 130, 152. **Open** from 6pm Mon-Sat; from 3pm Sun. **No credit cards. Map** p281 D10 **⑯**

Pull up a pin-head stool and try not to fall off as the dreadlocked DJ (and owner) spins his silky repertoire of classics. In this barely lit corner bar with moody red decor and a large terrace, the vibe is raw and punky – random characters pogo round the tables and there are stacks of on-sale vinyl on the shelves. Lively and unpretentious.

Gibraltar

Perú 895 (4362 5310). Bus 24, 29, 86. **Open** from 6pm-4am daily. **No credit cards. Map** p281 E9 **⑯**

If you've been in town long enough to know that a pub – a *real* pub – is as rare a commodity in Buenos Aires as a stringless teabag, then pull up a stool in the Gibraltar and put your wandering feet to rest. This increasingly popular San Telmo watering hole offers the precious combination of cheap beer in – gasp! – pint glasses, genuinely spicy curries, an exhaustive collection of whiskies and the friendliest bar-owners in the city; all of which explains why you'll find so many expat elbows on the bar here on any given night. There's a pool table out the back and a telly in the corner.

Pride Café

Balcarce 869 (4300 6435). Bus 22, 24, 29, 74. **Open** 10am-11pm daily. **No credit cards. Map** p280 D10 **⑰**

Bringing a taste of Palermo Hollywood to backstreet San Telmo, this café-bar's emphasis is less on Pride and more on understated *Wallpaper**-style modernity with the occasional gay-friendly flourish – like the ever-playing Robbie Williams and Beyoncé big-screen DVDs. After hours and Sunday afternoons are busiest, when a mixed crowd, both gay and straight, congregates.

Territorio

Estados Unidos 500 (4307 0896). Bus 5, 22. **Open** 5pm-1am Mon, Tue; 10am-2am Wed-Sat. **No credit cards. Map** p280 D10 **⑱**

With its dark wooden tables and tiny mosaic bar, Terrotorio typifies the ongoing transformation of this traditionally downbeat barrio. The very fact that such a sophisticated spot can thrive these days reflects the neighbourhood's changing demographic. Ponder on this with the aid of a fine cheese platter, home-made breads and wine by the *copa*-load.

Recoleta & Barrio Norte

La Biela

Avenida Quintana 600 (4804 0449). Bus 59, 60, 101, 102, 110. **Open** 7am-3am Mon-Thur; 7am-4am Fri, Sat; 8am-3am Sun. **Credit** V. **Map** p282 J11 **⑲**

Close to Recoleta Cemetery, the terrace of this pricy, historical, Parisian-style cafe is a good bet for some people watching. It's named after the 'connecting rod' in car engines, testimony to the fact that famous motor racing drivers hung out here in the 1950s. Nowadays, the massive rubber tree shelters a terrace full of tourists and Recoleta's most monied residents.

Eat, Drink, Shop

Gibraltar – who said South Americans don't like to cue?

BN Café

Peña 2300 (4805 6794). Bus 41, 61, 95, 101, 118.
Open 8am-7pm Mon; 8pm-midnight Tue-Sat; 11am-5pm Sun. **Main courses** AR$8-$14. **No credit cards. Map** p282 I11 ⓴
Fresh salads, sushi and a charismatic owner are just a few of the reasons why this slick corner café is doing so well. It's dressed like a typical New York deli with white walls, banquettes, chalk-boards, and glossy magazines strewn mock randomly across the tables. The menu changes regularly but Sundays are an established safe bet, with a generous daytime buffet spread across the back of the bar.

Milión

Paraná 1048 (4815 9925). Bus 29, 39, 102, 152.
Open noon-2am Mon-Wed; noon-3am Thur; noon-4am Fri; 7.30pm-4am Sat; 8pm-2am Sun.
Credit AmEx, V. **Map** p281 I10 ㉑
Milión's stunning transformation from stately townmansion to 21st-century 'it' bar has made it an emblem of cool in contemporary BA. While maintaining its original lavish form, the classic architecture is offset by dim lighting, cutting-edge art displays and projected visuals, bringing the space in line with its new, style-conscious clientele. Given its popularity, Milión's high-ceilinged rooms are often littered with reservation cards. But somewhere between the first floor terrace, picturesque garden and marble staircase you're bound to find a place to rest your weary tush.

Rubia y Negra

Libertad 1630 (4313 1125). Bus 17, 67, 102.
Open 6pm-2am Mon-Thur; 7pm-3am Sat.
Credit AmEx, MC, V. **Map** p282 I11 ㉒
It's probably the most common beer swigger's predicament: Saturday night is here, your girlfriend's all glammed up, you've promised her a night out somewhere plush and all you really want to do is sit home with a six-pack and the remote control. Enter Rubia y Negra, which straddles the divide between classy wine bar and local pub, with a line of gourmet beers brewed on the premises and served in a sophisticated setting. Check out the 12 per cent Barley Wine beer, aged for six months. The food – sushi and modern Argentinian – is excellent.

Shamrock

Rodríguez Peña 1220 (4812 3584). Bus 37, 39, 101, 124, 152. **Open** from 6pm Mon-Fri; from 8pm Sat, Sun. **Credit** AmEx, MC, V. **Map** p282 I11 ㉓
A genuine Irish bar – the owners hail from Cork – this BA institution sets itself apart with an open plan and thoroughly modern vibe that is closer in spirit to the contemporary Celtic tiger than its shamrock and shillelagh Microcentro counterparts. It's also good value, with a generous happy hour running from opening time until midnight. This and excellent music ensure that it's always jammed with hormonal hordes of twenty and thirtysomethings. Heavy drapes lead down to the heaving Basement Club (*see p183*), open from Thursday to Saturday.

Palermo & Palermo Viejo

Acabar

Honduras 5733 (4772 0845/4776 3634). Bus 39, 93, 111. **Open** from 8pm-4am daily. **Credit** MC, V. **Map** p279 O5 ㉔
Neon lighting, coloured corrugated-iron sheets, canteen-style food and board games galore. This bar of odds and sods is a circus-like frenzy of junkyard proportions. A dizzlingly extensive food menu is presented on easy-to-share laminated cards, although the dishes themselves are often less satisfying than the selection process. A bustling place to eat, drink and play.

Bangalore Pub & Curry House

Humboldt 1416 (47792621). Bus 93, 140, 168.
Open 6pm-4am daily. **No credit cards.**
Map p279 N5 ㉕
Think warm woods, soft chairs and ceiling fans and you've some idea what this classic colonial-style establishment has to offer. Another winner from the winning team that brought you Gibraltar (*see p143*), Bangalore is BA's first official pub and curry house and performs both functions with aplomb. Downstairs offers comfy seating and jugs of gin and tonic, while the upstairs dining area is an intimate hideaway in which to sample the sub-continental

Milión.

cuisine, including a *curry de calabaza* (pumpkin) that is so melt-in-the-mouth it'll probably have you speaking in tongues. With impeccable service and loving attention to detail, Bangalore provides the best value pub grub in town.

Carnal

Niceto Vega 5511 (4772 7582). Bus 39, 93, 184. **Open** 9pm-3am Tue, Wed; from 9pm Thur-Sat. **No credit cards. Map** p279 N4 26

Thursday nights' pre-Club 69 (at Niceto Club opposite; *see p184*) drinks are the big story in Carnal, particularly in summer when swarms of frisky locals invade the roof terrace and downstairs bar. There's a healthy dosage of pretension, but it's a friendly vibe, bustling with good-looking, flirtatious young *porteños*. Beware, though: it's a popular spot and the door policy has tightened up considerably. Make sure to book ahead or arrive before 10.30pm – it's not one to be missed.

Congo

Honduras 5329 (4833 5857). Bus 34, 55, 166. **Open** 8pm-3.30am Tue-Sun. **Credit** AmEx, V. **Map** p279 N5 27

One of the bar kings of the Palermo Viejo jungle, this popular drinking hole was opened by the owners of Niceto Club (*see p184*) in late 2004. For all the laid-back charm of the cosy, brown and beige leather-clad interior, the true magic of Congo resides in its gorgeous, spot-lit summer garden which ranks

Smart cookies go to **Mark's Deli**. *See p147.*

among the city's best outdoor drinking spaces. There's no better place to enjoy an icy Bossa Nova (rum, brandy, galliano, passion fruit and honey) as BA's sticky summer reaches boiling point. Tuesday is barbecue night, so follow your nose and join the hordes of carnivores in the garden.

El Diamante

Malabia 1688 (4831 5735). Bus 15, 110, 141, 160. **Open** from noon Mon-Sat. **Credit** AmEx, MC, V. **Map** p279 M4 28

While half of Argentina seems happier dwelling melancholically on its European roots, Palermo resto-bar El Diamante is a celebration of the eclectic mix of culture, music and colour that is South America. Modelled on a bar in Asunción, Paraguay, 'The Diamond's' intimate first-floor space and atmospheric Mexican styled terrace throw all things Latin (and a few things kitsch) into the proverbial melting pot in a homage to continental unity. The acoustics in the inside bar can be migraine inducing, so best to head straight for the roof, grab a Cuba Libre and lie back on a hammock above the blue mosaic fountain, taking in the view. Latin music prevails, with bossa nova nights on Mondays.

Dubliners

Humboldt 2000 (4771 6178). Bus 39, 93, 111, 168. **Open** from noon Tue-Fri; from 8pm Sat; 4-10pm Sun. **Credit** AmEx, MC, V. **Map** p279 N5 29

While this is one of the city's more authentic-looking Irish pubs, the table service and the incense burning at the bar suggest something other than a snug on O'Connell Street. That said, the huge Guinness posters, green ceilings and stained-glass windows assist a gratifying night of make-believe. With imported beers at up to AR$40 a bottle (for Duval), only the rich or foolish veer from local brews.

La Finca

Honduras 5147 (4832 3004). Bus 34, 39, 55. **Open** 11am-midnight Tue-Sun. **Credit** MC, V. **Map** p279 M5 30

There's been a slight change of location but it's boozy business as usual at this charming outlet for lesser-known Mendoza microwineries. Wine buffs will wet themselves at the array of vintage and limited-edition bottles. The rest of us can chin-wag at one of the four small tables, while sampling a glass of the hand-picked wine of the week. Tasty mixed *picadas* (cheese and meat platters) for AR$30 help absorb the bacchanalian blow.

Kim y Novak

Güemes 4900 (4773 7521) Subte D, Plaza Italia/34, 55, 93 bus. **Open** from 9.30pm Tue-Sun. **No credit cards. Map** p279 N6 31

Aptly named after the demure 1950s Hollywood vixen, idolised for her platinum blonde hair and come-hither attitude, this funky space invites a hip, colourful and predominantly gay crowd. Downstairs there's a lively dancefloor and Sundays are reserved for a gay party (*see also p197*).

Eat, Drink, Shop

Lelé de Troya

Costa Rica 4901(4832 2726). Bus 39, 55.
Open from noon daily. **Credit** AmEx, MC, V.
Map p279 M5 ㉜
Unlike her namesake Helen of Troy, proprietress Lelé's take on beauty is this vivid restaurant/bar. Colour-coded rooms vary as widely as the tasty, world-themed menu. In summer the terrace offers a panoramic view of the area, while sun loungers for stretching out on – with bottles of chilled white wine – satisfy the posturing vainglorious.

Mark's Deli

El Salvador 4701 (4832 6244). Bus 15, 39, 55.
Open 8.30am-9.30pm Mon-Sat; 10.30am-9pm Sun.
No credit cards. Map p279 M5 ㉝
Mark's is modelled along the lines of a hip New York deli. This bright, orange-hued café is favoured by trendsetting Palermo folk. Sip an icy lemonade and sink your teeth into a smoked salmon sandwich, or munch on giant choc-chip cookies and a latte while watching the fashion identicats at play. Cheap lunch-time menus are available on weekdays. **Photo** *p146.*

Mundo Bizarro

Guatemala 4802 (4773 1967). Subte D, Plaza Italia/34, 55, 93 bus. **Open** 8pm-3am Mon-Wed; 8pm-4am Thur; 8pm-5am Fri, Sat; 8pm-3am Sun.
No credit cards. Map p279 M6 ㉞
It's hard to go wrong with a bar that so proudly bares its maxim, 'In alcohol we trust.' A giant fly sculpture hovers above the bar, while 1950s artwork and funky photography adorn every wall and surface. It's probably not for your maiden aunt, but if you fancy an unhealthy dose of rock 'n' roll, dig yourself into one of the black leather booths and knock back a few Fuzzy Navels. Mondays are sushi night and, on Tuesdays, boys drink two for one. It's the girls' turn on Thursdays. The music – everything from Dolly Parton to Black Sabbath – is arguably still the best of any bar in Buenos Aires. Be warned: things don't heat up until after midnight.

Omm

Honduras 5656 (4774 4224). Bus 39, 93, 111.
Open from 6pm Mon; from 11.30am Tue-Sun.
Credit AmEx, MC, V. **Map** p279 N5 ㉟
Slick and intimate, Omm is a small, softly lit space filled with candles, chrome tables and attentive staff. It's a firm favourite for amorous couples and for small groups getting stuck into some quality tapas. The outside terrace is perfect for looking louche and uncaring as the world bustles by and the excellent cocktails are the best value in town.

Oui Oui

Nicaragua 6068 (4778 9614). Bus 39, 67, 152, 161.
Open 8am-8pm Tue-Fri; 10am-8pm Sat, Sun.
Main courses AR$10-$15. **No credit cards.**
Map p279 O5 ㊱
Until recently, most of BA's French eateries were expensive, formal bistros, more *7ème* than *5ème arrondissement.* Oui Oui, by contrast, offers honest, down-to-earth Gallic fare of the kind the French

actually eat as opposed to simply write about is making an impact. Thirty-year-old francophile Rocio Garcia Orza does wonders with hot filled croissants, fresh baguettes, vichysoisse and *pain au chocolat,* all options hastily scribbled on chalk-boards in a colourful environment.

Único Bar Bistro

Fitz Roy 1892 (4775 6693). Bus 39, 93, 111.
Open 8.30am-6am Mon-Fri; 8.30pm-6am Sat, Sun.
Credit MC. **Map** p279 N5 ㊲
Recently renovated, Unico continues its relentless crusade in the cause of round-the-clock intoxication. The jumble of tourists, regulars and celebrity spotters creates a perpetual buzz, while frenzied staff navigate the bar wielding burgers, beer and cocktails. It's a surefire bet for any night of the week, and the perfect spot for an early evening nibble, a full night of immorality, or a sneaky 6am top-up to propel you home.

Virasoro

Guatemala 4328 (4831 8918). Bus 36, 160, 168.
Open 7pm-3am Mon-Sat. **No credit cards.**
Map p279 M6 ㊳
In a glamorous, sometimes self-consciously trendy neighbourhood, Virasoro is a torch bearer for the unpretentious nightspot. Decorated with local art and record memorabilia, weekdays are tranquil affairs, with locals playing chess and board games or listening to poetry readings. But come weekends, it morphs into a popular live music venue (mostly jazz) – be sure to reserve a table in advance.

878

Thames 878, Villa Crespo (4773 1098). Bus 34, 140, 151, 168. **Open** from 10pm daily. **No credit cards.**
Map p279 M4 ㊴
Once a 'word of mouth' bar (in other words, a speak-easy), 878's now gone straight. Ring the bell at the unmarked door and you'll be invited into a slick, low-lit space with comfy couches and more than a few reminders of its early days as a carpentry workshop. It's a perfect spot for a sultry dinner-for-two or a hefty exploration of one of the best-stocked bars in the city. A nod to Julian, the ever effervescent owner and in-house whisky specialist, should clear any doubts over which cocktail to choose. One of the coolest, least publicised bars in the city.

Las Cañitas

Supersoul

Báez 252 (4776 3905/www.supersoul.com.ar). Bus 15, 29, 64. **Open** from 6pm Mon-Fri, Sun; from 7pm Sat. **Credit** V. **Map** p284 O9 ㊵
The 1970s-feel, sister bar of larger, redder Soul Café next door, Supersoul has a retro-glam swagger that's guaranteed to get your mojo working. Disco balls and psychedelic swirls breathe life into this cute and dinky space. Pull up a seat at the tangerine coloured bar, where the gorgeous staff will help you quench your thirst with a smile.

Eat, Drink, Shop

Shops & Services

The design, the stitch and the wardrobe.

In the immortal words of Bo Derek, 'Whoever said money can't buy happiness simply didn't know where to go shopping.' We like to think La Derek had Buenos Aires in mind. Shopping in this city is sheer pleasure. With elaborate window displays, custom-made leather goods, funky one-offs and, best of all, the devalued peso, BA is one big crazy discount store for dollar-toting tourists.

The increasingly hip and happening **Palermo Viejo** neighbourhood is a boutique wonderland showcasing the latest burst of creativity in Buenos Aires. Young *porteños* fresh out of design school have set up shop alongside established local and international names. The windows are dressed to perfection, and the interiors alone are excuse enough for a shop hop around this trendy barrio.

Downtown, a combination of old money and glitz has put Recoleta firmly on the retail trail. **Avenida Alvear** and nearby **Rodríguez Peña**, **Posadas** and **Libertador** are BA's Fifth Avenue equivalents. Here, international designers show off their latest collections beside art galleries and Parisian-style cafés.

Then there's the nostalgia factor. Buenos Aires revels in an old-school approach to shopping. This is a country where you'll still find shops dedicated to one type of product, with the stock behind the counter. Certain areas specialise in a particular type of goods. **Avenida Corrientes** is packed with bookshops, **Arenales** is noted for its interior decoration and furnishing shops, and **Arroyo** is dotted with art galleries and dealerships. The major antiques area is **San Telmo**.

Unlike Bo, not all of us are naturally equipped with retail radar. Enter the personal shopper. Doble M Gifts (4899 2853/www.argybargy. biz/dobleM) and Florencia Bibas (www.florencia bibas.com.ar) both offer services where those too busy to shop set the price and get gift-wrapped packages delivered to their hotel.

When you purchase Argentinian-made products worth at least AR$70 in a shop displaying a Global Refund/Tax Free Shopping sticker, don't forget to ask for the *factura* (bill) and the *cheque de reintegro*. When you leave the country, present both at Customs, which will send you to a *puesto de pago* where you will be given back the 21 per cent sales tax minus an administration fee.

Shopping centres

Abasto de Buenos Aires

Avenida Corrientes 3247, entre Agüero y Anchorena, Almagro (4959 3400/www.abasto-shopping.com.ar). Subte B, Carlos Gardel/24, 26, 124, 146, 168 bus. **Open** 10am-10pm daily. **Credit** AmEx, DC, MC, V. **Map** p282 J8.
This spectacular building – formerly a market – in an old tango district houses more than 200 shops. It caters primarily to locals, with most of the main Argentinian chains represented, although some top brands don't have outlets here. The complex also has a large food court and a cinema. **Photo** *p149.*

Alto Palermo

Avenida Santa Fe 3253, entre Coronel Díaz y Bulnes, Palermo (5777 8000/www.altopalermo.com.ar). Subte D, Bulnes/12, 15, 39, 64, 152 bus. **Open** 10am-10pm daily. **Credit** varies. **Map** p282 K9.
One of the oldest and most representative of the 'shoppings', but with one of the youngest crowds. Popular with families and gaggles of giggling mall rats, it contains most of the Argentinian chains, including Chocolate, María Vazquez and Rapsodia.

Galerías Pacífico

Florida 737, entre Viamonte y Córdoba, Microcentro (5555 5100/www.galeriaspacifico.com.ar). Subte B, Florida/6, 93, 130, 152 bus. **Open** 10am-9pm Mon-Sat; noon-9pm Sun. **Credit** varies. **Map** p281 G11.
In an elegant turn-of-the-century building, the fine frescoes in this Florida street mall were painted by five Argentinian muralists. You'll find famous brand names such as Christian Dior and Ralph Lauren, as well as local stars Sibyl Vane and Vitamina.

Paseo Alcorta

Salguero 3172, y Figueroa Alcorta, Palermo (5777 6500). Bus 67, 130. **Open** 10am-10pm daily. **Credit** varies. **Map** p282 L11.
Paseo Alcorta, considered by shopping buffs to be the best mall in Buenos Aires, contains the gigantic Carrefour hypermarket and four cinema screens. It's also home to the latest Argentinian designer wears and wares, from children's shops Cheeky and Mimo & Co to womenswear stores Ayres and Awada. You'll also find well-known brands such as Lacoste and Cacharel.

Patio Bullrich

Avenida del Libertador 750, entre Montevideo y Libertad, Recoleta (4814 7400/7500/www.shopping bullrich.com.ar). Bus 67, 92, 102, 130. **Open** *Shops* 10am-9pm daily. *Restaurants* 10am-midnight daily. **Credit** varies. **Map** p282 I12.

The oldest and most luxurious of all BA's malls (opened in 1988) was once the city's meat auction house. The elegance extends from the marble floors to the uniformed lift operators. Top-end boutiques include Trosman, Etiqueta Negra (menswear) and Jazmin Chebar, as well as Versace and Max Mara.

Antiques & collectibles

San Telmo – particularly Defensa street between Independencia and San Juan – has the biggest concentration of antiques dealers in the city. Serious collectors should go on weekdays, but for a casual browse go to the area's central square, **Plaza Dorrego**, on Sundays between 10am and 5pm.

Club de Tango

5th Floor, Office 114, Paraná 123, entre Bartolomé Mitre y Perón (4372 7251/www.clubdetango.com.ar), Congreso. Subte A, Sáenz Peña/29, 39 bus. **Open** 11am-6pm Mon-Fri. **No credit cards. Map** p281 G9.
Over 2,000 tango CDs, along with rare cassette recordings and a mountain of tango memorabilia, publications, artwork, books and more.

Gil Antigüedades

Humberto 1º 412, entre Defensa y Bolívar, San Telmo (4361 5019). Bus 24, 29, 126, 130, 152. **Open** 11am-1pm, 3-7pm daily. **Credit** AmEx, V. **Map** p280 D9.
The sheer volume of items here will dazzle vintage fashion victims. The speciality is Victorian clothing (exquisite handbags bordered with gems), but there are also German-made *mates* from 1880-90.

Guevara Art Gallery

Defensa 982, entre Carlos Calvo y Estados Unidos, San Telmo (4362 2418/). Bus 24, 29, 126, 130, 152. **Open** 11am-7pm daily. **No credit cards. Map** p280 D10.
For lovers of art deco and art nouveau, this gallery has around 2,000 WMF collector's items from 1850-1930, as well as Daum and Lalique pieces.

HB Antiquedades

Defensa 1016, entre Humberto 1º y Carlos Calvo (4361 3325). Bus 24, 29, 152. **Open** 10am-7pm Mon-Fri, Sun. **No credit cards. Map** p280 D9.
Stepping into this vast, upmarket emporium of top-of-the-range antiques is like walking into a slightly over-furnished palace. It's worth a look if only to take in the impressive centrepiece, an Italian pink chandelier that hangs regally from the high ceilings.

La Pasionaria

Godoy Cruz 1541, entre Cabrera y Niceto Vega, Palermo Viejo (4773 0563). Bus 39, 55, 111. **Open** 4-8pm Mon-Fri; 10.30am-8pm Sat. **No credit cards. Map** p279 N5.
In a huge warehouse, Pancho Salomón displays items from the 1920s to '50s. It's chaotic, though almost poetically so, and worth a visit just to see the hundreds of gems he's accumulated.

Silvia Petroccia

Defensa 1002, y Carlos Calvo, San Telmo (4362 0156). Bus 24, 29, 126, 130, 152. **Open** 10am-7pm daily. **No credit cards. Map** p280 D9.
Michael Jackson and Donna Karan have had their wallets out in this super cool store. The furniture is more old than antique, and has been touched up by Petroccia, but you can find amazing items rescued from old *porteño* palaces, as well as extra large mirrors and candelabra.

Bookshops

Porteños are well read and Buenos Aires has more than 1,000 bookshops. Avenida Corrientes is home to a number of stores selling both new and second-hand books. Many of these outlets are open till midnight. Elsewhere, look out for the **Cúspide** and **Yenny** chains.

Ateneo Grand Splendid

Avenida Santa Fe 1860, entre Callao y Riobamba, Barrio Norte (4811 6104/4813 6052). Subte D, Callao/12, 39, 152 bus. **Open** 9am-10pm Mon-Thur; 9am-midnight Fri, Sat; noon-10pm Sun. **Credit** AmEx, DC, MC, V. **Map** p282 I10.
This gloriously renovated theatre now contains the largest bookstore in South America. It includes an ample choice of English books and a café.
Other locations: Florida 340, Microcentro (4325 6801).

Abasto de Buenos Aires. *See p148.*

Eat, Drink, Shop

CHOCOLATE

El Club del Comic

Marcelo T de Alvear 2002, y Ayacucho, Barrio Norte (4966 1748/www.clubdelcomic.com.ar). Subte D, Facultad de Medicina/39, 101, 111, 132, 152 bus. **Open** 10am-8.30pm Mon-Sat. **Credit** AmEx, DC, MC, V. **Map** p282 I10.

Comics and fanzines galore from Europe, the United States, Japan and Argentina. Rifle through deep stacks of rarities and limited editions.
Other locations: Montevideo 355, Tribunales (4375 2323).

Gandhi Galerna

Avenida Corrientes 1743, entre Callao y Rodríguez Peña, Tribunales (4374 7501). Subte B, Callao/12, 24, 37, 60 bus. **Open** 10am-10pm Mon-Thur; 10am-midnight Fri, Sat; 4-10pm Sun. **Credit** AmEx, DC, MC, V. **Map** p281 G9.

Gandhi has long been the place where Buenos Aires' thinkers and talkers gather. It has a noteworthy music selection and an unrivalled choice of local journals and mags. Live music venue Notorious (*see p205*) is on the first floor.
Other locations: throughout the city.

KEL Ediciones

Marcelo T de Alvear 1369, entre Uruguay y Talcahuano, Recoleta (4814 0143/www.kel-ediciones.com). Bus 39, 102, 111, 152. **Open** 9am-8pm Mon-Fri; 9.30am-1.30pm Sat. **Closed** Jan. **Credit** MC, V. **Map** p281 H10.

KEL stocks English-language fiction, non-fiction, travel books and teaching materials.
Other locations: Conde 1990, Belgrano (4555 4005).

Rigoletto Curioso

Paseo la Plaza, Local 10, Avenida Corrientes 1660, entre Montevideo y Rodríguez Peña, Congreso (6320 5310/www.rigolettocurioso.com.ar). Subte B, Callao/ 12, 24, 37, 60 bus. **Open** 10am-10.30pm Mon-Thur; 10am-1am Fri; noon-1am Sat; 2-10.30pm Sun. **No credit cards. Map** p281 G9.

A real-life old curiosity shop piled high with rarities and out-of-print editions, from Italian anarchist tracts to gardening manuals. Armchair generals will enjoy the antique lead soldiers.
Other locations: Soler 4501, Palermo Viejo (4831 3649).

Walrus Books

Honduras 5628, entre Fitz Roy y Bonpland, Palermo Viejo (4777 0632). Bus 39, 93, 151. **Open** 2-8pm Wed-Sun. **No credit cards. Map** p279 N5.

Run from home by photographer Geoffrey Hickman and his wife Josefina, this bohemian bookshop stocks an eclectic range of titles both new and second-hand. All books are in English. The shop doesn't give on to the street; ring the bell.

Design & home accessories

For one-stop designer shopping for the home, head to **Buenos Aires Design** at Avenida Pueyrredón 2501, y Azcuénaga (5777 6000).

Located next to the Centro Cultural Recoleta, it has two floors with more than 60 interior design shops and thousands of take-home items.

Calma Chicha

Honduras 4925, entre Gurruchaga y Serrano, Palermo Viejo (4831 1818). Bus 39, 151, 168. **Open** 10am-8pm Mon-Sat; 2-8pm Sun. **Credit** AmEx, DC, MC, V. **Map** p279 M5.

Argentinian-produced board games and *pinguinos* (penguin-shaped wine jugs) are among the witty items in this busy Palermo emporium. Cowhide, leather, denim and woven textiles are fashioned on the premises into big beanbags, purses and more.

Capital

Honduras 4958, entre Gurruchaga y Serrano, Palermo Viejo (4834 6555/www.capitalpalermo. com.ar). Bus 39, 55. **Open** 11am-8pm Mon-Sat. **Credit** AmEx, DC, MC, V. **Map** p279 M5.

Capital stocks all sorts of hip home treats, including streamlined leather *mate* gourds, cool corkscrews and coffee sets, stylish kids' games and jigsaws and a range of designer furniture at designer prices.

Cubo

Armenia 1493, y Gorriti, Palermo Viejo (4833 7887). Bus 39, 55, 106. **Open** 11am-7pm Mon-Sat. **No credit cards. Map** p279 M5.

Designer Fernando Luvini is a kind of postmodern Geppetto, handcrafting wooden toys for boys of all ages. Robots, racing cars and spinning tops are among the objects carved and lathed in the shop.

Gropius

Honduras 6027, entre Arevalo y Dorrego, Palermo Viejo (4774 2094/4776 4420/www.gropiusdesign-1920-2000.com). Bus 39, 93, 111. **Open** 10am-8pm Mon-Sat. **No credit cards. Map** p279 O5.

In this slick showroom you'll find a fine selection of classic furniture replicas: pieces or entire ranges from Charles Eames, Gropius, Le Corbusier and Mies van der Rohe. The similarities are uncanny and the prices about one-fifth of the originals.

Laura O

Uriarte 1554, entre Gorriti y Cabrera, Palermo Viejo (4832 8778/www.laurao.com). Bus 15, 55, 57, 151, 168. **Open** 10am-8pm Mon-Sat. **Credit** AmEx, MC, V. **Map** p279 M5.

This warehouse-sized space is the place where trendy *porteños* have their wedding lists. Whites, creams, chocolate browns and camels in natural fabrics are the signature of Laura Orcoyen, one of Argentina's coolest interior decorators.

Materia Urbana

Defensa 707, entre Chile e Independencia, San Telmo (4361 5265/www.materiaurbana.com). Bus 24, 29, 126, 130, 152. **Open** 11am-7pm Tue-Sun. **Credit** AmEx, DC, MC, V. **Map** p281 E10.

Take an enjoyable meander through this grand second-floor apartment where each of the three rooms is dedicated to small-format art and designer objects from around 70 local artists.

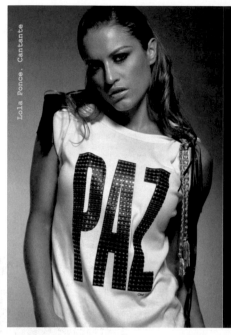

Milagros

Gorriti 5417, y las vías, Palermo Viejo (4899 0991/
www.milagrosdeco.com.ar). Bus 39, 55, 166.
Open 10am-8pm Mon-Sat; 1-7pm Sun.
Credit AmEx, MC, V. **Map** p279 N5.
Interior designer Milagros Resta's warehouse is
crammed with desirable objects, from recycled
antiques and patchwork bedcovers to embroidered
pillows and velvet-covered boxes.

Oda – Objetos de Artistas

Costa Rica 4670, entre Armenia y Gurruchaga,
Palermo Viejo (4831 7403). Bus 15, 39. **Open** 11am-
8pm Mon-Sat. **Credit** AmEx, MC. **Map** p279 M5.
Objetos by respected Argentinian artists are discern-
ingly arranged at this shop by curator Valeria
Fiterman. Boyo Quintana's sweet sculptures are a
worthy investment for any collector.

Papelera Palermo

Honduras 4945, entre Gurruchaga y Serrano,
Palermo Viejo (4833 3081/www.papelerapalermo.
com.ar). Bus 34, 39, 55, 168. **Open** 10am-8pm Mon-
Sat; 2-8pm Sun. **Credit** AmEx, MC. **Map** p279 M5.
With handmade paper in all shapes, sizes and textures, this super stationer's is a joy to browse
in. The walls are lined with brightly coloured rolls
of wrapping paper, and a tiny gramophone plays
scratchy tunes while you make your choices.

Puro Diseño

Terrazas de Buenos Aires Design, Local 1006,
Avenida Pueyrredón 2501, Recoleta (5777 6104/
www.purodiseno.com.ar). Bus 61, 67, 92, 93, 103.
Open 10am-9pm Mon-Sat; noon-9pm Sun.
Credit AmEx, MC, V. **Map** p282 J11.
With products from over 120 of Argentina's best
designers under one roof, Puro Diseño offers clothes,
furniture, jewellery, toys and all sorts of fashions
and fixtures including leather goods. **Photo** *p154.*

Ramos Generales

Ground Floor 'C', Cabello 3650, entre Scalabrini
Ortíz y Ugarteche, Palermo (4804 3524). Bus 10,
15, 21, 37, 160. **Open** 10.30am-7.30pm Mon-Sat.
Credit AmEx, V. **Map** p282 L10.
Luscious home linens in the very best fabrics and
colours abound at Ramos Generales. The quality
and selection are outstanding but it'll cost you.

Reina Batata

Gurruchaga 1785, entre Costa Rica y El Salvador,
Palermo Viejo (4831 7572/www.reinabatata.com).
Bus 34, 36, 55, 93, 161. **Open** noon-8pm Mon-Sat.
Credit AmEx, MC, V. **Map** p279 M5.
Essentially a trendy homeware shop, but don't turn
your nose up at the racks of glasses and plates. If
you fancy yourself as a barbecue expert, the bone-
handled carving set makes for a sharp souvenir.

Sabater Hermanos

Gurruchaga 1821, entre Costa Rica y Nicaragua,
Palermo Viejo (4833 3004/www.shnos.com.ar). Bus
15, 39, 55, 151. **Open** 10am-8pm Mon-Sat; 1-7pm
Sun. **No credit cards. Map** p279 M5.

Run by the third generation of Sabater family soap
makers, this funky shop/workshop is a soap version
of a pick 'n' mix counter. Select coloured soap flakes
to pack into a box, scoop out coloured soap shapes
and 'hundreds and thousands', and add in a long
thin stick made of… guess what? **Photo** *p163.*

Tavano Interior Architecture

Soler 4802, entre Nicaragua y Soler, Palermo Viejo
(4899 0978/www.alextavano.com). Bus 15, 39, 55,
93. **Open** 10.30am-8pm Mon-Sat. **Credit** AmEx, MC,
V. **Map** p279 M6.
Visionary Alex Tavano was one of the first to see the
potential in Palermo Viejo. His collection of artwork
and furnishings testifies to his range of interests: from
pop art prints to the latest in home design tendencies.

Wussmann

Venezuela 570, entre Bolívar y Perú, San Telmo
(4343 4707/www.wussmann.com). Bus 9, 10, 24,
29, 86. **Open** 10.30am-8pm Mon-Sat; 10.30am-2pm
Sun. **Credit** AmEx, V. **Map** p281 E10.
An exclusive paper shop, Wussmann's new San
Telmo store is housed in a renovated building that
is a work of art in itself. Beautiful leather journals,
photo albums and handcrafted paper with ancient
prints all make excellent gifts.
Other locations: Rodriguez Peña 1399, Recoleta
(4811 2444).

Fashion

Many international designers have a strong
presence in Buenos Aires, including Giorgio
Armani, Louis Vuitton, Ralph Lauren, Hermès,
Burberry and Versace – but imported luxury
brands sell for top dollar prices.

Designer

Cora Groppo

El Salvador 4696, y Armenia, Palermo Viejo (4833
7474/www.coragroppo.com). Bus 15, 39, 55, 151,
168. **Open** 11am-8pm Mon-Sat. **Credit** AmEx, MC, V.
Map p279 M5.
Wearable, sexy and chic, Cora's collections are also
sold abroad. Famed for her wedding gowns, this
young designer's evening wear is increasingly
sought after by Buenos Aires' fashion elite.
Other locations: Uruguay 1696, Recoleta
(4815 8516).

FFiocca

Cabello 3650, entre Scalabrini Ortíz y Ugarteche,
Palermo (4806 5637/www.ffiocca.com). Bus 37,
93,160. **Open** 11am-8pm Mon-Fri; 11am-2pm Sat.
Credit DC, MC, V. **Map** p282 L10.
Strong colours and bold, thematic designs characterise Florencia Fiocca's work. Her collections are
complemented by the jewellery on display from contemporary designers Massone, Pini, and Querio, who
work with leather and various metals to produce
original, striking accessories.

Jazmín Chebar

*El Salvador 4702, y Gurruchaga, Palermo Viejo
(4833 4242/www.jazminchebar.com.ar). Bus 34,
151, 168.* **Open** 10am-8pm Mon-Sat; 1-7pm Sun.
Credit AmEx, MC, V. **Map** p279 M5.
Young BA designer Jazmín Chebar brings a fresh
touch to classic styles. From relaxed tops through
to tailored jackets, Chebar plays with colours and
details to produce a classic look with a subtle twist.
Other locations: Paseo Alcorta (5777 6770) and
Patio Bullrich (4814 7424) shopping centres.

María Cher

*El Salvador 4714, entre Armenia y Gurruchaga,
Palermo Viejo (4832 3336/www.maria-cher.com.ar).
Bus 15, 39, 55, 151.* **Open** 10am-8pm Mon-Sat; 2-
8pm Sun. **Credit** AmEx, DC, MC, V. **Map** p279 M5.
María has quickly built up a solid reputation thanks
to her eclectic collections which she sells to the 'feminine, independent and mature' woman.
Other locations: Paseo Alcorta shopping centre
(5777 6541).

María Martha Facchinelli

*El Salvador 4741, entre Armenia y Gurruchaga,
Palermo Viejo (4831 8424/www.facchinelli.com).
Bus 15, 39, 151, 168.* **Open** 10.30am-8pm Mon-Sat.
Credit AmEx, MC, V. **Map** p279 M5.
This young designer – praised by Bazaar and Nylon
– has finally opened a boutique in Palermo Viejo.
Her creations exude a refinement rare among her
peers. Star pieces are dresses in gauze and natural
silk, and cashmere coats.

Puro Diseño. *See p153.*

Mariano Toledo

*Armenia 1564, entre Honduras y Gorriti, Palermo
Viejo (4371 5327/www.mtoledo.com.ar). Bus 15, 55,
151, 168.* **Open** 11am-8pm Mon-Thur; 11am-9pm
Fri, Sat. **Credit** AmEx, MC, V. **Map** p279 M5.
Opulent designs lie behind the oversized sliding
glass door at this Palermo boutique. The window
dressing and interior design are perhaps more
impressive than the clothes on offer, but a keen shopping eye may uncover some hidden treasure. Look
out for the waterfall 'wall'.

Nadine Zlotogora

*El Salvador 4638, entre Malabia y Armenia,
Palermo Viejo (4831 4203/www.sinfincreativos.com
/sites/nadine). Bus 15, 39, 55.* **Open** 11am-8pm
Mon-Sat. **Credit** AmEx, MC, V. **Map** p279 M5.
Zlotogora's idiosyncratic styling is an artful blend of
fantasy and romance. Her ethereal, other-worldly
clothes are distinctively feminine with satin, macrame
and embroidered pieces, each of which is individually dyed to ensure its uniqueness.

Pablo Ramírez

*Perú 587, entre Venezuela y Mexico, San Telmo
(4342 7154/www.pabloramirez.com.ar). Bus 12, 39,
102, 140.* **Open** 10.30am-7.30pm Mon-Fri; 10.30am-
3pm Sat. **No credit cards**. **Map** p279 E10.
The wunderkind of Argentinian design, thirty-something Ramírez has wowed top names like Isabella
Blow with his designs. Famous for his black and
white palette, the designer has been splashing out
on primary colours in his more recent collections.

Pesqueira

*Armenia 1493, y Gorriti, Palermo Viejo (4833
7218). Bus 15, 55, 151, 168.* **Open** 11am-8pm
Mon-Sat. **Credit** AmEx, MC, V. **Map** p279 M5.
One of the new generation of Argentinian designers,
Valeria Pesqueira's trademarks to date are animal
prints in modern cuts and fabrics. Plenty for the city-
chic shopper with a wild side.

Tramando, Martín Churba

*Rodríguez Peña 1973, entre Posadas y Alvear,
Recoleta (4811 0465/www.tramando.com). Bus
17, 61, 67, 92, 93.* **Open** 10.30am-6pm Mon-Sat.
Credit AmEx, DC, MC, V. **Map** p282 I11.
Martin Churba, a textile phenomenon, experiments
with printing and weaving techniques by applying
plastic and paint. The clothes are basic in shape but
extraordinarily well constructed. Homeware goods
like rugs, bowls and chairs are also manufactured
from this peculiar combination of pop and craft.

Trosman

*Patio Bullrich, Avenida del Libertador 750, entre
Montevideo y Libertad, Recoleta (4814 7411/
www.trosman.com). Bus 67, 92, 102, 130.*
Open 10am-9pm daily. **Credit** AmEx, DC, MC,
V. **Map** p282 I12.
Jessica Trosman (formerly half of the celebrated
Trosman-Churba label) is one of the international
queens of new Argentinian fashion. Her trademark

Eat, Drink, Shop

is elaborate collections using innovative materials like plastic and latex to create an edgy, chic look. **Other locations**: Armenia 1998, Palermo Viejo (4833 3058).

Varanasi

Libertad 1696, y Libertador, Recoleta (4815 4326/www.varanasi-online.com). Bus 17, 59, 93, 130. **Open** 10am-8pm Mon-Fri; 10am-6pm Sat. **Credit** AmEx, DC, MC, V. **Map** p282 I12.

Mario Buraglio and Víctor Delgrosso (who are both architects-turned-designers) combine sophistication and daring in equal measure, employing overlayered materials, experimental shapes and pairings of natural and synthetic fabrics. **Other locations**: El Salvador 4761, Palermo Viejo (4833 5147).

Mid-range

Adorhada Guillermina

El Salvador 4723, entre Armenia y Gurruchaga, Palermo Viejo (4833 2553). Bus 15, 57, 93, 161. **Open** 10am-8pm Mon-Sat; 2-7pm Sun. **Credit** AmEx, MC, V. **Map** p279 M5.

A lively and accessible range of everyday urban wear, with reasonably priced clobber for professionals and partygoers. **Other locations**: Arenales 1603, Recoleta (4814 4265).

Chocolate

Patio Bullrich, Avenida del Libertador 750, entre Montevideo y Libertad, Recoleta (4815 9530/www. chocolateonline.com.ar). Bus 102, 130. **Open** 10am-9pm daily. **Credit** AmEx, DC, MC, V. **Map** p282 I12.

A pioneer in local high street fashion with branches in the city's top shopping centres. Attracting discerning women shoppers since the 1980s, the chain has remained cool without feeling the necessity to open a branch in trendy Palermo Viejo. **Other locations**: Paseo Alcorta (5777 6544) and Alto Palermo (5777 8072) shopping centres.

Juana de Arco

El Salvador 4762, entre Armenia y Gurruchaga, Palermo Viejo (4833 1621/www.juanadearco.net). Bus 15, 39. **Open** 10.30am-8pm Mon-Fri. **Credit** AmEx, MC, V. **Map** p279 M5.

There's nothing conventional to be found at this homage to hippy and retro chic. Brash, bright and in your face, it's the kind of place you either love or loathe (the Japanese have given it the thumbs up and Juana de Arco now exports there). **Photo** *p161*.

Kosiuko

Avenida Santa Fe 1779, entre Callao y Rodríguez Peña, Recoleta (4815 2555/www.kosiuko.com.ar). Bus 37, 39, 152. **Open** 9.30am-8.30pm Mon-Sat. **Credit** AmEx, DC, MC, V. **Map** p282 I10.

The trailblazer for hipster jeans poses only one question – how low can you go? Bold, vivacious, figure-hugging clothes for aspiring pop stars. **Other locations**: throughout the city.

Lupe

El Salvador 4657, entre Armenia y Malabia, Palermo Viejo (4833 0730). Bus 15, 55, 151, 168. **Open** 11am-8pm Mon-Sat; 2-7pm Sun. **Credit** AmEx, DC, MC, V. **Map** p279 M5.

This expanded Palermo boutique is worth a peep for its casual designs at reasonable prices. In particular, check out the glitzy bling belts.

María Vazquez

Libertad 1632, entre Posadas y Libertador, Recoleta (4815 6333/www.mvzmariavazquez.com.ar). Bus 93, 130. **Open** 10am-8pm Mon-Fri; 10am-6pm Sat. **Credit** AmEx, DC, MC, V. **Map** p282 I12.

MV experiments with textures and colour, creating revealing and sexy clothes. Colombian superstar Shakira shops for her gold silk-screened jeans here. **Other locations**: throughout the city.

Mercer

El Salvador 4677, entre Malabia y Armenia, Palermo Viejo (4831 4891). Bus 15, 57, 110, 160. **Open** 11am-8pm Mon-Sat. **Credit** AmEx, MC, V. **Map** p275 M5.

The floor of this vast warehouse space is layered in rugs, eastern-style lanterns and fans hang from the roof and the changing rooms feature old cabinets filled with Oriental objects. In between the floral-painted pool table, drapes and furniture you'll find a varied selection of jeans, shirts and tops.

Ona Sáez

Avenida Santa Fe 1651, entre Montevideo y Rodríguez Peña, Recoleta (4813 2834/www.onasaez. com). Bus 10, 37, 39, 152. **Open** 10am-9pm Mon-Fri; 10am-8pm Sat. **Credit** AmEx, DC, MC, V. **Map** p282 I10.

A trendsetting, seductive and provocative clothing store for him and her, famed for its 'nice ass' jeans. Its creator, Santiago Sáez, also coordinates valuable local charitable schemes through the brand. **Other locations**: throughout the city.

Paula Cahen d'Anvers

Avenida Santa Fe 1651, entre Montevideo y Rodríguez Peña, Recoleta (4811 3176). Bus 10, 37, 39, 152. **Open** 10am-8pm Mon-Sat. **Credit** AmEx, DC, MC, V. **Map** p282 I10.

Vibrant colours, prints and oh-so-soft fabrics make this women's clothing line the closet favourite. The logo – an embroidered crown – is in high demand. **Other locations**: throughout the city.

Las Pepas

Avenida Santa Fe 1631, entre Montevideo y Rodríguez Peña, Recoleta (4811 7887/www.laspepas. com.ar). Bus 10, 37, 39, 152. **Open** 9.30am-9pm Mon-Fri; 9.30am-8pm Sat. **Credit** AmEx, DC, MC, V. **Map** p282 I10.

Vintage-inspired clothes fill this busy, on-the-button boutique. There are handbags, satchels and pointy shoes in bright colours, not to mention a kaleidoscope of leather jackets, coats and skirts. **Other locations**: Paseo Alcorta shopping centre (5777 6553).

Eat, Drink, Shop

KEY BISCAYNE

Rapsodia

Patio Bullrich, Avenida del Libertador 750, entre
Montevideo y Libertad, Recoleta (4814 7458/
www.rapsodia.com.ar). Bus 17, 67, 93, 130.
Open 10am-9pm daily. **Credit** AmEx, DC, MC,
V. **Map** p282 I12.
Model Sol Acuña and partner play with bright
colours to achieve a cowgirl-visits-the-crib look. The
jeans and denim jackets are current must-haves.
This highly successful chain now boasts two vintage stores selling old collections. **Photo** *p158.*
Other locations: Paseo Alcorta shopping centre
(4804 0084); El Salvador 4757, Palermo Viejo (4832
5363); Arguibel 2899, Las Cañitas (4772 7676).

Think Pink

Gurruchaga 1765, entre Costa Rica y El Salvador,
Palermo Viejo (4833 4499). Bus 15, 55, 151, 1
68. **Open** 10am-9pm Mon-Fri; 10am-8pm Sat.
Credit AmEx, DC, MC, V. **Map** p282 M5.
The girly girl's dream come true, Think Pink is
all about ruffles and ribbons.

Multi-brand boutiques

La Aurora

Honduras 4838, entre Armenia y Gurruchaga,
Palermo Viejo (4833 4965). Bus 39, 55. **Open**
11am-8pm Mon-Sat. **Credit** AmEx, DC, MC, V.
Map p279 M5.
Rubén Perlmutter has turned the front room of
his house into a multi-brand boutique, selling
Varanasi's conceptual designs, T-shirts from Ana
Fuchs and Dolores Elortondo and, of course, Birkin,
the casual line designed by Perlmutter himself.

Bendita Tu Eres

Thames 1555, entre Honduras y Gorriti, Palermo
Viejo (4834 6123). Bus 24, 55, 166. **Open** 11am-
8pm Mon-Sat. **Credit** AmEx, MC, V. **Map** p279 M5.
The name translates as 'you are blessed', which is how
you'll feel shopping here. The Agent Provocateur of
BA, Bendita's flirtatious collection of bras, knickers
and vests by local designer Florencia Rodrigo spells
sex, fun and all things naughty but nice.

Cat Ballou

Avenida Alvear 1702, y Rodríguez Peña, Recoleta
(4811 9792). Bus 17, 67, 92, 93, 130. **Open** 11am-
8pm Mon-Fri; 10.30am-4.30pm Sat. **Credit** AmEx,
MC, V. **Map** p282 I11.
Handcrafted objects and clothes at Cat Ballou go
together as if curated. Look for hand-painted stones
by the Argentinian sculptor Renata Shussheim, as
well as rugs, shawls and decorations.

Emme

Thames 1535, entre Gorriti y Honduras, Palermo
Viejo (4832 3037). Bus 34, 55. **Open** 10am-8pm
Mon-Sat. **Credit** AmEx, MC, V. **Map** p279 M5.
Pretty purchases from Emme are worth the pesos.
A pricey but gorgeous boutique oozing elegance and
femininity, this Palermo Viejo locale offers beaut-
ifully tailored tops, dresses and trousers.

Un Lugar en el Mundo

Defensa 891, entre Estados Unidos y Independencia,
San Telmo (4362 3836). Bus 20, 22, 24, 29.
Open 10.30am-8pm daily. **Credit** DC, MC, V.
Map p280 D10.
Independent on-the-rise Argentinian designers fill the
racks of this funky multi-brand San Telmo boutique.
With clothing and accessories for both sexes, items here
are original, colourful and cool. **Photo** *p169.*

Salsipuedes

Honduras 4814, entre Armenia y Gurruchaga,
Palermo Viejo (4831 8467). Bus 39, 55.
Open 10.30am-9pm Mon-Fri; 10.30am-8pm
Sat. **Credit** AmEx, MC, V. **Map** p279 M5.
Some 30 designers sell their unique designs at owner
Mariana's Salsipuedes (meaning 'get out if you can').
Look for Mariano Toledo's experiments with susp-
enders and Pablo Ramírez's denimwear.

SoldBA

Costa Rica 4645, entre Gurruchaga y Armenia,
Palermo Viejo (4833 7990/www.soldba.com). Bus 15,
39, 55. **Open** 3-8pm Mon, Tue; noon-8pm Wed-Fri;
noon-9pm Sat; 3-8pm Sun. **Credit** AmEx, V.
Map p279 M5.
Hip fashion and music *multiespacio* showcasing
more than 30 young and upcoming Argentinian
designers. Emerging talents like Pia Campiano and
Noscpick make it worth a look.

Tienda Tres

Armenia 1655, entre Honduras y El Salvador,
Palermo Viejo (4831 4193). Bus 5, 55, 151, 168.
Open 10.30am-8pm Mon-Sat; 1-6pm Sun. **Credit**
AmEx, MC, V. **Map** p279 M5.
Three local designers – Verónica Alfie, María
Lombardi and Flavia Martini – have grouped
together to display their work at this Palermo bou-
tique. Each has her own particular approach to fash-
ion, but the general emphasis is on floaty prints and
Argentinian cuts.

Street & clubwear

AY Not Dead

Soler 4193, y Julián Alvarez, Palermo Viejo (4866
4855/www.aynotdead.com.ar). Bus 36, 188. **Open**
11am-8.30pm Mon-Sat. **Credit** AmEx, DC, MC, V.
Map p282 L8.
A bright pink beacon of innovation, St Martin's
trained Angie Chevalier's first store is named in
homage to deceased Mafia boss Alfredo Yabrán.
Fusing religion, zebra prints and slogans from punk
and disco, designs are glamorous and trendsetting.

Cult

Gurruchaga 1776, entre Costa Rica y El Salvador,
Palermo Viejo (4833 3534/www.cultindustries.com).
Bus 34, 55, 93, 161. **Open** 11am-8pm daily.
Credit AmEx, DC, MC, V. **Map** p279 M5.
Attention all aspiring surfers: for the latest unique
designs in T-shirts, shorts and swimming trunks,
Cult is where it's at.

Eat, Drink, Shop

Galería Bond Street

*Avenida Santa Fe 1670, entre Montevideo y
Rodríguez Peña, Recoleta. Subte D, Callao/37, 39,
111, 152 bus.* **Open** 10am-10pm Mon-Sat. **Credit**
varies. **Map** p282 I10.

Underground teens (including punks, metal heads
and skaters) hone their look at this arcade; Galería
Bond Street is particularly great for fresh and funky
local T-shirt designs. If you smell burning flesh,
don't worry – needle artists are working hard drawing blood in the many tattoo parlours.

Galería Larreta

*Florida 971 or San Martín 954, entre Paraguay y
Marcelo T de Alvear, Retiro (4311 9112). Subte C,
San Martín/6, 26, 93, 130, 152 bus.* **Open** 8am-
8pm Mon-Fri; 8am-7pm Sat. **Credit** varies.
Map p281 F11.

This lively arcade is a mixed bag of collectibles (Te
Acordás Hermano), customised leatherwear from
Zoo (Units 12 and 13) and a constantly evolving roster of upcoming designers who have set up shop on
the second floor.

Red Store

*El Salvador 4801, y Gurruchaga, Palermo
Viejo (4833 4839). Bus 39, 55, 168.* **Open**
11am-8pm Mon-Sat. **Credit** AmEx, MC, V.
Map p279 M5.

At the Red Store you'll find mostly imported (and
therefore more expensive) street designs like Diesel
and Levi's (including the Engineered Jeans line) and,
occasionally, some groovy Italian watches. There's
also a good selection of the latest international trainers sold here – perfect for the super cool.

Colourful clothes at **Rapsodia**. *See p157.*

Menswear specialists

Balthazar

*Gorriti 5131, entre Thames y Uriarte, Palermo Viejo
(4834 6235). Bus 34, 55, 166.* **Open** 11am-8pm
Mon-Sat. **Credit** AmEX, MC, V. **Map** p279 M5.

Wise men should make the journey to this fun and
funky Palermo boutique. There's something here for
every mood and occasion, from classic dress shirts
to Day-Glo socks and accessories.

Bensimon

*Avenida Quintana 4924, y Ayacucho, Recoleta
(4807 5218/www.bensimon.com.ar). Bus 17, 101,
102.* **Open** 10am-8.30pm Mon-Sat. **Credit** AmEx,
DC, MC, V. **Map** p282 I11.

Putting together a great casual look, in bold colours
and soft cotton, Bensimon kits out staff at some of
the city's funkiest bars and restaurants. As a back-
handed tribute to its success, there are Bensimon
copies around.

Other locations: Paseo Alcorta, Galerías Pacífico,
Alto Palermo and Abasto shopping centres.

El Cid

*Gurruchaga 1732 entre El Salvador y Costa Rica,
Palermo Viejo (4832 3339/www.el-cid.com.ar). Bus
34, 55, 93, 161.* **Open** 10am-8.30pm Mon-Fri; 11am-
8.30pm Sat; noon-7pm Sun. **Credit** AmEx, DC, MC,
V. **Map** p279 M5.

Renowned local designer Nestor Goldberd combines
executive tailoring with hip and sophisticated accessories to achieve this classic collection. Browse
through top quality leather jackets and suits and
smart jeans and shirts.

Other locations: Reconquista 751, Microcentro
(4313-0610); Defensa 941, San Telmo (4300 6682).

Etiqueta Negra

*Dardo Rocha 1366, y Pringles, Martínez (4792
7373). Bus 60.* **Open** 10am-8pm Mon-Sat. **Credit**
AmEx, DC, MC, V.

After years of moving and shaking in BA's fashion
scene, Federico Alvarez Castillo opened this bold
and beautiful shop in the northern suburbs to sell
his super-chic but highly wearable menswear line.
It's also worth the trip to drool over his collection of
vintage sports cars and bikes parked in the store.

Other locations: Patio Bullrich shopping centre
(4814 7430).

Félix

*Gurruchaga 1670, entre El Salvador y Pasaje
Santa Rosa, Palermo Viejo (4832 2994/www.felixba.
com.ar). Bus 15, 39, 55.* **Open** 11am-8pm Mon-Sat;
2-7pm Sun. **Credit** AmEx, MC, V. **Map** p279 M5.

If you like Paul Smith and Pringle, you'll love Félix.
Details stand out but the price doesn't. Jeans, shirts,
boxers, wallets, belts and scarves – the stock is all
cool. To deck your kids out in the same look, pop
round the corner to the children's branch at El
Salvador 4742 (4833 3313).

Other locations: Libertad 1627, Recoleta
(4815 4087).

Packing a poncho

Strutting through designer boutiques on a Palermo Viejo spree, you'd be forgiven for forgetting you're in Latin America. But not everything on the BA retail run is a homage to cutting edge design and cool. You can also find shops dedicated to indigenous craftsmanship, authentic traditions and regional raw materials. Geared towards foreign visitors, these outlets sell products notable for their clean lines and vibrant colours, and with a 'one-of-a-kind' quality that is the antithesis of conveyor-belt homogeneity. So if you can't get out of the city to experience the spirit and diversity of rural Argentina, let rural Argentina come to you.

If you missed out on a trip to Misiones (home to the Iguazú Falls), the next best thing is a visit to **Del Monte** (Uriarte 1440, Palermo Viejo, 4881 6337). Run by two childhood friends, this is a tribute to the lush woodland and rich culture of their home province. A collection dominated by neutral shades and simple lines make this a refreshing find. Unusual leather placemats, corkscrews and sinkingly soft sheepskin rugs are all sourced from individual craftspeople and artists from this northern region.

Pasión Argentina (Emilio Ravignani 1780, 4777 7750, www.pasion-argentina.com.ar) was one of the first fair-trade companies in Argentina. Launched after training indigenous women from the north of Argentina in ethical, small scale manufacturing, it now works with more than 50 families. The result is stylish, ethnic products that also go some way towards salving your First World conscience after the commercial high has worn off. Look out for their sling-style leather bags, over-the-shoulder leather purses, and wooden tea caddies with weavings built into the lids.

If it's clothing you're looking for, just off Plazoleta Cortázar you'll find **Nann** (Serrano 1523, 4831 8835, www.nannargentina.com). This is the place to buy a poncho that you won't push to the back of your wardrobe once you get home. Owner Federico Nestrojil spent three months in Salta, Jujuy and Catamarca provinces looking for local craftsmen to work with. He's also spent time in London and New York – and it shows in the designs. This is native art that works at preserving Argentinian culture while adapting it for export.

Another essential stop-off is **Arte Etnico Argentino** (El Salvador 4600, 4833 6661, www.arteetnicoargentino.com), even if only for the window display. Products hail from the north-western province of Santiago del Estero and include rugs in brilliant fuchsias, bloody reds, screaming greens and deep browns, and chairs made of leather and wood.

Tierra Adentro (Thames 1900, 4773 9084, www.tierraadentro.info) is a celebration of Argentinian indigenous culture. Textiles, silver and coral jewellery, pottery and clothing are sourced from different locations around the country. In the process care is taken to respect ancient traditions and practices, while working to current trends and styles.

Eat, Drink, Shop

Giesso

Avenida Santa Fe 1557, entre Montevideo y Paraná, Recoleta (4811 3717). Subte D, Callao/39, 132, 152 bus. **Open** 9am-8pm Mon-Fri; 10am-8pm Sat. **Credit** AmEx, DC, MC, V. **Map** p282 I10.
Classic tailoring and more than 80 years in the business combine to make this Argentinian brand credible to executives of all ages.

Hermanos Estebecorena

El Salvador 5960, entre Ravignani y Arévalo, Palermo Viejo (4772 2145/www.hermanos estebecorena.com). **Open** 11am-9pm Mon-Sat. **Credit** AmEx, DC, MC, V. **Map** p279 O5.
These brothers are at the cutting edge of style, applying all the principles of industrial design to hip, comfy and functional items, from underwear and socks to all-weather coats. Their original range includes stylish shoes, shirts and trousers too. **Other locations:** Paseo Alcorta shopping centre.

Il Rêve

Gurruchaga 1867, entre Nicaragua y Costa Rica (4834 6432). Bus 34, 55, 93, 161. **Open** 11am-8pm Mon-Sat; 2-7pm Sun. **Credit** AmEx, MC, V. **Map** p279 M5.
Selling fresh, neo-retro clothes and accessories, Il Rêve has everything a guy needs to put together a casual look with a funky edge.

Key Biscayne

Armenia 1735, entre Costa Rica y El Salvador, Palermo Viejo (4833 2104/www.key-biscayne. com.ar). Bus 15, 110, 141, 160. **Open** 11am-10pm Mon-Sun. **Credit** AmEx, MC, V. **Map** p279 M5.
From the 'Philosophy' pop-up on their website to the ornamental interior patio at their Armenia street branch, it's clear that this growing Argentinian menswear chain is aimed squarely at the anti-corporate metrosexual. Hooded cardigans, tank tops and polos come in autumnal greys and browns, while the

LEATHER WOMENSWEAR

SHOES

BAGS

TROUSERS

SKIRTS

Las Peras

FASHION BOUTIQUE

UNICENTER
LOCAL 1065

PASEO ALCORTA
LOCAL 1044 / 45

ALTO PALERMO
LOCAL 0001

AV. SANTA FE 1631
BUENOS AIRES
ARGENTINA

T-shirts and sleeveless vests are bright and beach ready. For the urban *gaucho* there's a wide range of stylish, reasonably priced leather jackets. **Other locations**: Paseo Alcorta (4807 5282) and Alto Palermo (5777 8007) shopping centres.

Old Bridge
Gurruchaga 1715, entre El Salvador y Costa Rica, Palermo Viejo (4833 0327/www.oldbridge.com.ar). **Bus** 15, 55, 151, 168. **Open** 11am-8pm Mon-Sat. **Credit** AmEx, MC, V. **Map** p279 M5.
The clothes are probably the least interesting thing about this gallery-like shop. Take a peek, even if you've no interest in fun men's casualwear. Maps form a floor-to-ceiling wallpaper, and the outside space is decorated with hanging geraniums in shocking pinks and oranges.
Other locations: Abasto shopping centre.

Riccardi
Gurruchaga 1672, entre El Salvador y Costa Rica, Palermo Viejo (4833 7649). **Bus** 15, 55, 151, 168. **Open** 11am-8.30pm Mon-Sat. **Credit** AmEx, DC, MC, V. **Map** p279 M5.
A cut above the other mid-range men's boutiques in the area, this place stands out with its flashy but cool hand-painted tailored shirts by artist Federico Violante – perfect for wild nights out on the town and busting moves in one of BA's many clubs. The look here is otherwise quite classic, with linen shirts and soft sweaters in an array of colours.

Vintage & used clothing

Used clothes and accessories used to be for the lower ranks, but now there's a consignment of second-hand stores in every barrio. Keep your eyes peeled for vintage Italian handbags. **Juan Pérez** at Marcelo T de Alvear 1441 (4815 8442) is a great option if you're heading out and have forgotten to pack elegant shoes. Here you'll find perfect save-my-night heels.

Galería 5ta Avenida
Avenida Santa Fe 1270, entre Libertad y Talcahuano, Recoleta (4816 0451/www.galeria5ta avenida.com.ar). **Bus** 10, 39, 59, 152. **Open** 10am-9pm Mon-Sat. **Credit** varies. **Map** p281 H11.
This arcade is lined with used clothing shops and tattoo parlours, and boasts bargains galore for the the discerning shopper. For vintage eyewear, visit Hernán Vázquez at Optica Nahuel (4811 2837).

Children & maternity

Carolina Form
Ground Floor, Cabello 3650, entre Scalabrini Ortiz y Ugarteche, Palermo (4806 0935). **Bus** 10, 37, 64, 160. **Open** 11am-8pm Mon-Fri; 10am-1.30pm Sat. **Credit** AmEx, DC, MC, V. **Map** p282 L10.
Specialising in maternity wear, this slick Palermo boutique makes pregnancy look glamorous with a range of casual and evening wear for mums-to-be.

Cheeky
Avenida Santa Fe 1499, y Paraná, Recoleta (4813 1875/www.cheeky.com.ar). **Bus** 10, 59, 102, 152. **Open** 9am-8pm Mon-Sat. **Credit** AmEx, DC, MC, V **Map** p282 I10.
One of Argentina's most successful – and lovable – purveyors of adorable babies' and kiddies' wear.

Owoko
El Salvador 4694, y Thames, Palermo Viejo (4831 1259/www.owoko.com.ar). **Bus** 15, 57, 151, 168. **Open** 11am-8pm Mon-Sat; 3-7pm Sun. **Credit** AmEx, MC, V. **Map** p279 M5.
This bright and smiley kids' emporium makes clothes shopping an interactive experience. With every purchase you get a free story.

Fashion accessories

Abunda
Thames 1481 entre Gorriti y Cabrera, Palermo Viejo (4833 0076). **Bus** 15, 151, 168. **Open** 1.30-7.30pm Mon-Fri. **Credit** AmEx, MC, V. **Map** p279 M5.
A group of local designers came together to create this quirky box of treasures. Have fun browsing through the hand-made knick-knacks and T-shirts.

Carla Disí
Gorriti 4660, entre Malabia y Scalabrini Ortiz, Palermo Viejo (4832 1655/www.carladisi.com.ar). **Bus** 15, 55, 151, 168. **Open** 11am-8pm Mon-Sat. **Credit** AmEx, DC, MC, V. **Map** p279 M5.
For fans of vintage eyewear, this is a must. Carla's completely original collection of frames from the 1960s, '70s and '80s was sourced by her father, an optician. French and Italian styles dominate, but there are shades for all tastes, including sporty Spaldings, classic Catseyes and luminous Retro.

Juana de Arco. *See p155.*

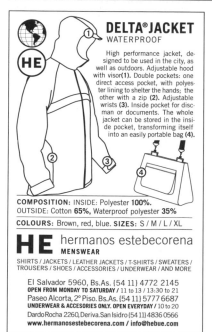
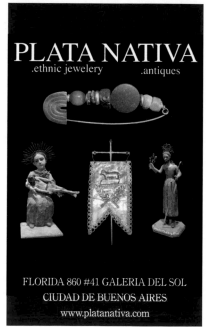

Condimentos

*Honduras 4874, entre Armenia y Gurruchaga,
Palermo Viejo (4833 9403). Bus 39, 55.*
Open 10.30am-9pm Mon-Fri; 10.30am-8pm
Sat. **Credit** AmEx, MC, V. **Map** p279 M5.
Designers Mariana Szwarc and Luna Garzon opened
this boutique in a converted garage. Well worth a
browse, Condimentos sells a come-hither range of
handcrafted and designer acces-sories. Essential
items to look out for include Mishal Katz's retro
bags, or those printed with Argentinian maps, and
the silver jewellery from Mineralia.

Etnia

*El Salvador 4792, entre Armenia y Gurruchaga,
Palermo Viejo (4831 9003/www.etniaonline.com.ar).
Bus 15. 55. 151, 168.* **Open** 11.30am-7.30pm Mon-
Sat. **Credit** AmEx, MC, V. **Map** p279 M5.
A girl can never have enough accessories, or at least
that's the kind of thinking that tends to take over as
soon as you step inside Etnia. In this girlie treasure
trove of jewellery, scarves and bags, you're sure to
find something to kick start your wardrobe into the
new season. The chunky gemstone earrings and
necklaces are particularly stunning.
Other locations: Abasto, Alto Palermo,
Galerias Pacifico and Paseo Alcorta shopping
centres.

Fahoma

*Libertad 1169, entre Santa Fe y Arenales, Recoleta
(4813 5103). Bus 10, 39, 102, 152.* **Open** 10am-
8pm Mon-Fri; 10am-1.30pm Sat. **Credit** AmEx, DC,
MC, V. **Map** p281 H11.
Women who know how to accessorise shop for their
striking jewellery and elegant handbags in this
Recoleta store. The shop is nearly always crowded,
in large part thanks to designer Julio Toledo's exclusive line of handbags.

Fitico

*5th Floor, Avenida Cabildo 2911, entre Congreso y
Quesada, Belgrano (4703 4316/www.fitico.com.ar).
Bus 59, 151, 152, 168.* **Open** 10am-6pm Mon-Fri.
No credit cards.
If you're on the hunt for novelty bags with a nation-
alistic theme, Fitico should be your first port of call.
The most striking is the Obelisk style leather *mochi-
la* (backpack) lined in the colours of the Argentinian
flag. You can design your own bag, or choose from
all sorts of off-the-peg sacks, including the envelope,
loo roll and telephone varieties.

Kristobelga

*Gurruchaga 1677, entre El Salvador y Honduras,
Palermo Viejo (4831 6677). Bus 15, 55, 140,
151, 168.* **Open** 11am-8pm Mon-Sat; 4-7pm Sun.
Map p279 M5.
Worth a look, if only for their effortlessly cool range
of famed Havaiana flip-flops. These Brazilian fashion
statements will cost you around AR$25, depending
on the size and style.

Las Juanitas

*Honduras 5120, entre Thames y Uriarte, Palermo
Viejo (4383 6772). Bus 34, 55, 166.* **Open** 11.30am-
8pm Mon-Sat. **Credit** AmEx, MC, V. **Map** p279 M5.
Calling all rockstars, real and wannabe – find the
perfect pair of shades here to help you dodge imagined paparazzi on the streets of Buenos Aires.
Continuing the rock 'n' roll theme, there's also an
extensive selection of silk-screened tops embossed
with the likes of Jimi Hendrix and James Brown to
get you 'feeling the funk'.

La Mercería

*Armenia 1609, y Honduras, Palermo Viejo (4831
8558). Bus 15, 57, 110, 160.* **Open** 9am-8pm Mon-
Fri; 9am-8.30pm Sat; 1-8pm Sun. **Credit** AmEx, MC,
V. **Map** p279 M5.

Sabater Hermanos. *See p153.*

Buttons and beads and all things nice can be found at this ultimate destination for retro chic accessories. Pretty sewing tidbits sit alongside fake fur scarves, felt hats, organza wraps and diamante brooches.

Jewellery

Celedonio Lohidoy

Unit 10, Silvio Ruggieri 2755, entre Cerviño y Cabello, Palermo (4803 7292/www.celedonio.net). Bus 37, 93, 110. **Open** 2-7pm daily. **No credit cards. Map** p282 L10.
Selling beautiful bijoux jewellery to the serious buyer (Sarah Jessica Parker included), Celedonio Lohidoy has outlets worldwide, most notably at Saks Fifth Avenue. To visit the Argentinian workshop you'll need to telephone ahead for an appointment. It's worth the trouble.

Jona

By appointment only (4432 8581/www.jona. omadesign.com).
Jona jewellery, designed by Cecilia Rosemberg, is made from all manner of weird and wonderful materials, including antique buttons, shells, crystal from old chandeliers and even fish scales. The results are delightfully unique pieces, delicate and decidedly different. Call for viewing appointments; Rosemberg will meet you at your hotel or take you to her Palermo showroom at Pasaje Lazo 3134.

Stylish leather at **Prüne**. *See p165.*

María Medici

Niceto Vega 4619, entre Scalabrini Ortiz y Malabia, Palermo Viejo (4773 2283/www.mariamedici .com.ar). Bus 15, 55, 151, 168. **Open** 11am-8pm Mon-Fri; 11am-3pm Sat. **No credit cards. Map** p279 M4.
Maria Medici's showroom brings a touch of Madrid style to this quiet corner of Palermo Viejo. Architect and jewellery designer Medici, who learned her craft in Spain, mixes a range of materials with her silver creations, including cow hide, semi-precious stones and coloured sand. The result is edgy, contemporary jewellery different to anything else in the city.

Metalistería

Borges 2021, entre Guatemala y Soler, Palermo Viejo (4833 7877/www.metalisteria.com.ar). Bus 34, 55, 93. **Open** 10.30am-1pm; 3-8.30pm Mon-Sat. **Credit** AmEx, MC, V. **Map** p279 M6.
Contemporary jewellery in unconventional designs, incorporating flower petals, mesh, leather and paper for a unique way to accessorise.

Nana Lou

Báez 283, entre Arévalo y Arguibel, Las Cañitas (4772 7826/www.nanalou.com.ar). Bus 10, 36, 160. **Open** noon-1am daily. **Credit** AmEx, DC, MC, V. **Map** p283 O9.
If you're heading for a late one in Las Cañitas, pop in to Nana Lou for a shop between courses. Nestled in between bustling bars and restaurants, this funky jewellery store stays open late.

Plata Nativa

Unit 41, Galería del Sol, Florida 860, entre Córdoba y Paraguay, Retiro (4312 1398/www.plata nativa.com). Subte C, San Martín/6, 26, 93, 132, 152 bus. **Open** 10am-7.30pm Mon-Fri; 10am-2pm Sat. **Credit** AmEx, MC, V. **Map** p281 G11.
This small, hidden gallery of indigenous and Latin American art also sells antique silver and contemporary ethnic accessories. The necklaces woven in agate and turquoise, inspired by Mapuche jewellery, are in a class of their own.

Leather goods

Bag hags will be thrilled to know that thanks to Argentina's cheap and plentiful leather, bags, like shoes, are sold nearly everywhere. On and around Florida street has become the main leather zone, though you'll have to contend with an overly zealous sales approach. Or check out Murillo street in Villa Crespo, where the leather wholesalers are gathered.

Blaqué

Galerías Pacífico, Florida 737, entre Viamonte y Córdoba, Microcentro (5555 5215/www.blaque. com.ar). Bus 28, 50, 130, 132, 152. **Open** 9am-8.30pm Mon-Fri; 10am-8pm Sat; 11am-7.30pm Sun. **Credit** AmEx, DC, MC, V. **Map** p281 G11.
Blaqué stocks wallets, bags, shoes and luggage in bold shapes with oversized silver buckles. Colour is

the key with most styles available in brown, camel, black, grey, green, and red. Ask for the DYMS range of overnight and weekend bags in soft dark brown, cherry red, camel and chocolate brown leathers. **Other locations**: Avenida Santa Fe 1587 (4811 8808) and Avenida Santa Fe 2390 (4827 3922).

Casa López

Marcelo T de Alvear 640 and 658, entre Florida y Maipú, Retiro (4311 3044/www.casalopez.com.ar). Subte C, San Martín/7, 10, 17, 152 bus. **Open** 9am-8pm Mon-Fri; 9.30am-7pm Sat; 11am-6pm Sun. **Credit** AmEx, DC, MC, V. **Map** p281 G11.
Old-lady leather at first glance, but look closer: you'll find pocketbooks, wallets, bags and briefcases designed with decadence and a modern edge. **Other locations**: Galerías Pacífico (5555 5241) and Patio Bullrich (4814 7477) shopping centres.

Humawaca

El Salvador 4692, y Armenia, Palermo Viejo (4832 2662/www.humawaca.com). Bus 15, 55, 151, 168. **Open** 11am-8pm Mon-Sat. **Credit** AmEx, DC, V. **Map** p279 M5.
Another architect who has made the logical transition to fashion design, Ingrid Gudman works principally with leather to produce original bags, purses and wallets. Her trademark is multi-use items, like her reversible tote and her divisible bag. The Argentinian-designed BKF 'butterfly chair' is the inspiration for her BKP backpack. The perfect place to pick up a gift that uses local products and reflects the city's latest wave of creativity.

Peter Kent

Avenida Alvear 1820, entre Callao y Ayacucho, Recoleta (4920 7624/www.peterkent.com.ar). Bus 17, 67, 93, 124, 130. **Open** 10am-8pm Mon-Fri; 9am-2pm Sat. **Credit** AmEx, DC, MC, V. **Map** p282 I14.
Wealthy *porteños* love this luxury leather store – and you can see why. Outstanding quality, with classics and modern styles that wouldn't look out of place in Harvey Nicks or Saks Fifth Avenue. **Other locations**: Paseo Alcorta shopping centre.

Prüne

Florida 961, entre Marcelo T de Alvear y Paraguay, Retiro (4893 2634/www.prune.com.ar). Subte C, San Martín/7, 10, 17, 152 bus. **Open** 10am-8.30pm Mon-Fri; 10am-8pm Sat; 11am-6.30pm Sun. **Credit** AmEx, DC, MC, V. **Map** p281 G11.
Formerly a wholesaler, Prüne has upped its game to unleash numerous styles and colours on the public. Design, colours and options are excellent and the prices are very reasonable. **Photo** *p164*.

Santesteban

Galería Promenade, Avenida Alvear 1883, entre Callao y Ayacucho, Recoleta (4800 1174). Bus 17, 67, 92, 93. **Open** 10am-8pm Mon-Sat. **Credit** AmEx, DC, MC, V. **Map** p282 I11.
Exquisitely sculptured bags and boots from designer Verónica Santesteban. Look for handbags decorated with polished cowhorn, or Louis XV-style shoes bordered with Czech glass.

Sybil Vane

Galerías Pacífico, Florida 737, entre Viamonte y Córdoba, Microcentro (4313 0239/www.sibylvane. com). Bus 50, 130, 132, 152. **Open** 10am-9pm Mon-Fri. **Credit** AmEx, DC, MC, V. **Map** p281 G11.
Bags, boots and more bags abound at this popular store. Leather products for all occasions, whether professional or party oriented. **Other locations**: Paseo Alcorta (5777 6603), Patio Bullrich (4814 7094) and Alto Palermo (5777 8017) shopping centres.

Uma

Honduras 5225, entre Uriarte y Godoy Cruz, Palermo Viejo (4832 2122/www.umacuero.com). Bus 39, 55. **Open** 11am-8pm Mon-Sat. **Credit** AmEx, DC, MC, V. **Map** p279 M5.
Uma is where to head for the youngest and freshest of looks in leather – from clothes to shoes and bags – in a striking range of colours, styles and finishes. Check out the cool little dresses for cutting a dash in the office, as seen in *Vogue*. **Other locations**: throughout the city.

Lingerie & swimwear

In shopping malls, look for **Caro Cuore** or visit **Juana de Arco** (*see p155*) for fun panties.

Amor Latino

Gorriti 4925, entre Serrano y Gurruchaga, Palermo Viejo (4831 6787/www.amor-latino.com.ar). Bus 39, 55. **Open** 11am-8pm Mon-Sat. **Credit** AmEx, MC, V **Map** p279 M5.
In Amor Latino, the matching undies and bras, and lacy nighties on offer are ultra sexy and feminine, if slightly impractical. Rummage through the goldfish bowls packed full of multicoloured g-strings to find something a little bit different.

Santillan

Gurruchaga 1638, entre El Salvador y Honduras, Palermo Viejo (4831 9988/www.santillanbsas.com). Bus 15, 55, 168. **Open** 11am-8pm Mon-Fri. **Credit** AmEx, MC, V. **Map** p279 M5.
A cute boutique offering unique, handcrafted swim suits at affordable prices and an elegant range of underwear to boot.

Shoes

If you need shoe repairs, **Fix Shoe** in Recoleta (Vicente López 1668, 4811 0226) can get most jobs finished in a day.

De María

Libertad 1655, entre Libertador y Posadas, Recoleta (4815 5001). Bus 62, 67, 92, 130. **Open** 10am-9pm Mon-Sat. **Credit** AmEx, DC, MC, V. **Map** p282 I12.
De María's hand-made shoes are exquisitely crafted and very affordable. The slick styles reflect a 1920s influence, but in the soul there's pure raunch and rock 'n' roll. Ring the bell to be let into the minimalist yet distinctly luxurious showroom.

Mishka.

Divia

El Salvador 6033, y Arevalo, Palermo Viejo (4777 6371/www.diviashoes.com). Bus 39, 93, 111, 161. **Open** 11am-8pm Mon-Sat. **Credit** AmEx, DC, MC, V. **Map** p279 O5.

This Palermo boutique lives up to its promise to provide 'sophisticated, exotic and delicate shoes'. It's the place to find your perfect pair of flirty heels, embellished with rhinestones, glitter or ankle charms to add sparkle to your step.

Josefina Ferroni

Armenia 1471, entre Gorriti y Cabrera, Palermo Viejo (4831 4033). Bus 39, 55, 106, 109. **Open** 3-8pm Mon; 11am-8pm Tue-Sat. **Credit** AmEx, DC, MC, V. **Map** p279 M5.

Ferroni's immaculately handcrafted range of boots makes her the queen of stylish footwear; each pair is extraordinary. The handbags and belts are also startlingly fresh and fashionable.

Mandarine

Honduras 4940, entre Borges y Gurruchaga, Palermo Viejo (4833 0094). Bus 39, 55, 151, 168. **Open** 10.30am-8pm Mon-Sat. **No credit cards.** **Map** p279 M5.

This small Palermo Viejo shop has a fine range of classic women's shoes, alongside others that reflect some of the current Argentinian footwear trends. Sweet details and great value.

Other locations: Armenia 1686, Palermo Viejo (4832 4862).

Mishka

El Salvador 4673, entre Armenia y Malabia, Palermo Viejo (4833 6566). Bus 39, 55. **Open** 11am-8.30pm daily. **Credit** AmEx, DC, MC, V. **Map** p279 M5.

Buenos Aires' best for shoes, Mishka can't be beaten for style or quality. The collection is small and chiefly designed for dainty feet, but it's happy days if you find your fit because these shoes are a guarantee of serious wow factor. Sophisticated lines and universally excellent finishing.

Paruolo

Alto Palermo, Avenida Santa Fe 3253, entre Coronel Díaz y Bulnes, Palermo (4551 1100) Subte D, Bulnes/12, 39, 152 bus. **Open** 10am-10pm daily. **Credit** AmEx, DC, MC, V. **Map** p282 K9.

If you're a fan of Sarah Jessica Parker, put Paruolo on your Buenos Aires 'must shop' list. From 'pointies' to round-toes, flats to wedges, this popular store is hard to beat for funky designs and a sexy, styled look. Argentinian designers are slowly moving away from black and neutral leathers, and Paruolo captures the latest trend for bold colours, using gold, bronze, and silver.

Ricky Sarkany

Paseo Alcorta, Salguero 3172, y Figueroa Alcorta, Palermo (4781 5629/www.rickysarkany.com). Bus 67, 102. **Open** 10am-10pm daily. **Credit** AmEx, DC, MC, V. **Map** p282 L11.

Glitz and glamour are all the rage at the busy store of headline-making local designer Ricky Sarkany. Now with outlets in the US and Spain, the BA original is the best place to buy a pair of Ricky's heels without paying international prices.

Other locations: Patio Bullrich shopping centre.

Food & drink

Bakeries, delis & health food

You will find *panaderías* (bakeries) on every high street, selling sandwiches, freshly baked bread, *facturas* (sweet pastries) and cakes of all shapes and sizes (*porteños* are notoriously sweet-toothed). As Argentinian regional produce grows in popularity, delis are becoming more common too. Two established names, with good selections of cold meats (*fiambres*) and cheeses and many locations, are **La Casa del Queso** at Corrientes 3587, Abasto (4862 4794) and **Al Queso, Queso** at Uruguay 1276, Recoleta (4811 7113).

Markets

All the fun of the *feria*

Even shopaphobes prone to running full force from your average high street locale can be persuaded to dabble in the experience if it involves open-air stalls under a blue BA sky. Luckily for them, the city has plenty of markets – flea and otherwise – selling local crafts and vintage finds, that double as hippy hangouts street parties.

The markets mentioned below are the best known in Buenos Aires, though you'll find stalls and stands of one kind or another in most of the city's squares and parks, like the weekend fair at **Plazoleta Cortázar** in Palermo Viejo and the **Cabildo Patio Feria** near Plaza de Mayo. Admission is usually free.

One of the oldest, both in terms of years and wares, is the **Feria San Pedro Telmo**, held on and around San Telmo's Plaza Dorrego every Sunday afternoon. Around 270 stalls groan with antique dolls, soda siphons, jewellery, tango memorabilia, toys and other collectibles. Something of the soul of old Buenos Aires endures here – in the lyrical wheeze of the *bandoneones* (the native button accordion), the shatterproof concentration of the over-rouged tango demonstrators and in the babble of different languages.

As a sort of side-show to the Sunday San Telmo event, the **Feria de la Baulera**, just a short walk up Defensa street, is housed within the historic Casa de la Moneda. It's one of BA's best weekend markets for vintage clothes, antique jewellery and accessories.

If you prefer hoedowns to heirlooms, you may be happier at BA's other great Sunday jamboree, the **Feria de Mataderos**. At this rural-style fete located in the far west of the

city, *gauchos* show off their skills with guitars and horses and day trippers indulge in country food and browse through the predominantly *gaucho*-themed flea market. Folk bands perform on a small central stage and locals join in the *chacareras* country dances.

For a little more arts and crafts, and plenty of youngsters lolling on the verges, **Feria Plaza Francia** is the best bet on a weekend afternoon. Handbags, handcrafted kitchen utensils, home-made jewellery, *mate* gourds, kaftans and plenty of tat are on sale at this two-day fair, also known as Feria Plaza Alvear. It's nestled beside the Recoleta Cemetary and the rolling green hills around it abound with *mate*-sipping *porteños* listening to live guitar players and watching Capoeirha demos.

Those who just enjoy ferreting through heaps of unsorted curios should visit the **Mercado de las Pulgas** (Spanish for 'flea market'). This chaotic warehouse is crammed full of second-hand furniture, junk and antiques. You'll find chandeliers and retro lamps, oversized glass jars, tin tea caddies, crystal cast-iron baths and old weighing scales. The older airline-hanger-scale building is slowly being replaced by a newer, more ordered building next door. Fingers crossed, it won't lose some of its charm.

Feria de la Baulera
Defensa 630, y México, San Telmo. Bus 24, 28, 86. **Open** 11am-8pm Sat, Sun. **Admission** AR$1. **No credit cards. Map** p281 E10.

Feria de Mataderos
Lisandro de la Torre, y Avenida de Los Corrales, Mataderos. Bus 55, 80, 92, 126. **Open** *Jan-Mar* 6pm-midnight Sat. *Apr-Dec* 11am-7pm Sun. **No credit cards.**

El Mercado de las Pulgas
Niceto Vega, y Dorrego, Palermo Viejo (no phone). Bus 140, 161, 168. **Open** 10am-5pm daily. **No credit cards. Map** p281 O4.

Feria Plaza Francia
Plaza Francia and Plaza Alvear, Avenida del Libertador y Pueyrredón, Recoleta. Bus 17, 110. **Open** 9am-7pm Sat, Sun. **No credit cards. Map** p282 J11.

Feria San Pedro Telmo
Plaza Dorrego, San Telmo. Bus 9, 10, 29, 195. **Open** 10am-5pm Sun. **No credit cards. Map** p280 D9.

Taura

*Republica Arabe de Siria 3073, entre Gutierrez y
Cabello, Palermo (4804 2080/www.taura.info).
Subte D, Plaza Italia/10, 59, 160, 188, 194 bus.*
Open 9am-8.30pm Mon-Sat. **Credit** AmEx, MC, V.
Map p283 M10.

This upmarket deli and butcher, created in 2003, is
beautifully designed and cheaper than many supermarkets. You can order free-range meats straight
from the farm with 48 hours' notice.

Valenti Especialidades

*Patio Bullrich, Avenida del Libertador 750, entre
Montevideo y Libertad, Recoleta (4815 3090/3080).
Bus 67, 92, 93, 130.* **Open** 10am-9pm daily.
Credit AmEx, DC, MC, V. **Map** p282 I12.

The best-quality cold cuts and cheeses from the
Valenti family: salmon from Scotland, true Greek
feta and Spanish *jamón ibérico de bellota*. It's a plea-
sure to shop at this top-notch deli or succumb to their
delicious sandwiches on homemade bread.
Other locations: Soldado de la Independencia 1185,
Belgrano (4775 2711); Vuelta de Obligado 1820,
Belgrano (4783 1933).

Speciality

Look out for *alfajores – dulce de leche* between
two cookies, dipped in chocolate. **Havanna** at
Avenida Santa Fe 3148, Barrio Norte (4822
1482) is a famous purveyor, with shops and
coffee bars across town.

Funky **Un Lugar en el Mundo**. *See p157.*

Dos Escudos

*Montevideo 1690, entre Quintana y Guido, Recoleta
(4812 2517/www.dosescudos.com.ar). Bus 17, 102.*
Open 7am-9pm daily. **Credit** AmEx, MC, V.
Map p282 I11.

If you want to make an impression when invited to
someone's house, buy a cake from Dos Escudos, an
institution among old-school patisseries.
Other locations: Juncal 905, Retiro (4327 0135); Las
Heras 3014, Recoleta (4805 4329).

El Gato Negro

*Avenida Corrientes 1669, entre Rodríguez Peña
y Montevideo, Tribunales (4374 1730). Subte B,
Callao/12, 24, 37, 60 bus.* **Open** 9am-11pm Mon-Fri;
9am-1am Sat; 3-11pm Sun. **Credit** AmEx, MC, V.
Map p281 G9.

A favourite of any cook keen on flavourings, the top
quality selection of herbs, spices and aromatic
seeds here is unsurpassed in the city. The best way
to appreciate the ambience is by taking tea at the
in-house café. The building's original 1928 archi-tec-
ture has resulted in El Gato Negro being awarded
protected heritage site status.

Tikal Chocolates

*Honduras 4890, entre Gurruchaga y Armenia,
Palermo Viejo (4831 2242/www.chocolatestikal.com).
Bus 39, 55.* **Open** 9am-9pm Mon-Sat. **Credit** AmEx,
DC, MC, V. **Map** p279 M5.

This lovely chocolate shop uses Venezuelan cacao.
The chocolate bonbons are faintingly delectable and
you can eat in or take them away.

Wine & spirits

La Brigada Cava

*Bolívar 1008, entre Carlos Calvo y Humberto 1º, San
Telmo (4362 2943/www.labrigada.com). Bus 24, 28,
29, 86.* **Open** 9.30am-1.30pm, 4.30-9pm daily.
Credit AmEx, MC, V. **Map** p280 D9.

With 32,000 bottles to choose from, La Cava, the new
drinks-focused branch of the wonderful La Brigada
steakhouse chain (*see p115*), stocks all the best
Argentinian wines, with world-renowned Angelica
Zapatas alongside the cheaper Weinert range.

Grand Cru

*Avenida Alvear 1718, entre Callao y Rodríguez Peña,
Recoleta (4816 3975/www.grandcru.com.ar). Bus 17,
67, 92, 93, 130.* **Open** 10am-8pm Mon-Fri; 10am-
6pm Sat. **Credit** AmEx, MC, V. **Map** p282 I11.

Sophisticated wine shop with an incredible cellar
harbouring some of the world's finest wines. Guaranteed to bring on an attack of oenophilia.

Parras

*Local 22 y 23, Galería Alvear, Avenida Alvear 1777,
entre Callao y Rodríguez Peña, Recoleta (4814 0011/
www.parraswines.com). Bus 17, 59, 67, 102.*
Open 10am-9pm Mon-Fri; 10am-6pm Sat.
No credit cards. Map p282 I11.

Gustavo, Parras's chatty owner, loves a Merlot as
much as Miles from hit wine movie *Sideways* hates

one. 'If only he could have tried Argentina's,' he enthuses. Like everything on sale here, the wines and champagnes are intentionally exclusive but, unlike other wine shops, Parras lets you taste absolutely anything on offer. Recommended.

Terroir
Buschiazzo 3040, entre Segui y Libertador, Palermo (4778 3443/www.terroir.com.ar). Bus 10, 37, 130. **Open** 10.30am-9pm Mon-Fri; noon-7pm Sat. **Credit** AmEx, DC, MC, V. **Map** p283 M10.
Like all the best boutiques, Terroir is easy to walk past; it's marked only by an unobtrusive sign and a shiny doorbell. But don't be intimidated; proprietors Claudio and Emiliano sell fine Argentinian and international wines to the wealthy and discerning, but an equally warm welcome awaits hoi polloi.

Winery
Corrientes 302, y 25 de Mayo, Microcentro (4394 2200/www.winery.com.ar). Subte B, Alem/26, 93, 99, 152 bus. **Open** 9am-8pm Mon-Fri; 9am-2pm Sat. **Credit** AmEx, MC, V. **Map** p281 F11.
A fast-growing chain with a modern look and an excellent selection of Argentinian wines. Several branches, including this one, have attractive on-premises wine bars.
Other locations: Avenida LN Alem 880, Retiro (4311 6607); Avenida del Libertador 5100, Belgrano (4774 1190); Avenida del Libertador 500, Retiro (325 3400); Avenida Juana Manso 800, Puerto Madero (4894 8204).

Health & beauty

All of the major shopping centres have health and beauty outlets. **Patio Bullrich** (*see p148*) has the **Beauty Shop** – an entire floor of make-up and pampering heaven.

Lulu of London
Rodriguez Peña 1057, entre Marcelo T de Alvear y Santa Fe, Recoleta (4815 8471/www.luluoflondon. com.ar). Subte D, Callao/39, 132, 152 bus. **Open** by appointment only. **No credit cards**. **Map** p282 I10.
An exclusive beauty salon run from the apartment of expat Jude O'Hara. Services include skincare, massages, waxing and aromatherapy. Gays and transvestites are welcome. Call in advance.

MB Centro de Belleza
4th Floor, Flat H, Avenida Santa Fe 1592, entre Montevideo y Paraná, Recoleta (4816 7755). Bus 10, 37, 39, 59, 152. **Open** 9am-8pm Mon-Sat. **Credit** MC, V. **Map** p282 I10.
This no-frills beauty salon is efficient and excellent value. The 'all you can wax' promotion is a godsend if you need smoothing off for summer.

The Nail Company
Arenales 1739, entre Rodriguez Peña y Callao, Barrio Norte (4815 2139). Bus 10, 12, 61, 110, 124. **Open** 9.30am-8.30pm Mon-Sat. **Credit** AmEx, MC, V. **Map** p282 I10.

Armed with the latest in beautifying technology, the Nail Company leaves your hands in tip-top condition. Massages and exfoliation offered too.

Hairdressers

Cerini
Marcelo T de Alvear 1471, entre Paraná y Uruguay, Recoleta (4811 1652/www.cerini.net). Bus 39, 102, 111, 152. **Open** 8am-10pm Mon-Sat. **Credit** AmEx, DC, MC, V. **Map** p282 I10.
Cerini is a super-modern and incessantly bustling salon. Appointments are not essential, but if you come in the after-work period, you'll have to wait.

Glam
Quintana 218, entre Montevideo y Rodríguez Peña, Recoleta (4812 4578). Bus 17, 102. **Open** 9am-10pm Mon-Sat. **Credit** AmEx, DC, MC, V. **Map** p282 I11.
Slick semi-exec/semi-punk salon with an emphasis on edgy looks and a cool vibe.

Via Vargas
Cerrito 1058, entre Marcelo T de Alvear y Santa Fe, Barrio Norte (4816 4439/www.viavargas.com.ar) Bus 5, 10, 39, 111, 152. **Open** 9am-9pm Mon-Fri. **Credit** AmEx, DC, MC, V. **Map** p281 H11.
Cool blue decor isn't the only thing that sets Via Vargas apart. Add a bar and a pilates gym and you'll see why cuts here are a whole life experience.

Opticians

Vision Express (freephone 0800 555 0182) offers service in one hour; there are branches at Florida 713 (4314 4155) and in several of the shopping centres.

Infinit Boutique
Thames 1602, y Honduras, Palermo Viejo (4831 7070/www.infinitnet.com). Bus 39, 55. **Open** noon-8pm Mon; 11am-8pm Tue-Sat. **Credit** AmEx, MC, V. **Map** p279 M5.
This is the first sunglass manufacturer designed and made in Argentina to open up a shop. There's a great range of styles and fine craftsmanship is assured.

Pfortner Cornealant
Avenida Pueyrredón 1706, y Juncal, Recoleta. (4827 8600). Subte D, Pueyrredón/41, 60, 62, 118 bus. **Open** 9am-6.30pm Mon-Fri; 8am-noon Sat. **Credit** AmEx, DC, MC, V. **Map** p282 J10.
Excellence in lenses as far as the eye can see. This optician has been in business for nigh on 60 years and is considered by many the best in town.

Pharmacies

FarmaCity
Florida 474, entre Corrientes y Lavalle, Microcentro (4322 6559/www.farmacity.com). Subte B, Florida/10, 59, 111 bus. **Open** 24hrs daily. **Credit** AmEx, DC, MC, V. **Map** p281 F11.

Gola Palermo.
See p172.

A mega-chain with 35 well-stocked stores across the city – and growing. There's a good range of imported products, the pharmacists are skilled professionals, and staff are helpful. But remember that some prescriptions cannot be filled outside your home country. Most branches are open 24 hours and all offer delivery services.
Other locations: throughout the city.

Spas

Many of the city's best spas are located in the city's luxury hotels (*see pp35-58* **Where to Stay**). For wholly Ayurvedic treatments, try the spa at **Home Hotel Buenos Aires** (see *p55*).

Aqua Vita Medical Spa

Arenales 1965, entre Riobamba y Ayacucho, Barrio Norte (4812 5989/www.aquavitamedicalspa. com). Bus 10, 12, 21, 29, 39, 132 152. **Open** 9am-9pm Mon-Sat. **Credit** AmEx, DC, MC, V. **Map** p282 I10.
Treat yourself and indulge in a range of delicious treatments – facial purification, aromatherapy massage, shiatsu, reflexology or half-day head-to-toe programmes, including anti stress treatments – in this aesthetically calming spa centre.

Evian Agua Club & Spa

Cerviño 3626, entre Scalabrini Ortíz y Ugarteche, Palermo (4807 4688/www.aguaclubspa.com). Bus 10, 37, 59, 60, 93. **Open** 7.30am-10.30pm Mon-Fri; 10am-9pm Sat, Sun. **Credit** AmEx, DC, MC, V. **Map** p282 L10.
One of the best places to get away from the city while you're still in it. This spa has a fitness centre, solarium, spa services, massage pool, relaxation room, a doctor and a bistro. It also offers day packages that can be adapted to your particular needs.

Music

Musimundo

Avenida Santa Fe 1844, entre Callao y Riobamba, Barrio Norte (4814 0393/www.musimundo.com) Bus 10, 37, 39, 152. **Open** 10am-10pm Mon-Thur; 9.30am-10pm Fri, Sat; 11am-10pm Sun.
Credit AmEx, DC, MC, V. **Map** p282 I10.
Argentina's own, Musimundo has a good, mainstream selection of music from around the world and stocks plenty of Argentinian rock and folklore music. Some branches also sell audio and computer equipment and have ticket sales outlets.
Other locations: throughout the city.

Zival's

Avenida Callao 395, y Corrientes, Tribunales (4371 7500/www.zivals.com). Subte B, Callao/12, 24, 37, 60 bus. **Open** 9.30am-10pm Mon-Sat. **Credit** AmEx, DC, MC, V. **Map** p281 H9.
Claiming to stock the widest selection of music in South America, Zival's (also an excellent bookshop) has all genres, but specialises in classical, jazz, folk, tango and hard-to-find independent local recordings.

Photography

There's a fast colour processing lab in every barrio in the city. For professional needs, use **Buenos Aires Color** at Piedras No.980, San Telmo (4361 4831), which provides a wide range of services from larger formats to black-and-white processing to digital imaging. For professional equipment, go to **Cosentino** at Bartolomé Mitre No.845 (4328 3290/www. opticacosentino.com.ar). It stocks a number of hard-to-find brands like Mamiya and Hasselblad, alongside an excellent collection of Canon, Nikon and Leica goods.

Sports & outdoor gear

Adidas

Avenida Santa Fe 1774, entre Callao y Rodriguez Peña, Barrio Norte (4815 3479). Subte D, Callao/ 10, 17, 39, 152 bus. **Open** 9am-9pm Mon-Sat. **Credit** AmEx, DC, MC, V. **Map** p282 I10.

An outlet of the brand famous for its three stripes, this Adidas store stocks a complete range of all the usual trainers, tracksuits and tops. Most tempting is the retro section upstairs with racks of 1970s tracksuits, and French football shirts from the golden era of Michel Platini, Jean Tigana and company.

Converse

Avenida Pueyrredón 1920, entre Peña y Pacheco De Melo, Recoleta (4806 6298). Bus 41, 61, 95, 101, 118. **Open** 10am-8pm Mon-Thu; 10am-6pm Fri. **Credit** AmEx, V. **Map** p282 J10.

Converse All Stars are practically uniform for young Argentinians. The 'original performance basketball shoe' and its more recent incarnations can be picked up for around a third of the price they go for abroad.

Gola Palermo

Russel 4924, entre Gurruchaga y Borges (4833 2474). Bus 34, 36, 55, 93, 161. **Open** 11am-8pm Mon-Sat. **Credit** AmEx, MC, V. **Map** p279 M5.

Gola is the latest newcomer on the Palermo retro sportswear scene. Tucked away on a quiet side street, the latest styles are displayed in a setting that reflects the brand's 100-year history. The spirit of its early days as a small bootmaker in Leicester, England, is captured by exposed brick walls and a tin roof. But the trainers and clothing range are moving with the times. **Photo** *p171.*

La Martina

Paraguay 661, entre Florida y Maipú, Retiro (4576 0010). Subte C, San Martín/7, 10, 17, 152 bus. **Open** 10am-8pm Mon-Fri; 10am-2pm Sat. **Credit** AmEx, DC, MC, V. **Map** p2817 G11.

La Martina has a polo team, a polo training camp and a brand of polo clothing and equipment. It's been said that Sting, Sophia Loren and Ali MacGraw all shop here. This branch sells clothes, boots, helmets and saddles (all made in Argentina).
Other locations: Galerías Pacífico (5555 5234) and Patio Bullrich shopping centres.

Nike Soho

Gurruchaga 1615, entre El Salvador y Honduras, Palermo Viejo (4832 3555). Bus 15, 57, 110, 160. **Open** 10am-8pm Mon-Sat. **Credit** AmEx, DC, MC, V. **Map** p279 M5.

Nike have decked out this colonial-style corner shop with vintage wall hangings, chandeliers and flea-market finds. More like a museum of sporting memorabilia than a clothes shop, the vintage collections, in particular the baseball jackets, are the main attraction.
Other locations: Pierina Dialessi 360, Dique IV, Puerto Madero Este (4315 5556), Avenida Santa Fe 1665 (4811 5223).

Wildlife

Hipólito Yrigoyen 1133, entre Salta y Lima, Congreso (4381 1040). Subte A, Lima/29, 59, 64, 67, 86 bus. **Open** 10am-8pm Mon-Fri; 10am-1pm Sat. **Credit** AmEx, DC, MC, V. **Map** p281 F9.

Camping, outdoor and extreme sports gear – new and second-hand – for climbers, anglers, campers, parachutists and more, with expert staff. It's also a great source of information on where to practise.

Travel

Argentina Travel Services

9th Floor, Office 904, Suipacha 190, entre Perón y Bartolomé Mitre, Microcentro (4326 6907/www.ats-travel.com.ar). Subte D, Diagonal Norte/17, 24, 29, 111 bus. **Open** 10am-7pm Mon-Fri. **Credit** AmEx, MC, V. **Map** p281 F10.

For tailor-made trips and adventure holidays, consult the English-speaking experts at Argentina Travel Services. This central agency, the owners of which previously worked for British Airways, offers excursions to destinations all over the country.

Bieule-Pueyrredón Viajes

14th Floor, Office 5, Avenida Santa Fe 1780, entre Callao y Rodriguez Peña, Barrio Norte (4815 9177). Bus 10, 12, 37, 39, 150, 152. **Open** 10.30am-6pm Mon-Fri. **Credit** AmEx, MC, V. **Map** p282 I10.

An accommodating English-speaking travel agency that organises trips around Argentina, specialising in Patagonia, Salta and Buenos Aires province. Bieule-Pueyrredón Viajes arranges accommodation, transport and various activities.

Curiocity

4th Floor, Juncal 2021, entre Junín y Ayacucho, Recoleta (4803 1112/www.curiocitytravel.com). Bus 10, 39, 111. **Open** 10am-7pm Mon-Fri. **No credit cards. Map** p282 I10.

Specialising in tailor-made holidays for the young and wealthy, Curiocity also produces a brochure full of all the coolest ways to blow your savings.

Equinoxe

Avenida Callao 384, 3rd Floor, y Corrientes, Tribunales (4371 5050). Subte B, Callao/12, 24, 60 bus. **Open** 9am-7pm Mon-Fri. **Credit** AmEx, DC, MC, V. **Map** p281 G9.

The professional and multilingual staff at Equinoxe arrange onward travel throughout Argentina, including packages to destinations such as the Iguazú Falls, Patagonia. They also organise *estancia* (ranch) holidays and book your international flights.

Say Hueque

Viamonte 749, Office 1, 6th Floor, entre Esmeralda y Maipú, Microcentro (5199 2517/20). Subte C, Lavalle/10, 17, 59 bus. **Open** 10am-6.30pm Mon-Fri; 10am-1pm Sat. **Credit** varies (depending on itinerary). **Map** p281 G11.

An experienced travel agency geared towards the backpacking brigade. Say Hueque also specialises in adventure holidays.

Arts & Entertainment

Features

Festivals & Events

Fashion shows, cattle markets and the Day of the Noodle Maker.

Buenos Aires is a city for all seasons. In winter, it's time for huddling over hot chocolate in cafés and strolling round art galleries. The chilly spell is brief and by the time the blossom is on the trees, BA turns its attention to weightier matters like catwalks and open-air dance festivals. In the summer (Christmas till March), schools and colleges close, and with them most of the city. As tanned *porteños* return in the autumn, BA cranks up for the new academic year, theatres and concert halls inaugurate their new seasons and – most eagerly anticipated of all – competitive football kicks off again.

Argentinians can find an excuse to celebrate anything and everything – there's a day for all sorts of occupations. Festive days include Día del Amigo, Día de la Secretaria, Día de las Mascotas (Pets' Day) and even a Día del Obrero del Fideo (Day of the Noodle Maker).

Whatever the event, organisation can be haphazard and sometimes non-existent; so check websites (*see p265*) for the latest information. Otherwise, newspapers (especially on Fridays) or tourist information points are your best sources. Events supported by the local government are detailed on its website at www.bue.gov.ar, or call 0800 3378 4825.

January-March

Chinese New Year
Along Arribeños 2000-2200 blocks, Belgrano (Chinese Embassy 4541 5085). Bus 15, 29, 60, 64. **Map** p285 S9. **Date** Jan or Feb.
This small-scale festival is an explosion of colour and clamour in Belgrano's tiny Chinatown, known locally as Barrio Chino. Local restaurants set up stalls on the streets and dole out dim sum.

Carnaval
Plazas & social clubs throughout Buenos Aires (tourist information 4313 0187). **Date** Feb.
Don't expect Rio or New Orleans – here, it's small scale, with teams of *murga* drummers and dancers performing on some plazas. The best carnivals in the region are in the Uruguayan capital, Montevideo (*see p238*), while in Argentina the main action is in Gualeguaychú in Entre Ríos province. That said, the 2006 BA festivities were the best attended in living memory, with Avenida de Mayo used as a parade route for the first time in more than a decade.

Abierto de Tenis de Buenos Aires
Buenos Aires Lawn Tennis Club, Olleros 1510, y Libertador, Palermo (4772 0983). Bus 15, 29, 59, 60. **Map** p285 Q9. **Date** Feb.

Fashion Buenos Aires. *See p175.*

BA's annual Tennis Open gives locals the rare opportunity to watch their own players slug it out on the red dust of the city's premier tennis arena. Homesters Guillermo Coria, Gastón Gaudio and clay court specialists Gustavo Kuerten and Carlos Moya are all regular racket swingers.

Buenos Aires Tango Festival

Various theatres & cultural centres (www.festival detango.com.ar). **Date** late Feb-Mar.

This is the big one: it's the city's – and therefore the world's – most important tango festival, a nine-day extravaganza of concerts, shows, free classes, exhibitions, open-air *milongas* (Avenida Corrientes is closed for an evening) and other tango-associated festivities. If you're in town, don't miss it. If you're a fan of tango, you should plan your trip around it.

Opera Season

Teatro Colón, Libertad 621, entre Tucumán y Viamonte, Tribunales (box office 4378 7300/4378 7301/www.teatrocolon.org.ar). Subte D, Tribunales/ 29, 39, 59, 109 bus. **Map** p281 G10. **Date** Mar-Dec.

The Colón (*see p198*) officially opens its curtains in early March, with ballet, opera and classical concerts. Look out for brilliant pianist/conductor Daniel Barenboim's annual return.

Fashion Buenos Aires

Predio La Rural, Avenida Santa Fe 4201, y Avenida Sarmiento, Palermo (4784 3205/www.grupopampa. com). Subte D, Plaza Italia/10, 29, 39, 60, 152 bus. **Map** p283 M9. **Date** Mar & Sept.

The latest fashions from local designers grace the catwalk in Buenos Aires' twice-yearly, four-day fashion week: the winter collection is presented in March, the summer one in September. With over 30 labels represented at the 2005 summer show, the 'BAF' hosted up to 13,000 guests per day. Pay AR$10 at the door and step into a strobe-lit world of willowy beauties, catty *fashionistas* and all kinds of other people who would think nothing of blowing a week's wages on a tank top.

St Patrick's Day

Pubs all over Buenos Aires. **Date** 17 Mar.

Traditionally a day for the Irish, Argentinians have adopted this as one of their own. Almost every pub jumps on the green bandwagon, but the epicurean epicentre is in and around the many Irish pubs on Reconquista street in the Microcentro.

April-June

Festival Internacional de Cine Independiente

Hoyts Abasto & other cinemas (www.bafilmfest.com). **Date** Mid-late Apr.

Highly popular ten-day showcase for non-Hollywood films from all over the world, including the work of local directors. It attracts one or two name directors and high profile actors usually seen only at the likes of the Cannes or Berlin film fests.

Feria del Libro

Predio La Rural, Avenida Santa Fe 4201, y Avenida Sarmiento, Palermo (Fundación El Libro 4374 3288/ www.el-libro.com.ar). Subte D, Plaza Italia/39, 60, 152 bus. **Map** p283 M9. **Date** mid Apr-May.

The three-week-long annual BA Book Fair is a monster event. It's geared more towards readers than publishers and attracts hundreds of thousands of *porteño* bookworms and a handful of world famous authors. As well as the stands, there are plenty of readings, special performances, book signings and debates. Not for claustrophobes.

ArteBA

Predio La Rural, Avenida Santa Fe 4201, y Avenida Sarmiento, Palermo (4816 8704/www.arteba.com). Subte D, Plaza Italia/10, 29, 39, 60, 152 bus. **Date** mid May. **Map** p283 M9.

National and international galleries, specialist publishers, artists and collectors, not to mention 100,000 paying punters, group together for this week-long art fair, which has evolved into one of the best attended and most hyped cultural events in Latin America. It displays the works of hundreds of artists from Argentina and overseas.

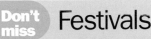

Don't miss **Festivals**

Abierto Argentino de Polo

Displays of daring, style and skill. And that's just the crowd. *See p177.*

Fashion Buenos Aires

One of Latin America's most prestigious fashion events, attracting top models and gawking punters. *See left.*

Buenos Aires Tango Festival

It takes two hundred thousand to tango in this, the dance's most important international showcase. *See left.*

Opera Season, Teatro Colón

If you only have one night out in Buenos Aires, make it at the Colón, one of the world's great opera houses. *See left.*

South American Music Conference

BA's most important dance music event, with live sets and workshops by DJs your gran has probably heard of. *See p176.*

▶ For more festivals, see our specialist **Arts & Entertainment** chapters. For a list of public holidays, *see p262.*

Arts & Entertainment

Aniversario de la Revolución de Mayo

Plaza de Mayo (Museo del Cabildo 4334 1782). Subte A, Plaza de Mayo or D, Catedral or E, Bolívar/24, 29, 64, 86, 152 bus. **Map** p281 E11. **Date** 25 May.

The humble celebration of the day of the 1810 revolution begins the preceding midnight when people gather in front of the Cabildo to sing the national anthem. At 8pm on 25 May the crowds mass again for another patriotic singalong.

July-September

Día de la Independencia

Across Argentina. **Date** 9 July.

Although the main events are held in freedom's birthplace in the north-western city of Tucumán, cafés along Avenida de Mayo participate in the festivities, serving up traditional hot chocolate with *churros* (doughnuts) for breakfast. A solemn Mass at the Cathedral is attended by the President, who is forced to sit through a tongue-lashing homily delivered by the city's archbishop.

Marcha del 26 de Julio

City centre streets & plazas. **Date** 26 July.

To mark the anniversary of the death of Evita, their spiritual leader, loyal Peronists stage torch-lit marches through the city centre and hold graveside vigils in Recoleta Cemetery.

La Rural

Predio La Rural, Avenida Santa Fe 4201, y Sarmiento, Palermo (4324 4700 ext 780/www.rural arg.org.ar). Subte D, Plaza Italia/10, 29, 39, 60, 152 bus. **Map** p283 M9. **Date** end July-Aug.

The Exposición de Ganadería, Agricultura e Industria Internacional – known as La Rural – is the nation's supremely important two-week agro fair. Lambs, rams, pigs and other farm animals get a look-in, but it's the bulls who are most respected. The best events are the madly macho *gaucho* stunts.

World Tango Championships

Various theatres and cultural centres (www.mundialtango.com.ar). **Date** mid Aug.

Prequalifying stages, strict rules and an eagle-eyed jury are just a few of the hurdles awaiting those couples attempting to become the World Tango Champions. The prize money is small (AR$5,000 for the best Stage Tango couple and the same for the best Salón Tango couple) but the prestige is priceless.

Fiesta del Inmigrante

Museo de la Inmigración, Avenida Antártida Argentina 1355, y de los Inmigrantes, Puerto Madero (4317 0285/www.fiestadelinmigrante). Bus 6, 20. **Map** p281 G12. **Date** weekend closest to 4 Sept.

Ethnic groups celebrate the flavourful food, music, dance and sacrifices of their immigrant ancestors.

Feria de Vinos y Bodegas

www.argentinawines.com. **Date** 7-10 Sept.

A wine fair – the biggest of its kind in BA – for the connoisseur, with over 250 bodegas decanting and sweet-talking over the week. Check website for venue.

Festival Internacional de Buenos Aires

Teatro San Martín & other theatres (festivaldeteatro ba.com.ar). **Date** every 2yrs in Sept; next Sept 2007.

Buenos Aires' major performing arts festival, this is a fortnight of mainly Latin American theatre, dance and musical performances.

Nokia Trends

Predio La Rural, Avenida Santa Fe 4201, y Sarmiento, Palermo (4784 3205). Subte D, Plaza Italia/10, 29, 39, 60, 152 bus. **Map** p283 M9. **Date** late Sept.

Now established as one of BA's biggest and best open-air music fests; the 2005 event was headlined by Moby. Tickets cost around AR$80.

October-December

Casa Foa

Venue varies (www.casafoa.com). **Date** Oct-Nov.

Going strong for over two decades, this sizeable exhibition attracts scores of local and international firms from the design and decor industry.

Código País

Venue varies. **Date** Nov.

An annual art and design fair showcasing fresh local talent. Código País also includes live DJs, music and art workshops, talks, theatre and fashion shows, plus stalls selling the latest in innovative alternative clothing and accessories. **Photo** *p177.*

Festival Martha Argerich

Teatro Colón, Libertad 621, entre Tucumán y Viamonte, Tribunales (4378 7300/www.teatrocolon. org.ar). Subte D, Tribunales/29, 39, 59, 67, 100, 109 bus. **Map** p281 G10. **Date** Oct.

Renowned Argentinian pianist Martha Argerich wows her legions of fans during this high-profile ten-day celebration of fine classical music. The programme ranges widely, from Argerich's virtuoso solo performances to ensemble pieces that feature famous guest musicians. In a typical BA snafu, the festival was cancelled in 2005 due to industrial action by the Colón's technical staff. Normal service will hopefully have resumed by 2006.

Maratón de Buenos Aires

Information *www.maratondebuenosaires.com.* **Date** Oct.

Roadrunners clog Avenida 9 de Julio in this annual marathon. The start and finish line is the Obelisco.

South American Music Conference

Centro Costa Salguero, Avenida Rafael Obligado, y Sakguero, Costanera Norte (4806 9749/www. samc.net). Bus 33. **Map** p278 L12. **Date** mid Oct.

This world-class event has helped establish BA as the dance capital of South America, with techno workshops, seminars and an end-of-event party to end all end-of-event parties. Tickets from AR$70.

Festival BUE
Club Ciudad de Buenos Aires, Avenida del Libertador 750, y Manzanares, Nuñez (www.festivalbue.com). Bus 28, 29, 130. **Date** late Oct.
Perhaps only in Argentina would a music festival called Buenos Aires Urban Electronica book Elvis Costello as a headliner – but that's what happened in 2005 and the bespectacled legend went down a storm. The Strokes were there too. Expect equally strong line-ups in future years.

Marcha del Orgullo Gay
Plaza de Mayo (www.marchadelorgullo.org.ar). Subte A, Plaza de Mayo or D, Catedral or E, Bolívar/24, 64, 86, 152 bus. **Map** p281 E11. **Date** 1st Sat in Nov.
BA's growing Gay Pride March gathers gays, lesbians, trannies, and heteros for serious protest and an even more serious party.

Alvear Fashion & Arts
Along Avenida Alvear, Recoleta (4807 0545). Bus 17, 67, 93, 124, 130. **Map** p282 I11. **Date** early Nov.
A one-week, red-carpet exhibition of local painters, sculptors and photographers held at the top-flight boutiques on BA's Fifth Avenue.

Día de la Tradición
Feria de Mataderos, Lisandro de la Torre y Avenida de Los Corrales (4687 5602). Bus 55, 80, 92, 126. Also San Antonio de Areco, BA province (Tourist Office 02326 453165). **Date** weekend nearest 12 Nov.

Local talent at **Código País**. *See p176*.

The annual *gaucho* day has regional food and music and brave shows of horsemanship. The town of San Antonio de Areco (*see p231*), 113 kilometres (70 miles) north-west of the capital, or BA's Feria de Mataderos (*see p104*), are the places to be.

Creamfields
Dique 1, Costanera Sur (www.creamfieldsba.com.ar). Bus 2, 3. **Map** p280 C10 **Date** 12 Nov.
Better known as 'Mudfields', this is the one date in the BA calendar for which rain is all but guaranteed. But with 30,000 revellers jumping around and some of the best in international DJ talent behind the decks, no one complains. Expect global names like Paul Oakenfold and Deep Dish, while local-DJ-turned-international-superstar Hernán Cattáneo is now almost a given. Just don't wear your best trainers.

Gran Premio Nacional
Hipódromo Argentino de Palermo, Avenida del Libertador 4101, y Dorrego, Palermo (www.palermo.com.ar). Bus 10, 36, 160. **Map** p283 O10. **Date** mid Nov.
First run in 1884, Argentina's top annual horse race attracts hardcore punters and social climbers alike. In recent years it's become a day-long event with plenty of course-side entertainment and celebrity ligging. Dress appropriately – for men, the jumper draped louchely over the shoulders is a *sine qua non*, though deck shoes are optional.

Abierto Argentino de Polo
Campo Argentino de Polo, Avenida del Libertador 4000 y Dorrego, Palermo (Asociación Argentina de Polo 4343 0972/www.aapolo.com). Bus 10, 64, 130, 160. **Map** p283 O9. **Date** mid Nov/mid Dec.
Talking of horses, Argentina has long been polo's spiritual home, producing the world's top stars both on four legs and two. Held at Palermo's magnificent 16,000-capacity Campo Argentino de Polo, the Argentinian Polo Open is the sport's annual highlight. If the games aren't entertaining enough, the half-time tradition of stomping the divots is a networker's dream.

Festival Buenos Aires Danza Contemporánea
Teatro San Martín & other theatres (www.buenos airesdanza.com.ar). **Date** held every 2yrs in Dec; next in Dec 2006.
For two weeks only, once every two years, tango takes a back seat and BA's overlooked modern dance scene is centre stage at theatres presenting the best in local as well as international talent.

Festival Buen Día
Plaza Palermo Viejo, Costa Rica y Armenia (www.festivalbuendia.com). Bus 15, 39, 55. **Map** p279 M5. **Date** late Dec.
Fashion, shopping, electronica dance music and cocktail mixing are fused in this low-culture, youth-oriented open-air party from noon to midnight. Local bands and DJs provide the soundtrack while punters snack at the food stalls around the plaza.

Arts & Entertainment

Children

Big fun for small people.

Argentinians love children. Dragging your offspring around Buenos Aires is a genuine pleasure; there always seems to be a passerby handy to gurn and coo at your kids. Far from the seen-and-not-heard school of thought, *porteños* are only too happy to accommodate your little ones at most restaurants, cafés and public spaces, and you'll get none of that eyes-to-heaven intolerance you might have come to expect from fellow diners at home.

But despite the fact that *porteños* go gaga over kids, there's still a downside to taking your tykes around BA. Sidewalks lack ramps, so pack a sturdy pushchair: negotiating the pot-holed pavements and kerbs can be a challenge. Also be prepared to change your routine; evening meal times, in particular, are much later than you may be accustomed to, so it's not a bad idea to incorporate siestas into your daily plans, especially in summer.

There are a number of restaurants that particularly appeal to children and families. Among them are **Cumaná** (*see p119*) where kids can scribble on the table cloths, and **Pizza Banana** (Avenida Costanera Rafael Obligado y La Pampa, 4314 9500) where they can work up an appetite on the bouncy castle. Many eateries have kids' options, or will prepare a special menu to satisfy the fads of your pride and joy.

Most hotels are also family-oriented, and there are many apartment hotels with large living spaces and kitchenettes. There are no babysitting agencies, but major hotels such as the Four Seasons (*see p49*) have child-minding services, while others will be able to put you in touch with a trusted local babysitter.

BA has excellent markets, museums, cinemas and theatres for families, and Children's Day celebrations in August. For more information on kids-related events, consult newspaper supplements or *Planetario* (4704 0635, www.revistaplanetario.com.ar), a free monthly magazine available from the Recoleta and San Martín cultural centres. They also organise the annual **Feria de los Chicos** (Children's Fair). It usually takes place in April; the venue varies, so check under '*eventos*' on their website.

The language barrier will be less of an obstacle for kids than for their parents. Many events feature clowns, jugglers and musicians. Look out in particular for **Caracahumba**, a well-established puppeteer collective.

Outdoors

Built-up though the city is, there are still plenty of green areas where kids can safely burn off excess energy. Most parks, recreation areas and plazas have playgrounds for children, although some may not be in the best state of repair.

For a family day out with a range of sporting facilities, pools and outdoor space, try the all-inclusive multi-sport venues (*see p212*). Recoleta, with its open-air market, though not exclusively aimed at youngsters, has such diverting attractions as street performers, fire-eaters, living statues, puppeteers and jugglers.

The biggest expanse of greenery is Palermo's **Parque Tres de Febrero** (*see p95*). Here, kids will run out of puff before they run out of park and it's one of few places largely free of dog mess. Hire a bike with child seats (AR$7 per hour) or rollerblades (AR$10 per hour) and discover the area at your own pace. Or float out on the lake in a pedalo or rowing boat (AR$14

Pedal hard at **Parque Tres de Febrero**.

See the stars at the **Planetario Galileo Galilei.** *See p180.*

per hour). At weekends, there are rides in *mateos*, horse-drawn carriages found dotted around the park; AR$35 for 30 minutes.

Also in this area is the lovely **Jardín Japonés** (*see p95*), which hosts puppet shows on weekends from 4-5pm, as well as a series of recycling workshops. Your kids will love feeding the shoals of insatiable (and acrobatic) koi carp. Palermo park is also home to the city's **Jardín Zoológico** (*see below*) and the excellent planetarium (*see p180*).

Another escape from the crowded streets is the **Reserva Ecológica** (*see p101*). The circuit around the reserve is quite long on foot, especially for under-fives, but you can hire bicycles at the entrance. The reward at the end of the walk is a spectacular view of the River Plate. A little further north, open-air leisure complex **Parque Norte** on the Costanera Norte (4787 1382, www.parquenorte.com) has four good-sized pools with slides, and a separate pool for children. The tram ride in the barrio of Caballito (*see p99*) is also a family favourite.

For wannabe cowboys or cowgirls, a visit to the *gaucho* themed **Feria de Mataderos** (*see p104*) in the far west of the city is a must. Look out also for street theatre from **Grupo Catalinas Sur** in La Boca (www.catalina sur.com.ar) and **Las Calandracas** in Barracas.

For a family day out with a difference, it's Holy Week every day of the year at the world's best (or, rather, only) religious theme park, **Tierra Santa** (*see p102*).

Jardín Zoológico de Buenos Aires

Avenidas Las Heras y Sarmiento, Palermo (4806 7412). Subte D, Plaza Italia/15, 36, 37, 60, 152 bus. **Open** *Jan, Feb* 10am-6pm daily. *Mar-Dec* 10am-5.30pm Tue-Sun. **Admission** AR$4-$8.50, free under-12s, concessions. **Credit** V. **Map** p283 M9.
This city zoo houses over 350 species, plus aquariums and an educational farm, where kids are taught to bake, milk cows and recycle paper. Indigenous animals include the llama, vicuña and guanaco (don't get too close – they spit). Arachnophobes should give the tropical house a wide berth.

Indoors

On cold or wet days, museums, cinemas, cultural centres, theatres and shopping centres are great ways to keep the kids entertained. During the school holidays (particularly the January-March summer break), the **Malba** modern art museum (*see p95*) and the **Teatro Colón** (*see p202*) both run special – and top quality – programmes for children. The Abasto shopping centre (*see p148*) is tailor-made for kids. As well as the excellent **Museo de los Niños** there are restaurants, games arcades and play areas, and a fully functional indoor amusement park equipped with roller coaster, swinging pirate ship, video games and even a Ferris wheel. Well worth a whirl.

Cine Los Angeles (Corrientes 1770, Tribunales, 4372 2405) specialises in children's movies, although they are shown dubbed in

Arts & Entertainment

Spanish. Most cinemas, however, do show English versions of the latest animated movies, but check before purchasing a ticket.

La Calle de los Títeres

Centro Cultural del Sur, Avenida Caseros 1750, y Baigorri, Constitución (4305 6653/4306 0301). Bus 45, 59, 67. **Open** Puppet shows *Mar-Dec* 3pm Sat; 3pm, 4pm Sun. **Closed** Jan, Feb. **Map** p281 E7.

'The puppet street' presents free shows and puppet-making in the picturesque patio of an old mansion.

Museo Argentino de Ciencias Naturales Bernardino Rivadavia

Avenida Angel Gallardo 470, entre Warnes y Marechal, Caballito (4982 1154/4494/www.macn. gov.ar). Subte B, Angel Gallardo/55, 65, 112, 105, 124 bus. **Open** 2-7pm daily. **Admission** AR$2. **No credit cards. Map** p280 L3.

This old-fashioned natural history museum thrills kids who are dotty about dinosaurs. The star skeleton on display belongs to an ex-carnotaurus, the 'bad guy' in Disney's *Dinosaur* movie.

Museo de los Niños

Level 2, Corrientes 3247, entre Agüero y Anchorena, Abasto (4861 2325/www.museoabasto.org.ar). Subte B, Carlos Gardel/24, 26, 124, 146, 168 bus. **Open** 1-8pm Tue-Sun. **Admission** AR$5; AR$12-$18 family ticket; free under-3s. **Credit** AmEx, DC, MC, V. **Map** p282 J2.

This mini-adult world is perfect for curious young-sters. They can operate a crane on a building site, test their medical skills in the hospital or run a TV studio.

Museo Participativo de Ciencias

1st Floor, Centro Cultural Recoleta, Junín 1930, y Quintana, Recoleta (4807 3260/4806 3456/www. mpc.org.ar). Bus 10, 17, 60, 67, 92, 110. **Open** *Jan, Feb* 3.30-7.30pm Tue-Sun. *Mar-Dec* 10am-5pm Tue-Fri; 3.30-7.30pm Sat, Sun. **Admission** AR$6; free under-4s. **No credit cards. Map** p282 J11.

'*Prohibido no tocar*' (it's forbidden not to touch) is the motto of this science museum in the Recoleta cultural centre, where kids can explore the mysteries of physics and have fun at the same time. It's best for children over seven.

Planetario de la Ciudad de Buenos Aires Galileo Galilei

Parque Tres de Febrero, Belisario Roldán y Avenida Sarmiento, Palermo (4772 9265/4771 6629/www. planetario.gov.ar). Subte D, Plaza Italia/37, 67, 130, 160 bus. **Open** *Museum* 10am-6pm Mon-Fri; 1-7.30pm Sat, Sun. *Shows* 3pm, 4.30pm, 6pm Sat, Sun. **Admission** *Museum* free. *Shows* AR$4; free under-5s, concessions. **No credit cards. Map** p283 N11.

The spaceship-shaped planetarium is in the middle of Palermo's main park. Shows (best for age seven and up) are in Spanish, but the visuals have a literally universal appeal. They include images from the Hubble space telescope. Particularly impressive – and unique in Latin America – is their special programme designed for the blind and hard of hearing (check the website for more details). **Photo** p179.

Outside Buenos Aires there are a number of child-friendly attractions that can be enjoyed as part of a day trip. The best is groundbreaking wildlife park **Temaikèn** (*see p236*), where 200 species live in the open air. A visit to an *estancia* (ranch – *see p237*) or to Tigre (*see p231*) are other worthwhile family outings. The following are also good fun for the family:

Parque de la Costa

Vivanco 1509, y Mitre, Tigre (4002 6000/www. parquedelacosta.com.ar). Tren de la Costa to Delta/ 60 bus. **Open** 11am-8pm Thur-Sun. **Admission** *Park* free. *Shows & rides* AR$18; AR$9 3-12s; AR$6 concessions; free under-3s. **Credit** AmEx, DC, MC, V.

This attractive amusement park is beside the Delta station in Tigre (to find it, just follow the screams), the terminus on the Tren de la Costa (*see below*). There are fairground and boat rides, roller coasters, theme restaurants and a lake with a dancing fountain show – something for all ages and sizes.

Tren de la Costa

Avenida Maipú 2305, Olivos (4002 6000/www.trende lacosta.com.ar). From Retiro, Ramal 2 train on Mitre line to Olivos/59, 60, 71, 152 bus. **Open** 6.30am-11pm Mon-Fri; 8am-midnight Sat, Sun. **Return ticket** AR$3; free under-3s. **Credit** AmEx, DC, MC, V.

On this delightful 25-minute train ride from Olivos to Tigre, you can get on and off at stations along the route, where there are cinemas, restaurants and shops. San Isidro station has the most options.

Feel the thrill at **Parque de la Costa**.

Arts & Entertainment

Clubs

Trust the hype: BA is now Latin America's top clubbing destination.

Unless you pine for nightclubs staffed entirely by dwarves, featuring cabaret interludes of dominatrices chasing red indians – as was once the case at legendary BA dive Nave Jungla – you will probably think the *porteño* club scene has come a long way in the last few years. In fact, Buenos Aires is now considered Latin America's leading dance destination.

One nation under a groove? Not quite. In December 2004 a fire claimed the lives of 194 people in the overcrowded República Cromagnon nightclub, forcing authorities to take a hard – and long overdue – look at club safety. After a year of rigorous inspections, closures and overhauls, the city's nightlife is now recovering. But the situation is still very volatile; try to check local listings and flyers before heading to a club. For more on the Cromagnon fire and its aftermath, *see p182* **Shock of the new**.

Regular visits from big name foreign DJs, complemented by the talents of local mix masters, continue to feed a growing appetite for beats. Names to look out for include Javier Zuker, Cristóbal Paz, Space Ibiza resident Elio Riso, Bad Boy Orange and Romina Cohn, not forgetting Argentina's most successful DJ export, London resident Hernán Cattáneo. Check out Surface Bookings (www.surfacebookings.com) for DJ listings and information.

In addition to regular club nights, outdoor events – including sporadic full moon parties and raves in the city's parklands or along the river – and one-offs cater to the increasingly exacting demands of clubbers who only a few years ago were still clinging to a middle-of-the-road musical diet. Look out in particular for Moon Park, SouthFest and Brahma Beats events (www.2netproducciones.com.ar), all of which attract international DJs. October is the month of the **South American Music Conference** (www.samc.net), the southern cone's answer to Miami's world-renowned event (*see p176*). The SAMC is up there with November's regular dance event, **Creamfields** (*see p177*), the popular Argentinian version of the UK's classic mega-rave. It's held on a patch of wasteland behind Puerto Madero.

CLUB CULTURE

When planning a night out, pace yourself and be prepared to travel. Venues are split between central locations and the Costanera Norte along the river. Clubs get lively late (after 3am) and go on until they run out of people. Popular places, especially those with outside terraces like **Mint** and **Big One**, rumble on past breakfast the next day, whereupon after-hours venues like **Caix** keep the party going until mid afternoon.

Though there is rarely a strict dress code in any club, *porteños'* slavery to fashion makes them militant about following style commandments. Yet this enthusiasm for all that is hip reaps handsome visual rewards – BA's clubbers are a good-looking and flirtatious lot. The places that succeed are invariably packed with stylish, chatty people who never tire of foreign visitors. There's a friendly, non-aggressive vibe, partly owing, no doubt, to how little the locals drink. Dancefloor fisticuffs are mercifully rare, and anyone turning up at a club queue drunk or boisterous will be frowned upon by doormen and clubbers alike.

PRICES & INFORMATION

Though still affordable for tourists, entrance fees for many of the city's top nightspots have soared since the Cromagnon tragedy, though

Niceto Club.
See p184.

Shock of the new
The Cromagnon tragedy

For many *porteños* 30 December 2004 will forever be the day the music died. In Argentina's worst ever non-natural disaster, 194 people, mostly teenagers and young adults, burned or suffocated to death in a fire in the República Cromagnon nightclub, a big and perennially overcrowded live music venue in the Once neighbourhood. They were attending a gig by Callejeros, a local rock band with a large cult following.

Since then political discourse in BA has become virtually synonymous with the tragedy. The former mayor of Buenos Aires, Aníbal Ibarra, was relieved of his duties in March 2006 after an impeachment committee ruled he should carry the can for the city's inept and corrupt health and safety bureaucracy. Omar Chabán, the nightclub's former owner – a man about as popular in BA as Osama Bin Laden is in New York – is holed up on a remote island on the Tigre Delta awaiting trial.

But closure is still a long way off for the victims' families. News programmes still replay the harrowing footage of that evening: youngsters dying on the pavement outside the nightclub while friends and passers by fanned their faces with T-shirts and pieces of cardboard; paramedics giving CPR; sirens wailing. The first anniversary of the tragedy was marked by a candlelit procession from Once to Plaza de Mayo, with silent ranks of mothers brandishing photos of their dead children and carrying the sneakers the kids were wearing when they died. It's encore time for Argentina's most wretched historical leitmotif – mothers whose only demand is for someone to tell them why their children are dead.

In the midst of all this it seems rather banal to be discussing Cromagnon's effect on BA's club scene, an effect that has, nonetheless, been profound and far-reaching. The most visible consequence of the disaster has been

the permanent closure of many of the city's less salubrious *boliches* (slang for discos), their owners unable or unwilling to comply with new safety regulations. The more tourist-friendly venues like Mint and Pachá have been forced to reduce their capacities, provoking a rise in prices and a more comfortable – if less adrenal – experience for clubbers. Few will argue that these changes are anything but overdue; most would contend that they are 194 young lives too late.

But the process won't end there. This is, after all, Buenos Aires, the Freudian mother lode, where solving a problem is only marginally more important than understanding how and why the problem arose. At the heart of the matter is BA's partly self-created reputation as a hedonistic arcadia, an unpasteurised, supercaffeinated, chainsmoking, crash-helmets-are-for-sissies society where the pursuit of pleasure is taken very seriously indeed and risk is often discounted with an ironic shrug.

So is it time for Buenos Aires to sober up and get serious? Some think so. Or simply to file Cromagnon under 'shit happens' and party even harder? That's another school of thought.

And then there is the fear, etched into the faces of those grieving, furious parents, that the Cromagnon disaster will fade from memory, its lessons ignored and, eventually, forgotten. That safety inspectors will again start to take bribes. That greedy promoters will again chain up fire escapes to keep non-paying punters from sneaking in. That risking other people's lives will again be preferable to all that pesky paperwork.

The most resonant phrase in all Argentinian literature is the title of the 1984 report into the fate of those who 'disappeared' under the military dictatorship: *Nunca Mas* (*Never Again*). It can only be hoped that the epitaph to the Cromagnon tragedy is similarly steely and uncompromising.

a foreign accent and a good appearance still help get you in pretty much anywhere. The admission price to smaller venues ranges from AR$5 to AR$15 (women usually pay less than men and sometimes get in for free), with larger clubs charging AR$20-$40 depending on who's in the booth. As a rule, credit cards are not accepted for admission, although if there's a restaurant you may be able to use plastic (sometimes to pay your bar tab too). A drink, usually a bottle of beer, is often included with the cost of entrance: look out for flyers saying 'con consumición' or 'con trago'. Many bars work on an annoying double queue system; pay for your drink at the cashier and get your receipt before you begin your fruitless attempts to make eye contact with the elusive bar staff.

The best source of information on the BA scene, and a good place to purchase CDs of local DJs, is www.buenosaliens.com – check the site once in town for the week's schedule. New site www.clubber.com.ar has good forums but is only accessible to those with sufficient Spanish to follow the threads. You can also pick up flyers (which sometimes offer discounted admission) from **Galería Bond Street** (*see p158*), various boutiques dotted around Palermo Viejo or downtown bars like **Dadá** (*see p139*).

Upmarket tour agency **Curiocity** (*see p172*) offers a useful personalised service – they can take you out on the town, get access to the city's best clubs and secure tables in the VIP sectors.

Venues

Asia de Cuba

Pierina Dialessi 750, y Macacha Güemes, Puerto Madero Este (4894 1328/www.asiadecuba.com.ar). Bus 2, 130, 152. **Open** *Restaurant* 12.30pm-1am daily. *Club* 1-5am Tue-Sat. **Map** p281 E12.
At this flashy dockside spot (open all day as a restaurant) in hip Puerto Madero Este, you can dine on sushi, sweat it out on the dancefloor, or just enjoy the slightly mob-scented scenery while relishing a decent drink. The best part is the end, when you heroically slide past the security guards, a Martini and companion in hand, to stroll by the river.

Azúcar

Avenida Corrientes 3330, entre Agüero y Gallo, Abasto (4866 4439/www.azucarsalsa.com). Bus 24, 26, 124, 146, 168. **Open** from midnight Fri, Sat. **Map** p278 J5.
This small salsa venue verges on the tacky, with one wall painted with cartoon images of salsa's famous names, but it has energy to spare, an enthusiastic crowd and a cadre of resident – and impossibly cool – Cuban dance instructors. The dancefloor is small but there are plenty of places to sit and sup. The venue has daily dance classes (not on Mondays) in a variety of styles; check the website for schedules.

Bahrein

Lavalle 345, y Reconquista, Microcentre (4315 2403/www.bahreinba.com). Subte B, L.N. Alem/ 6, 22, 28, 93, 152 bus. **Open** from 12.30am Tue, Wed, Fri, Sat. **Map** p281 F11.
Since its opening in late 2004, Bahrein hasn't exactly been short of customers. Now one of the most happening clubs in the city, it draws a mixed crowd that flits between the swish top-floor restaurant and chillout area, the more commercial 'Funky Room' and the heavier grooves of the basement's 'XSS'. Cages, chandeliers and stained-glass windows may sound like a bizarre mix but it works well, each floor with a very distinct vibe. Weekends are perpetually rammed, and come Tuesdays, it plays host to BA's most prominent drum and bass night – '+160', fronted by local talent Bad Boy Orange.

The Basement Club

The Shamrock, Rodríguez Peña 1220, entre Juncal y Arenales, Recoleta (4812 3584, www.thesham rockbar.com). Bus 37, 39, 124, 152. **Open** from midnight Thur; from 1am Fri, Sat. **Map** p282 I10.
Beyond the curtains to the basement of this ever popular bar awaits another world – fresh sounds, a giant glitter ball and disco floor lights. An energetic vibe emanates from residents Waltie, Lucas Ferro and DJ Boro, with Cristóbal Paz making regular appearances on Thursday nights. On two Sundays per month, a rock 'n' roll party offers up some good old-fashioned fun.

Big One

Adolfo Alsina 940, entre Bernardo de Irigoyen y Tacuari, Monserrat (4331 1277/www.palacio buenosaires.com). Bus 10, 17, 59, 64, 86. **Open** from 1.30am Fri, Sat. **Map** p281 F10.
On Saturdays, Palacio Alsina hosts Big One, the capital's heaviest night of electronica. It's a vast venue that feels more like a cathedral than a disco. An upper balcony kitted out with tables and sofas allows a brief respite from the heaving mass of messy dancers below. Progressive house and techno are the orders of the night. Fridays are gay night (*see p197*).

Caix

Centro Costa Salguero, Avenida Rafael Obligado y Salguero, Costanera Norte (4806 9749). Bus 37, 45. **Open** from 1am Fri, Sat; 9am-3pm Sun. **Map** 282 L12.
A popular weekend haunt, Caix – situated close to a putting green, an evangelist temple, the city airport and the river's most polluted waters – is as surreal as the BA club scene gets. The place is at its most charged when the rest of the city is fully wound down. At 9am on Sunday morning, hundreds of indefatigable clubbers descend into a world of unrepentant hedonism, and most remain until the DJ pulls off his headphones sometime around 3pm. The action takes place upstairs where a brew of high-octane build-ups and releases keep the sweat-sodden crowd in raptures. If it gets too hot, try the airier second dance room which looks out across the heads of a scattering of bewildered fishermen.

CBGB

Bartolomé Mitre 1552, entre Montevideo y Paraná, Tribunales (no phone). Subte A, Sáenz Peña/6, 7, 24, 29, 39, 180 bus. **Open** from 12.30am Fri, Sat. **Map** p281 G9.

Relatively unknown and seriously underground, CBGB is a small but decent venue dedicated to live performances – predominantly hard rock and metal. Friday nights, though, afford a rare glimpse into the city's hip-hop subculture.

Club Aráoz

Aráoz 2424, entre Güemes y Santa Fe, Palermo (4833 7775). Subte D, Scalabrini Ortiz/36, 39, 106, 152 bus. **Open** 1.30-7am Fri, Sat. **Map** 278 L6.

Called 'Lost Clubbing' on Friday nights, this venue draws an A-list roster of acclaimed homegrown spinners, courtesy of Surface Bookings, the top DJ talent agency in Buenos Aires. Among the names who've dropped in for the night in Lost's booths are Martín García, Hernán Cattáneo, and the godfather of drum 'n' bass, Grooverider. It's a smaller, more intimate and therefore more selective club than Mint or Big One; so you can dive into the middle, flounder around, and come out still breathing.

Crobar

Paseo de la Infanta, Avenida del Libertador 3883, y Infanta Isabel, Palermo (4778 1500/www.crobar. com). Bus 10, 34, 36. **Open** from 9.30pm Thur-Sat. **Map** p283 N10.

This is the one BA clubbers have been waiting for. After a long delay, North American megaclub chain Crobar – whose slogan exhorts clubbers to 'claim your nightlife' – opened its fourth branch (the others are in New York, Chicago and Miami) here in March 2006 with a set by DJ extraordinaire, Tiesto. This is a huge space, with multiple VIP areas, chillout zones and a retractable roof. Don't miss it.

Jet

Avenida Rafael Obligado 4801, Costanera Norte. Bus 37, 160 (no phone). **Open** from 12.30am Fri, Sat. **Map** p282 K12.

Another monosyllabic venture from the team behind the VIP area at top BA club Mint, Jet is considerably less hectic than its better known elder brother, with the focus falling more towards the people than the music. The dancefloor is patrolled by cute twenty-somethings, but the older and/or plainer won't feel awkward. In any case, you can always retreat to one of the comfy booths, sip a well-mixed drink and take in the blend of mainstream indie and disco remixes.

Maluco Beleza

Sarmiento 1728, entre Rodríguez Peña y Callao, Tribunales (4372 1737/www.malucobeleza.com.ar). Bus 12, 24, 26, 60, 146. **Open** from 10pm Wed, Fri-Sun. **Map** p281 G9

Maluco Beleza is a little slice of Brazil in the centre of town. The music shows a typically Brazilian disregard for genre (mixing Dire Straits into samba), and the people an equally typical desire to have a good time. Sunday nights gather a great crowd, but

you're guaranteed some fun whenever you show up. The disco gets going after 1am; before then, there's lambada or, on Wednesday, a supper-show.

Mint

Avenida Costanera Rafael Obligado, y Sarmiento, Costanera Norte (4806 8002/www.mint-argentina. com.ar). Bus 37, 160. **Open** *Feb-Dec* from 1.30 Fri, Sat. **Closed** Jan. Map p283 M12.

One of the top high-maintenance dancefloors on the Costanera Norte, Mint fills out with a colourful fauna of college kids, rich young things and tourists, while providing a stage for local and international guest DJs spinning techno to progressive house. Fridays are for the real fanatics – an enthusiastic crowd lured by the promise of prominent international DJs and willing to fork out the extra AR$10-$30. Saturday's are generally less serious, less expensive but always good *craic*. Before you melt on the dancefloor, escape to the riverside terrace and kick back on the beds set out for the occasion. Groups can rent a cosy muslin-screened box for up to AR$250, no extras included. Even mintier inside is ExtraMint: a VIP sector where champagne is the main commodity. **Photo** *p185*.

Museum

Perú 535, entre Mexico y Venezuela, San Telmo (4771 9628/www.museumclub.com.ar). Bus 2, 9, 10, 22, 24, 29. **Open** 8pm-2am Wed; from 10pm Fri-Sun. **Map** p281 E10.

Wednesday's after-office parties are Museum's biggest, but a suit is usually a prerequisite. Teeming with an assortment of attractive thirtysomethings, it's a definite mid-week highlight. Girls get in free before 10pm. Designed by Gustave Eiffel (who also had a hand in some tower in Paris), it's a top venue for a night's boogying, kitted out with some of the best sound and lighting in the city. Fridays and Saturdays also bring in a crowd, with the added attractions of occasional trapeze artists and other entertainments as well as the usual DJ fare. Downstairs there's a popular preamble of dinner and show (anything from live music to strippers) until the DJ kicks in around 3am. Upstairs, you'll find a fairly standard mix of house and techno.

Niceto Club

Niceto Vega 5510, entre Humboldt y Fitz Roy, Palermo Viejo (4779 9396/www.nicetoclub.com). Bus 39, 93, 151, 168. **Open** from 12.30am Thur, Fri; from 1am Sat. **Map** p279 N4.

Still BA's most happening dance spot, Niceto Vega hosts Thursday's notorious frenzy, Club 69. Greeted by a fanfare of transvestite hostesses and a Rocky Horror-style stage show (from 3am), the more conservative may be forgiven for making a dash for the nearest exit. However, by 4am, the main room is rammed with punters, sweating it out to sets of house and techno. Add some impressive visuals and a few licentious podium dancers and the recipe's almost complete. For a change of pace, battle your way to room two for funk and hip-hop. Fridays and Saturdays are less established, but commercial house and funk continue to draw a sizable crowd. Before 1.30am, you can catch a live gig from local or international talents, ranging from flamenco shows to Jamaican ska and electropop. **Photo** *p181*.

Pachá

Avenida Costanera Rafael Obligado, y La Pampa, Costanera Norte (4788 4280/www. pacha-ba.com). *Bus 37, 160.* **Open** Mid Feb-Dec from midnight Fri; from 2am Sat. **Map** p285 R11.

It was Saturday night's Clubland@Pachá that put Buenos Aires on the global clubbing map and it's still considered one of the best clubs in town. Closed for several months after the Cromagnon fire, this key player on the Buenos Aires scene could not remain out of the picture for long. Despite its huge size and multiple dancefloors, Pachá is usually packed well into the morning – saying hello to the sun on the glorious riverside terrrace is bog standard so pack your sunnies. Arrive just before dawn so you can catch the sunrise and the musical zenith (a crescendoing mix of prog trance and techno). Regular visits from major international players like the Chemical Brothers keep the club news, though now that local DJ svengali Martin Gontad is less involved, the bigger local names tend to be special guests rather than regulars.

Podestá Súper Club de Copas

Armenia 1740, entre El Salvador y Costa Rica, Palermo Viejo (4832 2776/www.elpodesta.com.ar). *Bus 15, 39, 110, 140.* **Open** from 11pm Fri, Sat. **Map** p279 M5.

Podestá retains a resolutely underground feel while attracting a loyal crowd of regulars. The atmosphere comes mainly from the blend of alternative rock in the lively ground-floor bar and upbeat house and techno in the lofty converted upstairs studio. While fairly gritty below, the second floor has benefited from a recent overhaul and now attracts an array of new punters in addition to the art student crowd.

Podestá Versión Discoteca

Alvarez Thomas y Federico Lacroze, Colegiales (4832 2776/www.elpodesta.com.ar). *Bus 19, 39, 45 93, 112, 168.* **Open** from 12.30am Sat. **Map** p279 P4.

The Podestá team seems to have hit upon a good formula, but if the Palermo Viejo venue (*see above*) isn't up your street, Saturday nights in this spacious converted theatre are definitely worth a look. It's a hugely impressive building with a big capacity and the perfect spot for a beat-hungry mob to dance away a few hours. The interior is split-level; the DJ, unusually positioned above and behind the crowd, spins a mix of commercial and hard house. Call ahead to secure a pass for the plush VIP section, kitted out with its own dancefloor and sofa area.

Rumi

Avenida Figueroa Alcorta 6442, y La Pampa, Núñez (4782 1307). *Bus 37, 130.* **Open** from 1.30am Wed-Sat. **Map** p285 R10.

Despite being a recent additon to the Buenos Aires dance scene, Rumi has already been incorporated into the northern suburbs' 'must go' list for Fridays and Saturdays. It pulls in the laid-back, Diesel jean wearing type, with the average age dropping from the mid thirties on Thursday's Noche de Revival to a younger, friskier crowd on the weekends, when resident DJ Martín Diaz is in the booth. Earlier in the evening (from 9pm), Rumi serves up decent sushi platters, and cocktails that, at AR$12 each, are worth savouring before you venture out on to the floor.

Mint. *See p184*.

Film

To understand BA, you need to see the bigger picture.

The majority of their cinemas are either old and decaying or brand new and soulless, but *porteños* are, and have always been, in thrall to the silver screen. For proof look no further than the booming **Festival Internacional de Cine Independiente** (*see p175*) which takes place in mid-April. From mid-morning to midnight, for ten days of cinematic frenzy, the state-of-the-art Hoyts Abasto multiplex and other city cinemas screen more than 180 films from the most diverse sectors of the international indie scene. There's a fierce official competition as well as late night screenings of bizarre cinema.

NEW ARGENTINIAN CINEMA

If Hollywood is characterised by conformity and copycat, the 'new wave' of Argentinian cinema is a marvellously messy bag of directors, ideologies and settings. Local media talk of a school of '*cine*', but all they really have in common is an excess of creativity and the gumption to make interesting feature films on a shoestring. There is also a healthy contempt

for parabolic plots and pat endings, which gives many of the Argentinian films of the last decade a 'slice of life' quality. It may be this that has made the grittier films so successful in Europe and on the US arthouse circuit – they take audiences back to the kitchen sink dramas of the 1960s and away from the brain-addling slush of special effects and big name actors.

Thus it wasn't computer-enhanced wizardry that made Carlos Sorín's 2003 Patagonian road movie *Historias mínimas* one of the joys of that year – just a dog, a cake, an endless highway and a cheesy TV quiz show. More whimsical and eloquent than most of the films set in manic BA, the film's interwoven 'minimal stories' went on to win a Goya and a host of other prizes. In some ways, the title of the film defines the prevailing ethos of Argentinian realism. Sorín's latest flick, *Bombón el perro* (Bombón the Dog, 2004), another warm, deadpan take on the everyday foibles of the human (and canine) condition, won the Fipresci prize at the San Sebastián film festival.

Carlos Sorín's *Bombón the Dog* (*left*) and Lucrecia Martel's *The Holy Girl*.

Sorín, as you may have surmised, likes working with dogs – perhaps because they tend to waive their fees. In general, though, Argentinian 'new wave' directors prefer to home in on strictly human frailties. Two outstanding contemporary Argentinian directors working in this mode are Daniel Burman and Lucrecia Martel, who regularly share platforms at international film festival fringe events. Burman's acclaimed *El abrazo partido* (*Lost Embrace*, 2004) charts the struggle of Ariel, a young, aimless Jewish *porteño*, as he tries to come to terms with his father's departure for Israel in the early 1970s to fight in the Yom Kippur war. Uruguayan Daniel Hendler, who plays the lead, won Best Actor at the 2004 Berlin festival, while the film took the Jury Grand Prix. Burman's latest film, also starring Hendler, is *Derecho de familia* (*Family Law*, 2006), a sharp comedy-drama about a dazed and confused thirtysomething lawyer going through a premature mid-life crisis.

Martel's *La niña santa* (*The Holy Girl*, 2004), her follow-up to the harrowing *La ciénaga*, is the story of the sexual awakening – and subsequent Catholic guilt – of a 16-year-old choir girl. It was shown as part of the official selection at Cannes 2004 and has since been screened all over the world.

Whichever way you look at it, viewing Argentina through the eyes of local directors is usually more rewarding than seeing it from the perspective of foreign auteurs. Spaniard Carlos Saura's Oscar-winning dance film *Tango* (1998) and Wong Kar Wai's gay holiday movie *Happy Together* (1997) get away with their tango-laced effusions, but Robert Duvall's *Assassination Tango* (2002) and Christopher Hampton's *Imagining Argentina* (2003), starring Emma Thompson and Antonio Banderas no less, should be avoided at all costs.

Independent cinema continues to thrive in Argentina and 2005 saw a number of noteworthy developments. After scooping up various prizes at international festivals, Jorge Gaggero's acclaimed *Cama adentro*, is a smartly written film about a middle class woman marooned with her maid during Argentina's 2001 economic crisis. Juan Solanas, son of esteemed director Fernando 'Pino' Solanas, unveiled his first full-length feature, *Noroeste*, at Cannes. The film explores the north-eastern region of the title through the eye of a foreigner, a French woman travelling north to adopt a baby. After making the dense neo-realist drama *El asadito* (1999), veteran Gustavo Postiglione reared his head again with two other productions, *Impanema* and *Miami*, the latter first released as a short, and later lengthened and released as *Miami Rmx*.

Cinemas

Buenos Aires has always had two classes of cinema: those in the city centre – around Avenidas Santa Fe, Corrientes, Callao and on the pedestrianised stretch of Lavalle – and those in the outlying neighbourhoods. These days, shiny new multiplexes offering state-of-the-art technology and US-style facilities draw most of the audiences. Smaller cinemas are fading at an alarming rate, though a handful of art house venues and amateur cine clubs thankfully still thrive.

INFO, TIMINGS AND TICKETS

Nearly all films are shown in their original version with Spanish subtitles. Children's films are the only exception, and even then original versions are often shown at selected venues. Some cinemas have late-night showings (*trasnoches*) beginning around 1am on weekends. Tickets cost almost half-price on Wednesdays and at many early showings.

Check the *Espectáculos* sections of local papers for cinema listings. As English-language film titles are often translated and end up bearing no resemblance to the original, it helps to buy the *Buenos Aires Herald*, which publishes English-language listings. The Friday edition includes capsule reviews of recommended films. Celluloid lovers who can read Spanish should pick up long-running film magazine *El Amante*. The website www.cinenacional.com is a superb Spanish-language resource on Argentinian cinema, with an exhaustive, searchable database. Free weekly listings mag *Llegás* (available in shops and bars) has trenchant reviews and excellent information on art-house screenings. If you have cable TV, tune in to Volver channel, with its classic reruns. I-SAT channel also shows hard-to-find classics and indie movies.

The film rating system in Argentina has four different categories: ATP (suitable for all ages); SAM13 (suitable for under-13s, only if accompanied by an adult); SAM16 (no under-16s); and SAM18 (no under-18s).

City centre

Listed below are the best of the downtown cinemas; others are old and lacking in facilities. New releases include Hollywood blockbusters, European art-fare and Latin American cinema.

Atlas Lavalle

Lavalle 869, entre Suipacha y Esmeralda, Microcentro (4328 6643/www.atlascines.com.ar). Subte C, Lavalle/10, 17, 70 bus. **Open** from noon daily. **Tickets** AR$10 Thur-Sun; AR$6 Mon-Wed. **No credit cards. Map** p281 G11.

This once-historical cinema has been split up into five smaller screens, but is still a bit of a relic. It mostly features Hollywood new releases.

Atlas Santa Fe
Avenida Santa Fe 2015, entre Ayacucho y Junín, Barrio Norte (4823 7878/www.atlascines.com.ar). Subte D, Callao/39, 60, 111, 124, 152 bus. **Open** from noon daily. **Tickets** AR$11 daily; AR$7 first showing daily. **Credit** AmEx, V. **Map** p282 I10.
This Barrio Norte movie house is a two-screen cinema, last renovated in the 1980s, showing new releases.

Espacio INCAA KM 0 – Gaumont Rivadavia
Rivadavia 1635, entre Rodríguez Peña y Montevideo, Congreso (4371 3050). Subte A, Congreso/12, 37, bus. **Open** from noon daily. **Tickets** AR$3 concessions. **No credit cards. Map** p281 G9.
This three-screen cinema, and the Complejo Tita Merello at Suipacha No.442 (4322 1195), are supported by INCAA (the National Film Board). They only show new Argentinian releases (no English subtitles). The Gaumont is the better equipped.

Lorca
Avenida Corrientes 1428, entre Paraná y Uruguay, Tribunales (4371 5017). Subte B, Uruguay/24, 26, 102 bus. **Open** from 2pm daily. **Tickets** AR$8 Thur-Sun; AR$5 Mon-Wed. **No credit cards. Map** p281 G10.
One of the most traditional cinemas on Corrientes, Lorca is one of BA's best options for independent film, showing an excellent pick of local and foreign non-mainstream movies on its two screens.

Nuevo Cine Metro
Cerrito 570, entre Tucumán y Lavalle, Tribunales (4382 4219). Subte D, Tribunales/29, 39, 109 bus. **Open** from 12.30pm daily. **Tickets** AR$10 Thur-Sun; AR$6 Mon-Wed. **No credit cards. Map** p281 G10.
Recently refurbished, the Metro is a decent and centrally located cinema option, although it may not be the most high-tech in town. Fronting on Avenida 9 de Julio, it boasts three screens showing mostly new releases from mainstream cinema.

Multiplexes

Cinemark 8
Alicia Moreau de Justo 1920, y San Juan, Puerto Madero (4315 5522/www.cinemark.com.ar). Bus 4, 64, 130 152. **Open** from noon daily. **Tickets** AR$13; AR$8.50 Mon-Wed, before 4pm Thur-Sun, under-12s, concessions. **Credit** AmEx, MC, V. **Map** p280 D10.
This modern complex down in the docklands has eight screens and a restaurant. It shows a mixture of Hollywood and Latin American new releases. A ten-screen branch, conveniently located near the Alto Palermo shopping centre, opened in 2001. **Other locations**: Cinemark 10, Beruti 3399, Palermo (4827 5700/4827 9500 information).

Village Recoleta
Vicente López 2050, y Junín, Recoleta (0810 444 66843/credit card booking 4800 0000/www.village cines.com). Bus 10, 130. **Open** from 11am daily. **Tickets** AR$15; AR$9.75 before 12.30pm and all day Wed, under-12s, concessions. **Credit** AmEx, DC, MC, V. **Map** p282 J11.
This huge complex near Recoleta Cemetery includes bars, restaurants, a food court, games arcade, bookshop, Tower Records and a 16-screen cinema on three floors. The childcare facility at weekends for two- to 12-year-olds is a big draw for cinephile parents.

Repertory & art-house

Malba (*see p95*) hosts excellent cinema events: new indie releases, outstanding retrospectives with restored 35mm prints and lectures by filmmakers. San Telmo's **Museo del Cine** also features film cycles and home-grown films, and the **British Arts Centre** (*see p74*) screens movies focused on British culture. Opening hours vary – call or check websites for details.

Alianza Francesa de Buenos Aires
Avenida Córdoba 946, entre Suipacha y Carlos Pellegrini, Microcentro (4322 0068/01/www.alianzafrancesa.org.ar). Subte C, Lavalle/59, 99, 106, 132. **Open** movie showings from 8pm Tue. Closed Jan, Feb. **Tickets** free. **Map** p281 G11.
The respected French-language institution doubles as a prestigious cultural centre offering riveting cycles of international cinema in its refined and comfortable auditorium.

Centro Cultural Ricardo Rojas
Avenida Corrientes 2038, entre Junín y Ayacucho, Once (4954 5521/www.rojas.uba.ar). Subte B, Callao/24, 26, 60, 124 bus. **Tickets** AR$2-$5. **No credit cards. Map** p281 H9.
This lively cultural centre shows interesting arthouse and experimental fare in its one cinema.

Cosmos
Avenida Corrientes 2046, entre Ayacucho y Junín, Once (4953 5405/www.cinecosmos.com). Subte B, Callao/24, 26, 60 bus. **Tickets** AR$9 Thur-Sun; AR$5 Mon-Wed, before 4pm Thur-Sun. **No credit cards. Map** p281 H9.
A film buff's paradise, Cosmos features new Argentinian releases, as well as retrospectives and auteur films from all over the word.

Sala Leopoldo Lugones
10th Floor, Teatro San Martín, Avenida Corrientes 1530, entre Paraná y Montevideo, Tribunales (freephone 0800 333 5254/www.teatrosanmartin. com.ar). Subte B, Uruguay/24, 26, 60, 102 bus. **Tickets** AR$5. **No credit cards. Map** p281 G9.
Named after one of Argentina's most important cultural figures, the poet Leopoldo Lugones, this cinema is located within the San Martín theatre complex. The historical auditorium offers screenings of first-rate art-house movies from all over the world.

Shock of the new Argentinian cinema

How often it is that the worst of times brings out the best in filmmakers! The golden age of Hollywood coincided with the Great Depression. British cinema shone brightest during the dark days of World War II. And when, in late 2001, Argentina stared into its own abyss, the cameras were there to capture the moment, both literally and metaphorically. 'New Argentinian cinema' was born. Or, to put it more accurately, *christened*. For in fact Argentinian cinema had been thriving since the mid 1990s, when a booming economy and a raft of government measures put state cash into the coffers of independent production companies for the first time. Argentina has never lacked for creative writers and directors, but a shoestring will only stretch so far. Decent investment and a proper support structure were the fertilising influences needed for Argentinian cinema to blossom into a bona fide film industry.

And so it did. Filmmakers like Martín Reijtman – director of *Rapado* (1992) and *Los guantes mágicos* (2003), and in many ways the movement's spiritual father – and Alejandro Agresti (*Pizza, birra, faso*, 1997) began to deal directly with the vicissitudes of contemporary life, appealing to a new generation of film-goers.

What distinguished these films was their deftly satirical approach to narrative and the way they turned a cold, objective eye on Argentina's troubling social issues without throwing ideological dogma at the viewer. If all Argentinians had wanted to do was find out what was going wrong in the country on any particular day, they could simply switch on the evening news. What 'new Argentinian cinema' offered, and still offers, is a fresh, sometimes allegorical and often deliberately distorted snapshot of the national mood.

Would the world have cared about, or even noticed, 'new Argentinian cinema' but for the economic and social crisis of 2001? I would like to think so. Most of the filmmakers mentioned here have looked at Argentina's political present only obliquely; to misquote St Paul, through a camera lens, darkly. My own movies are about the search for identity in an atomised society, a theme that runs through all of Argentinian history. But more importantly they are comedies, extended riffs on universal themes like fatherhood and ethnicity. Lucrecia Martel's *La niña santa* (*The Holy Girl*, 2004) is set in a dingy conference hotel in the boondocks; it happens to be in the north of Argentina but it could just as well be in West Virginia. Carlos Sorín's *Bombón el perro* (*Bombón the Dog*, 2005) is set in a Patagonia that is depressed by unemployment and worker discontent. But at heart it's a touching story about the relationship between a man and his dog – and who doesn't love *that*?

What these examples illustrate is that new Argentinian cinema is not a 'movement' as such. Unlike the Dogma group of the 1990s, we set ourselves no stylistic strictures, nor do we cleave to a political manifesto. Although that kind of approach has its uses – it can produce great cinema – it also has 'straight to DVD' stamped all over it.

Instead, we want to make cinema that reflects Argentina's diversity, the exuberance and dark humour of its people and their penchant (some would say fetish) for self-analysis. We'll leave it to others to hold up the proverbial 'mirror to society'. We're happy simply to point a camera.

Daniel Burman, director of *Derecho de familia* (*Family Law*, 2006; *pictured*).

Arts & Entertainment

Galleries

Rich pickings for culture vultures.

It's a good time to be either an artist or an art buyer in Buenos Aires. The happy coincidence of the prostrate Argentinian peso and a thriving local scene has led bargain-hunting international dealers to take a closer look at *porteño* art; and even the casual tourist has enough spending power to make quality acquisitions.

The flagship for the city's burgeoning art market is the annual **arteBA** fair (*see p175*), held every year in May since 1991. This week-long event has evolved into one of the best attended and most hyped cultural events in Latin America, pulling more than 100,000 buyers and enthusiasts in 2005.

Geographically, Palermo Viejo, San Telmo and Abasto now compete with traditional art zones Recoleta and Barrio Norte. Fringe venues in these areas are flourishing. Complementing this expansion in non-traditional spaces is a growing interest by local artists in using non-traditional methods – particularly the technology-heavy fields of video and digital art, and photography. Outstanding local artists working in these media include Sergio Loof, Liliana Porter and Sara Facio, the latter celebrated for her feminist viewpoint and exquisite portraits. To see the work of photographers and video and digital artists, **Arte x Arte** gallery is unmissable.

Sharp-eyed entrepreneurs and corporate sponsors are getting in on the action too. Businessman and philanthropist Eduardo Costantini's prestigious venture, **Malba (Museo de Arte Latinoamericano de Buenos Aires;** *see p95*), has, in the space of five years, established itself as one of the most exciting cultural hotspots in the capital, successfully challenging the hegemony of traditional, state-managed – which often means mismanaged – institutions such as the **Museo Nacional de Bellas Artes** (*see p91*) and the **Museo de Arte Moderno** (*see p80*).

INFORMATION

The websites www.ramona.org.ar, www.arte baires.com.ar and www.arsomnibus.com.ar provide listings for most galleries. Look for an *inauguración* (opening) or a *muestra* (show). For less mainstream happenings, flyers can be picked up in places as diverse as downtown bars and cafés or Palermo Viejo boutiques. Alternatively, head for specialist bookshops like Libros de Arte (Libertad 1384, Recoleta, 4812 0023) or try shops within the major museums.

Galleries

Galleries do not charge admission or take credit cards unless otherwise stated. Many of them are closed during the summer vacation (January and February). Look out for the 'Gallery Nights' programme which runs between March and November: over 60 galleries open their doors to the public (from seven to 11pm).

180° – Arte Contemporáneo

Basement, San Martín 975, entre Paraguay y Marcelo T de Alvear, Retiro (4312 9211/www. 180gradosarte.com.ar). Subte C, San Martín/ 10, 93, 130, 152 bus. **Open** 1pm-midnight Mon-Fri; 1-4pm Sat. **Map** p281 G12.
An underground art gallery in the literal sense, this well-lit and intelligently put together space in the basement beneath Filo restaurant (*see p111*) is devoted to photography, video and digital art.

Arroyo

Arroyo 830/834, entre Suipacha y Esmeralda, Retiro (4325 0947/www.galarroyo.com). Subte C, San Martín/17, 59, 61, 67, 92 bus. **Open** 11am-8pm Mon-Fri; for auctions Sat, Sun. **Map** p281 H12.
Arroyo's real strength is its monthly auctions. They offer a wide range of works by renowned artists at relatively affordable prices.

Arte x Arte

Lavalleja 1062, entre Córdoba y Lerma, Villa Crespo (4772 6754/4773 2738/www.artea.com.ar/artexarte). Bus 15, 92, 106, 109, 168. **Open** *Apr-Dec* 1-7pm Mon-Sat. Closed Jan-Mar. **Map** p278 L4.
Arte x Arte claims to be the largest South American gallery space – 1,800 square metres (19,355 square feet) – dedicated exclusively to photography, video and digital art. Here, you'll find six exhibition spaces, a library and a bar.

Belleza y Felicidad

Acuña de Figueroa 900, y Guardia Vieja, Almagro (4867 0073/www.bellezayfelicidad.com.ar). Subte B, Medrano/19, 24, 26, 124, 127 bus. **Open** 11am-7.30pm Mon-Fri; 11am-4pm Sat. **Map** p282 K7.
Beauty and happiness? It's an old-fashioned view of the function of art but a trip to Belleza y Felicidad should put a smile on your face. The two spaces are appealingly anarchic – is that an installation or a running repair? – and showcase local artists.

El Borde

Uriarte 1356, entre Niceto Vega y Cabrera, Palermo Viejo (4777 4573/www.el-borde.com). Bus 34, 140, 151, 168. **Open** 2-8pm Mon-Sat. **Map** p279 M4.

Opened in June 2003, this metal shop turned gallery is an attractive and original space in which to check out contemporary artwork from less commercial, upcoming BA artists. The single exhibition room showcases a wide range of media – photography, video art, painting and installation.

Centro Cultural Borges

Galerías Pacífico, Viamonte, y San Martín, Retiro (5555 5449/www.ccborges.org.ar). Subte C, San Martín/10, 17, 152 bus. **Open** 10am-9pm Mon-Sat; noon-9pm Sun. **Admission** AR\$2. **Map** p281 G11.

It's not an art gallery per se (the eclectic events programme also includes independent cinema and experimental theatre) but the Borges centre has hosted many of *the* must-see exhibitions of recent years. These included the 2005 Andy Warhol show, the city's most visited exhibition of that year.

Centro Cultural de España

Basement, Florida 943, entre Paraguay y Marcelo T de Alvear, Retiro (4312 5850/www.cceba.org.ar). Subte C, San Martín/10, 17, 152 bus. **Open** *Jan, Feb* 10.30am-4.30pm Mon-Fri. *Mar-Dec* 10.30am-8pm Mon-Fri. **Map** p281 G11.

This centre promotes visual arts and media by both Argentinian and Spanish artists. There are also music events and poetry readings.

Centro Cultural Recoleta

Junín 1930, y Quintana, Recoleta (4803 1040/ www.centroculturalrecoleta.org). Bus 10, 17, 60, 67, 92, 110. **Open** 2-9pm Tue-Fri, 10am-9pm Sat, Sun. **Admission** free; AR\$1 suggested contribution. **Map** p282 J11.

Long established as the darling of the Buenos Aires art scene, the scope of CCR's 20 exhibition spaces ranges from children's drawings to work produced by psychiatric patients, as well as shows featuring well-established artists. Its largest space, Cronopio, is used for major retrospectives or group shows and has displayed artists as diverse as Yoko Ono, Liliana Porter and León Ferrari.

Dabbah Torrejón Arte Contemporáneo

Sánchez de Bustamante 1187, entre Córdoba y Cabrera, Palermo (4963 2581/www.dabbahtorrejon. com.ar). Bus 99, 109. **Open** 3-8pm Tue-Fri; 11am-2pm Sat. Closed Sat in Jan, Feb. **Map** p278 K6.

Since September 2000, this cutting-edge gallery, occupying a converted house near Abasto, has promised to be 'a bridge between creativity and the public' – and it has kept its pledge. Exhibiting works by a stable of promising young artists – including the likes of Fabián Burgos, Alejandra Seeber, Sergio Avello and Mariana López – the gallery is becoming accustomed to rave reviews.

Daniel Abate

Pasaje Bollini 2170, entre French y Peña, Recoleta (4804 8247/www.danielabategaleria.com.ar). Bus 10, 21, 37. **Open** noon-7pm Tue-Sat. **Map** p282 K10.

Voted best local exhibitor at arteBA 2005, Daniel Abate's gallery is considered one of the best nurseries for young and original Argentinian art talent. Look out for the children's-book-illustrator-on-acid paintings of Mariano Grassi and Sandro Pereira's half-cute, half-scary giant rubber duckies.

Contemporary creepy-crawlies at the **Centro Cultural Recoleta**.

Arts & Entertainment

Fabulous *fileteado*

Buenos Aires, which talks up tango and brags about Borges, is surprisingly bashful about promoting its unique contribution to the visual arts, the decorative style known as *fileteado*. When asked about it, most *porteños* will reward you with a blank stare.

Which is strange when you consider that *file* (as it is usually known) is a fundamentally public and popular art genre. It was never meant for museum walls. Indeed, the originators of *file*, who lived in BA in the late 19th century, weren't even artists – they were immigrants, mostly of Italian background, employed as engineers and bodywork finishers in the city's transport workshops.

They weren't paid to paint. But, upon deciding that their vehicles should look good as well as run smoothly, paint they did, using cheap acrylics and their own ingenuity. With the side panels of *colectivos* (city buses), handcarts and delivery vans as their canvasses, workers like Salvador Venturo and Vicente Brunetti developed the signature style of fileteado: brightly coloured decorative whorls and vortices, flower motifs, calligraphic flourishes and tendril-like lines that resolve themselves into the heads of fabulous creatures. (If Gustav Klimt had lived to design an early Grateful Dead album cover, he might have come up with something like this.) Pithy phrases and maxims were often incorporated into the design, making *file* a sophisticated precursor of the bumper sticker.

Up until the mid 1970s, therefore, the main audience for *file* consisted of commuters. It was steadfastly ignored by the *porteño* art elite – perhaps because it wasn't elitist enough. Then, showing the same disregard for aesthetics as they did for human rights, the use of *file* on city buses was banned by the military dictatorship. Buenos Aires entered a darker period in more ways than one.

But the good news for lovers of colour is that *fileteado* is making a comeback. Once dismissed for being grassroots and 'native' (there is a parallel with tango here), *file* is now lauded for exactly those reasons. It is reappearing on the walls of concert venues (for example, San Telmo's Torquato Tasso centre; pictured), on book covers, in ad campaigns and as part of interior design schemes. A good example of the last-named is the painted floor of the El Mercado restaurant at the super-trendy Faena Hotel + Universe.

The artist commissioned by the Faena, and the leading contemporary exponent of *fileteado*, is Alfredo Genovese. A passionate cheerleader for *file*, he has recently published a book about it; the English translation is called *Fileteado Porteño* and is available in all major BA bookshops. For more information go to www.fileteado.com.ar.

Daniel Maman Fine Arts

Avenida del Libertador 2475, entre Bulnes y Ruggieri, Palermo (4804 3700/www.danielmaman.com). Bus 10, 37, 59, 60, 102. **Open** 11am-7pm Mon-Fri; 11am-8pm Sat. **Map** p282 L10.

Openings at Daniel Maman's chic and good-looking gallery attract a chic and good-looking crowd. With an uncanny flair for selecting talented and charismatic figures, such as Rómulo Maccio, Alicia Penalba, Nicolás García Uriburu and Karina El Azem, Maman's shows always make waves.

Dharma Fine Art

1st Floor, Door 1, Rue des Artisans, Arenales 1239, entre Libertad y Talcahuano, Recoleta (4814 4700/ www.dharmafinearts.com). Bus 17, 102. **Open** 2-8pm Mon-Fri. **Map** p281 H11.

A first-rate gallery and interactive space, where artists and sponsors get together to create new projects. The thoughtful shows exhibit works by Argentinian masters, as well as the newest 'Young Turks'.

Elsi del Río

Arévalo 1748, entre Honduras y El Salvador, Palermo Viejo (4899 0171/www.elsidelrio.com.ar). Bus 39, 55. **Open** Feb-Dec 3-8pm Tue-Fri; 11am-2pm Sat. Closed Jan. **Map** p279 O5.

This former butcher's shop opened as a gallery in 2000 and continues energetically to promote young and emerging artists, both local and international. Its exhibitions always manage to exude a sense of play no matter how serious the messages therein, and the gallery boasts a varied annual programme of individual and group exhibitions.

Espacio Fundación Telefónica

Arenales 1540, entre Montevideo y Paraná, Recoleta (4333 1300/www.fundacion.telefonica.com.ar/ espacio). Bus 10, 37, 59, 102. **Open** *2-8.30pm Tue-Sun.* **Map** *p281 H10.*

Opened in late 2003, this two-floor contemporary centre has both artistic and educational ambitions. Sophisticated multimedia technology is used to present the visual arts alongside social projects and research. There are media labs and educational activities on site alongside the exhibition space.

Fundación Alberto Elía/ Mario Robirosa

Ground Floor, Studio A, Azcuénaga 1739, entre Pacheco de Melo y Las Heras, Recoleta (4803 0496). Bus 10, 37, 41, 101, 102. **Open** *Mar-Dec* 2-8pm Mon-Fri. Closed Jan, Feb. **Map** p282 J10.

The owners of this small, smart space have minds of their own and aren't afraid to show it. The place stages coherent exhibitions by contemporary artists such as painter Carlos Gorriarena and filmmaker Jorge Polaco. The guest list at openings reads like a *Who's Who* of the Buenos Aires art world.

Fundación Federico Jorge Klemm

Basement, Marcelo T de Alvear 626, entre Maipú y Florida, Retiro (4312 4443/www.fundacionfjklemm. org). Subte C, San Martín/10, 17, 70, 152 bus. **Open** 11am-8pm Mon-Fri. Closed Jan. **Map** p281 G11.

This important downtown gallery, once run by the late mega personality/TV presenter/art patron/artist Federico Klemm (and now administered by the National Fine Arts Academy), houses many key Argentinian works (including some Bernis) and an impressive international collection (Picasso, Dali, Warhol, Mapplethorpe). At the back, Klemm's own creations (imagine an even more self-obsessed Andy Warhol) and his collection of 20th-century pop arcana – costumes worn by Nureyev and dresses owned by Evita – are on permanent display.

Fundación Proa

Avenida Pedro de Mendoza 1929, y Del Valle Iberlucea, La Boca (4303 0909/www.proa.org). Bus 29, 64, 152. **Open** 11am-7pm Tue-Sun. **Admission** AR$3; AR$1-$2 concessions. **Map** p280 A8.

Since setting-up in a recycled building on the La Boca riverfront in 1996, Proa has presented some of the most stimulating and insightfully curated shows in Buenos Aires. Six major annual exhibitions and other cultural events keep the premises bustling, while the inviting roof terrace affords great views of the filthy, but nonetheless iconic, Riachuelo. Some memorable recent shows have included Sol Lewitt, Diego Rivera, 'Metropolitan Icons', 'Scenes of the 1980s' and 'Art in La Boca'.

Praxis

Arenales 1311, y Talcahuano, Recoleta (4813 8639/www.praxis-art.com). Bus 10, 39, 152. **Open** 10.30am-8pm Mon-Fri; 10.30am-2pm Sat. **Map** p281 H11.

Praxis is a local gallery with international reach, with spaces in Buenos Aires, the US and Brazil. Dedicated to contemporary figurative works, it's one of the driving forces in promoting Argentinian art. **Other locations**: Arroyo 858, Recoleta (4393 0803).

Rubbers

Avenida Alvear 1595, y Montevideo, Recoleta (4816 1864/1869/www.rubbers.com.ar). Bus 17, 61, 67, 92, 93. **Open** 11am-8pm Mon-Fri; 11am-1.30pm Sat. **Map** p282 I11.

Directed by Natalio Povarché (who founded the business in 1957), this gallery has (paradoxically, given its name) always been synonymous with solidity in art. The Alvear gallery opened in 2003 with a spectacular Berni exhibit; the other location is in the stunning Ateneo bookshop (*see p149*). **Other locations**: 3rd Floor, Santa Fe 1860, Barrio Norte (4816 1782).

Ruth Benzacar

Florida 1000, y Marcelo T de Alvear, Retiro (4313 8480/www.ruthbenzacar.com). Subte C, San Martín/10, 17, 132, 152 bus. **Open** 11.30am-8pm Mon-Fri. **Map** p281 G11.

Founded in 1965 by the late Ruth Benzacar – and now run by her daughter Orly – this well-located gallery was the jewel in the crown of swinging 1960s Buenos Aires. Young artists are enthusiastically received and the forceful gallery remains one of the leaders of the pack. Also opens Saturday mornings in March only (10.30am-1.30pm).

Stimulating sights at **Fundación Proa**.

Gay & Lesbian

Big parties, bargain prices, beautiful people – what more do you want?

The people are sexy, the scene is diverse, the seat of government is painted pink – no wonder BA is replacing Rio and São Paulo as the gay capital of South America. São Paulo may have better clubs and Rio has its beaches, but for its effortless style, range of attractions and, above all, the insatiable hedonism of its inhabitants, the Argentinian capital brooks no rivals.

Current estimates put the amount of gay tourists visiting Buenos Aires at around 20 per cent of the overall total, and that percentage promises to rise as the word spreads. And it's no surprise. The city offers a variety of services aimed at gay visitors, including bars, clubs, restaurants, accommodation options and even clothing stores and beauty parlours – and all at knock-down prices. While not every locale is solely aimed at the gay market, many are gay-friendly – as are the vast majority of the city's relatively progressive and respectful inhabitants. Even the city government's official website, www.bue.gov.ar, includes a link to direct you to the gay scene.

Gays and lesbians now have all kinds of organisations and services at their disposal, from travel agencies such as **Pride Travel** (2nd floor, Office E, Paraguay 523, 5218 6556/www.pride-travel.com) and gay city tour guides, to tango teachers at gay *milongas*.

There's even a 'gay map' backed by the city government's tourist office. You can find it at gay bars and most tourist information points. Also look out for the city's first five-star gay hotel, as yet unnamed but scheduled to open in San Telmo in early 2007. The city's most visible event is November's **Marcha del Orgullo Gay** (Gay Pride; *see p177*), first staged in 1992. It has been growing in size since its inception and now attracts more than 10,000 revellers.

WHERE'S THE PARTY?

For daytime cruising, head to Plaza Palermo Viejo – especially the café Bartok, on the corner of Armenia and Costa Rica. This is a relaxed part of the city, close to many hip boutiques and designer shops. Plaza las Heras and the Jardín Botánico are also cruisy; or get active with roller skating and other sports around the Rosedal park in Palermo.

Although defining specific queer areas is tricky, the neighbourhoods of Palermo and Barrio Norte form part of a notional 'Gayland'. Historic San Telmo is also gay-friendly and the

Sunday Antiques Market is as busy as it is cruisy. Try **Pride Café** at Balcarce 869 (*see p143*) or **La Farmacia** at Bolívar 898 (*see p141*).

The bar-café **El Olmo**, on the corner of Santa Fe and Pueyrredón, continues to be a meeting spot for gays. On weekends, between midnight and around 2.30am, it's around here that you'll find flyers and discount passes for the main clubs and pubs in town, as well as info on events such as the meetings of the Bears' Club (Club de los Osos). For those into leather, check www.fierroleather.com.ar.

While BA boasts a great gay clubbing scene, it can often be hard to track down. The scene here is generally more mixed than its London or New York counterparts. Gay men and women are happy to dance with straights at the best events in town. To find out if there is a party this weekend, check the listings and reviews at www.thegayguide.com.ar, an excellent resource with a decent English translation.

Cool coffee house **Pride Café**. See p143.

SAFETY & INFORMATION

Though the general guidelines on safety while being in BA apply to the queer scene, there are a few specifics. The one simple rule is that sex with anyone under the age of 18 is illegal (gay or straight). Street prostitution is also illegal, so picking up a hustler could lead to arrest. Few venues supply condoms, so always carry them with you. If you need information about health, safety or resources in Buenos Aires, contact the organisations listed below. Most of them will have someone who can get by in English. For up-to-the-minute information on BA's queer scene, check out *La Otra Guía* and *Queer* (free in pubs and clubs), or buy *ImperioG*, the best gay magazine around.

Resources

As well as the important gay and lesbian organisations listed below, **Lugar Gay de Buenos Aires** (*see below*) is another useful information point.

Comunidad Homosexual Argentina (CHA)

Tomás Liberti 1080, y Irala, La Boca (4361 6382/ www.cha.org.ar). Bus 10, 24, 39, 70, 93. **Open** phone advice 1.30-8pm Mon-Fri; otherwise, call first. **Map** p280 B9.
Argentina's oldest and most politically influential queer organisation. Go here for advice, information and an exhaustive library of books, videos, films, newsreels and press clippings.

La Fulana

Avenida Rivadavia 3412, entre Sánchez de Bustamente y Billinghurst, Almagro (4867 2752/ www.lafulana.org.ar). Subte A, Loria/52, 86, 132, 151 bus. **Open** 6-10pm Tue-Sat. **Map** p280 I4.
The most useful and efficient community centre for lesbians and bisexual women in Argentina.

Sociedad de Integración Gay-Lésbica Argentina (SIGLA)

Pasaje del Progreso 949, y Salas, Parque Chacabuco (4922 3351/www.sigla.org.ar). Train to E Mitre/26, 86 bus. **Open** 3-6pm Mon, Wed, Fri; 5-10pm Sat.
SIGLA provides legal advice, health information, workshops and recreational activities for gays and lesbians. The website has listings of all the upcoming parties and events.

Where to stay

Many of the city's hotels are gay-friendly, and while they may welcome gay visitors they often lack contact with the community. For more information on gay and gay-friendly hotels in BA, check out www.bestfriendlyhotels.com. Those looking for a longer stay should get in touch with either **El Conventillo Tango Club**

(4373 3995, www.conventillotango.com.ar) or **BAires Rental** (4829 1605, www.bairesgay rental.com.ar). They both offer smart apartments close to the city centre. Otherwise, try these gay owned-and-run bed and breakfasts.

Bayres B&B

Córdoba 5842, entre Carranza y Ravignani, Palermo Viejo (4772 3877/www.bayresbnb.com). Bus 39, 93, 111, 151, 168. **Rates** US$25-$60 single/double. **No credit cards. Map** p283 N7.
Close to top gay bars and clubs such as Amerika and Bach Bar, this cosy B&B is as good as it gets. There's breakfast any time you want, free internet access, plus air-con and cable TV in all five rooms.

Big House

Bolívar 920, entre Estados Unidos y Carlos Calvo, San Telmo (4362 0701/www.bighousefriendly. com.ar). Bus 22, 28, 126. **Rates** US$35-$60 single/double. **Map** p280 D9.
This cosy San Telmo B&B invites guests to make themselves at home. With only five rooms there's a warm, homey feel to the place, and while specifically aimed at the gay market, owner Pedro welcomes all comers, whatever their sexual orientation.

Lihuel Calel Bed & Breakfast

1st Floor, Reconquista 755, entre Viamonte y Córdoba, Microcentro (4893 1060/www.lihuel-calel.com). Subte B, LN Alem/22, 26, 130 bus. **Rates** US$55-$75 single/double. **Map** p281 F11.
For a proper *porteño* immersion, Lihuel Calel's thematic rooms are perfect: they're named after legendary Argentinians such as Borges, Evita, Che Guevara and Carlos Gardel. But the impeccable decor means this downtown accommodation option falls just on the right side of cheesy.

Lugar Gay de Buenos Aires

Defensa 1120, entre Humberto 1º y San Juan, San Telmo (4300 4747/www.lugargay.org). Bus 24, 29, 126. **Rates** US$45-$55 single/double. **No credit cards. Map** p280 D9.
In the heart of picturesque San Telmo, the place is best known as a meeting point; it hosts workshops on literature, gay issues, film and music. Now they offer bed and breakfast too – seven simple but functional rooms with cable TV.

Palermo Viejo Bed & Breakfast

Niceto Vega 4629, y Scalabrini Ortiz, Palermo Viejo (4773 6012/www.palermoviejobb.com). **Rates** US$45 single; US$55 double. **Map** p283 M7.
Under the roving eye of its hands-on owner, this perfectly located and friendly B&B has a number of well-decorated rooms.

Bars & clubs

The action in most bars doesn't start until past midnight, and clubs don't get frisky until after 3am. Many bars feature singers, strippers and drag queens. There's usually a cover charge

Gender bending **Club 69**.

or minimum spend in bars (AR$2-$10) and an admission charge in clubs of up to AR$20. None of these venues accepts credit cards. Gay men enjoy greater visibility than lesbians.

A number of special nights are arranged on a more ad hoc basis and tend to move around from venue to venue. Look out for **Brandon Gay Day** (www.brandongayday.com.ar), a monthly event in which a funky young crowd gathers to drink, dance to electronic music or just chill. Check the website for details on forthcoming parties.

Alsina

Adolfo Alsina 940, entre Bernardo de Irigoyen y Tacuarí, Monserrat (4331 1277/3231/www.palacio buenosaires.com). Bus 59, 64, 86. **Open** from 1.30am Fri, Sat; 8pm-1.30am Sun. **Map** p281 F10.
Hot, clean-cut guys gather in this huge, stylish venue to swing their well-built bodies to dance and house. Saturdays are a straighter affair called Big One (*see p183*). Sundays tend to be better than Fridays and attract the city's hippest, best-looking gay men and women. Only in Buenos Aires would the Sunday tea party get going at 11pm.

Amerika

Gascón 1040, entre Rocamora y Córdoba, Almagro (4865 4416/www.ameri-k.com.ar). Bus 26, 106, 109, 140, 168. **Open** from 1am Fri, Sat. **Map** p278 K5.

It used to be BA's gay mega-disco, but these days Amerika is more straight than gay, so you can pretty much forget about scoring – unless, that is, you head to the darkroom after hours of putting them away at the free beer bar. Not as much fun as it was before it got confused about its identity.

Bach Bar

Cabrera 4390, y Alvarez, Barrio Norte (15 5877 0919, www.bach-bar.com.ar). Bus 26, 106, 151, 168. **Open** from 11pm Tue-Sun. **Map** p282 L7.
One of the few venues serving the BA lesbian scene, Bach is best after 12.30am on Fridays and Saturdays. The music is predominantly cheerful, cheesy pop and the bar is a lot of fun, attracting women (and some men) from across the social spectrum.

Bulnes Class

Bulnes 1250, entre Cabrera y Córdoba, Barrio Norte (4861 7492). Bus 26, 106, 109, 140. **Open** from 6pm Thur; from 11pm Fri, Sat. **Map** 282 K8.
This recently opened venue attracts an older gay crowd. It's a big, brightly painted bar, owned by the same people who brought us Sitges and Glam. It still needs to find its feet – and a few more punters – but early signs are promising.

Club 69

Niceto Vega 5510, entre Humboldt y Fitz Roy, Palermo Viejo (4779 9396/www.nicetoclub.com). Bus 39, 93, 151, 168. **Open** from 1am Thur; last Sat of mth. **Map** p282 K8.
This is a very gay-friendly club that attracts a huge, alternative, young gay crowd when it plays at Niceto Club on Thursday nights (things get going after 2.30am). The atmosphere is pure decadence, making it one of the essential entries on your weekly partying agenda. *See also p184.*

Contramano

Rodríguez Peña 1082, entre Marcelo T de Alvear y Santa Fe, Recoleta (no phone). Bus 12, 37, 39, 124, 152. **Open** from midnight Wed-Sun. **Map** p282 I10.
A pioneer of the Buenos Aires gay scene, Contramano transcends fads. For your musical delight, there's cheesy pop, golden oldies and Latin beats. Older gay men – and plenty of younger ones – have been getting it together here for over two decades now.

GLAM

Cabrera 3046, entre Laprida y Agüero, Barrio Norte (4963 2521/www.glambsas.com.ar). Bus 29, 109, 111. **Open** from 1am Thur, Fri, Sat. **Map** p282 J8.
This spacious, colonial-style house is one of the best gay bars in town, especially after 2.30am on Thursday and Saturday nights. It has three bar areas plus a patio. Hip, sexy boys, lesbians and straight women happily gyrate till late to great tunes. It has cruisy areas along the passageways and it's easy to score. Saturdays can be unbearably crowded.

Kim y Novak

Güemes 4900, y Godoy Cruz, Palermo Viejo (4773 7521). Bus 29, 39, 111, 152. **Open** from 9pm Wed-Sun. **Map** p283 N9.

Arts & Entertainment

Brokeback Buenos Aires?

Long before *Brokeback Mountain* (*pictured*) vaulted rural man love into the limelight, gay men in the pampas were making the pilgrimage to Zona X, a small club in the heart of the dairy land. Making no effort to hide itself, the pink-brick building with a large silver 'X' splashed on the front sits right off the highway. Despite its bold visibility and nearly eight years in business, most have chosen to ignore the club's existence. But lately, due in part to *Brokeback*'s success, increased press coverage has set tongues wagging about this '*rancho gay*', opening a debate on Argentina's greatest sexual taboo: fornicating *gauchos*.

Perhaps what most illuminates the sexual oppression in the pampas is the almost total absence of any historical record of homosexuality in the area. Conventional wisdom insists that the *gaucho*, the ultimate pillar of Argentinian virility and masculinity, did not have sex with other gauchos. And while civil gay unions are recognised in Buenos Aires, the province is light years away from such legislation, and not surprisingly, many gay men choose to move to the city.

But for gay men who want to stick around, the going can be tough, and Zona X looks to provide a bit of relief. Slap bang on Ruta 5, which runs through the bucolic western part of the province of Buenos Aires, it's just two kilometres from Suipacha, a town whose entrance is framed by an archway proclaiming it to be 'The Sensitive City'. The route takes you through massive fields of soy, sunflowers and corn; dairy cows munch next to the highway where *gauchos* bump slowly along in old Ford Falcons and battered trucks, their wide-brimmed hats filling the windshields. Nestled next to a gas station and popular family grill, Zona X sits framed in palm trees. The original dirt floor and straw roof have been replaced with concrete and corrugated steel, and Thursday, Friday and Saturday nights find the club packed with an eclectic mix of pampas party people.

Five pesos gets you through the door and in to the dimly lit, inconspicuous hallway. Once inside, a bar serving reasonably priced beer and cocktails divides a small dance floor and a stage. In the back, close to the bathrooms, there's a dark room for the shyer customers – of which there are many.

Recently, Zona X has become fashionable for late night outings by wealthy gays from the city, but despite this, it's far from a sophisticated, Castro District free-for-all. While transvestites prance about and couples grind on the dance floor, the darker reaches of Zona X are filled with young men – some charmingly decked out in traditional *gaucho* garb but most in street wear – peering nervously around the room. You'll also find older men fidgeting and drinking alone. The sometimes stilted atmosphere perhaps testifies to the difficulties that come with being gay in rural Argentina.

Zona X opens late and usually fills to capacity at around 3 or 4am, at which point the team of formidable, statuesque in-house transvestites take to the stage, executing spectacular karaoke versions of classic *boleros* and *rancheras* (country ballads). It more than makes up for the lack of mountains, Brokeback or otherwise, around these endlessly flat Argentinian plains.

(To get to Zona X from Buenos Aires, we recommend you hire a taxi; it will cost around AR$150 one way. It's best to go with a local.)

Zona X

Ruta Provincial 5, km 128, near Suipacha (no phone). **Open** from 10pm Thur-Sat. **Admission** AR$5. **No credit cards.**

This tiny bar doesn't get going until 2.30am, though it serves good food earlier on. The crowd is around 75 per cent gay and the basement has a dancefloor.

El Olmo
Santa Fe 2502, y Pueyrredón, Barrio Norte (4821 5828). Subte B, Pueyrredón/39, 41, 61, 118, 152 bus. **Open** 7am-2am Mon-Thur, Sun; 24hrs Fri, Sat. **Map** p282 J9.
El Olmo is a classic BA *confitería* by day that mutates into a meeting spot for gay men by night. The atmosphere is relaxed and friendly. One of the best spots for picking up club promotion flyers.

Simón en tu laberinto
Bolívar 860, entre Independencia y Estados Unidos, San Telmo (4361 4529). Bus 22, 28. **Open** from 6pm Tue-Fri; from 12.30am Sat, Sun. **Map** p280 D10.
Mexican dishes spice up this bar, theatre and art space, which offers exhibitions and poetry recitals alongside the enchiladas.

Sitges
Córdoba 4119, entre Palestina y Pringles, Palermo Viejo (4861 3763/www.sitgesonline.com.ar). Bus 109, 168. **Open** from 10.30pm Wed-Sun. **Map** p282 L7.
Sitges is a mainstay of the Buenos Aires gay and lesbian scene. It's packed after 1am on weekends and attracts gay men and women from all walks of life.

Titanic Club
Callao 1156, entre Santa Fe y Arenales, Recoleta (4816 1333/www.the-titanic-club.com.ar). Bus 10, 37, 39, 101, 124, 152. **Open** from 9pm Mon-Sat. **Map** p282 I10

This kitschy, cutesy pub caters to a mixed, mostly male crowd of twenty- to fifty-somethings. Don't be fooled by the name, though – it ain't that big.

Gyms & saunas

American Hot Gym
Ayacucho 449, entre Corrientes y Lavalle, Once (4951 7679). Subte B, Callao/12, 60 bus. **Open** 8am-midnight Mon-Fri; 9am-9pm Sat. **Admission** AR$12 per day. **No credit cards.** **Map** p281 H9.
This fully equipped gym caters to a mainly gay clientele and has a good range of facilities.

Buenos Aires A Full *p.281*
Viamonte 1770, entre Callao y Rodríguez Peña, Tribunales (4371 7263/www.afullspa.com). Subte D, Callao/12, 29, 37, 60 bus. **Open** noon-3am Mon-Thur; 24hrs Fri-Sun. **Admission** AR$30. **No credit cards.** **Map** p281 H10.
This spacious sauna pulls a sexy crowd and has a bar, jacuzzi, steam rooms and gym.

Tom's
Basement, Viamonte 638, entre Maipú y Florida, Microcentro (4322 4404/www.buenosairestoms.com). Subte C, Lavalle/26, 99, 109, 132 bus. **Open** noon-3am Mon-Thur, Sun; 24hrs Fri-Sat. **Admission** AR$7-$8. **No credit cards.** **Map** p281 G11.
Strictly speaking Tom's isn't a sauna – but it is a steamy place for easy scoring. Dimly lit hallways with private cabins and peep holes lead on to two labyrinthine, busy darkrooms. There's also a comfy chill out area and some video booths.

Spicy, sexy **Empire Thai** restaurant and bar: popular with the local gay crowd. *See p113.*

Arts & Entertainment

Music

Buenos Aires sounds almost as good as it looks.

Classical & Opera

After winning political independence from Spain, Argentinians set about asserting their cultural identity. The arts blossomed in Buenos Aires, and by the turn of the 20th century, this 'golden age' had left the city with no fewer than five opera houses. From the original five, two remain standing – the **Teatro Colón** and the **Teatro Coliseo** (Marcelo T de Alvear 1125, Tribunales, 4816 3789), though only the former maintains a regular opera season. Beyond staging world-class operas, the iconic Colón also hosts ballets, concert cycles and intimate recitals and experimental workshops (*see p202* **Theatre of dreams**).

Despite its status as the key classical music centre in South America, BA still doesn't have a venue devoted to symphonic concerts. Instead, these are performed across the city in places like the **Teatro Avenida** (*see p226*), **Museo Isaac Fernández Blanco** (*see p74*) and **Teatro Margarita Xirgú** (*see p201*), among others.

There is a year-round music scene. Normally, Colón's season runs March to December, but some programming continues in summer, including opera. However, recent renovation projects, scheduled to continue for an undisclosed but most likely lengthy period of time, have unfortunately limited shows at this breathtaking venue.

A large part of the classical music scene is in the hands of private professional and amateur groups, including important associations such as Mozarteum Argentino (www.mozarteum argentino.org) and Festivales Musicales (www.festivalesmusicales.org.ar). The Buenos Aires Philharmonic holds a sell-out season of around 20 concerts at the Colón. There are also more modest, unsubsidised institutions – like **La Scala de San Telmo** (Pasaje Giuffra 371, 4362 1187, www.lascala.com.ar) – which open their doors to talented performers. For complete information on everything from classes to concerts, take a look at www.musicaclasica argentina.com. Also in San Telmo, the beautiful **Galería Wussmann** (*see p153*) hosts occasional classical concerts (www.wussmann.com).

Classical music's status has been bolstered by keen critics, especially Marcelo Arce, whose lectures are attended by thousands of fans, plus classical radio stations such as Radio Cultura Musical (100.3FM), Radio Cultura (97.9FM) and Radio Nacional Clásica (96.7FM). Social clubs, libraries, museums and cultural centres also occasionally screen ballet and opera videos: try the **Círculo Italiano** (Libertad 1264, Recoleta, 4815 9693, www.circuloitaliano.com.ar).

If gala nights at the Colón are still occasions for tiaras and tuxes, interest in opera extends beyond BA's aristocracy. Performances take place not only at the Colón, but also at more intimate venues like Margarita Xirgú and even **La Manufactura Papelera** (*see below*) – a former paper factory where several groups stage rarely performed works.

Outside the capital, the most impressive venue is the **Teatro Argentino** (Calle 51, 0221 429 1746) in La Plata (56 kilometres/35 miles from BA; free buses from Callao 237, Tribunales, 4373 2636). It seats 2,300 in the main Alberto Ginastera auditorium, and the smaller Astor Piazzolla Auditorium accommodates 500 more. The Teatro Roma (Sarmiento 109, 4205 9646) in Avellaneda – ten minutes from downtown – is a small opera house with good acoustics and an offbeat repertoire, featuring the likes of Verdi's *Corsario* or Bellini's *Capulets and Montagues*. Finally, in Zona Norte, try the first-rate Sacred Music series on Sunday afternoons at the **Catedral de San Isidro** (*see below*).

These are all places where opera fans can sate their appetite thanks to the efforts of Juventus Lyrica, Buenos Aires Lírica, Casa de la Opera, Peco o Peco, and Opera del Buen Ayre. There are many locally trained, talented performers, directors and designers, including conductor/pianist Daniel Barenboim (now an Israeli citizen) and pianist Martha Argerich (a festival named after her is held at the Colón; *see p176*). Tenors José Cura and Marcelo Alvarez are also acclaimed at home and abroad.

Catedral de San Isidro
Avenida del Libertador 16199, y 9 de Julio, San Isidro (4743 0291). Train Mitre or de la Costa to San Isidro/60, 168 bus. **Open** 8am-8pm Mon, Fri; 8am-10pm Sun. **Admission** free.
Performances are usually at 4pm, from April to December; arrive early to secure a good seat.

La Manufactura Papelera
Bolívar 1582, entre Brasil y Caseros, San Telmo (4307 9167/www.papeleracultural.8m.com). Bus 24, 29, 39. **Shows** 6pm or 8.30pm Thur-Sun. **Closed** Jan. **Tickets** AR$7-$40. **No credit cards. Map** p280 C9.

Teatro Margarita Xirgú
Chacabuco 875, y Estados Unidos (4300 8817/
www.mxirgu.com.ar). Bus 10, 17, 29, 59, 156.
Open *Box office* 2-8pm Tue-Sun. **Tickets** AR$5-$40.
Credit AmEx, DC, MC, V. **Map** p281 E9.

Rock, Folk & Jazz

Most people think tango when they think Buenos Aires, but if you tot up the number of gigs in any given week, it seems that Argentina prefers to rock. Trad rock, folk and jazz are played, while fusion bands mix genres and spice up their music with diverse influences ranging from Eastern European polka to Caribbean rhythms.

KEEP ON ROCKIN' IN THE NEW WORLD

Brazilians and Mexicans might beg to differ, but local legend says that Latin American rock was born in BA – and Argentina's *rock nacional* is preferred by many to the imported version. Since the mid 1960s, more than 1,000 bands have released albums in this genre.

Mirroring the hard-living rocker lifestyle, *rock nacional* has experienced peaks and valleys. After gaining a toehold in the early 1970s, many rockers, labelled subversive by the military dictatorship, were censored or forced to leave the country in the 1970s and early 1980s. During the Malvinas/Falklands War, English-language music was banned, giving local bands more airtime. The strange turn of events gave local talent the exposure it needed, and with the return of democracy, the scene took flight. By the end of the 1980s, Argentinian rock had spread across Latin America, aided by Rock & Pop (95.9FM) radio station. Tours of up-and-coming groups, such as Los Enanitos Verdes and the now-disbanded Soda Stereo caused mass hysteria wherever they played.

Despite this passion for Argentinian rock, most local hipsters still consider the Rolling Stones to be the definitive band. 'Los Stones' generated a fashion cult in Argentina, with musicians copying the Ronnie Wood hairdo and Mick Jagger skinny T-shirts of the 1970s, and music fans christening their own lifestyle 'Rolling'. And that lips logo is ubiquitous in the city. An opposing fan group is (almost) as passionate about Los Beatles.

This love of the Stones has influenced local bands such as La 25, Intoxicados (formerly Viejas Locas) and La Mancha de Rolando. Others, such as Expulsados, were influenced by US proto-punk outfit the Ramones – punk and metal are still popular in BA, and ska, reggae, swing, poodle metal (check out Whitesnake copyists Rata Blanca), rockabilly and even oi! music have small but devoted followings.

Many bands inspire the same fanaticism as local football teams, engendering self-styled 'tribes' who bellow insults at the followers of rival bands. This was particularly the case at concerts by Patricio Rey y Los Redonditos de Ricota, a cult band forced into retirement by the very passion it created. After four years off the circuit, their mythical leader, El Indio Solari, played the first show of his new solo career in 2005 in front of 50,000 fans in La Plata.

Other established acts such as Divididos and La Renga continue to ignite fervour in their followers, while the upshot Jovenes Pordioseros have enjoyed instant cult status.

COOL AS FOLK

The musical customs of successive waves of diverse immigrant groups have mixed with native sounds to create an incredibly rich folk tradition in Argentina. At one time considered the old-fashioned music of country bumpkins and ageing hippies, the local styles from the northern provinces and outlying pampas now attract huge numbers of followers. Folklore's boom owes much to a long list of *rock nacional* bands that have incorporated the genre's instruments and beats into their popular music. The social and political force of the lyrics attract

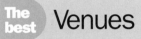

The best Venues

El Caberet, Faena Hotel + Universe
The biggest local acts in BA's trendiest concert venue. *See p57.*

Club del Vino
Wine, women and song – only without the women. *See p204.*

ND/Ateneo
If you didn't think folk music could have a cutting edge, think again. *See p204.*

Notorious
Or rather, famous – for its daily shows from the city's most accomplished musicians. Tasty food and drinks too. *See p205.*

Teatro Colón
Peerless acoustics and splendid aesthetics in one of the world's great opera houses. *See p202.*

Thelonious Bar
This bar honouring Sr Monk doubles up as a jiving, jamming jazz joint. *See p206.*

Theatre of dreams

The Teatro Colón is unquestionably BA's greatest cultural monument. Described by ballet dancer Mikhail Baryshnikov as 'the most beautiful of all the theatres I know', its spectacular architecture and hear-a-pin-drop acoustics are rivalled by only a handful of the world's opera houses.

The Colón was inaugurated in 1908 with a performance of Verdi's *Aida*. It had successfully overcome one or two teething problems: the first Italian architect had died before completing the project and his successor was murdered by the valet he'd recently sacked.

The building was described by Meano (the architect with the staffing issues) as incorporating 'the characteristics of the Italian Renaissance, the solidity of German architecture and the decorative charm and variety of French architecture'. The stunning mosaics were brought over from Venice, and the foyer houses a display of musical instruments including violins by Stradivari.

The cavernous auditorium is a sensuous medley of red velvet and gilt. It can seat 3,000 guests, and when the upper standing areas

– paraiso (gods), *inferno* (hell) and *gallineros* (not in Dante – it means 'chicken sheds') – are brimming, it has been known to hold more. To the right and left of the stalls, covered in black grilles, are boxes originally intended to house opera-crazy widows who couldn't be seen in public during their grieving period.

Perpetually buzzing with activity, the Colón now houses its own orchestral choir, children's choir and ballet, and plays host to the BA Philharmonic Orchestra and numerous artists of international fame. It has seen first night performances conducted by, among others, Strauss and Stravinsky, and both Maria Callas and Rudolf Nureyev have trod its boards. A contemporary superstar, Argentinian pianist and conductor Daniel Barenboim, returns to BA once a year to lead concerts at the Colón.

Following Argentina's 2001 economic crisis, the Colón adopted a price-freezing policy. During the season (March to December) a special Monday-night concert series, 'The Colón for Two Pesos', has tickets on sale for... well, you guessed it. And even the most expensive opera seats cost no more than AR$220.

Guided tours of the building are available hourly in Spanish and English, offering the opportunity not only to gasp at the main auditorium but also to explore the underworld of workshops, studios, set stores and practice rooms in the theatre's basements.

An extensive multi-million dollar renovation plan is due to be completed in 2008. (But like all construction projects in Buenos Aires, it isn't over till the fat lady sings.)

Teatro Colón

Cerrito, entre Tucumán y Viamonte, Tribunales (box office 4378 7344/tours 4378 7132/ www.teatrocolon.org.ar). Subte D, Tribunales/ 29, 39, 59 bus. **Open** *Box office 9am-8pm Mon-Sat; 10am-5pm Sun.* **Tickets** *Ballet AR$35-$45. Concerts AR$10-$20. Opera AR$20-$170.* **Credit** *varies.* **Map** *p281 G10.*

many, as does the fact that folklore lends itself to a good ol' wine-soaked hoe-down.

There are hundreds of different styles. Many are based on dances – the *chacarera*, *zamba* or *chamamé* – which are now played by megastars like El Chaqueño Palavecino. Legendary folk figures such as the late, great Atahualpa Yupanqui, Cuchi Leguizamon and Eduardo Falú (who still occasionally performs) transformed and

enriched these traditional rhythms, providing folklore with a new virtuoso dimension.

Interpreter Mercedes Sosa, one of the *grandes dames* of classic folk music, has performed regularly in Argentina and Europe, often joined on stage by other legendary Argentinian musicians. Folklore's greatest ambassador, popular folk/rock artist Leòn Gieco, combed rural Argentina from tip to tail in a 'rolling studio'. Recording artists on the spot, the result is an epic four-disc panorama of regional sounds, *De Ushuaia a La Quiaca*, produced by Oscar nominee Gustavo Santaolalla.

La Folklórica (98.7FM) radio can be received almost anywhere in the country. It airs folk music round-the-clock and attracts a wide audience. But to catch these earthy sounds live, the best places are the *peñas* (*see p206*), or venues such as **La Trastienda** (*see p204*), **Clásica y Moderna** (*see p139*) or ND/Ateneo (*see p204*), which have regular folk cycles. The traditional Sunday fair, **Feria de Mataderos** (*see p104*), is an open-air alternative for those willing to head out to the capital's western limits.

THE BEAT IS ON

At the end of the 1990s, dance music hit town, and it hasn't left yet. Big-name DJs from Buenos Aires such as Javier Zuker, Carlos Alfonsín and international star Hernán Cattáneo play clubs and festivals for an ever-expanding audience. Following the lead of pioneers such as Daniel Melero and ex-Soda Stereo leader Gustavo Cerati, electrónica has seeped into rock; Leo García is a well-liked exponent of experimental electrónica, and numerous other local bands such as Victoria Mil are following his lead.

Simultaneously, local popular dance music – or *música tropical* – is gaining wider acceptance. This music was originally confined to *bailantas* (improvised and often quite seedy concert venues) but has broken class barriers to become one of the most profitable sectors of the Argentinian music industry. The premature deaths of star performers Gilda in 1996, Rodrigo in 2000 and Walter Olmos in 2002 have only served to boost the phenomenon. The spots where they died have been turned into shrines by mourning fans.

Another hugely popular sub-genre from the urban fringes is *cumbia villera*, a sound that sprang from the culture of drugs, crime and despair in BA's poverty-stricken slums. A provocative offspring of a bastardised version of Colombia's noble cumbia sound, *cumbia villera* is a fusion of Latin beats, punk attitudes and gangsta rap morality. Approaches to the villa life differ, with noble destitution and anti-heroism reflected in the lyrics of pioneers Rafaga and Guachin, while wildly popular bands like Pibes Chorros and Damas Gratis are more likely to spin unadulterated tales of sex, drugs and violence.

Jazz is also enjoying a boom. The local jazz scene contains some outstanding artists, such as guitarist Valentino, bass player Javier Malosetti, trumpeter Fats Fernandez, pianist Adrian Iaies and bass quintet leader Alejandro Herrera. Visits from jazz heavies from across Latin America are on the rise, and living legends such as Wynton Marsalis sometimes make appearances. Jam

sessions, usually advertised under the English nomenclature, are increasingly prominent and there's even a government initiative to promote live jazz, known as the **La Ruta del Jazz** (*see p205*).

GIGS & FESTIVALS

Despite the continuing exchange-rate challenge, BA is beginning to make its presence felt on the international concert circuit. A number of top bands hit the capital in 2006, including U2, the Rolling Stones and Oasis.

The festival scene is also kicking. In 2006 Cosquín Rock (in the province of Córdoba) opened with a scorching performance by ex-Redondos guitarist Skay Beilinson and closed with a tribute to recently deceased guitar hero Pappo; some 40,000 enjoyed five days of power chords. Electronic music bleeped its way on to the bill at Cosquín too: a tent dedicated to DJs infiltrated what was once a rock-only affair. Many other rock festivals, including Epecuén Rock and Gesell Rock, take place inland and on the Atlantic coast during the summer.

To placate those poor souls who can't make it to the beach, the BA city government (www.buenosaires.gov.ar) often subsidises free outdoor summer concerts in places like the Rosedal in Palermo (*see p92*), while over the water, Uruguay hosts a first-class jazz festival in Punta del Este. Keep an eye out also for posters advertising smaller, impromptu festivals that often feature more diverse styles such as reggae, punk and rockabilly.

Buenos Aires boasts a huge number of live music venues. In this chapter we list places that have at least two shows a month; call ahead in January and February since some places put their programmes on ice over the summer. As with so many city spaces, music venues are often multifunctional – a place listed under 'Jazz' might have a folk evening on Tuesday, tango classes on Thursday and an occasional art exhibition.

Many venues, especially clubs, are unlikely to accept credit cards. However, you can buy tickets using major credit cards at the following agencies: **Ticketek** (5237 7200, www.ticketek.com.ar, nine locations), and **Ticketmaster** (4321 9700, two locations). The booking fee is usually ten per cent of the ticket price.

Rock and folk venues

Major venues

Megastars – whether local heroes like Los Piojos or international top dogs like U2 – play the city's football stadiums. The main locations for live concerts are River Plate, Vélez Sarsfield, Ferro Carril Oeste and La Bombonera. It's better

Arts & Entertainment

(and cheaper) to buy a ticket for the main ground – *el campo* – rather than the stands, since the number of large screens is often limited. For details of sports stadiums, *see pp208-14* **Sport & Fitness**. Below is a list of other major venues, less monumental, but each with its own pros and cons. Look out also for jazz concerts at the **Teatro Coliseo** (*see p200*).

Estadio Obras Sanitarias

Avenida del Libertador 7395, entre Núñez y Manuela Pedraza, Núñez (4702 3223/www.estadioobras. com.ar). Bus 15, 29, 130. **Box office** Feb-Dec noon-8pm Mon-Fri. **Closed** Jan. **Tickets** AR$20-$65. **No credit cards**.

The so-called Temple of Rock, and a favourite with Argentinian rock fans, can hold 5,000 souls. Eric Clapton, James Brown, Megadeth and Manu Chao, along with BA's hottest bands, have all played here. Recently renovated toilets and a very welcome new air-conditioning system have relieved the place of some of its traditional drawbacks.

Luna Park

Bouchard 465, entre Corrientes y Lavalle, Centro (4311 5100/4312 2135/www.lunapark.com.ar). Subte B, LN Alem/26, 93, 99, 152 bus. **Box office** 10am-8pm Mon-Sat; varies Sun. **Tickets** AR$15-$110. **Credit** AmEx, DC, MC, V. **Map** p281 F11.

Ray Charles, Norah Jones and Franz Ferdinand are among the stars to have graced the dressing rooms of this boxing stadium. It's a good space for enthusiastic audiences, but there are some drawbacks: thick columns can block views and the dodgy sound system has been known to make top acts sound like shambling amateurs.

Teatro Gran Rex

Avenida Corrientes 857, entre Suipacha y Esmeralda, Centro (4322 8000). Subte B, Carlos Pellegrini or C, Diagonal Norte or D, 9 de Julio/10, 17, 24, 29, 70 bus. **Box office** 10am-10pm daily. **Tickets** AR$20-$75. **No credit cards**. **Map** p281 F10.

Ideal for artists who require the attention of a comfortably seated audience; past performers include Brazilian Caetano Veloso and Boy George. It holds 3,500 punters who can choose between the stalls (*platea*), the mezzanine (*super pullman*) or the dress circle (*pullman* – cheaper seats, worse sound). The Gran Rex is also a venue for musicals, and has its own car park and coffee shop.

Teatro Opera

Avenida Corrientes 860, entre Suipacha y Esmeralda, Centro (4326 1335). Subte B, Carlos Pellegrini or C, Diagonal Norte or D, 9 de Julio/10, 17, 24, 29, 70 bus. **Box office** 10am-8pm daily. **Tickets** AR$20-$60. **Credit** varies. **Map** p281 F10.

Opposite the Gran Rex, Teatro Opera is one of BA's classic-style auditoriums. Since it opened in 1872, many great local artists have performed here, including tango stars Hugo del Carril and Edmundo Rivero, as well as international greats such as Louis Armstrong and Ella Fitzgerald.

La Trastienda

Balcarce 460, entre Belgrano y Venezuela, San Telmo (4342 7650/www.latrastienda.com). Subte A, Plaza de Mayo or D, Catedral, or E, Bolívar/24, 29, 126, 130 bus. **Box office** Jan 4-8pm daily. Feb-Dec noon-8pm Mon-Sat; 3pm-8pm Sun. **Tickets** AR$10-$60. **Credit** DC, MC, V. **Map** p281 E10.

In the ruins of an old mansion dating from 1895, the Trastienda holds 400 people seated at small tables and another 1,000 standing. A mecca for serious musicians and discerning fans, it attracts cutting edge local bands, established Latin American talent and international groups such as groovers Medeski, Martin and Wood. For younger audiences there are concerts by the likes of Stereolab and Café Tacuba, plus occasional free events.

Smaller venues

Club del Vino

Cabrera 4737, entre Armenia y Malabia, Palermo Viejo (4833 0048). Bus 15, 39, 110, 141, 168. **Open** *Shows* from 9.30pm Tue-Sun. *Restaurant* noon-3pm, 8pm-1am Mon-Sat. **Tickets** AR$10-$35; free jazz Tue, tango Wed. **Credit** AmEx, MC, V. **Map** p281 M5.

A statue of Bacchus dominates the patio and sets the tone. With its restaurant, wine bar and 200-seat auditorium, this is one of the best spots in the city for lovers of good grape and classy music. During the show you can order cold cuts and cheeses, along with wines by the glass. A special US$45 package for tourists includes transport to and from your hotel, dinner, the show and a bottle of wine to take home with you. Although the restaurant stays open all summer, there are no shows in January.

Mitos Argentinos

Humberto 1º 489, entre Bolívar y Defensa, San Telmo (4362 7810/www.mitosargentinos.com.ar). Bus 24, 29, 126, 130, 152. **Open** from 9.30pm Fri, Sat; from 12.30pm Sun. **Tickets** AR$5 women Fri, Sat, all Sun; AR$8 men Fri; AR$10 men Sat. Free before 11pm. **Credit** AmEx, DC, MC, V. **Map** p280 D9.

Local rock and blues bands play in this old San Telmo house, and though most are barely known, they're wisely selected, so it's worth the experience. Dinner is available on Fridays and Saturdays (10.30pm), and on Sundays lunch is served while tango shows and classes take place. After hours, dancing continues until the sun comes up.

ND/Ateneo

Paraguay 918, y Suipacha, Retiro (4328 2888). Subte C, San Martín/10, 59, 109, 152 bus. **Box office** Feb-Dec noon-8pm Mon-Sat. **Closed** Jan. **Tickets** AR$15-$40. **No credit cards**. **Map** p281 G11.

Reopened in 2002 with hugely improved acoustics, this traditional theatre is now a key venue for all musical genres, from folklore and tango to rock and jazz. There are concerts most Thursdays to Sundays, mainly by talented Argentinian performers or other Latin American artists. There are also occasional film screenings, theatre performances and poetry recitals.

Templum

Ayacucho 318, entre Sarmiento y Corrientes, Once (4953 1513). Subte B, Callao/24, 37, 60, 124 bus. **Open** Feb-Dec from 10pm Sat, Sun. **Closed** Jan. **Tickets** AR$7-$10. **No credit cards. Map** p281 H9.

This early 20th-century house hides a cultural centre inside. It's principally devoted to theatre but, on Saturday nights at 11pm, there are carefully chosen ethnic, jazz or world music gigs. One spacious room, seating 60 people, is used as the concert hall.

Vaca Profana

Lavalle 3683, y Bulnes, Abasto (4867 0934/ www.vacaprofana.com.ar). Bus 26, 168. **Open** from 9pm Tue-Sun. **Tickets** AR$7-$15. **No credit cards. Map** p278 K5.

Vaca Profana is quickly becoming a major stopping point for quality local bands. Small and intimate with good drinks and tapas, it's a prime spot to relax and get a close view of the musicians. A quirky , cult venue with a devoted following.

Jazz & blues venues

Buenos Aires' jazz scene is gaining momentum, both in terms of musicians and venues, while outside the capital, events like the La Plata Jazz Festival or Bariloche Jazz Festival attract ever-increasing audiences.

More and more places are dedicated to jazz and blues, and as a result the city of Buenos Aires has organised and is promoting a jazz circuit called **La Ruta del Jazz** (the Jazz Route). It's an attempt to bring together dozens of formal and informal joints – often bars and restaurants – where some kind of jazz, fusion, ethnic, R&B or Caribbean/Latin jazz takes place

Legendary *rock nacional* star **Fito Páez**.

at least once a week. As well as places listed in this chapter, other venues on the Ruta in Palermo Viejo include **Bar Abierto** (Borges 1613, 4833 7640), **Cala Bistro** (Soler 4065, 4823 0413) and **El Gorriti** (Bonpland 1411, 4777 0242, www.elgorriti.com). If you're in the San Telmo area, try **El Perro Andaluz** (Bolívar 852, 4361 3501).

Blues Special Club

Avenida Almirante Brown 102, y Pilcomayo, La Boca (4854 2338). Bus 29, 53, 64, 93, 168. **Open** from 10pm Fri-Sun. **Tickets** AR$5; international shows AR$15 (1wk in advance), AR$20 (on the door). **No credit cards. Map** p280 C9.

This soulful establishment is a classic for *porteño* blues fans. Affable owner Adrián regularly brings new artists over from the US. On Fridays, there are lawless '*zapadas*' (jam sessions).

No Avestruz

Humboldt 1857, entre El Salvador y Costa Rica, Palermo Viejo (4771 1141/www.noavestruz.com.ar). Bus 39, 93, 111. **Open** *Jan, Feb* from 10pm Fri, Sat. *Mar-Dec* 8pm-1am Thur-Sat, 7-11pm Sun. **Tickets** AR$8-$15 **No credit cards. Map** p279 N5. Jazz is played once or twice a week in this spacious warehouse. The scattered couches and chairs make for an informal atmosphere.

Notorious

Avenida Callao 966, entre Marcelo T de Alvear y Paraguay, Barrio Norte (4816 2888/www. notorious.com.ar). Subte D, Callao/12, 39, 60, 111 bus. **Open** 8am-midnight Mon, Tue; 8am-1am Wed, Thur; 8am-3am Fri; 10am-3am Sat; 6pm-midnight Sun. **Tickets** AR$10-$20. **Credit cards** (restaurant only) AmEx, DC, MC, V. **Map** p281 H10.

Arts & Entertainment

Pure sax appeal at **Thelonius Bar**.

Notorious has daily live shows by respected local jazzers such as Fats Fernandez and Adrian Iaies, as well as occasional new folk and world music acts. The stage is close to the tables, so you can catch every groan and moan during the improvs – but reserve ahead to be as near to the front as possible. The new branch – above classic bookstore Gandhi (see p149) – offers a similarly eclectic live programme and simple, decent food, but the view from the back tables is poor. **Other locations**: First Floor, Gandhi, Corrientes 1743, Tribunales (4371 0370).

El Samovar de Rasputín

Del Valle Iberlucea 1251, entre Lamadrid y Magallanes, La Boca (4302 3190). Bus 29, 53, 64, 152. **Open** Shows from midnight Fri-Sat; from 6pm Sun. **Tickets** free, minimum spend. **No credit cards. Map** p280 A8.
This mythic joint in the heart of La Boca is managed by Napo, a blues obsessive who often hangs around until dawn spinning yarns – some of which may be true – from his hippie glory days. Taj Majal, James Cotton and BB King's band have all played here. There are tango classes on Sunday afternoons (2-9pm), and good barbecued meats are available.

Thelonious Bar

Salguero 1884, entre Güemes y Charcas, Palermo (4829 1562/www.theloniusclub.com.ar). Subte D, Bulnes/29, 39, 111, 152 bus. **Open** 9.30pm-4am Tue-Sat. *Shows* 10.30pm Tue-Sat. **Tickets** from AR$8. **No credit cards. Map** p282 L9.

If you're after the best local jazz, this is the place. Every night, you can hear some of the most talented musicians in the country, while nibbling on tapas or Mediterranean platters. Sound quality is excellent; less so the seating comfort levels.

Other venues

Pubs & bars

If you want to cry into your beer to the melancholy strains of tango, or twirl a cocktail stick to a bossa nova beat, BA has plenty of suitable venues. **El Cabaret** at the Faena Hotel + Universe (*see p57*) attracts some of the city's top talent. It's expensive, AR$100 and upwards, but you can get up close to legends like Nacha Guevarra, Fito Páez and Charly Garcia. In the city centre, **La Cigale** (*see p137*; free live shows on Thursdays) is the place to enjoy well-prepared drinks while listening to the latest in electronic music, pop and retro rock. **Bartolomeo**, in Congreso (Bartolomé Mitre 1525, 4372 2843), has local music (tango, jazz, blues and latino) from Thursdays through Saturdays, and theatre performances in the basement on Thursdays. Tickets cost AR$3-$5. **Milión** (*see p145*) in Recoleta uses a small part of its large mansion to provide an intimate setting for live music on Wednesday nights, while **Imaginario** (www.imaginariocultural. com.ar) at Bulnes and Guardia Vieja in the heart of Abasto, has a basement where funk and rock bands play through a permanent fug of 'cigarette' smoke.

Peñas

Peñas are where you can experience the typical folklore sounds and taste the regional cuisines of Argentina's interior provinces.

Peña del Colorado

Güemes 3657, entre Salguero y Vidt, Palermo (4822 1038/www.delcolorado.com.ar). Subte D, Bulnes/29, 39, 92, 111, 152 bus. **Open** from 8pm daily. *Shows* 10pm Fri, Sat. **Tickets** AR$8-$10. **No credit cards. Map** p282 L9.
Between sips of *mate*, customers strum and sing their own traditional sounds within the brick walls of this welcoming, warm (too warm in summer) venue.

La Peña del Abasto

Anchorena 571, entre Lavalle y Pasaje Carlos Gardel, Abasto (5076 0148). Subte B, Gardel/ 24, 26, 124, 168 bus. **Open** Shows 10pm Fri-Sun. **Tickets** AR$8-$12. **No credit cards. Map** p278 J5.
At this folklore centre in the heart of the tango district, you may be lucky enough to hear guitar player Luis Salinas and other virtuosi pushing the trad envelope. If the music moves you, there's dancing to be done.

Arts & Entertainment

The rock 'n' roll hall of fame

THE LIVING

Charly Garcia

With a genius for self-promotion Madonna would envy, the ability to crank out catchy rock anthems, perfect pitch and caustic wit, Charly Garcia is *the* Argentinian rock star. Politicians aside, Charly is one of two Argentinians – Maradona is the other – who does what he wants, when he wants, with complete impunity. Charly's shows are slaves to his moods, some times offering hours of musical virtuosity and pure rock, other times lasting a song or two before a tantrum leads to broken equipment and subsequent silence. The anecdotes are endless. His best known escapade was a leap from the ninth floor of a hotel in Mendoza into a small pool. Within days, Buenos Aires was papered with promotional posters showing Charly's emaciated figure unbelievably high in the air and the name of his new song: 'Me Tirè por Vos' ('I Jumped for You').

Andres Calamaro

Another musical prodigy, Calamaro is Charly's 'best enemy'. A running dispute, either over artistic dominance or Calamaro's ex-wife or both, once led Calamaro to wait by Charly's door with a baseball bat. When Charly didn't appear, Calamaro entered a nearby music store and destroyed Garcia's disks. First gaining fame in the late 1970s as the front man of seminal band Abuelos de la Nada, and then playing with Garcia, Calamaro migrated to Spain and headed the successful Los Rodriguez. The solo discs *Alta Suciedad* and *Honestidad Brutal*, released at the end of the 1990s, are packed with Dylanesque *bons mots*. After all but disappearing at the beginning of the millennium, 2005 marked the return of Calamaro. He was named Argentina's Person of the Year in *Rolling Stone* magazine and wrapped up December with sold-out shows promoting his new CD, aptly named *El Regreso* (*The Return*).

THE DEAD

Luca Prodan

Although not Argentinian, Luca Prodan came to represent '*argentinindad*' like few others. Born in Italy to an extremely wealthy family and sent to study in Scotland, Prodan's short life was a fast, fierce rebellion against his upper-class past. To escape a heroin addiction, Luca arrived in Argentina in 1981, where he took up heavy drinking and formed the legendary band Sumo. Despite almost instant fame, Luca prowled the streets with the homeless, drinking in plazas and train stations and railing against what he saw as the hypocrisy of *rock nacional*. His dissolute lifestyle and apparent rootlessness struck a chord in this nation of immigrants and led to a unique sound with elements of punk, reggae and rock. Many claim that his most famous song, 'Mañana en el Abasto', better captures the soul of the old *porteño* neighbourhood than anything by Carlos Gardel. Death from cirrhosis at the age of 34 solidified his cult status, and members of Sumo broke off to form the popular bands Los Divididos y Las Pelotas.

Pappo

Noberto 'Pappo' Napolitano's hard-rocking blues riffs were a *rock nacional* staple for over three decades. A fan of leather jackets, long black hair and mean looks, Pappo moved in the grey area between blues and heavy metal, playing with greats from both genres such as BB King and Motörhead's Lemmy. Tragically, but somehow predictably, he died in a motorcycle accident in February 2005.

THE MORIBUND?

Sandro

Rumoured to own the world's largest collection of women's undergarments, Roberto Sanchez, aka Sandro, is Argentina's answer to Elvis Presley. Like the King, Sandro thrust his pelvis to fame and then starred as heartthrob in a number of B-movies in the 1960s and 1970s. Unlike the King, and perhaps improbably, he is still alive, having hit 60 in 2005. Despite recent 'secret surgery', hard living ('I treated myself worse than anyone,' he has said in the past) has lead to serious lung problems. But age and illness haven't dampened the desire of his religiously devoted fans, older women he still affectionately calls '*las nenas*' or 'the girls'. In 2004 Sandro wheezed through his sets at the Gran Rex with an oxygen tube taped to his microphone. Donning his signature red robe and digging deep for the sensual tenor of his youth, he set an unofficial new record for the number of bras thrown on stage at an Argentinian concert.

Sport & Fitness

Buenos Aires is kicking (and punching, and throwing, and riding...)

Sport in Argentina is a life-affecting endeavour, treated with a religious fervour that borders on the obsessional, and it has frequently been the catalyst for massive outpourings of national joy or despair. Of course, Argentinians want their country to prosper, to achieve stability, to be free from chronic unemployment, corruption and crime. But winning the football World Cup – well, that's pretty good too.

Although most of the myths and triumphs revolve around 'the beautiful game', with rising stars like Lionel Messi ensuring the country maintains its reputation as a hotspot for top players, there's much more to Argentinian sport than football. Las Leonas ('the Lionesses') are one of the world's top women's hockey teams; Los Pumas are a respected, if not quite top rank, national rugby outfit; NBA basketball star Emanuel 'Manu' Ginóbili is a key player for the San Antonio Spurs; and, of course, the world's best polo players are Argentinian (see p210 **Horse play**). Most recently, the buzz has been around a group of brilliant young tennis players known locally – no one quite knows why – as 'the Argentinian legion'. The only real sporting disappointment is that most of the top athletes have taken to strutting their skills outside the country, although they're always back to represent Argentina when it really counts.

Despite today's glut of talent, there's an overwhelming sense of nostalgia. Walk down Lavalle Street on any given day and you'll find scores of men gesticulating excitedly at televised replays of sporting events from years ago. Visually, the city is plastered with sports memorabilia – on newsstands and in bars, collectors' emporia and the stadiums themselves. Investment has also been made in two new sports museums, one dedicated to Boca Juniors football team (see p81) and a rugby museum in San Isidro (see p106). River Plate football team are planning to open their own museum in late 2006.

Football is the main event for spectators (see pp27-30 and p209), though basketball continues to grow in popularity (see below). Any week in Buenos Aires (except during January) offers a huge choice of football matches and venues.

On the other side of the tracks, both geographically and socially, is polo (see p211). All equestrian sports are popular, generally speaking, and there is an in-town race track, plus a grass track in San Isidro (see p211).

For shops selling sporting goods, see p172.

Spectator sports

Basketball

The Argentinian basketball team had their finest hour in the 2002 World Championships, when they became the first foreign squad to beat the US Dream Team in international competition, a feat they repeated on their way to winning the gold medal in the 2004 Athens Olympics. NBA star Emanuel Ginóbili (he plays for the San Antonio Spurs) is probably the most popular sports personality in the country after soccer legend Diego Maradona.

On the local scene, the phenomenon is more pronounced in Buenos Aires province than in the capital, which has only a handful of important teams. The best to watch are Boca Juniors (whose home court is La Bombonerita) and Obras Sanitarias. La Liga Nacional de Básquetbol (the national league) runs from October to June; matches are usually on Friday and Sunday evenings at 8 or 9pm.

Estadio Luis Conde (La Bombonerita)
Arzobispo Espinoza 600, y Palos, La Boca (4309 4748/www.bocajuniors.com.ar). Bus 29, 33, 53, 64, 86, 93, 152, 168. **Tickets** AR$7-$15. **No credit cards. Map** p280 B9.

Club Atlético Obras Sanitarias de la Nación
Avenida del Libertador 7395, entre Crisólogo Larralde y Campos Salles, Núñez (4702 4655/ 4702 9467/www.clubosn.com.ar). Bus 15, 29, 130. **Tickets** AR$8-$15; free under-12s. **No credit cards. Map** p285 T9.

Boxing

Boxing was very much part of the local sporting calendar until the mid 1980s. **Luna Park** (see p204), BA's answer to Madison Square Garden, used to attract enormous crowds. Today, it's mostly used as a concert venue, attracting international names like the White Stripes and Oasis in recent times, though since early 2003 the red carpet has been rolled out every month or so for the slightly less glamorous ritual of the Saturday night fight. Smaller matches are held at the stadium of the Federación Argentina de Box, which has a capacity of 3,000.

Federación Argentina de Box

Castro Barros 75, y Rivadavia, Almagro (4981 8615). Subte A, Castro Barros/86, 128, 160 bus. **Closed** mid Dec-mid Jan. **Tickets** AR$10-$25. **No credit cards. Map** p278 J3.
Can also recommend boxing instructors for lessons.

Football

Each club has its own stadium, and there are at least five top-flight matches to choose from at weekends. There are two annual league championships – the *Apertura* (Opening) from August to December and the *Clausura* (Closing) from February to July. Games for other regional championships, like the Copa Libertadores and the Copa Nissan Sudamericana are also often played in Buenos Aires.

Seeing a match live, especially at Boca Juniors' Estadio Alberto J Armando, known as La Bombonera or 'Chocolate Box', is an unforgettable experience. Come kick off, a cacophonous cocktail of fireworks and abuse greets players and ref alike, and the dancing and singing are a constant all the way through. Buy your ticket in advance and get a seat in the *platea* (seated area). Down in the terraced *popular*, it's more tribal. It's also worth noting that the better a team is doing, the higher the *platea* price; standard ticket prices are AR$10-$40, rising to AR$100.

Dress casually, don't carry valuables or potentially dangerous implements and keep your wits about you when leaving the stadium at night. You can buy tickets for Boca or River matches through **Ticketek** (5237 7200, MasterCard only), or for any team at their ground (cash only). Go with a local fan or with one of the companies that escort tourists to matches (they guarantee good seats and transport for a premium price of US$35-$50). Of these, **Curiocity** (*see p172*) and **Go Football** (4816 2681, www.gofootball.com.ar) are recommendable options.

For more on BA's unique football culture, see *pp27-30*.

Estadio Alberto J Armando (La Bombonera)

Brandsen 805, y la Vía, La Boca (4309 4700/ www.bocajuniors.com.ar). Bus 10, 29, 53, 64. **Map** p280 B9.
Watching a game here is a unique and vertiginous experience: the concrete stands vibrate and at the higher levels you feel like a wrong move will tip you out on to the pitch itself. The *platea baja* in the stands area is your recommended vantage point. There's also a museum, plus guided tours of the grounds; *see p81*.

River Plate fans cheer on their team at Boca Juniors' **La Bombonera** stadium.

Horse play

It's easy to look at polo through blinkers and see only Britain's Prince Harry riding through a field. But if you want to experience the chukkas and champagne first hand, Argentina in springtime is the perfect place. The world's oldest team sport, polo found its way from India to Europe in the mid-19th century, and was brought to its spiritual home of Argentina by British ranchers and engineers in 1875.

Nowadays, the best players in the world are Argentinian; nine of them currently with a perfect ten handicap, which is more than all other nationalities combined. The best ponies are also bred in Argentina: an intelligent, agile cross between thoroughbreds and local *criollo* horses.

Glance at the team sheets and you might wonder if it's only the horses that are bred to win. Out of the five brothers that make up the Novillo Astrada clan, four saddle up for the prize-winning La Aguada team, and there are six Heguys scattered across the country's other top teams. While polo in Argentina isn't as confined to the semi-aristocracy as it is elsewhere, it's still dynasties with *dinero* that deliver results.

Not that player background will affect your enjoyment; at its best polo can be genuinely thrilling to watch. Once the teams have bullied off, the concept is pretty simple: use the sticks to hit the ball into the goal, or set up your mount for a crowd pleasing 'pony goal'. There are six chukkas of seven minutes each in a match, with the four players on each team changing horses every chukka (the best without touching the ground). The teams change ends after each goal, which both minimises wind advantage and confuses inattentive newcomers – you've been warned. If the game isn't entertaining enough, the half-time tradition of stomping the divots is a networker's dream.

The drama isn't always confined to the pitch. When the 'Maradona of Polo' (but think Beckham on a horse rather than the not-particularly-equestrian Diego) Adolfo Cambiaso – a Grand Slam winner too many times to count, captain of 2005 champions La Dolfina and polo's most swooned over pin-up – mentioned in an interview that he hoped his father's favourite football team, Nueva Chicago, would be promoted, he could never have envisaged the results: appreciative Nueva

Estadio José Amalfitani

Avenida Juan B Justo 9200, y Jonte, Liniers (4641 5663/5763/www.velezsarsfield.com). Train from Once to Liniers/2, 52, 86, 106 bus.

Renovated for when Argentina hosted the 1978 World Cup and well maintained ever since, this comfortable stadium is the home ground of Velez Sarsfield who beat Milan in 1994 to become World Club Champions. It also hosts matches between smaller clubs and bigger, more popular teams.

Estadio Monumental

Avenida Figueroa Alcorta 7597, y Udaondo, Nuñez (4789 1200/www.cariverplate.com.ar). Bus 12, 29, 42, 107, 130. **Map** p285 T10.

The Monumental – home to Club Atlético River Plate, eternal rivals of Boca Juniors – was the setting for the opening and the final of the 1978 World Cup. It's the largest stadium in the country and, thanks to its location in the swish, upper-class barrio of Nuñez, probably the safest. It's also the only all-seater stadium in Buenos Aires that comes close

to meeting FIFA standards. Big name international musicians like U2, and the Red Hot Chili Peppers have also played at the Monumental. to crowds of 60,000 and upwards.

Horse racing

Introduced by the British, horse racing – known here by the English word 'turf' – is one of the city's oldest sports. Turf's main venue, the elegant **Hipódromo Argentino** (which can accommodate 100,000 spectators) is in Palermo. The palatial building housing the main stands and *confitería* was designed by French architect Faure Dujarric and opened in 1908.

Even if you don't end up backing the winner, you'll enjoy the eccentric cast of characters who gather here on race days to fritter away their inheritances or hard-earned cash on the gee-gees. The biggest day on the racing calendar is the Gran Premio Nacional, held annually in

Chicago *barra brava* fans (hardcore football supporters) began transferring support from the terraces to the cathedral of Polo during the Argentinian Open finals, invading the pitch and rowdily getting behind team and particularly their captain. The culture clash left Cambiaso's reputation, at least among the politely clapping rich, in tatters, but it certainly helped bring the formerly elitist sport to the masses.

Three big teams make up the coveted Triple Crown: Tortugas (end of October at Tortugas Country Club); Hurlingham (mid-November at Hurlingham Polo Club); and season climax, the Argentinian Open, held at Palermo's magnificent 16,000 capacity Campo Argentino de Polo in November/December. The eight-team Open features teams with handicaps of 28-40 (the sum of their individual player handicaps). Tickets for all tournaments are available from Ticketek (5237 7200).

Cambiaso's family run **La Martina**, one of several *estancias* close to Buenos Aires where you can learn the game (*see p238*). If you're lucky you may catch a glimpse of the great god of the polo field himself, perhaps mucking out the stables or – far more likely – waxing his Porsche.

November, although there are around ten regular meetings per month, usually on Mondays, Saturdays and Sundays. The other big race on the calendar is the Gran Premio Carlos Pellegrini (*see p177*), run in November at the smart **Hipódromo de San Isidro** in Zona Norte, the only grass track in Argentina. It also hosts flat races on Wednesdays and weekends.

Hipódromo Argentino de Palermo
Avenida del Libertador 4101, y Dorrego, Palermo (4778 2800/www.palermo.com.ar). Bus 10, 37, 160. **Tickets** AR$5-$10; free under-12s and women. **No credit cards. Map** p283 O10.
Under-18s must be accompanied by an adult. For guided tours of the Villa Hípica, telephone 4778 2820.

Hipódromo de San Isidro
Avenida Márquez 504, y Santa Fe, San Isidro (4743 4019/4743 4011/www.hipodromosanisidro.com.ar). Train from Retiro to San Isidro. **Tickets** AR$1-$5. **No credit cards.**

Motor racing

Though you can no longer hear the roar of Formula 1 racing at the Autódromo, the layout is exactly the same as it was in the days of Juan Manuel Fangio, a national sporting idol who won the world championship five times in the 1950s. These days, Argentinian motor racing (*automóvilismo*) lacks any really outstanding drivers on the international scene but still maintains an attractive local calendar, with two main categories: Turismo Carretera (with very powerful cars that must be more than 25 years old to race) and the TC 2000, for souped-up saloon cars.

Autódromo de la Ciudad de Buenos Aires Oscar Gálvez
Avenida Roca 6700, y Ave Gral Paz, Villa Lugano (4605 3333). Bus 21, 28, 114, 141. **Tickets** AR$15-$90. **No credit cards.**
Races are held most Fridays, Saturdays and Sundays, and there is stock car racing some Fridays at 8.30pm.

Pato

Although *pato* is officially Argentina's national sport, most people in Buenos Aires have never seen it, let alone played it. The game is a bizarre cross between polo and a previously popular, but now extinct sport, *pelota al cesto*. Originally played with a dead duck wrapped in leather straps, a ball has now replaced the unfortunate fowl. If you can catch a match, it's a unique spectacle; the main tournament runs in November/December. The ground is 50 minutes outside town – entrance is usually free.

Campo Argentino de Pato
Ruta 8, at km 30, Campo de Mayo, San Miguel (information 4331 0222/www.fedpato.com.ar). Train from Chacarita to Sargento Cabral. **Games** Sat, Sun.

Polo

Polo is played in Buenos Aires from September to November, which is the golden month when the venerable **Abierto Argentino de Polo** (Argentinian Open – *see p177*) is contested. Top teams include La Aguada, Ellerstina, Indios Chapaleufú I and II and La Dolfina. (*See also p210* **Horse play**).

Beginners and experienced players can have polo lessons at several *estancias* in Buenos Aires province: **La Martina** (*see p238*) is top notch.

Campo Argentino de Polo de Palermo
Avenida del Libertador 4300, y Dorrego, Palermo (4777 6444/www.aapolo.com). Bus 15, 29, 55, 60, 64. **Tickets** AR$12-$55; *Argentinian Open* AR$15-$60. **Map** p283 O9.

A wonderful polo field, in the heart of the city, with capacity for 45,000. The Argentinian Open tournament is over 100 years old. You get purchase tickets for all tournaments from Ticketek (5237 7200).

Rugby

These days the national team, Los Pumas, are a handful for even the best international teams, and an impressive display in the 2004 World Cup cemented that reputation.

In the normally genteel world of international rugby, watching Los Pumas in Argentina is a unique experience; fans boo during the opposing team's national anthems and blow cow horns as the enemy attempts a conversion. Major rugby internationals are played at Estadio Monumental (*see p210*). On the domestic scene, two teams from the northern suburb of San Isidro dominate: Club Atlético de San Isidro (CASI) and the San Isidro Club (SIC). The season runs from April to October.

Club Atlético de San Isidro

Roque Sáenz Peña 499, y 25 de Mayo, San Isidro (4743 4242/www.casi.org.ar). Bus 168/ train from Retiro to San Isidro. **Tickets** AR$7; AR$3 13-18s; free under-13s. **No credit cards.**

San Isidro Club

Blanco Encalada 404, entre Sucre y Darregueira, San Isidro (4776 2030/4763 2039/www.sanisidro club.com.ar). Bus 60 (Panamericana line). **Tickets** AR$5; AR$2.50 7-15s; free under-7s. **No credit cards.**

Tennis

In recent years, Argentinian tennis players have been numbered among the world's best. Guillermo *'el Mago'* Coria, the 2004 French Open champion Gastón *'el Gato'* Gaudio (who beat Coria in the epic final) and David 'no nickname' Nalbandian are the leading racketeers.

The city's biggest tennis tournament is the **Abierto de Tenis de Buenos Aires** (Buenos Aires Tennis Open), which takes place in mid February (*see p174*) at the Buenos Aires Lawn Tennis Club.

Buenos Aires Lawn Tenis Club

Olleros 1510, y Libertador, Palermo (4772 0983). Train to Lisandro de la Torre/59, 60 bus. **Tickets** AR$18-$100. **No credit cards. Map** p285 Q9.

Participation sports

Buenos Aires is a paradise for budding Beckhams. On any open space you'll find children, teenagers and adults playing in improvised pitches, shouting *'golaaaaaazo'* every time the ball slips through the posts.

At weekends, the parks are full of people playing *picados*, as informal games are called. If you want to play, just ask.

There is also a host of multi-sport venues (*centros deportivos*). Three with good locations and facilities are **Punta Carrasco** (Avenida Costanera Rafael Obligado, y Sarmiento, 4807 1010, www.puntacarrasco.com.ar) and **Parque Norte** (Avenida Cantilo, y Guiraldes, 4787 1382), located in Costanera Norte or, closer to the centre, **Club de Amigos** at Avenida Figueroa Alcorta 3885, Palermo (4801 1213, www.clubdeamigos.org.ar). All of the above have outdoor swimming pools, tennis courts and football pitches.

Not surprisingly, with a huge river lapping at its edges, Buenos Aires boasts lots of water-related sports – though you'll need to head out to the less polluted waters of Zona Norte. **Perú Beach** at Elcano 794, Acassuso (4793 8762, www.peru-beach.com.ar) is one of the best. As well as kite surfing and windsurfing, it offers climbing, roller hockey and skateboarding. For the thirsty, the lazy or the indifferent, there's also a popular bar serving drinks and snacks.

Cycling

Buenos Aires is by no means a bicycle-friendly city, but there are decent guided tours organised by **Bike Tours** (4311 5199, www.biketours.com.ar) from US$25. They offer a choice of circuits, as well as bike hire. Another option is **La Bicicleta Naranja** (4362 1104, www.labicicletanaranja.com.ar) which organises both thematic and area tours. Alternatively, try the cycle paths in Palermo's Parque Tres de Febrero. Bike hire is available close by at **Bicicleterías Saúl** (Salguero y Cabello or San Benito y Libertad, 4867 6706) for AR$4 per hour (take along ID). The **Reserva Ecológica** is a great spot too, but you'll need your own wheels.

Fishing

There's stunning fly-fishing far from the city, in Patagonia and other regions, but fishing in the River Plate is a dirty (and unpredictable) business. Although you will see some locals throwing out a line on the Costanera Norte – and there is a fishing club for members only. You should head upriver, or deeper into the basin, for any action. Your best option is San Pedro, 150 kilometres (93 miles) up the coast where you can fish for two feisty local species – dorados and *surubíes*. Daniel Beilinson (4311 1222, dbeilinson@flyfishingcaribe.com) is an experienced guide who can take you there on a day trip (US$400 for two adults, tackle, transport and lunch included).

Football

If you want more than a kick around in the park look for the words *cancha de fútbol* (football pitch); there are hundreds of them. Pitch hire will set you back around AR$60-$80 per hour. Two of the bigger and better five-a-side centres are **Catalinas Fútbol y Paddle** (Avenida Eduardo Madero 1220, 4315 1138) and **Claudio Marangoni** (Coronel Diaz and French, 4805 4210, www.claudiomarangoni.com.ar).

Golf

Campo de Golf de la Ciudad de Buenos Aires

Avenida Torquinst 6397, entre Olleros y Alsina, Palermo (4772 7261/7576). Bus 42, 107, 130. **Open** 7am-5pm daily. **Rates** AR$10-$30; AR$8-$10 under-18s. **No credit cards. Map** p285 Q10.
This well-located, popular 18 holer is challenging in terms of length (6,585 yards) and bunker placements. Club hire costs AR$35 extra, carts are AR$5-$10, and you'll have to buy balls from the shop (AR$15 for six). Information on other golf courses further afield in Argentina is available at www.aag.com.ar.

Horse riding

Most of the *estancias* (ranches) in BA province offer day and weekend packages that include as much riding as your backside can stand. Two stand-out options are **Las Artes Endurance Country Club** (*see p237*) and **Los Dos Hermanos** (*see p238*). Alternatively, try one of the two centres below.

Club Alemán de Equitación

Avenida Dorrego 4045, y Lugones, Palermo (4778 7060/www.robertotagle.com). Bus 37, 130, 160. **Open** 9am-noon, 3-7pm Tue-Sun. **Rates** AR$40 per class for 45 mins. **No credit cards. Map** p283 O11.
This club offers instruction for all standards (including showjumping). Individual and group lessons offered, geared according to your level.

Club Hípico Buenos Aires

Avenida Figueroa Alcorta 4800, entre Roldán y Dorrego, Palermo (4778 1982/4777 8777/www. escuelahipocampo.org). Bus 37, 130, 160. **Open** 8am-9pm Tue-Sun. **Rates** AR$35-$45 per class for 45 mins. **No credit cards. Map** p283 O11.
An expertly run school offering classes, showjumping training, a pony club and, once a month, a full-day or night-time ride for AR$75 – call for details.

Karting

Circuito 9

Avenida Costanera R Obligado, y Salguero, Costanera Sur (5093 8210/www.circuito9.com.ar). Bus 33, 45. **Open** 4pm-1am Tue-Thur; 4pm-2am Fri, Sat; 4pm-midnight Sun. **Rates** AR$25-$45. **No credit cards. Map** p282 L12.

Baking and shaking at **Parque Norte**. *See p212.*

Arts & Entertainment

Up to ten drivers can compete in races of up to 25 laps, once the pecking order is established. The price includes all the extras – racing overalls with elbow and knee pads, gloves and helmet.

Racquet sports

The *centros deportivos* (*see p212*) also have tennis and squash courts.

Catedral Squash

1st floor, Defensa 267, entre Alsina y Moreno, Monserrat (4345 5511). Subte A, Plaza de Mayo or D, Catedral or E, Bolívar/29, 130, 152 bus. **Open** 8am-10pm Mon-Fri; 11am-7pm Sat. **Rates** AR$16-$22. **No credit cards. Map** p281 E10.
There are five courts on the first floor, rackets available to rent (AR$2), but rather manky balls. We advise you to buy your own ball beforehand. Day use of the gym facilities costs just AR$10.

Salguero Tenis

Salguero 3350, y Figueroa Alcorta, Palermo (4805 5144). Bus 37, 67, 102, 130. **Open** 8am-midnight Mon-Sat; 10am-9pm Sun. **Rates** *Tennis* AR$22-$27; *squash* AR$14-$18; *paddle* AR$14-$20. **No credit cards. Map** p282 L11.
Tennis (open-air clay courts), squash and paddle (a cross between the two) are on offer, plus free parking.

Running

The Palermo Parque Tres de Febrero and Parque Thays (for both, *see chapter* **North of the Centre**) are popular with joggers and runners. However, there are no clay tracks, so you have to alternate between grass and pavement. Around the Palermo lakes, there are marked paths for runners and cyclists, but they are not much respected by other users. If you are downtown, the best bets are the flat promenades along Puerto Madero, down into the lovely, red-earth Reserva Ecológica (*see p101*).

Swimming

Whatever you do don't swim (or fish) in the River Plate anywhere near the city centre – it's way too polluted. Most gym chains have at least some centres with pools – **Megatlón** (*see below*) has several. Hotel pools are generally open to non-guests for a daily or monthly fee. The loveliest outdoor pool is at the **Hilton** (*see p57*; day use of pool and spa AR$65-$90), for undercover swimming, head to the stunning Le Mirage pool and spa on the 23rd floor of the **Panamericano Hotel & Resort** (*see p39*; day use of pool only AR$80). The **Marriott Plaza Hotel** (*see p39;* day use of pool, gym and spa AR$90) boasts a small but pretty pool slap bang in the city centre overlooking leafy Plaza San Martín.

Watersports

Most of the aquatic and nautical activities on the River Plate are concentrated in Zona Norte, 45 minutes from downtown. In addition to Perú Beach (*see p212*), there's **Renosto Nautica y Deportes** in San Fernando (Avenida del Libertador 2136, 4725 0260, www.wakeboard.com.ar), where you can take lessons in waterskiing and wakeboarding. A 25-minute class, using one of the school's boats, costs AR$45. Add AR$35 to cover ski hire, lifejackets and ropes and handles.
Of course, with BA's tranquil waters, sailing is also big. With a recognised helmsman's certificate, you can charter a boat for a reasonable AR$300-$500 per day. Contact skipper **John Wright**, who operates out of Puerto Madero (4361 5403). If you are still learning, you can take sailing lessons out of Dársena Norte. Call the Yacht Club Argentino (4314 0505/www.yca.org.ar).

Fitness

Gyms & spas

Buenos Aires gyms are generally well-equipped and fashion conscious. It's cheapest to go to one of the multi-sport complexes (*see p212*), though most of the larger hotels allow non-guests to use their health facilities for a fee. Alternatively, try one of these health clubs:

Megatlón

Rodríguez Peña 1062, entre Marcelo T de Alvear y Santa Fe, Recoleta (4816 7009/www.megatlon.com). Subte D, Callao/37, 39, 111, 152 bus. **Open** 24hrs from 7am Mon-8pm Sat; 10am-6pm Sun. **Rates** AR$15 per day; AR$80-$90 per mth. **Credit** AmEx, DC, MC, V. **Map** p282 I10.
Slick, clean and busy, the Megatlón chain has all the latest hamster wheels and a wide range of classes. **Other locations:** throughout the city.

Le Parc Gym & Spa

San Martín 645, entre Tucumán y Viamonte, Microcentro (4311 9191/www.leparc.com). Subte B, Florida/6, 93, 130, 152 bus. **Open** 7am-11pm Mon-Fri; 10am-8pm Sat. **Rates** AR$20 per day; AR$175 per mth. **Credit** AmEx, DC, MC, V. **Map** p281 F11.
One of the city's most exclusive health clubs, with computerised exercise machines, swimming pool, squash courts and beauty treatments.

Yoga

All the city's main gyms offer yoga classes (*see above*). Alternatively go to major specialist centre **Fundación Hastinapura** (Venezuela 818, Monserrat, 4342 4250, www.hastinapura.org.ar). It teaches all levels, with variants of Hatha yoga on offer.

Tango

Sadness and ecstasy, sex and solitude: the world still needs tango.

The recent renaissance of tango shouldn't really have happened – or it should have been just a blip. There are no longer great cabarets in BA, no authentic tango bars, no grand salons. There is no Astor Piazzolla to innovate, much less a Carlos Gardel to emulate. The *milonga* (dance hall) scene is esoteric and obsessive, a secret world of men and women who slip furtively from one club to another, searching less for the next conquest as much as the perfect figure-eight step. Tango, like flamenco, attracts an eccentric minority and comes with a baggage of dusty nostalgia that always seems about to crush its very soul.

Yet despite all this – and the not insignificant competition that comes from rock, pop and club music – the grand old rhythm of the River Plate now enjoys a popularity that it hasn't seen since the 1970s. Left-leaning sociologists say that the effects of economic hardship have forced *porteños* to look inward and explore their identity and reality through the arts. A less romantic view is that tango satisfies the tourist image of the city, and the city government's launch of an annual festival back in 1999 has had knock-on effects on the subculture.

A lot of the energy comes from a handful of savvy, largely sincere singers and songwriters who want a tango that is daring and also popular with younger audiences. In the front line is Daniel Melingo, a one-time rocker who does a downbeat dub tango in a style somewhere between Lou Reed's lyricism and Tom Waits' loucheness. The diva of the day is Adriana Varela, a vampish fortysomething who came to singing late in life and brought just the right balance of drinking and smoking on the one hand and professionalism on the other. A glut of electronica bands has given tango big drum beats and a rasping, danceable bass groove, or, alternatively, slowed down and muted its swing to create stylish chill-out music (*see p217* **Going electric**).

Traditional tango music is very much alive. In any one week there will be concerts by local heroes like Julio Pane, who plays the *bandoneón* (the button accordion which is quintessential to tango), and European-based stars like Juan Carlos Caceres and Dino Saluzzi, as well as several orchestras playing live at municipal theatres, cultural centres or even on the streets of San Telmo. If you're lucky, some superstar act like Daniel Barenboim or the veteran outfit

Sexteto Mayor may be in town showcasing lavish classical tango at the Colón theatre. At the other end of the spectrum, you'll hear tango buskers on the Subte and tango on every other taxi-driver's radio: the FM station 2X4 (92.7) is dedicated exclusively to tangos past and present (www.la2x4.gov.ar).

FROM ROOTS TO RICHES

First appearing around 1880, the dance had its debut in Buenos Aires' outlying immigrant quarters, where Italians, Spaniards, blacks and *gaucho criollos* uprooted from the pampas brought together elements of *habanera*, polka, Spanish *contradanza* and Argentinian *milonga* (country songs) to create a new beat. Tango historians have tended to whiten the history, but in a new book, *Tango: The Art History of Love*, Yale professor Robert Farris Thompson makes a strong case for the African influence. Thompson argues that many of the dance's most idiosyncratic gestures – the swaying torso, the funereal air, the way the lower legs go berserk, and so on – were born in West Africa.

Mixing with these blacks, the local white *compadritos* (small-time hoods) forged a lively

The best · Tango spots

Centro Cultural Torquato Tasso
Top live acts, and the Sunday night *milonga* sees out the weekend in style. See p220.

Centro Región Leonesa
Its Thursday night trad *milonga,* known as Niño Bien, is a gem. See p220.

La Esquina de Carlos Gardel
Take your maiden aunt. See p222.

La Nacional
One of the oldest tango halls in the city and still one of the best. See p220.

Salon Canning
Parakultural on Mondays and Tuesdays draws youthful *tangueros*. See p220.

San Telmo barrio
Nowhere else evokes the turn-of-the-century tangopolis so well. See pp79-81.

Arts & Entertainment

bop, which simulated the violent knife fights that characterised life in the city margins. It was in this milieu that *lunfardo* – BA's unique street slang – evolved, as the semi-literate *compadritos* modified the Spanish language, mixing in Italian and Genovese words and, occasionally, the names of products or local businesses.

In the city's southern barrios of Pompeya, La Boca and Barracas, life moved to the rhythm of tango. From these humble beginnings, with gatherings taking place mainly in bars and in social and football clubs, tango moved to more central salons and the richer residents of Recoleta and Palermo began to take an interest in the new fashion. Between 1870 and 1910, the dance was transformed from a morally dubious jig of the underclass into the latest craze of the *niños bien* (rich kids). To become truly acceptable to the upper classes, tango had to be shown worthy of European culture. As early as 1906, tango scores had travelled to France, and by 1910 tango had been consecrated as the preferred dance of the Parisian bourgeoisie. London and New York were quick to follow suit. This excursion overseas sealed it for Buenos Aires, and tango was no longer a scandalous, proletarian affair. By the time the brothels were banned in 1919, tango was already as respectable as the waltz – but far more exciting.

Tango took a new musical turn with *tango canción* (tango song) when Carlos Gardel recorded 'Mi Noche Triste' in 1917. Though tango-like songs had been set to music before, this is recognised as the first true sung tango in terms of its structure and Gardel's vocal style (*see p218* **Tango's holy trinity**).

At the same time, the musical form moved on, trios becoming sextets to provide a richer sound for the dance halls. By the late 1930s, *orquestras típicas* – four *bandoneóns*, four violins, piano and double bass – were the darlings of the salon and dozens of them played the circuit. Conservatory-trained Italians, such as Juan de Dios Filiberto and Julio de Caro, brought more sophistication into tango, Filiberto in a traditional vein and De Caro exploring tango's potential as an evolving, experimental form. Just as the adoption of tango by the middle classes conveniently ignored its origins, so the importance of the dance's black roots was forgotten as tango shed its folksy origins and took on classical airs and graces.

From the 1920s on, tango was the 'in' thing in Buenos Aires and the artists of this period – all those named above as well as conductor Osvaldo Fresedo, lyricist Enrique Santos Discépolo and Francisco Canaro – make up the bulk of its most famous exponents. Booms in film, radio and the recording industry helped its success. In the late 1930s and '40s, new talents emerged, among them two giants: composer

and bandoneón player extraordinaire Aníbal Troilo and composer Osvaldo Pugliese (*see p218* **Tango's holy trinity**).

PIAZZOLLA AND THE NEW TANGO

The young *bandoneón* player Astor Piazzolla worked with Troilo, but wanted to take tango even further – in a direction that would leave dancers cold but thrill music lovers. Exploring tango's affinity with jazz, he successfully fused the two forms and created Nuevo Tango. With poet Horacio Ferrer, he took tango into the modern world, attracting a new international audience and leaving traditionalists in BA to debate whether his highly lyrical, often frantic and explosive sound was tango at all.

In the 1970s and '80s, Piazzolla spent time in Italy and toured the US and Japan, moving increasingly towards jazz fusion. *Milongas* continued to draw the tango faithful and since young professional dancers still sought a challenge, an era of exportable shows began. Choreographer Juan Carlos Copes' bestselling show *Tango Argentino*, which boomed in Buenos Aires before opening Broadway in the 1980s, created a new international fashion in tango shows that has been re-imported into the capital by the burgeoning tourist industry.

If it is through the great composers and lyricists that tango's history can be traced, then it is the dance that offers an opportunity to explore the roots of the *porteño* psyche. Many commentators cite memorable, pithy expressions for tango – 'the vertical expression of a horizontal desire' – or wax excitedly about the dance's sensuality. But it has many shades, which can be read as an index of social, sexual and emotional traits: the playful suggestiveness, the decorous codes, the repressed hysteria, the absence of frivolity and let-it-all-go sexuality – in tango there is nothing of the explosive, orgiastic energy of Brazilian rhythms.

THE TANGOPOLIS

As well as being a visible, audible, danceable cultural expression, tango is a set of myths and traditions. BA poet, librettist and songwriter Horacio Ferrer has coined the term 'tangopolis', alluding to the city's essential soul.

This includes the iconography of the songs – street lamps, corners, old bars, dancers in split skirts strutting their stuff on the cobbled streets. Carlos Gardel is to tango what Elvis Presley was to rock 'n' roll, so, unsurprisingly, his mug is ubiquitous – smiling from murals, shop windows, posters and magazines. In the sprawling Chacarita cemetery, there's a bronze of his body; there are also Gardel pharmacies, a Gardel Subte station and sections of the Abasto shopping centre named after his songs.

Going electric

When Astor Piazzolla electrified tango in the late 1950s, allowing a plugged-in guitar and modern-sounding keyboards on to the stage, traditionalists threatened to kill him. No doubt the detractors of much modern tango wish these guardians of the faith could come back to gun down the dozens of young knob-twirlers and wave-warpers currently splicing old tango tunes into their laptop compositions and mixing them with dance beats and dub loops.

From the band names it's sometimes hard to fathom who's behind the new music. In the record stores around the capital you'll find discs by the likes of Otros Aires, Tanghetto, Narcotango and Tango Crash. They are not all synth-obsessed. Tangoloco (aka the Daniel García Quinteto), for instance, do a strange mix of MoR, prog rock and guitar solos, and one of their albums is an electrotango exploration of Beatles classics. Yes, it's that bad. Tango Crash play real instruments and have released an impressive acoustic-electronic fusion record in Europe.

Few of these artists can muster more than a dozen dance steps or even cock their fedoras in the right fashion, but the very best arrangements are filled with the passionate intensity of tango. Narcotango – aka Carlos Libedinsky – waves in lots of wonderful *bandoneón* over the rolling drum and bass, and Otros Aires feature samples of singers who hark back to the 1920s and 1930s in their nasal tones and ironic delivery.

Some cynics – especially French ones – argue that all these musicians are merely spin-offs of Gotan Project (*pictured*), the Franco-Suizo-Argentinian trio behind the acclaimed 1999 album *La Revancha del Tango* (not to mention countless TV idents and ad jingles). But Gustavo Santaolalla, the Oscar-winning producer (he wrote the soundtrack for *Brokeback Mountain*) behind the Grammy-winning Bajofondo Tangoclub collective, says he was already exploring the possibilities of electrotango when Gotan surprised him with their debut.

Gotan and Bajofondo's productions are still the classiest. The former have gone on to create a stunning live show, exploring tango's countless clichés and using video images of the dance steps to good effect. Gotan guitarist, Eduardo Makaroff, has launched his own label, Mañana, dedicated to bringing a variety of new tango sub-genres to audiences in Europe. Bajofondo has splintered into its composite parts, and Luciano Supervielle's 2005 self-titled debut album is a stylish, pounding throb of urbane tango. Another band member, Javier Casalla, has recorded a wonderful album of his exploits on the rarely used Stroh violin, which leans more towards new classical music than the nightclub.

Tango's holy trinity

Iconoclasts and modernizers of tango get a lot of press, but serious traditionalists will tell you that the likes of Astor Piazzolla, Dino Saluzzi and Adriana Varela are but mortal maestros when compared to the three gods of tango: singer Carlos Gardel (1890-1935), bandoneón-player Aníbal Troilo (1914-1975) and pianist Osvaldo Pugliese (1905-1995).

These three legends encapsulate their eras more than any of their fellow poets, bandleaders, composers and performers. Gardel (*pictured right*) was the Bing Crosby of the 1920s, a superstar; night owl Troilo (*far right*) was the undisputed supremo of the *bandoneón* (button accordion) during the 1950s-1970s; and Pugliese (*far right, below*) was the doyen of dancers and a brilliant pianist.

The father of tango canción

Born in Toulouse, Gardel was an immigrant made good with a to-die-for tenor voice. He could please the middle classes and dazzle the workers. His dreams, sorrows, travels and tribulations were theirs, and as the man who created *tango canción*, he gave words to define the muddled identity of the modern, non-creole Argentinian.

His best recordings – whether numbers he penned himself such as 'Volver' (a sublime ode to exile) and 'Mi Buenos Aires Querido', or covers of 'Yira, yira' and 'A media luz' – can be compared to Frank Sinatra's legendary Atlantic recordings, both for the lush musicality of Gardel's powerful voice and for the importance of the songs for his compatriots.

It's easy from a distance of over 80 years to imagine Gardel as some kind of establishment figure. But before he became an icon he was an innovator. Films, radio and new recording technologies, and his likeable, laddish personality helped no end, but Gardel had a musical gift of the first order and helped tango to evolve and expand as a genre.

When he was killed in an air accident at Medellin airport in Colombia, the whole of Latin America mourned his passing. His name is a synonym for style and moral greatness in Argentina and everyone believes the motto, 'Gardel sings better every day.'

It's not all about the main man though. Street corners, plazas and streets are dedicated to Enrique Santos Discépolo, Homero Manzi and, since late 2003, Astor Piazzolla. In barrios that have adopted tango – La Boca, San Telmo and Boedo all claim a key role in its genesis – there are bars and cafés named after tango stars. Dusty, off-the-beaten-track holes and themed bars are now part of tango mythology. Even when there are no shows, concerts or lone strummers, there's a *tanguero* nostalgia hanging in the air like French tobacco.

You can study for a tango degree at the **Academia Nacional del Tango** (*see p221*). Several radio shows play lots of tango, and the Solo Tango cable TV channel allows fans to live and breathe the rhythms of the city while they do the ironing or get togged up for a night out. All major record shops have tango sections, and specialists such as **Zival's** (*see p171*) and **Casa Piscitelli** at San Martín No. 450, Microcentro (4394 1992) have an amazing range.

For the more dedicated tangophile, specialist shops such as **Chamuyo** (Sarmiento 1562, Tribunales, 4381 1777) and **Fattomano**

(Guatemala 4464, Palermo Viejo, 4823 3156) supply dancers with stilettos and a range of belle époque accoutrements. You can even stay in a tango hotel, with all-inclusive packages of lessons, outings, *milongas* and shows – check out the **Mansión Dandi Royal** (*see p47*) for a live-in monument to kitsch nostalgia.

If you want to see tango exhibits, there are a few places to check out. The **Casa del Teatro** at Avenida Santa Fe No.1243 (4813 5906) has a small Gardel room, open Tuesday and Thursday afternoons from 4-6.30pm, and **Botica del Angel** (Luis Sáenz Peña 541, Congreso, 4384 9396) is a 'living museum' of tango and folklore, but can only be visited via prearranged guided tours. **Piazzolla Tango** (*see p222*) downtown has a small museum and photo gallery, and the adjacent and revamped **Museo Casa Carlos Gardel**, where the star was born, is well worth visiting. Round the corner from this last, on Zelaya, are a number of colourful murals venerating the Gardelian image.

After all the tombs and artefacts, you might even feel like dancing. The annual **Buenos Aires Tango Festival** (*see p175*) in February

Son of a bitch

When people saw Aníbal Troilo perform, they were spellbound by the Buddha-like intensity with which he played the bandoneón and by his fluid tangos that switched so naturally from staccato to legato figures. An enigmatic bandleader, he created his own distinctive sound. He was also a good bloke, and enjoyed a few drinks (and maybe more) with his mates and fellow musicians.

Troilo cut his teeth playing *bandoneón* behind Ciriaco Ortiz, Julio De Caro, Angel D'Agostino and Enrique Santos Discépolo before founding his own orchestra in 1937. During the 1940s he was a star of the BA tango scene and his evolutionary style laid the groundwork for the emergence of the so-called *'nuevo tango'* of the 1950s. Songs such as 'Barrio de tango', 'Sur' and 'Che, bandoneón' by Troilo and his brilliant collaborator Homero Manzi enjoy hymnal status in Buenos Aires.

Troilo is known by most people as 'Pichuco', the nickname his father gave him, or simply as El Gordo (Fatso). No other *tanguero* is remembered with such warmth, affection and awe.

The spirit of modernity

If you've seen Osvaldo Pugliese's tomb at Chacarita cemetery (*see p99*), you may have the impression he was a cerebral stiffo who played gentle tango airs. But behind that aloofness lay a talent for innovation and an ear for addictive dance rhythms.

Pugliese rose to prominence in the late 1920s as ivory-plinker for the leading orchestras of Roberto Firpo and Pedro Maffia, before joining forces with violinist Elvino Vardaro to tour Argentina. Consolidating his fame in BA's Café Nacional he became a hero for fans of daring dance tango. His vast repertoire covered all sounds and hues, but Pugliese's liveliest tangos mix the walking beat of salon tango with a rich concert-style envelope of sounds. Numbers like 'Malandraca' and 'La Yumba' are often played later in the evening when the dancers want to dance more impressionistically. His work also suits modern dancers who like a challenge.

is the city's main tango extravaganza. Free classes build up to the week-long event, which involves hundreds of shows and tango-inspired events, when the whole city moves to the rhythm of its native sound. It takes place just after the Rio carnival, meaning lovers of spectacle and sexy thighs can do both in a single trip – or at least this is what the canny BA culture mandarins would *like* you to do.

In 2005, Gustavo Santaolalla and Walter Salles, the director of *Central Station* and *The Motorcycle Diaries*, teamed up to produce a tango film along the lines of Wim Wenders' *Buena Vista Social Club*. The film, *Café de los Maestros*, promises to be a fascinating portrait of the older generation of tango maestros – including Virginia Luque, Leopoldo Federico, Atilio Stampone and Nelly Oma – at work and play in studios and concert halls. The album soundtrack, a handsome boxed double under the same title, is already on sale around the city.

INFORMATION

Finding your way round such a thriving scene isn't easy. A foldout leaflet called 'Tango Map', found in San Telmo bars, is packed with

milonga info and makes navigating straightforward. Targeting younger readers and with some articles in English, free monthly *El Tangauta* contains a supplement with information on classes and *milongas*. Both are available in tourist information offices and kiosks. *Guía Trimestral* (quarterly, AR$2 from kiosks) includes just about everything related to tango. You should also check newspaper listings and free paper *Llegás* (available in cafés and bookshops). Government-sponsored website www.tangodata.com.ar always has useful listings, and www.todotango.com is an excellent bilingual site with news, essays and listings – its links pages are extensive.

Where to dance tango

Milongas

A clampdown on dancehalls following the tragic fire at the Cromagnon nightclub in late 2004 (*see p182*) saw many of the traditional *milongas* – dance nights which at best combine the neighbourliness of a social club with the faded elegance of a 1930s ballroom – suspended in early 2005. But nothing can stop *porteños* from dancing, and many of the old-style *milongas* are once again back in full swing. They mostly attract an older generation who prefer to dance *al suelo*; that is, feet pegged to the floor, legs discreetly doing tricks as couples shuffle through steps called backward-eights, little sandwiches and sit-downs with ghostly subtlety. Classes are often held prior to *milongas*.

Any *milonga* worthy of the name plays tangos according to the following ritual code: three sets (*tandas*) separated into straight tangos, more playful *milongas* (country songs) and waltzes. Nods and signals are used to find a partner – the man leading the way, as he does in the dance. While the couple wait for the first few bars to be over before moving, they locate each other's hands as they make eye contact – anything more obvious is considered amateurish and unrefined. The music is usually piped in – which might sound cheesy but it can add to the nostalgic atmosphere. *Milongas* go on late (5-6am at weekends, earlier on weeknights).

Note that many *milongas* either close completely or run a limited programme in January and February; check in advance.

Centro Cultural Torquato Tasso

Defensa 1575, entre Caseros y Brasil, San Telmo (4307 6506). Bus 24, 29, 39, 93, 130. **Open** from 4pm daily. *Milonga* 10pm Fri-Sun. *Classes* 8pm daily. **Admission** AR$5-$15. **No credit cards. Map** p280 C9.
This is a serious tango venue, with respected artists performing regularly. Friday and Saturday's events have live music, often including renowned orchestras such as Sexteto Mayor.

Club Gricel

La Rioja 1180, entre Humberto 1° y San Juan, Boedo (4957 7157/8398/www.clubgricel.com). Subte E, Urquiza/41, 53, 101 bus. **Open** 10am-10pm Mon-Fri; 10am-5pm Sat; 6.30pm-2am Sun. *Milonga* from 11pm Fri-Sat; from 8.30pm Sun. *Classes* 6pm, 8.30pm Mon; 7pm, 9pm Tue, Thur, Sun; 8pm Fri, Sat. **Admission** *Milonga* AR$5 Fri; AR$3 Sat, Sun. *Classes* AR$5-$10. **No credit cards.**
On Friday night Club Gricel is packed and lots of fun, with regulars coming back again and again with fixed table reservations.

La Nacional

Adolfo Alsina 1465, entre Sáenz Peña y San José, Congreso (4307 0146/www.la-nacional.com.ar). Subte A, Sáenz Peña/39, 60, 98, 168 bus. **Open** *Milonga* 11pm-4am Wed. *Classes* 9-11pm Wed. **Admission** *Milonga* AR$5. *Classes* AR$7. **No credit cards. Map** p281 F9.
This is one of BA's oldest tango venues, but the Wednesday night *milonga* is as popular as ever. If you don't fancy dancing, grab a drink and admire the setting. Reservations a must. **Photo** *p221.*

Centro Región Leonesa

Humberto 1° 1462, entre San José & Luis Sáenz Peña, Constitución (15 4147 8687). Subte E, San José/39, 60, 168 bus. **Open** *Milonga* after classes Thur. *Classes* 9-10.30pm Thur. **Admission** *Milonga* AR$5. *Classes* AR$5-$12. **No credit cards. Map** p281 E8.
An elegantly old-school *milonga* at 9pm on Thursdays (known as Niño Bien), where couples get dressed up for the occasion. New *milongas* with live orchestras are being planned for the weekends.

Nuevo Salón La Argentina

Bartolomé Mitre 1759, entre Callao y Rodríguez Peña, Congreso (4371 6767). Subte A, Congreso/ 12, 37, 60 bus. **Open** *Milonga* after classes Tue, Thur; 10.30pm Fri; after class & 10.30pm Sat; 8pm Sun. *Classes* 4pm Tue, Thur, Sat. **Admission** *Milonga* AR$6 men, AR$4 women. *Classes* AR$7. **No credit cards. Map** p281 G9.
Plenty of young dancers in an attractive 1930s building. There's a live orchestra on Saturdays.

Salón Canning

Scalabrini Ortiz 1331, y El Salvador, Palermo Viejo (4832 6753). Bus 29, 39, 168. **Open** *Milonga* 11pm-4am Mon-Fri. *Classes* 8pm-11pm Tue; 8pm-10pm Sun.* **Admission** *Milonga* AR$5. *Classes* AR$10. **No credit cards. Map** p282 L8.
This large hall gets taken over by a variety of different *milongas*. The Monday and Tuesday night event, known as Parakultural and organised by cult MC Omar Viola, is particularly popular and draws a young and trendy crowd.

Sin Rumbo

Tamborini 6157, y Constituyentes, Villa Urquiza (4571 9577). Bus 112, 117, 140. **Open** from 8pm daily. *Milonga* 10pm Tue, Wed, Fri-Sun. *Classes* 8pm Tue, Wed, Fri-Sun. **Admission** *Milonga* AR$5 Fri. *Classes* AR$7. **No credit cards.**
It's worth a trip to the edge of town to Villa Urquiza to get the feel of a genuine neighbourhood *milonga*. It's small, friendly and welcomes foreigners. Private classes are available and cost from AR$40.

La Viruta

Armenia 1366, entre Cabrera y Niceto Vega, Palermo Viejo (4774 6357/www.lavirutatango.com). Bus 15, 55, 168. **Open** from 8pm Wed-Sun. *Milonga* midnight Fri-Sun. *Classes* varies; check website. **Admission** AR$7-$9. **No credit cards. Map** p279 M5.
Milonga nights in a homely community centre. Lots of ages happily come together for tango, with a sprinkling of salsa and even rock 'n' roll dancing, as well as classes in all styles.

Classes and information

All of the above *milongas* have resident teachers, and hundreds of couples offer private – and considerably more expensive – classes (look for adverts in the specialised magazines).

Estudio La Esquina (4th Floor, Sarmiento 722, 4394 9898) offers two-hour classes for all levels, with experienced (and patient) teachers. The **Confitería Ideal** (Suipacha 384, Microcentro (5265 8078), an historic and gorgeous – though scandalously dilapidated and slightly smelly – old café, holds afternoon tango classes for beginners, and the **Mansión Dandi Royal** hotel (*see p47*) organises daily classes. Mora Godoy, currently one of the best known tango dancers in BA, now has her own school, the **Mora Godoy Tango Escuela** (2nd Floor, Avenida Pueyrredón 1090, 4966 1225, www.moragodoy.com). Below are some other recommended options.

Academia Nacional del Tango

1st Floor, Avenida de Mayo 833, entre Piedras y Tacuarí, Monserrat (4345 6968/6967). Subte A, Piedras/10, 70, 86 bus. **Open** 2-9pm Mon-Fri. *Classes* from 6pm Mon-Fri. **Admission** free. *Classes* from AR$7. **No credit cards.** **Map** p281 F10.
As well as running classes, this is Argentina's very own 'university of tango' and an excellent source of information and tango lore. A well-stocked research library is open Tuesday and Thursday from 5-7pm, and the World Tango Museum is open daily from 2-6pm (AR$3.50); entry to the museum is via Rivadavia 830.

Centro Cultural Konex

Avenida Córdoba 1235, entre Libertad y Talcahuano, Tribunales (4813 1100/www.centroculturalkonex.org). Subte D, Tribunales/29, 39, 109 bus. **Open** *Jan-Feb* 2-9pm Mon-Fri. *Mar-Dec* 10am-10pm Mon-Fri; 4-9pm Sat. *Classes* 4pm, 5.30pm, 7pm. **Admission** free. *Classes* AR$10; AR$5 Wed. **Credit** AmEx, DC, MC, V. **Map** p281 H10.
This well-known city centre cultural complex offers 90-minute tango classes with English-speaking teachers, as well as courses and seminars on the history and culture of tango.

Tanguería El Beso

1st Floor, Riobamba 416, entre Corrientes y Lavalle, Once (4953 2794). Subte B, Callao/37, 60, 124 bus. **Open** *Classes* 8.30pm Mon, Wed, Fri; 8pm Sun. *Milonga* 11pm Tue, Wed, Sat, Sun. **Admission** *Classes* AR$12 per class; AR$48 for 8 classes. *Milonga* AR$7. **No credit cards.** **Map** p281 H9.
This is the name of a respected academy run by Susana Miller, who also teaches in the US. Her own schedule is complicated, so call for information – and expect the style to be salón tango, close and free from showy tics. All the group classes are great and have a personal element.

Where to hear tango

For the wooden-legged, there is, of course, tango music and not all of it is made for dancing. There is a classical tradition, which goes back to early composers such as Juan de Dios Filiberto, and is kept up today by *bandoneón*-playing Piazzolla disciple Rodolfo Mederos and virtuoso

pianists Pablo Ziegler and Sonia Possetti. Also look out for Julio Pane on *bandoneón*, and guitarist Juanjo Dominguez. Singer Adriana Varela's strong, sensual shows are exceptional while Lidia Borda can pack a punch with her moody singing with a strong French lilt. Both **La Trastienda** and **ND/Ateneo** (for both, *see p204*) are serious venues for folk music and tango.

Outside the ever-evolving mainstream, there's a new, more experimental scene led by Daniel Melingo, grumpy-voiced Omar Mollo and Latino fusioneers La Chicana. Several orchestras and smaller outfits are committed to keeping alive the spirit of salón tango; among the best are Sexteto Mayor and El Arranque.

These are just the cool ones. Assorted Latino crooners with an eye for fashion (and hard cash) from Julio Iglesias to Shakira have also been giving tango a whirl. Remember 'Everybody Salsa'? Well, be warned – somewhere a misguided pop band is probably recording 'Everybody Tango' right now.

Where to watch tango

These are the city's best dinner shows. **Bar Sur** and **El Viejo Almacén** are intimate, atmospheric venues. **Chiquín** (Perón 920, Microcentro, 4394 5004) is a painstakingly

Old-school moves at **La Nacional**. See p220.

Tango on...

...solitude

'Nostalgia/To hear her laugh out loud/
To feel her lips on mine/Like fire, her
breathing/Anguish/To feel abandoned/
To know another is by her side/Soon,
soon he'll whisper his love.../From this
sorrowful loneliness I see the truth/
The fall of the dead roses of my youth.'
Enrique Cadícamo, '**Nostalgias**'

...drinking, drugs and whoring

'I know it's bad for me/I know I'm doing
me wrong/With this wino's tearful
song/But it's that old flame,
bandoneón/That burns, and yearns/For
booze that wipes me out/The drink that
brings/An end to the show/Drawing the
curtains/Over the heart.' **Cátulo Castillo**,
'**La última curda [The Last Piss Up]**'

'In the back streets of my 'hood/Was a
man who got laid, he was looking good/
He snorted so much they called him The
Nose/He came home in the mornings to
change his clothes/That boy lived a life
sunk by troubles and woes.' **Daniel
Melingo**, '**Narigon [The Nose]**'

...love

'Corrientes 348/Take the lift to the second
floor.../No caretaker, no neighbours/
Inside, cocktails and amor.../Everything in
the half light/What an enchantress is
love/Kisses in the half light.../Everything
in shadow/The twilight up above/Smooth
as velvet/The half light of love.' **Carlos
César Lenzi**, '**A media luz [At half light]**'

...Buenos Aires

'Barrio silver in the moonlight/Rumours of a
dance/It's everything you need/Barrio!
Barrio!/Your soul trembles.../Sorrows! I cry
out/In this lowlife slum/For a sweet tango
to hum.' **Alfredo Le Pera and Mario
Battistella Zoppi**, '**Melodia de arrabal
[Song for the slums]**'

'Sur/A blank wall and then.../Sur/The light
of a corner shop.../You'll never see me
again as you once saw me.../My stars will
no longer shine light/On our meandering
walks/Through Pompeya at night.../The
streets and the suburban moon/And my
love in your window.../Everything is dead,
I know...' **Homero Manzi**, '**Sur [Southside]**'

restored historic venue with an excellent menu
and a star-studded show. For a tourist-oriented
dose of razzle and dazzle, try **Piazzolla Tango**
or **La Esquina de Carlos Gardel**. But for a
highly stylised, razzmatazz introduction to the
dance – that locals have deprecatingly dubbed
'tango for export – you can go along to the likes
of: **La Esquina Homero Manzi** (Avenida San
Juan 3601, Boedo, 4957 8488); **El Querandí**
(Perú 302, Monserrat, 5199 1770); **Sabor a
Tango** (Perón 2535, Abasto, 5953 8700,
www.saboratango.com.ar); and the most
spectacular spectacular of all, **Señor Tango**
(Vieytes 1653, Barracas, 4303 0231, www.
senortango.com.ar). The latter regularly fills
to its 1,500 capacity, with customers paying
from AR$150 per head.

Bar Sur

*Estados Unidos 299, y Balcarce, San Telmo (4362
6086/www.bar-sur.com.ar). Bus 29, 93, 130.* Open
8pm-3am daily. **Show** every 2hrs. **Tickets** AR$80-
$160. **Credit** AmEx, DC, MC, V. **Map** p280 D10.
The show is fairly fancy, but the intimate bar and
emphasis on participation makes this a fun and
friendly little joint. Used in films, the setting – both
inside and out on the street – evokes the Buenos
Aires of cobbled streets and streetcorner men.

La Esquina de Carlos Gardel

*Pasaje Carlos Gardel 3200, y Anchorena, Abasto
(4867 6363/www.esquinacarlosgardel.com.ar).
Subte B, Carlos Gardel/24, 26, 124, 168 bus.*
Open 8.30pm-12.30am daily. **Tickets** AR$120-$350.
Credit AmEx, DC, MC, V. **Map** p278 J5.
OK, so it's a show. But the venue is grand, the
dancers sexy and showbizzy, and the food is big
steaks and the wine blood-red. Leave your cynicism
hanging in the cloakroom and enjoy – at least until
they offer you a Gardel T-shirt.

Piazzolla Tango

*Florida 165, entre Mitre y Perón, Microcentro
(0810 333 82646/www.piazzollatango.com). Subte D,
Catedral/10, 29, 64, bus.* **Open** noon-midnight Mon-
Sat; varies Sun. *Classes* 5pm, 8pm Mon-Sat. *Dinner*
8.30pm, show 10.15pm Mon-Sat. **Tickets** AR$6.
Classes AR$12. *Show* from AR$150 stalls; AR$350
box. **Credit** AmEx, DC, MC, V. **Map** p281 F10.
Theatre, gallery and museum, this new venue in one
of the city's most gorgeous buildings – the Galería
Güemes – is also a good place to take classes.

El Viejo Almacén

*Avenida Independencia 300, y Balcarce, San Telmo
(4307 7388/4300 3388/www.viejoalmacen.com).
Bus 29, 93, 130, 152.* **Open** 2pm-2am daily. *Dinner*
8pm, show 10pm daily. **Tickets** AR$110-$135.
Credit AmEx, DC, MC, V. **Map** p280 D10.
A charming colonial venue and a tourist favourite on
the corner of atmospheric Balcarce street. In 1968
singer Edmundo Rivero took over the building as a
refuge for musicians, dancers and, as a plaque in the
doorway states, 'those who have lost their faith'.

Theatre & Dance

Boom or bust, the show must go on.

Theatre

With more than 150 weekly productions and a steady stream of premiéres, Buenos Aires is quickly becoming a world-class theatre town. A massive and diverse group of theatre-goers attend a wide range of plays, from big-budget, over-the-top Broadway-style musicals to no-budget, low-key independent productions by local playwrights. You'll also be able to catch an aerial interpretation of Spanish-language Shakespeare and an experimental troupe reciting local classics in a pitch-dark theatre.

The *porteño* obsession with theatre goes back to the end of colonial times, when picaresque satires were the barely tolerated medium through which the *criollo* elite could poke fun at its incompetent Spanish rulers. Over time, new styles and genres developed, with subsequent social developments giving birth to a generation of innovative thespians. The most recent political and economic convulsions have proved no different. The fringe theatre scene, after experiencing an explosion in the wake of the December 2001 economic and social crisis, has seen a steady increase in the number of venues and productions. Ironically, given the anti-establishment bent of much independent theatre, this budding renaissance is in no small part thanks to government subsidies for small playhouses and companies.

The traditional spotlight, though, shines on Avenida Corrientes. The 'street that never sleeps' was for many years Buenos Aires' answer to Broadway, though at some point the glittering neon billboards began to fizzle out and several magnificent playhouses were pulled down to make room for car parks and other more profitable businesses.

For the old-time theatres that escaped the bulldozers, the big attraction is the *revista porteña*, a type of 'skits and tits' cabaret revue show, currently staging a big comeback. Starring scantily clad showgirls known as vedettes, and slapstick comedians – most of whom are also recognisable television personalities – they draw huge crowds. Between monologues, sketches and dance routines, *capo cómicos*, as the comedians

> ▶ For information on **tango shows** and **tango classes**, *see pp215-222* **Tango**.

Cabaret combo El Rebenque at the **Faena Hotel + Universe**. See p57.

are known, pull off mordant satires of local politics – neither the feathers nor the beautiful girls can dilute the vitriol that is aimed at the country's political leadership. Tired of simply mimicking presidents from the stage, comedian Nito Artaza, the genre's number one showman, flirted with running for the top job himself under the banner of his fledgling 'Swindled Argentinian Savers' movement. Enrique Pinti is the other most visible figure within the *capo cómico* genre.

Thanks to the success of home-grown and imported musicals, *porteños* have warmed to a genre that was previously unknown to them. And although devaluation means that expensive imports like Bob Fosse's *Chicago* (which was given a dazzling local production) are no longer affordable, the musical is still very much alive thanks to a new, energetic generation of writers, directors and singer-dancers.

Reflecting the burgeoning popularity of independent theatre, a number of smaller, multi-purpose spaces featuring experimental, crossover works have appeared on Corrientes and elsewhere to compete with mainstream or state-run theatres. Many of these new venues, in lieu of charging an entrance price, let viewers in for free and then pass round the *gorra* (hat) when the 'curtains' close. It's not only a sign of Argentina's economic reality but also of the actors, and playwrights' confidence in the quality and impact of their works. Just about every space imaginable – including living rooms, abandoned warehouses, occupied factories, plazas and Subte carriages – are regularly co-opted as alternative performance venues.

It's this non-mainstream scene – known as Off-Corrientes and Off-Off-Corrientes – that is expanding from Abasto to other barrios such as Almagro, Villa Crespo and even trendy Palermo Hollywood. Fringe productions are keeping alive Buenos Aires' passion for theatre – that and the seemingly limitless pool of talent (perhaps a result of confronting so much drama in their everyday lives) from which BA theatre producers can draw. Slowly, many Off-Corrientes productions are gaining popularity and creeping into the limelight. The circus-based humour of the Los Macocos, once a fixture on the independent circuit, can now be seen – if in a watered-down version from their early days – on Corrientes. After playing for two years in smaller theatres, Javier Daúlte's *Nunca Estuviste tan Adorable* (You were never so adorable) cut through Corrientes' glitz and glam to bring a more thoughtful tone to the masses.

FESTIVALS

Theatre and dance festivals are usually of the highest quality in terms of performance, but often a bit disorganised. The most important theatre and dance event is the biannual

Festival Internacional de Buenos Aires (*see p176*). The festival attracts artists from around the world, but showcases Argentinian talent, and is the best venue for locals looking to take their works abroad. An alternative yearly event, helping to keep alive the traumatic memory of Argentina's 'Dirty War' of the late 1970s, is known as **Teatro x la Identidad** (Theatre for Identity, www.teatroxlaidentidad. net). This sober and moving festival usually takes place in August, with works touching on the sensitive issue of the identity of children abducted from their 'disappeared' parents.

TICKETS AND INFORMATION

You can buy tickets at the *boletería* (box office) of the venue itself (often cash only) or, for major productions or venues, by phone through **Ticketek** (5237 7200, www.ticketek. com.ar) and **Ticketmaster** (4321 9700); local credit cards are accepted and booking fees apply. Discounted tickets – 30 to 50 per cent off – for plays, musicals, supper shows and films are available at: **Cartelera Lavalle** at Lavalle 742, Microcentro (4322 1559, www. 123info.com.ar); **Cartelera Baires** at Unit 24, Avenida Corrientes 1382, Tribunales (4372 5058, www.cartelera-net.com.ar); and **Unica Cartelera** at Unit 27, Lavalle 835,Microcentro (4370 5319, www.unica-cartelera.com.ar). You can reserve seats by phone but must pay in cash when you go to collect the tickets.

Venues

State-run theatres

There are two main theatre centres funded by the national government. The 80-year-old **Teatro Cervantes**, a work of art in its own right, seats 1,000 people in two auditoriums and shows Latin American and Spanish theatre and some dance. Grouped together as the **Complejo Teatral de Buenos Aires** is a complex of five separate venues which stage principally, but not exclusively, contemporary works. The complex includes the centrally located Alvear, Regio and Sarmiento theatres, and the picturesque Teatro de la Ribera in La Boca, but the flagship is the **Teatro San Martín** on Avenida Corrientes. Renowned for the quality and eclecticism of its programmes, ranging from cast-iron classics to avant-garde experiments, it incorporates three discrete auditoriums with a combined capacity of around 1,700. Those who feel like they've seen one *Swan Lake* too many should check out their acclaimed contemporary ballet company.

At the Teatro San Martín you can pick up a programme for all five theatres in the complex. You can buy tickets in person, or online at www.teatrosanmartin.com.ar.

Teatro Cervantes

Libertad 815, entre Córdoba y Paraguay, Tribunales (4815 8880/8884 ext 121 box office/www.teatro cervantes.gov.ar). Subte D, Tribunales/29, 39, 109, bus. **Box office** *Feb-Dec* 10am-8pm Tue-Sun. Closed Jan. **Tickets** AR$8-$15. **No credit cards.** **Map** p281 G10.

Teatro San Martín

Avenida Corrientes 1550, entre Paraná y Montevideo, Tribunales (freephone 0800 3335254/www.teatro sanmartin.com.ar). Subte B, Uruguay/24, 60, 102 bus. **Box office** 10am-10pm daily. **Tickets** AR$4-$10 children's shows; from AR$7 adult shows. Half-price Wed. **Credit** AmEx, MC, V. **Map** p281 G9.

Other major venues

Also on Avenida Corrientes are the venerable **Teatro Opera** and **Gran Rex** (for both, *see p204*), used mainly for concerts. The **Teatro Nacional** at No.960 (4326 4218), was restored and reopened in March 2000.

Belisario

Avenida Corrientes 1624, entre Rodríguez Peña y Monevideo, Tribunales (4373 3465/www.belisario teatro.com.ar). Subte B, Callao/24, 26, 60, 102 bus. **Box office** *Jan, Feb* 4-9pm Wed-Sat. *Mar-Dec* 4-9pm Thur-Sun. **Shows** *Jan, Feb* Fri, Sat. *Mar-Dec* Thur-Sun. **Tickets** AR$8-$12. **No credit cards.** **Map** p281 G9.

Home to the best experimental theatre around, including improv shows where actors take their cue from audience requests.

Ciudad Cultural Konex

Avenida Sarmiento 3131, entre Jean Jaurés y T M de Anchorena, Abasto (4813 1100/www.ciudadcultural konex.org). Subte B, Carlos Gardel/26, 168, 180 bus. **Box office** *Jan, Feb* 2-9pm Mon-Fri. *Mar-Dec* 9am-10pm Mon-Fri. **Shows** *Jan, Feb* Fri, Sat. *Mar-Dec* Mon, Wed, Fri, Sat. **Tickets** AR$10-$15. **No credit cards.** **Map** p274 I5.

After an auspicious pre-opening festival in 2004, this exciting new Abasto venture (nerve centre of the Fundación Konex) fell prey to administrative difficulties. Shows started up again in early 2006, but long-term programmes have yet to be finalised.

Multiteatro

Avenida Corrientes 1283, y Talcahuano, Tribunales (4382 9140). Subte B,Uruguay/26, 60, 102 bus. **Box office** 10am-10pm daily. **Shows** 9pm Wed-Sun. **Tickets** AR$25-$30. **No credit cards.** **Map** p281 G10.

In its three smallish auditoriums, Multiteatro regularly stages provocative one-person shows as well as local adaptations of contemporary classics.

Teatro Astral

Avenida Corrientes 1639, entre Montevideo y Rodríguez Peña, Tribunales (4374 5707/9964). Subte B, Callao/12, 24, 37, 60 bus. **Box office** 10am-10pm daily. **Tickets** AR$25-$35. **Credit** AmEx, DC, MC, V. **Map** p281 G9.

Argentina's most famous feather-clad showgirls have swayed their hips on the stage of Astral, the main revue theatre on Corrientes.

Teatro del Pueblo

Avenida Roque Sáenz Peña 943, entre Carlos Pellegrini y Suipacha, Microcentro (4326 3606/ www.teatrodelpueblo.org.ar). Subte B, Carlos Pellegrini or C, Diagonal Norte or D, 9 de Julio/17, 24, 59, 67 bus. **Box office** 3.30-8pm Wed-Sun. **Shows** from 8.30pm Fri-Sun. **Tickets** AR$12; AR$5 concessions. **No credit cards.** **Map** p281 G10.

Founded in 1930, this was one of the first independent theatres in Latin America. It stages works by Argentinian playwrights, past and present.

Teatro Liceo

Avenida Rivadavia 1494, y Paraná, Congreso (4381 4291/box office 4381 5745). Subte A, Sáenz Peña/86, 102, 168 bus. **Box office** 10am-8pm Mon; 10am-11pm Tue-Sun. **Tickets** AR$15-$40. **No credit cards.** **Map** p281 G9.

This 700-seater, 140-year-old venue is the oldest in the city and still going strong.

Off-Corrientes

There are some companies, playwrights and performers whose work you should look out for. Playwright/directors such as Rafael Spregelburd, Javier Daúlte, Federico León and

Teatro San Martín: contemporary spirit.

Alejandro Tantanián are quality innovators who have opened doors for new forms of expression within the city's expanding theatre underworld. Along the way, they have raised an exciting new generation of young, multi-talented thespians whose works are defining a solid and unique style in Buenos Aires. In this group, look for the names Santiago Gobernori, Mariana Chaud, Matías Feldman, Mariano Pensotti and Lola Arias. Although most productions from this group are confined to the independent theatres named below, Daúlte, for one, has forced his way in to more popular venues.

Most Off-Corrientes venues (including those listed here) are in and around the Abasto neighbourhood, although the scene is expanding geographically. The **Actors Studio** is on Avenida Corrientes itself, but way up at No.3565/71 (4867 6622, www.actors-studio.org) in an old house converted into a restaurant-cum-theatre. It features new versions of classics and a diverse selection of outrageous new works and performers. **El Camarín de las Musas** at Mario Bravo No.960 (4862 0655, www.elcamarin delasmusas.com.ar) is a hip, comfortable multipurpose space that gets rave reviews for its highbrow productions. You can catch a meal or drink before descending to the basement theatre. **Espacio Callejón** at Humahuaca 3759 (4862 1167) is one of the best BA showplaces for gutsy new productions and it also offers evening classes in singing and theatre for amateurs. For the most complete and up-to-date information on independent theatre, go to www.alternativateatral.com. Tickets at all these venues cost AR$5-$10.

Dance

While tango tends to dominate dance in BA, diverse immigrant groups drew on deep-rooted customs to forge their own dances. *Milonga*, the quicker-stepping and more marginal relative of tango, is popular. Traditional dances such as *zamba* and *chacarera*, both solidified in their present form in the province of Salta, are prevalent in the west and north of the country. These dances can be seen and practised at *peñas* (folk music venues; *see p201*), as well as at cultural centres specialising in music and dance from the interior provinces.

Spanish dance enjoyed a following until the middle of the 19th century, and the first academic classical ballet company in South America started in the school of the Teatro Colón in the 1920s, just a few years after the Argentinian elite had been bowled over by visits from Anna Pavlova and Isadora Duncan.

Ballet remained the preserve of a few connoisseurs until Julio Bocca arrived on the scene in 1985. With his dance partner Eleonora Cassano, Bocca succeeded in bringing classical ballet to the masses with hugely successful open-air performances in such non-conventional stages as Avenida 9 de Julio and the Boca Juniors stadium. His choreography to Astor Piazzolla's tango music was equally audacious. In 1990, Bocca founded his own company, the Ballet Argentino, which tours the world, and together with the school of the Teatro Colón, churns out new ballet dancers. Nowadays, Argentinian dancers – such as Paloma Herrera, Maximiliano Guerra, Iñaki Urlezaga and Herman Cornejo – have become, in their field, as famous as football stars.

Modern dance isn't as popular as classical but BA has a first-rate company in the Teatro San Martín's resident ensemble, Ballet Contemporáneo. Directed by Mauricio Wainrot, the troupe has attracted new audiences with productions such as a version of Anne Frank's diary. Their production of Carl Orff's *Carmina Burana* gets reruns upon popular request whenever the theatre's schedule permits.

The Resident Ballet of the **Teatro Argentino** in La Plata, under the aegis of choreographer Oscar Aráiz, formerly with the Ballet Contemporáneo, dabbles in both classical and modern dance. Also keep an eye open for the work of Tangokinesis and Roxana Grinstein's El Escote, two avant-garde companies renowned for their absurdist take on tango. The popularity of De la Guarda has turned on BA's theatregoers to aerial dance. Original choreographies and interpretations of tango classics are just a part of what can be seen 'off the ground'.

Murgas, neighbourhood groups that combine dance with drums and theatre, can be seen in plazas and parks, especially during the carnival season (February and March; *see p174*).

Venues

Argentina's best contemporary dance troupes perform at the **Teatro San Martín** (*see p225*). Other venues worth checking out for modern dance are the **Alvear** (part of the Complejo Teatral de Buenos Aires) and the **Centro de Arte y Cultura** (Guardia Vieja 3783, 4866 2671), home to Maximiliano Guerra's Ballet del Mercosur. Alternative venues include Espacio Callejón, the **Teatro del Sur** at Venezuela No.2255, San Cristóbal (4941 1951) and **El Ombligo de la Luna** at Anchorena No.364, Abasto (4867 6578). Flamenco and Spanish dance fans should check the listings for the **Teatro Astral** (*see p225*) and the **Teatro Avenida** (Avenida de Mayo 1222, Congreso, 4381 0662), and look out for *tablaos* at Spanish restaurants.

Tripping the light elastic

For around two centuries, Argentinian cows have been forced to share the pampas with another species of migrant animal – circus performers. These nomadic shows – known as *circo criollo* – feature acrobats, clowns, jugglers, freaks and the dizzying aerial feats of trapeze artists. This backwoods, low-budget tradition spawned an urban, high-concept genre: impact theatre.

Argentinian aerialism took off in the 1980s when the Organizaciòn Negra, an underground theatre group, began using innovative props – rubber cords connected to mountaineering harnesses – to put on electrifying performances. When it dissolved in 1992, former members Diqui James and Pichòn Baldinu broke to form the now world-renowned De la Guarda (*pictured*).

James and Baldinu began fabricating elaborate sets: cranes, towers, pulleys, stages on wheels, and paper ceilings that fell like confetti. They added dazzling lights, water and fire to a soundtrack of live, primal drumming textured by electronic music.

By 1995 the duo's vision had taken them to New York; their show *Villa Villa* ran off-Broadway for six years, attracting over a million spectators. Deliberately rejecting unsettling material, De la Guarda's act chimed with the rave culture hedonism of the 1990s. Their mission statement reads: 'The language is not intellectual, it goes straight to the body, straight to the senses, straight to the soul.'

Although James and Baldinu have since parted ways, the craze continues. Baldinu stayed with De la Guarda, opening the group's own theatre, Sala Villa Villa in the Centro Cultural Recoleta (*see p191*).

In 2005 James launched his solo career with a show called *Fuerzabruta*. Using the techniques he developed with De la Guarda, James added more electronic music and a heavy dose of carnival sounds. *Fuerzabruta*'s high energy and feats of engineering – including a massive, transparent pool hanging over the crowd – attracted big crowds and a media buzz.

Now everyone's doing it. With varying degrees of success and coherence, an increasingly large percentage of BA's stage shows involve performers hanging from the ceiling. Part of Diego Maradona's 2005 chat show, *La Noche del Diez*, involved several shit-scared showgirls bobbing ineptly from the ceiling, nervously kicking at a huge, transparent soccer ball. This was also the year when high-wire went highbrow, the Teatro San Martín staging an Oberon-on-elastic interpretation of *A Midsummer Night's Dream*.

The list, and the dangling, goes on. These days no BA event is complete without someone floating in the air or bouncing off the walls. If all this aerial activity has you pining for a chance to head skyward, don't despair: you too can experience zero gravity first-hand, at Brenda Angiel's long-running aerial dance school (www.danzaerea.com.ar).

For more information on De la Guarda and *Fuerzabruta*, check out their websites at www.delaguarda.com and www.fuerzabruta.com.

Trips Out of Town

Features

Getting Started

Even the best cities have their limits.

If there's one thing *porteños* love more than Buenos Aires it's getting the hell out of Buenos Aires. A slight rise in temperature is all the excuse they need to pack a hamper, slap on some sunblock and head for the country or the coast. Those who have to sweat it out in the city during the humid months of January and February are viewed with a mixture of pity and disdain. And just to rub it in, no nightly news bulletin is complete without a 'beach report', delivered with the kind of gravitas most media outlets reserve for earthquakes and terrorist attacks.

There's no need for tourists to miss out on the fun. Depending on the season and your interests, BA serves as a great hub for seeking out sun, sand, history and horses. We've divided Argentinian trips thematically, into different physical environments – river destinations, countryside retreats and beaches on the Atlantic Coast in southern Buenos Aires province. You can even visit another country for the day or longer – as a separate chapter, we have grouped together a handful of top destinations in neighbouring Uruguay.

The first section – **Upriver** – is centred around the continuation of a very *porteño* presence in the brown waters of the Río de la Plata. North of BA beyond the city limits, riverside **Tigre** is a gateway to another world: the islands and waterways that make up the **Delta**. Rivers also provide one of South America's most spectacular experiences. Further than the typical short-trip destination, but eminently accessible from Buenos Aires, is the superlative-inducing **Cataratas de Iguazú**, a network of stunning waterfalls in the jungle border region of Argentina, Brazil and Paraguay.

If you prefer to head inland to enjoy the wide open spaces of the **Country**, picturesque **San Antonio de Areco**, just a couple of hours from BA, is where you can pick up the trail of Argentina's legendary *gauchos*. Throughout Buenos Aires province you can explore the pampas on horseback, or just kick back and let someone do the hard work of stoking the barbecue at one of the region's beautiful, historical *estancias*, as ranches are known.

Of course, you may simply want to hit the **Beach**. If you are visiting between November and April, the chances are you'll get enough sunshine to make you yearn for some sand between your toes. If you can't be bothered with

border crossings, you need to go south to the Atlantic coast for the sound of the surf and all the fun of resort life. **Mar del Plata**, **Pinamar** or **Mar de las Pampas** and **Mar Azul**, all offer varying degrees of sun-soaked action among the crowds or soporific summer solitude.

Just a short one-hour ferry across 'the puddle', as the River Plate is affectionately known, will get you to Uruguay. Popular **Colonia de Sacramento** is a World Heritage Site that marries time travel with tranquillity, and further north is the even more secluded tiny town of **Carmelo**. Uruguay feels like an oversized *pueblo* and even its capital, **Montevideo**, exudes a small-town feel. Once you slip into its easygoing groove though, you'll be pleasantly surprised by its diversity and sophistication. Throughout Uruguay, small beaches line the river shore from Colonia to Montevideo and beyond, but the country's contender for queen of the beach scene is **Punta del Este**, one of Latin America's favourite and most fashionable summer retreats.

Information

The local tourist office for each destination is given at the end of each relevant section.

Administración de Parques Nacionales
Avenida Santa Fe 690, entre Maipú y Marcelo T de Alvear, Retiro (4515 1365/www.parques nacionales.gov.ar). Subte C, San Martín/10, 17, 59, 152 bus. **Open** 10am-5pm Mon-Fri. **Map** p281 G9.

Provincia de Buenos Aires
Casa de la Provincia de Buenos Aires, Avenida Callao 237, entre Perón y Sarmiento, Tribunales (4371 7045/3587/www.vivalaspampas.com.ar). Subte B, Callao/12, 24, 26, 60 bus. **Open** 9.30am-7pm Mon-Fri. **Map** p281 G11.

Provincia de Misiones
Casa de la Provincia de Misiones, Avenida Santa Fe 989, entre Carlos Pellegrini y Suipacha, Retiro (4322 0677/www.misiones.gov.ar). Subte C, San Martín/10, 17, 59, 152 bus. **Open** *Jan, Feb* 9am-6pm Mon-Fri. *Mar-Dec* 9am-5pm Mon-Fri. **Map** p281 G11.

Uruguay Tourist Information
Embajada de Uruguay, Avenida Las Heras 1907, Recoleta (4807 3040/www.embajadadeluruguay. com.ar). Bus 10, 37, 59, 60, 101. **Open** 9.30am-5.30pm Mon-Fri. **Map** p282 J11.

Upriver

Merrily up the stream.

Tigre & the Delta

If you're looking to escape from Buenos Aires and don't have enough time to head for the hills, Tigre and the nearby Delta make for a perfect day or overnight retreat. Only 30 minutes from the capital, a network of over 10,000 kilometres (6,500 miles) of canals, brooks, rivers and islands makes up this peaceful region.

The town of Tigre serves as both port and gateway to the Delta. At the end of the 19th century Tigre was enjoying its belle époque; BA's high society used it as a summer playground, hosting extravagant galas and balls. Soon after though, with improved transport links, the aristocrats abandoned their summer homes in Tigre for the beaches of Mar del Plata.

It's taken over a century, but Tigre and the Delta are currently enjoying a revival. Today, an average of 80,000 *porteños* and visitors head there each weekend.

Tigre and the Delta are most easily reached by car, or by train from Retiro station. There is a direct train, or you can make one change and travel for the final part of the journey on the delightful Tren de la Costa (*see p180*).

On arrival in Tigre, visit the tourist office (*see p232*) to pick up a map and then head to the **Mercado de Frutos** (Sarmiento y Perú) where incense perfumes the air and stalls stacked high with fruits and wicker furniture trade from dawn till dusk. A peaceful stroll is rather spoilt by the wild screams from the nearby **Parque de la Costa** amusement park (*see p180*) – though there are great views from the park's Big Wheel.

Heading past the **Estación Fluvial** – starting point for boat trips to the Delta – you'll come to the bridge that crosses to the delightful Paseo Victorica, a leafy promenade where people come to eat, stroll and smooch. Facing the green verges are Italian restaurants, *parrillas*, ice-cream parlours, bars, and, in the backdrop, the splendid site of the **Club de la Marina**, built in 1876.

THE DELTA

If it's a sunny day, your best bet is to get out on to the Delta rather than hang around in Tigre. Waterside restaurants, uninhabited islands, hotels lost in thick vegetation, rare flora and fauna – these waterways have it all. Go to Estacion Fluvial Stand 7 for river taxis to the most important Delta islands.

The Delta.

Find everything except fruit at the **Mercado de Frutos**. *See p231.*

Around these islands numerous boats weave in and out of the watery channels, brushing past the overhanging willows. You can jump off at various points, accessible via the jetties that stretch out from the banksides.

For a fun and informative Delta boat tour with an English-speaking expert at the helm, contact **Barba Charters** (4824 3366/15 4403 2829/www.barbacharters.com.ar), run by local expert Santiago Bengolea.

Where to eat & drink

The most interesting options for food are out in the Delta. The bohemian hangout **Beixa Flor** (Arroyo Abra Vieja 148, 4728 2397, main courses AR$12-$22) has good home-made food. **El Gato Blanco** (Río Capitán 80, 4728 0390, main courses AR$15-$25) is one of the biggest eateries on the Delta, able to seat 150 people. For superb seafood in Tigre itself, try **María Luján** (Paseo Victorica 611, 4731 9613, main courses AR$18-$35).

Where to stay

In Tigre, **Villa Julia Hotel** (Victoria 800, 4749 0242, www.villajulia.com.ar, doubles US$45) is set in a fabulous house dating back to 1913,

carefully restored preserving the original features. This is a place in which to dine, sleep and relax in elegance. **Casona la Ruchi** (Lavalle 557, 4749 2499, www.casonalaruchi. com.ar, doubles US$45) is a family-run bed & breakfast with enormous wood-floored bedrooms, huge balconies and a swimming pool.

In the Delta, **Hostería Los Pecanes** (54 11 4728 1932, www.hosterialospecanes.com, doubles US$50) is a typical Delta house which has been converted into a cosy family-run *hostería*. For sheer indulgence, reserve a room at **La Pascuala Delta Lodge** (4728 1253, www.lapascuala.com.ar, US$137 per person all inclusive). Hidden under thick foliage, the Pascuala – built entirely from wood from its own island – includes 15 luxury cabins, a pool, gourmet cuisine and a self-service cocktail bar. A newcomer on the Delta scene is the **Rumbo 90 Delta Lodge & Spa** (15 5006 4341, www.rumbo90.com.ar, US$150-$300), which offers a wide range of spa treatments as well as great food and rooms with jacuzzis

Tourist information

Ente Municipal de Turismo de Tigre
Estación Fluvial de Tigre, Mitre 305 (4512 4497/ www.tigre.gov.ar). **Open** 9am-5pm daily.

Getting there

By bus

The *colectivo* (bus) No.60 from BA takes between 1hr 15mins and 1hr 45mins depending on traffic, and costs AR$1.35 one way.

By train

There are two possibilities: BA's Retiro station, direct to Tigre; or, the much better option, taking the train from Retiro to Bartolomé Mitre and then hopping on the Tren de la Costa (*see p180*) to Tigre.

Cataratas de Iguazú

Having got everything else out of the way, God must have spent the eighth day creating the dazzlingly beautiful Cataratas de Iguazú – the Iguazú Falls. One of the true wonders of the natural world, the 23 kilometres (14 miles) of foaming waterfalls dropping into a 70-metre (230-foot) high river canyon are as spectacular as an eco-spectacular can get. And being just an hour and a half's plane ride from Buenos Aires, this jewel of the jungle tops the list of weekend breaks to be had outside the capital.

The falls lie in the glorious setting of the **Parque Nacional Iguazú**, at the northern tip of the province of Misiones on Argentina's frontier with Brazil and Paraguay. Puerto Iguazú, the small town on the Argentinian side where planes and buses from BA arrive, is the best place to stay for a two- or three-day visit. There are bus services every half-hour (US$4 return) to the park gates, 15 minutes away, where you pay US$10 admission per day.

Visits to this jaw-dropper of a national park begin at its reception area and information centre, just beyond the entrance, from where excursions can be organised. The centre is worth a visit for an overview of the area's flora and fauna. From here, head by eco-train or by foot – car access is prohibited – to one of the three main trails offering views of the falls.

Numerous travel agencies in Buenos Aires offer package tours to Iguazú, including flights, lodging and excursions. As a guideline expect to pay US$400-$600 for a three-day/two-night deal, depending on the standard of accommodation.

BOAT TRIPS & EXCURSIONS

To get up close to the falls, visit the office of **Iguazú Jungle Explorer** in the information centre. They run various excursions, including the Gran Aventura (US$26), which takes you through the jungle by open-top truck, before speeding you by motorboat towards the falls. **Explorador Expediciones** (421632), also in the information centre, runs the Safari Fotográfico, a two-hour overland photo safari. Prices start at US$20.

Where to eat & drink

For daytime in the park, there are three restaurants and various snack stands. Back in Puerto Iguazú for the evening, try El Charo (Avenida Córdoba 106, 421529, main courses AR$10-$30), for a grilled surubí river fish. For outdoor eats and live music, Tío Querido (Bonpland 124, 420570, main courses AR$8-$20) is the nicest-looking, though there are several basic beer-and-pizza places with terraces on Avenida Victoria Aguirre near the plaza.

Where to stay

Inside the park, the **Sheraton International Iguazú** (420296/4200748, www.starwood hotels.com/sheraton) has five-star comforts, but is expensive (from US$300, depending on view). In Puerto Iguazú the best three-star hotel is the **Hotel Saint George** (Avenida Córdoba 148, 420631, www.hotelsaintgeorge.com, doubles US$75-$85), a couple of minutes from the bus terminal, with pool and air-con. Another excellent option is **Hotel Orquideas Palace** (Ruta 12, km 5, 420472,www.orquideashotel. com, doubles US$45-$70), situated on the outskirts of town on the road to the National Park. It has a gorgeous patio fringed with tropical fauna, and a pool.

Budget travellers should seek out the Swiss-owned **Hostería Los Helechos** (Calle Paulino Amarante 76, 420829, www.hosterialos helechos.com.ar, doubles US$20-$25).

When to go

The mean temperature in Iguazú is a pleasant 23°C (73°F), although extremes can range from zero in July to 40°C (103°F) in January.

Tourist information

Secretaria de Turismo

Avenida Victoria Aguirre 311, y Brañas, Puerto Iguazú (03757 420800). **Open** 8am-midnight daily.

Getting there

By air

There are several direct daily flights with Aerolineas Argentinas to Puerto Iguazú from Buenos Aires' Jorge Newbery airport. The flight takes 1hr 30mins and costs about US$250 return.

By road

From Posadas, the provincial capital of Misiones, Iguazú can be reached via Rutas Nacionales 12 and 9. Buses leaving Retiro bus station in BA take a whopping 21hrs to get to Puerto Iguazú (various operators; from AR$100 one way).

Country

Hop on a horse and get down with the *gauchos* in the Argentinian pampas.

San Antonio de Areco

San Antonio de Areco is at the epicentre of *gaucho* lore, not simply because walking around the cobbled streets you are as likely to pass a cowboy trotting on horseback as a child pedalling a bicycle, but because this was the home of author Ricardo Güiraldes and his semi-mythical *gaucho* hero, Don Segundo Sombra. Around 113 kilometres (70 miles) from Buenos Aires, with a population of 20,000, this popular weekend tourist destination is a mass of one-storey, century-old buildings surrounded by seemingly limitless grassy plains. Perfect, then, for brushing up on old horse-riding skills in the company of a few of these genuine Latin cowboys.

Begin your tour with a stroll along the town's main drag, Alsina, through to the town's centre and the charming square, **Plaza Ruiz de Arellano**. This central plaza is overlooked by the Iglesia Parroquial, built in 1728 by the town's original settlers in honour of San Antonio de Padua. Directly opposite the church, in the centre of the plaza, is a statue of Vieytes, commemorating a visit from former Irish president Mary Robinson and the Sociedad Argentino Irlandesa of San Antonio de Areco. It's ironic that, in an area central to the gaucho mystique, an Irish community predating Güiraldes's novel by over a century should have been so pivotal to the evolution of the town.

One thing that strikes you as you walk through San Antonio de Areco is the separation of town and country, sharply divided by the Areco River that marks a border between the stone streets and the pampas. The easiest way to cross this divide is via **Puente Viejo**, one of the country's first toll bridges and the unofficial symbol of the town. Passing over the bridge to the north of the town you will arrive at the **Parque Criollo** and the **Museo Gauchesco Ricardo Güiraldes**. Within the park's boundaries you'll find the atmospheric **Pulpería la Blanqueada**, a tavern/general store that Güiraldes wrote about in *Don Segundo Sombra*. The museum, which opened in 1938, is a homage to Güiraldes himself, exhibiting early editions of *Don Segundo Sombra*, photographs of the real-life characters of the book and random curiosities such as an old and regal safety deposit box and a bed that once belonged to General Rosas. To the east of the museum, on A Pazzaglia street, you can get a real feel for the *gaucho* lifestyle with horses for hire by the hour (US$4). Thankfully, the owners (but probably not the horses) are more than happy to chaperone those who've spent more time in bars than barns.

Tradition is everywhere in San Antonio de Areco and many of the structures remain exactly as they were a century ago, albeit a little worse for wear. One must-see building is the **Los Principios** grocery store, located to the west of the town centre at Bartolomé Mitre 151. The dusty, old, dark-wood store is a throwback to 1922, the year it opened, and the present owner, Américo Fernandez, has been selling his wares there for more than 60 years. Sweets and confectionery of all kinds are weighed out on ancient metal scales and the rolling ladder is still the only way to reach the paint thinners and spirits that line the very highest shelves.

The town is small enough to get around on foot, though most of the locals travel by moped or bicycle. If you want to save time or are heading straight to an *estancia*, your best bet is a car service. Remis Zerboni (453288) operates 24 hours a day.

If this quiet town has a high season it's in November, when a buzz of rural activities leads up to the spirited *gaucho* festivities of the annual **Día de la Tradición** (*see p177*). Exhibitions of the traditional *gato* (cat) dance and performances by folkloric bands are coupled with feats of country skills and horsemanship, in a busy programme spread out over two weeks. The celebrations culminate in the Día de la Tradición itself and a procession of *gauchos* in full regalia, riding horses adorned with silver and gold. If you want to be a part of the festivities, book hotel rooms early to avoid disappointment.

Parque Criollo & Museo Gauchesco Ricardo Güiraldes

Camino al Ricardo Güiraldes, y Camino al Parque (02326 455839). **Open** 11am-5pm Mon, Wed-Sun. **Admission** AR$2; free under-12s. **No credit cards.**

Where to eat & drink

The pick of the town's restaurants is **Almacén de Ramos Generales** (Zapiola 143, 456376, main courses AR$10-$18), a popular *parrilla* joint designed in the style of an old general

It's a wonderful wildlife

When is a zoo not a zoo? When it's a magnificent wildlife park like Temaikèn (a native Tehuelche word meaning 'land of life') in Buenos Aires province.

It's hard to believe that any of the 200 species that inhabit the open-plan spaces here are anything other than comfortable. An interesting selection of land mammals, including tigers and pumas roam the vast expanses, while river and marine creatures can be viewed in huge water tanks. There's also an exotic array of reptiles and 1,500 species of birds (including pelicans, penguins and flamingos) in and around the outdoor pools and artificial lakes. Bird lovers get an extra bonus: Temaikèn was created beside the Granja Heladería Munchi's, a bird sanctuary set up on the farm belonging to an ice-cream manufacturer (Route 25 y Miguel Cané, Belén de Escobar, 03488 4436 800). Temaikèn's entrance fee includes admission to both attractions (but not vice versa).

The park is thoughtfully planned and designed. Sturdy wooden, rope and bamboo walkways and platforms connect the exhibits. They blend in naturally with the environment and allow elevated views of the wildlife. In the aquarium the designers have built sections of the tank in the ceiling so that sharks and stingrays can be observed gliding effortlessly above your head. In the cinema, educational films are projected on a 56-metre-wide (184-foot) screen completely surrounding the audience.

Just 30 minutes away (around AR$60 by taxi) from downtown Buenos Aires, Temaikèn is a great day-trip option. As is normal with theme parks, you can't take your own food, but there's plenty inside the park from fast-food shacks and ice-cream parlours to reasonably priced cafés and restaurants. Just don't feed the animals.

Parque Temaikèn

Ruta Provincial 25, km 1, Escobar (03488 436900/www.temaiken.com.ar). **Open** 10am-7pm Tue-Sun. **Admission** *Wed-Sun* AR$15; AR$5 3-10s, concessions. *Tue* AR$8; AR$2 3-10s, concessions. **Credit** AmEx, DC, MC, V.

store, or *almacén*. For something a bit more authentic, head to **Puesto la Lechuza** (Sdo. Sombra y Bolivar, 454542, main courses AR$8-$16), a covered-terrace restaurant serving traditional country fare with regular folkloric shows. If you're just in need of a drink, **Barril** (San Martín 381, no phone) is a typical downtown pub, with outdoor seating. The house speciality of fried cheese with Worcester sauce may sound odd, but it makes for a fine imitation of cheese on toast.

Where to stay

For a town with a burgeoning tourist reputation, the accommodation choices in San Antonio de Areco are actually quite limited. Don't expect five-star pomp and circumstance on your visit here, since even the recommended hotels have small rooms, small pools and a minimal level of amenities. **Hotel Los Abuelos** (Zerboni y Zapiola, 4563900, doubles AR$70) has motel-like rooms, with ceiling fans, cable TV and a pool that's just about big enough for a duck under water. (The fact that its name translates as the Grandparents' Hotel tells you most of what you need to know.) Directly opposite, **Hotel San Carlos** (453106, www.hotel-sancarlos.com.ar, doubles AR$60) has smaller rooms and the option of six-person apartments with air-conditioning.

Tourist information

Dirección de Turismo de la Municipalidad

Boulevard Zervoni, y Arellano (02326 453165/ www.arecogaucho.com.ar). **Open** 8.30am-7pm Mon-Fri; 8am-8pm Sat, Sun.
The English-speaking staff will provide you with brochures and maps pointing out the town's historic sites. They can also organise a three-hour tour of the town in English for AR$60.

Getting there

By road

San Antonio de Areco is 1hr 30mins from BA on Ruta Nacional 8. A taxi from BA will cost around AR$160. If you're travelling by bus, Chevallier (4314 3639) offers the most frequent daily service, about once an hour, AR$12 each way, from Retiro bus terminal. The journey takes about 2hrs. Upon arrival in San Antonio, ask at the station for the departure schedule.

Estancias

In the 19th century, European immigrants flocked to Argentina to take advantage of a vast, fertile, untapped territory, building *estancias* throughout the countryside. Many ranches have been in the same family for generations and still raise cattle and crops. In the past decade, more and more of these homes opened to the public as agro-industry replaced the family farm and owners faced the choice of shuttering large homes that were too expensive to run or opening them as upmarket B&Bs.

Buenos Aires province has the highest concentration of these ranches, ranging in style from Tudor castles to Italian villas. Choose from a one-day Día de Campo package – often including all-you-can-eat *asado* (barbecue), horse riding and a folk music or *gaucho* show – to a weekend or longer stay. Many *estancias* host corporate events or weddings, so enquire first to avoid your tranquillity being breached by smiling salesmen or drunken relatives. It may look expensive at first, but horse riding and all your food (which is usually excellent) are included – though some drinks and activities may be extra – and children generally pay half-price. Many also offer rides in horse-drawn carriages and some have pools. They will cater for vegetarians, but tell them in advance. Bring insect repellent in summer to ward off the area's voracious bugs and mosquitos.

Owing to its popularity as a tourist destination, many of the *estancias* we've listed below are located near San Antonio. Most of the rest are within 125 kilometres (78 miles) of Buenos Aires. Reservations are a must: call the *estancia* direct or book through knowledgeable BA-based travel agent **José de Santís** (Office 313, Avenida Roque Sáenz Peña 616, Microcentro, 4343 2366, www.estanciasargentinas.com) or **Lan & Kramer Travel** (14th Floor, Florida 868, Retiro, 4748 4440, www.estanciastravel.com). If driving, ask for directions when you book.

Las Artes Endurance Country Club

Mercedes (in BA 4811 6024/www.lasartes endurance.com). **Rates** per person US$120 Día de Campo (riders); US$60 (non-riders). **No credit cards.**
A day at Las Artes gives riders the chance to see the pampas from atop a competition-standard Arabian horse. Friendly, multilingual owners Reinhard and Cristina host full-day programmes for small groups (maximum of six) and welcome non-riders. The cost includes all rides, food and drink. They can also arrange transfer from BA.

La Bamba

San Antonio de Areco (in BA 4732 1269/02326 456293/www.la-bamba.com.ar). **Rates** US$180 double; US$40 Día de Campo. **Credit** AmEx, MC V.
La Bamba is one of the San Antonio region's most traditional *estancias* offering an authentic window into the country's *criollo* past. An 1830s main house, painted bloody red, was the backdrop for the

Look out for the Latin cowboys.

legendary Argentinian film *Camila*. Comfortable rooms are furnished in the same colonial style, the most romantic being the main one with an open fireplace. The food is also top notch.

Bella Vista de Guerrero
Castelli (0245 481234/in BA 4778 9599/www.bella vistadeguerrero.com). **Rates** per person US$175; US$70 Día de Campo. **No credit cards**.
More of a mansion than a farmhouse, Bella Vista has manicured lawns, crisp, clean air and – as the name implies – great views of the pampas. If you can't decide between being a cowboy and an aristocrat, you can cover both bases here.

La Candelaria
Lobos (02227 424404/www.lacandelaria.com.ar). **Rates** per person US$50-$60; US$33 Día de Campo. **Credit** MC, V.
When travelling, 19th-century aristocrats Rebeca Piñeiro and Manuel de Fraga fell in love with a castle in France, they tracked down the architect and brought him back – along with plenty of French, German and English furniture – to the pampas. The result, after nine years of construction, is the most regal, if slightly out of place, of Argentinian *estancias*. Landscape architect Carlos Thays' vast gardens are equally magnificent, but the rather worn bedrooms don't quite match up to the truly awesome first impressions created from the stunning exterior.

La Cinacina
San Antonio de Areco (02326 452773/02326 452045/www.lacinacina.com.ar). **Rates** per person US$12 Día de Campo. **No credit cards**.
Located about eight blocks from Plaza Ruiz de Arellano in San Antonio, La Cinacina is more of a *gaucho* theme park than a country estate, but its Día de Campo packages are among the most affordable. Always busy at the weekends. **Photo** *p239*.

Los Dos Hermanos
Zárate (03487 438903/in BA 4765 4320/www. estancialosdoshermanos.com). **Rates** per person US$95; US$50 Día de Campo. **No credit cards**.
Just 55 minutes by car from BA, Dos Hermanos is run by the wonderful Ana and Pancho Peña and is one of the best options for a horse-riding day-trip out of the capital. They have 50 horses, so whether you're a Lester Piggott or a Sancho Panza, they'll match you up with a suitable steed. Great barbecue, too.

Dos Talas
Dolores (02245 443020, www.dostalas.com.ar). **Rates** per person US$125; US $50 Día de Campo. **Credit** MC, V.
In the Luro family since 1858, the current generation of Sara and Luis de Elizalde offer guests a luxurious rural experience worthy of the belle époque. The gardens were designed by Charles Thays, Argentina's most celebrated landscaper. A magical place.

La Encantada
Capilla del Señor (02323 492063/www.posada laencantada.com.ar). **Rates** per person US$40-$60; US$20 Día de Campo. **No credit cards**.
The small but picturesque country house was built in 1856. If the weather conditions are favourable you can take a 50-minute hot-air balloon ride for AR$240 and there's also a swimming pool and horse riding. La Encantada is probably best for a day trip, since it doesn't offer many other attractions and is relatively close to Buenos Aires. During summer months, there is a programme of teatime classical music concerts in the garden.

La Martina
Vicente Casares (02226 430777/www.lamartinapolo. com). **Rates** per person US$350 for polo-playing guests; US$170 for non-polo-playing guests. US$60-$85 Día de Campo. **No credit cards**.
Adolfo Cambiaso – one of the world's leading players – runs a top-flight polo school for foreigners out of this century-old *estancia* 45 minutes from downtown BA. Cambiaso breeds all the ponies and he can often be found playing an exhibition match on one of the ranch's three full-size polo fields. (*See also p206* **Polo play**.)

El Ombú de Areco
San Antonio de Areco (4710 2795/02326 492080/ www.estanciaelombu.com). **Rates** per person US$110; US$45 Día de Campo. **Credit** V.
About six kilometres (four miles) from San Antonio, El Ombú was built in 1880 in the style of an Italian

villa for Indian-slayer General Juan Pablo Ricchieri, but in the ensuing century has taken on a more *criollo* look. It's the ultimate stress reliever with an unpretentious working-ranch feel. Walls are covered in ivy and its sizable acreage of soya bean fields and cattle pasture border the Areco River. There's a games room with a pool table, backgammon and a TV, and a small pool, and the delicious home-made eats include unforgettable empanadas. The owner speaks English and German.

El Rocío
San Miguel del Monte (02271 420888/www.estancia elrocio.com). **Rates** US$175 double; US$100 Dia de Campo. **No credit cards.**
If you want to horse around in style, saddle up at exclusive equestrian ranch, El Rocío. The cost of the Dia de Campo includes a polo class. Have a go, it's not as difficult as it looks. (But then, it looks impossible.) For overnight or weekend stays, there are comfortable, colourful rooms decorated with keepsakes from the owners' extensive travels, and the guest house has its own private kitchen. Demonstrations of horse-training and *pato*, the official national sport, are organised for guests on request. If it all sounds like too much huffing and puffing, there's a pleasant pool provided for the more sedentary traveller.

El Rosario de Areco
San Antonio de Areco (02326 451000/www.rosario deareco.com.ar). **Rates** per person US$110; US$50 Dia de Campo. **No credit cards.**
Former stables house the bedrooms, and the dining room and lounge are in an old barn. The owners raise polo horses and have an official polo field; the Polo Week package is offered during Argentina's Polo Open tournament in November, for US$250 per night. Anyone can participate and they teach you how to play. El Rosario is on the small side and a bit pricey, but there's a ten per cent discount for online bookings. English, French and Italian spoken.

Santa Rita
Antonio Carboni, Lobos (4804 6341/02227 495026/ www.santa-rita.com.ar). **Rates** per person US$60 double; US$30 Dia de Campo. **No credit cards.**
This mini, magical estate's first construction, a chapel for converting the local native population, dates from the colonial era – the main house was built in 1790. All the rooms have their charm, but the front-facing one on the first floor has an incredible panoramic view of the leafy grounds. Horseback rides across the property to a quiet rivulet are a must. There's also the chance to see farm activities being carried out, and a swimming pool can be used during summer months.

Villa María
Máximo Paz (4322 7785/02274 450909/www. estanciavmaria.com.ar). **Rates** per person US$130; US$60 Dia de Campo. **No credit cards.**
Celebrity Argentinian architect Alejandro Bustillo, also responsible for Buenos Aires' Banco Nación, built this monumental Tudor mansion in 1925 for beef baron Celedonio Pereda. Sixteen bright, elegant rooms look over an impressive artificial lake and immaculate grounds designed by Carlos Thays. There's a swimming pool and cosy billiard hall, as well as horse riding and carriage rides. The high prices reflect its popularity with a jet-set clientele.

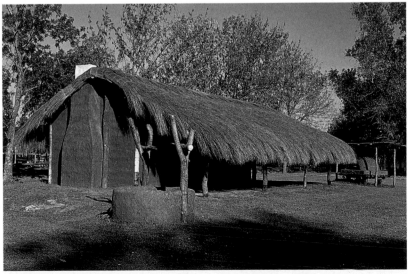

Get back to nature and save some *pesos* at **La Cinacina**. *See p238.*

Trips Out of Town

Beach

Sand, sea and sun.

Mar del Plata

For many Argentinians, beach holidays are synonymous with the coastal resort of Mar del Plata. It's a big seaside city in all its tack and glory, and people come in droves year after year. A huge chunk of Buenos Aires life – cultural events, football matches, even TV productions – decamps to the coast for summer.

The city – 400 kilometres (250 miles) south of Buenos Aires, with a year-round population of 650,000, swelling to over a million in summer – was founded in 1874. It was once a refuge for the *porteño* aristocracy; now it's the Argentinian middle-class tourist destination par excellence.

To the south, 20 kilometres (12 miles) beyond the lighthouse, lie the most exclusive beaches: **La Reserva**, **Del Balcón** and **La Caseta**. Continuing south on Ruta 11 brings you to Miramar, with magnificent views, woodland and 20-metre-high (65-foot) cliffs running down to the ocean. This is the best spot for surfing; for more information, see www.elsurfero.com.

The seafront boardwalk, **La Rambla** – constructed in 1940 by architect Alejandro Bustillo, who also built the casino – and the San Martín pedestrian area are the most popular walkways. The *puerto* (port) is full of pervasive odours from the fishmeal factories and old, rusting yellow boats. In the south docks there's a large colony of sea lions (the symbol of Mar del Plata), and you can take a one-hour boat trip to view the main beaches from the sea. At night the port fills with people visiting the dozen or so local restaurants serving seafood specialities.

For a blast of Mardel's past, walk through the barrios of Stella Maris, Playa Grande, Los Troncos and Divino Rostro. There you'll find the **Centro Cultural Victoria Ocampo** (Matheu 1851, 0223 4920569), open from 3-9pm daily. Also known as Villa Victoria, it's an English-style mansion that was once home to writer and literary patron Victoria Ocampo.

Where to eat

The all-you-can-eat *tenedor libres* concentrated in the San Martín area are extremely cheap and usually have queues outside the door. **Montecatini Alpe** (Belgrano 2350, 0223 4943446, main courses AR$10-$18) has decent, cheap nosh featuring fish and pastas and a recommended *sorrentinos gratinados*. In the port, check out **Chichillo** (Avenida Martínez

Mar del Plata.

de Hoz y 12 de Octubre, 0223 4896317, main courses AR$12-$26), where the *mejillones a la provenzal* (mussels with garlic sauce) are highly recommended. But if you only have time to try one seafood restaurant in Mar del Plata, head straight to **Viento en Popa** (Avenida Martínez de Hoz 257, 0223 4890220, main courses AR$18-$32) which serves simple but exquisite cuisine.

Where to stay

Mar del Plata boasts an enormous variety of accommodation options. Opposite Playa Grande is the five-star **Hotel Costa Galana** (Boulevard Maritimo Patricio Peralta Ramos 5725, 0223 4860000, www.hotelcostagalana. com.ar, doubles US$145-$195). The slightly cheaper **Hotel Amsterdam** (Boulevard Maritimo Patricio Peralta Ramos 4799, 0223 4515137, www.hotelamsterdam.com.ar, doubles U$70-$85) is housed in a 1920s family home and comes with spacious, well-equipped rooms. For something cheaper still, try the lovely and, of course, sea-facing **Hotel Guerrero** (Diagonal Juan B Alberdi 2288, 0223 4958885, www.hotel guerrero.com.ar, doubles US$45-$85); their out-of-season promotions arc fantastic value.

Tourist information

Centro Informacion Turistica

Boulevard Maritima Jose Peralta Ramos 2270 (0223 495 1777/www.mardelplata.com). **Open** 8am-8pm daily.

Getting there

By air

Mar del Plata is served by daily flights from BA (55 mins). The city's **Aeropuerto Brigadier Gral Bme de la Colina** (Ruta 2, km.386, 4785811) is 40 mins from the city centre.

By road

Numerous hourly services make the 5hr trip from BA's Retiro station to Mar del Plata's main terminal (Alberti 1600, 451 5406). Buses also run from Retiro to Pinamar (5hrs) and other resorts along the coast. Those driving to Mar del Plata from BA (4hrs), should take the RN2. Up to 4 people can take a taxi for around AR$300 one way.

Pinamar, Cariló & Ostende

Pinamar – located 340 kilometres (211 miles) south of BA – is surrounded by dunes and fragrant pine forests. It clings to a reputation as the most exclusive beach resort in Argentina, but don't expect peace: the resident population of 22,000 explodes to 600,000 during the summer months of January and February.

A couple of kilometres from Pinamar is the exclusive resort of **Cariló**. It's a separate and far more peaceful world of red brick houses set among woodland. Eight kilometres (five miles) from Pinamar is **Ostende**, a small resort with one of the best beaches in the area. It was founded at the beginning of the 20th century by a group of homesick Belgians.

Where to eat

In Pinamar, **Green Mango** (Quintana 56, 02254 407990, main courses AR$14-$25) is a good bet for classy drinks and delicacies plucked from the sea. Pinamar is renowned for good fish; local classic **El Viejo Lobo** (Avenida del Mar y Bunge, 02254 483218, main courses AR$16-$28) also has a good wine list.

Where to stay

In Cariló, the **Hotel Marcin** (Laurel y el Mar, 02254 570888, www.hotelmarcin.com.ar, doubles US$88-$200) is ideally situated on the beachfront. **Cariló Village** (Carpintero y Divisadero, 02254 470244, www.carilovillage.com, doubles US$100-$163 all inclusive) is a large hotel complex with 59 bungalows. In the centre of Pinamar is one of the coolest accommodation options in the entire region: **Hotel Las Calas** (Bunge 560, 02254 405999, doubles US$45-$116). Each of the 16 fully equipped boutique suites sleeps up to four. In Ostende, the **Viejo Hotel Ostende** (Biarritz y El Cairo, 02254 4860810, www.hotelostende. com.ar, US$35-$100 per person) opens January to March, over Easter week, and for long weekends.

Tourist information

Secretaría de Turismo

Avenida Bunge 654, entre Marco Polo y Libertador, Pinamar (02254 49 1680/www.pinamar.gov.ar). **Open** *Jan, Feb* 8am-10pm daily. *Mar, Dec* 8am-8pm daily. *Apr-Nov* 8am-8pm Mon-Sat; 10am-6pm Sun.

Getting there

To reach Cariló and Ostende, most people take a taxi or a minicab from Pinamar.

By bus

Buses from Pinamar depart daily from BA's Retiro (AR$30-$45 one-way, AR$50-$72 return); companies include **Río de la Plata** (4305 1405) and **Plusmar** (4287 2000). The trip takes 5hrs.

By car

For Pinamar, take Ruta 2 to Dolores, Ruta 63 to Esquina de Croto, Ruta 11 to General Conesa, Ruta 56 to Madariaga, then Ruta 74 to Pinamar. A taxi for up to 4 people costs around AR$240 one-way.

Trips Out of Town

Make your way through the deep pine forests to catch the rays at **Mar de las Pampas**.

Mar de las Pampas & Mar Azul

Emerging out of the thick pine forests bordering the coast, **Mar de las Pampas** is how Pinamar was 25 years ago: quiet and beautiful. Cul-de-sacs and sandy roads limit the speed of passing vehicles and strict building laws keep the pine trees standing

The village is neatly split into three zones: commercial, residential and hotel. On the beach, **El Soleado** is where people come to buy refreshments, relax and shelter from the winds.

Mar Azul is even smaller, even quieter and equally paradisaical. The village is little more than a clutch of sandy roads centred around cabin-style lodgings, a hotel and a supermarket.

Where to eat

In Mar de las Pampas, **Amorinda Tutto Pasta** (Avenida Cerchunoff, 02255 479750, main courses AR$10-$18) is a village classic. **Cabaña Huinca** (Querandies, entre Avenida Lucero y El Ceibo, 02255 479718, main courses AR$25-$30, closed weekdays in winter) serves up delightful culinary treats, though Osvaldo, the owner, is proudest of his home-made beer.

Tiny Mar Azul has fewer dining options but boasts an excellent sushi restaurant – **Apart Heiwa** on Calle 34 (02255 453674, main courses AR$30-$40). For meat, try **El Rodeo** (Calle 35 y Mar Azul, main courses AR$18-$25).

Where to stay

In Mar de las Pampas, metres from the beach, are the *cabañas* of **Rincón del Duende** (Virazón y Cuyo, 02255 479866, www.rincondelduende.com, rental for four people US$1,000 per week). As well as a fine restaurant, the complex boasts a swimming pool and tennis court. The plush, white **Miradores del Bosque** (JA Roca y Hudson, 02255 452147, www.miradoresdel bosque.com) doesn't quite blend in with the sylvan style of the village, but the apartments with individual terraces are luxurious and there is a spa. Rates are US$850-$1200 per week for two-six people, 40 per cent less out of season.

Just off the crossroads in Mar Azul, and 100 metres from the beach, are the *cabañas* of **Puerto de Palos** (Calle 35 y Mar del Plata, 02255 470311, US$37-$100 per day). A mini complex of log cabins set in the woods, with a pool, this is the best value option in the area. For a seafront location, check out **Rincón del Mar** (Calle 30 y La Playa, 02255 456003, www.rincondelmar.com.ar). A two-person studio costs US$800 per week in high season.

Tourist information

In Mar de las Pampas: *Avenida 3, y Rotunda (02255 470324).* **Open** Jan-Mar, Dec 10am-6pm.

Getting there

The closest town to Mar de las Pampas is **Villa Gesell**, 10km (6 miles) away and AR$15-$20 by taxi. Add another AR$7 by taxi to Mar Azul, 5km (3 miles) further on. There's a regular bus service running from Villa Gesell to Mar de las Pampas and Mar Azul (AR$1.80 one-way).

By air

There are flights from BA to Villa Gesell (Jan, Feb only) with **Aerolineas Argentinas** for AR$150-$180 one-way.

Uruguay

For deserted beaches and crowded nightclubs, try Uruguay.

Colonia del Sacramento

The closest place to BA across the River Plate is also the loveliest: Colonia del Sacramento, founded in 1680. This tiny town with a huge history – it was declared a UNESCO World Heritage Site in 1996 – is ideal for an escape from urban chaos. Exploring its cobbled streets, lined with colourful, picture-perfect, colonial houses and surrounded on three sides by water, is like travelling back in time.

You'll arrive at the port, just blocks from the heart of the **Barrio Histórico** (old town). It's easy to cover Colonia on foot, but there are also bicycles, mopeds, cars and even golf carts for rent at the port's entrance. But the real pleasure of Colonia is just walking. Explore the **Calle de los Suspiros** (Street of Sighs) with its huge cobbles and typical colonial houses; the active lighthouse, amid the ruins of the 17th-century Convento de San Francisco; and around the limits of the Barrio Histórico along the river, past the disused railway station and on to the Bastión del Carmen, the old town fortification.

Once you're all walked out, throw yourself down in a plaza or head to the beach on the **Rambla Costanera**, which is clean enough for

bathing. Colonia can become relentlessly hot in summer, so any watery relief offers respite.

Finally, and for something truly strange, head for **Real de San Carlos**. Located five kilometres (three miles) out of town along the coastal road are the 100-year-old remains of an Argentinian playboy's dreams of a leisure complex. You can see the ruins of the Moorish-style bull ring (where just eight fights were held from 1910 to 1912, before the sport was outlawed) and *pelota* court, also used as a theatre. The racetrack, which opened later, in 1942, still functions. The area is currently undergoing something of a renaissance: next door to the track, a luxury Sheraton resort opened in 2005 (*see p244*).

Where to eat

Colonia is full of average places to eat; as in Buenos Aires, it's hard to escape *parrilla* and pizza, but you pay more for second-rate versions of the big city equivalents. A local favourite is *chivito*: in BA, this is baby goat, but in Uruguay, it's a beefsteak sandwich with mounds of ham, cheese, egg and more. To try it, head for any of the *cantinas* on General Flores.

Colonia del Sacramento.

Colonia is famous for its cobbled streets.

In the old town take a table on the terrace of colourful **El Drugstore** (Portugal 174, 00 598 52 25241, main courses US$4-$7) for a variety of tapas, salads and sandwiches. For pizza, **La Bodeguita** (Del Comercio 167, 00 598 52 25329, main courses US$3-$7) has tasty varieties and a lively deck on the water. It opens for dinner and, from April to November, weekend lunches. The restaurant of the discreet **Club de Yachting y Pesca** (Puerto de Yates, 00 598 52 22197, closed Wed, main courses US$7-$17) offers fresh seafood for lunch and dinner.

Where to stay

The finest lodging in the old town is at the **Plaza Mayor** (Calle del Comercio 111, 00 598 52 23193, www.hotelplazamayor.com.uy, doubles US$76-US$130), a historic house with well-appointed rooms, a lovely patio and a small garden near the river. Another classy option is the **Hostal del Sol** (Solis 31, 00 598 52 23349, doubles US$50), which has spacious, antique-adorned rooms. Otherwise, **Posada Casa de los Naranjos** (18 de Julio 219, 00 598 52 24630, US$25-$40) is an attractive colonial house, with garden and pool. Outside the old town, the **Sheraton Colonia** (Continuación de la Rambla s/n, 00 598 52 29000, doubles from US$205)

opened in 2005. For cheap stays, try the youth hostel at General Flores No.440 (00 598 52 30347, US$7 per person dorm).

Getting there

By boat

From its Puerto Madero terminal in Buenos Aires, **Buquebus** (www.buquebus.com) has at least two fast crossings per day to Colonia (1hr US$61 return) on a comfy hydrofoil, and two slow ferries (3hrs, US$35 return), both with room for cars. Buses then connect Colonia to Carmelo (1hr).

Tourist information

Oficina de Turismo General
General Flores y Rivera (00 598 52 23700).
Open 8am-8pm daily.

Carmelo

Just 40 kilometres (25 miles) north-east of Buenos Aires and 77 kilometres (48 miles) along the coast from Colonia, the sleepy backwater town of Carmelo is situated where the River Uruguay broadens to become the River Plate.

Carmelo is in the heart of Uruguay's little explored wine country. Among the handful of wineries receiving tourists – by appointment – is **Los Cerros de San Juan** (00 598 481 7200), the country's oldest, on the R21 between Colonia and Carmelo. Founded in 1854, it still stores its wines in a century-old stone warehouse. After a visit, there's a sampling of local delicacies served with a glass of Tannat, Uruguay's answer to Argentina's Malbec.

In this oasis of tranquillity, and nestled in a pine forest outside town on Ruta 21, is the stunning **Four Seasons Carmelo Resort** (in BA 4321 1711, 00 598 542 9000, www.four seasons.com/carmelo, doubles US$330-$520), Carmelo's budget-busting, big draw. With 20 Zen-inspired bungalows around a gigantic pool, plus deluxe spa and golf course, it's the nearest thing to Bali on the River Plate. For something less flash, stay in town at the **Hotel-Casino Carmelo** on Rodó street (00 598 542 2314/2333, doubles US$50). From there, it's a short walk across the swing bridge – built in 1912 – to the golden beaches that are Carmelo's fame and the main motive for any visit to this sleepy town.

Close by, a few minutes towards Nueva Palmira, is the delightful **Finca Narbona** (Ruta 21, km 267, 00 598 540 4778; www.fincaygranja narbona.com), a restaurant, cheese factory and bakery in a converted 1909 general store. For about US$17, feast on a cheese and meat spread followed by lamb cooked in an adobe oven. Be sure to visit on an empty stomach.

Tourist information

Dirección de Turismo

Casa de Cultura, 19 de Abril, y Rodríguez (00 598 542 2001). **Open** *Jan, Feb* 10am-noon, 5-9pm Mon-Thu; 9am-9pm Fri-Sun. *Mar-Dec* 8am-6pm Mon-Thur; 9am-3pm Fri-Sun.

Montevideo

At first sight, the Uruguayan capital appears the spitting image of Buenos Aires, from which it is separated by only a 40-minute flight or short ferry ride. But the similarities are barely skin deep. Unlike BA, where temptation abounds, mellow Montevideo's main attraction is its absence of frenzied activity, undoubtedly helped by its 23 kilometres (14 miles) of sandy beaches.

The city has not lost its colonial spirit, and its historical fortifications seem to have protected it from the assault of the 21st century.

Although tagged as a cruise liner stopover, Montevideo was, until the 1930s, every bit BA's rival and the architectural richness of its **Ciudad Vieja** (Old City) is even more notable. Economic stagnation has left much of the city's grandeur, like its many vintage cars, in a dilapidated state reminiscent of old Havana. At its apogee, though, Montevideo was the world's largest importer of French tiles. More than 2,000, belonging to architect Alejandro Artucio Urioste, are housed in the impressive **Museo del Azulejo** (Calle Cavia, Pocitos, 00 598 2 709 6352).

Palacio Salvo, built in 1928 on Avenida 18 de Julio and Convención, is the non-official symbol of the capital and was for decades the highest structure in South America. Owing to Montevideo's low skyline, the office building appears even more majestic than its elder twin, the Palacio Barolo in Buenos Aires (*see p67*).

Another belle époque showpiece is the **Teatro Solís** (Buenos Aires 652, 00 598 2 950 3323). It was built in 1841 with red pine from Russia, gold from Genoa and marble from across the world. Puccini, Caruso, Vittorio Gassman, Sarah Bernhardt and Isadora Duncan have all graced its stage.

If you're in Montevideo on a Sunday, don't miss the **Feria Tristán Narvaja** (Tristán Narvaja y 18 de Julio), up there with the world's great outdoor markets such as London's Portobello Road. Every Sunday from 9am to 2pm seven blocks of Tristán Narvaja Street are lined with antique dealers. Market-lovers should also visit the bustling **Mercado del Puerto** (Piedras y Yacaré, 00 598 2 915 4178) in the port. It's open every day from 10.30am to 5pm and 9pm until 1am.

Fitting for a country so out of synch with global corporate capitalism, Uruguayan handicrafts are top notch. With five locations in Montevideo, including its showroom in a colonial house at Reconquista 587 (00 598 2 915 1338), artisan co-op **Manos del Uruguay** (www. manos.com.uy) sells wool sweaters, homespun yarn and a range of other quality handicrafts.

Sitting on the dock of the bay in **Montevideo**.

Trips Out of Town

Where to eat & drink

One of Montevideo's attractions is the many photogenic bars and cafés. In the Ciudad Vieja, look for art nouveau **Café Brasilero** (Ituzaingó 1447, 00 598 2 915 8120) and **Baar Fun Fun** (Ciudadela 1229, 00 598 2 915 8005), whose house shot, the sugary sweet Uvita, was praised in a tango by patron Carlos Gardel. It fills up Wednesday through to Saturday, when there is live music.

If you like a bit of action while you eat, head to the Mercado del Puerto. Among the many *parrillas*, **La Posada Don Tiburón** (00 598 2 915 4278, main courses US$5-$8) on Piedras street is comfy with terrace tables, while **El Palenque** (Pérez de Castellano 1550, 00 598 2 915 4704, main courses US$7-$12) pulls in international celebs and local politicians. For upscale but still relaxed dining, there's a growing bar and restaurant scene surrounding the one-block pedestrianised street of Bacacay in the Ciudad Vieja.

From Thursday to Sunday, the five dance floors of **W Lounge** (00 598 2 712 5287) surrounding Parque Rodó rival those of Buenos Aires for fun and fashion, and are where much of the scene is concentrated. Just below the Montevideo World Trade Center, **Lotus** (Luis A. de Herrera y 26 de Marzo, 00 598 2 628 1379) is a late-night hipster hangout.

Where to stay

The **NH Columbia** (Rambla Gran Bretaña 473, 00 598 2 916 0001, www.nh-hoteles.es, doubles US$65), part of a stylish Spanish hotel chain, is in a strikingly refurbished building with attractive rooms and river views. For luxury, **Belmont House** (Avenida Rivera 6512, 00 598 2 600 0430, www.belmonthouse.com.uy, US$130), in the stylish Carrasco barrio, is an elegant B&B full of antiques. The refurbished **Hotel Lafayette** (Soriano 1172, 00 598 2 902 4646, www.lafayette.com.uy, doubles US$35) is excellent value.

Getting there

By air

Aerolíneas Argentinas, **Aerovip** and Uruguayan airline **Pluna** fly several times a day to from BA to Montevideo (40mins). Flights depart from BA's **Aeropuerto Jorge Newbery** and arrive at Montevideo's **Carrasco** airport (604 0272), 10km/6 miles from the city centre.

By boat

From its Puerto Madero terminal (Av. Cordoba y Madero, www.buquebus.com) in BA, **Buquebus** has at least two boats a day to Montevideo (2hrs 35mins).

Tourist information

Centro de Información Turistica

Explanada Palacio Municipal, Avenida 18 de Julio, y Ejido (00 598 2 1950 1830). **Open** 10am-6pm Mon-Fri; 9am-5pm Sat, Sun.

Punta del Este

If Buenos Aires is the Paris of South America, Punta is its Saint Tropez. Brazen, cool and shamelessly obsessed by aesthetics, the narrow peninsula straddling the Atlantic Ocean and Rio de la Plata is one of the world's top resorts.

Every year Punta stirs up its own brand of sex, sensation and no lack of trivial gossip. 'Who's dating who?' and 'Where's the best party?' are the most debated topics. Of course, none of it really matters to any normal folk, but the headlines and the photos make for sizzling front covers for the tabloids

The fact that it is staggeringly expensive, even by European standards, has never seemed to bother its exclusive holidaymakers. Indeed, in the land of indulgence, it has always been part of the attraction: punters seem genuinely proud to be paying US$100,000 to rent out a luxury home. What is changing, however, is the tourism demographic. As fewer and fewer Argentinians cross the Delta, they're replaced by more and more Europeans, Americans, Brazilians and Mexicans, and passengers from visiting cruise ships. By the end of 2006, over 50 liners (including the 3,000-berth *Queen Mary II*) will have dropped anchor off the coast in that year alone. Most only stay for a day, but spend huge, so it's all good for Punta.

On maps, at least, the once exclusive peninsula remains the central reference point, dividing Punta into two zones: **Playa Mansa**, to the west, lapped by the still waters of the River Plate; and **Playa Brava**, to the north, extending up the Atlantic coast.

As you travel north out of the peninsula the beaches become progressively less populated, and the high rises replaced by mansions and exclusive resorts. After about ten kilometres (six miles), the panorama abruptly changes at Punta's most happening patch: **La Barra**. Among the main strip you'll find clubs, bars, restaurants, galleries, modelling agencies, and even an exclusive Nike shop on Ruta 10, where products are specially designed for Punta's picky clientele. **Bikini Beach**, at the hub of La Barra, resembles the Cannes Film Festival – only without the movies.

If La Barra is for the brash, **José Ignacio**, some 40 kilometres (25 miles) north of Punta, is more discreet. This tiny, former pirates' hideaway is a must-visit for its white sands, dusty roads and internationally acclaimed restaurants. Like Punta, the populace hibernates from March to December, but several restaurants stay open throughout the year making a trip worthwhile out of season.

The region's single greatest attraction is located 14.5 kilometres (nine miles) west of Punta del Este. **Casapueblo** (Ruta Panorámica, Punta Ballena, 42 578611), local painter and philanthropist Carlos Páez Vilaro's labour of love, is a hotel-cum-art museum that tumbles down the rocky cliff face of Punta Ballena. The building's exterior is a surrealist's dream, taking its inspiration from the *hornero* (oven bird) – Uruguay's national bird – and from white, turreted Moorish architecture, while inside is an eight-floor labyrinth of endless curves where each room is more unusual than the last.

But the real point to Casapueblo is the sun. It pops up in his paintings and behind the walls, and when it dips into the blue bay of Portozuelo each night, a silent, ritual tribute is performed.

Where to eat & drink

Around Punta's seaport, try **Kikas** (Rambla, entre Calles 27 y 28, 00 598 42 440951, main courses US$5-$7) for tourist-friendly menus, and **El Mejillón** (Rambla & Calle 11) for *licuados* (smoothies) with an ocean view. Also on the peninsula, **Lo de Charlie** (Calle 12 y 9, 00 598 42 444183, main courses US$7-$10) takes the local Punta fare (fish & seafood) and elevates it to the almost sublime, with Basque and Mediterranean variations – the red tuna carpaccio alone is worth a visit.

Fifteen minutes from the seaport, **La Bourgogne** (Pedragosa Sierra y Avenida del Bar, 00 598 42 487873, main courses US$8-$15) is considered one of Punta's best eateries. Star chef Jean Paul Bondoux picks the herbs from the restaurant's organic garden to spice up traditional dishes like rack of lamb, and rabbit in mustard sauce.

In La Barra, two established places on the main strip are **Baby Gouda** (00 598 42 771874, main courses US$6-$8), with its Moroccan/Asian menu, and the Punta branch of **Novecento** (00 598 42 772363, main courses US$7-$9). Half a block off the main drag, towards the beach, **Le Club** (00 598 42 770246, main courses US$8-$12) is a swish hotel-cum-bar-cum-restaurant with a sea-view deck for cocktails.

In Manantiales, overlooking model-packed Bikini Beach, **Cactus y Pescados** (00 598 42 774782, main courses US$5-$7) is perfect for a late, post-beach lunch. Every summer famed Argentinian chef Francis Mallman – the visionary who put José Ignacio on the map

back in the 1970s – returns from NYC to preside over his sublime **Los Negros** (Faro de José Ignacio, 00 598 48 62091, main courses US$15-$25). **La Huella** (Playa Brava, José Ignacio, 48 62279, main courses, main courses US$12-$20) is a fantastic fish/sushi/*parrilla* restaurant.

Everyone brags about where the best nightlife is, but look out for **Purple**, **Mint Xtra**, **Budabar** and the perennial hotspot, **Tequila** in La Barra. You may well bump into the likes of a holidaying Naomi Campell, DiCaprio or Kate Moss, but as is always the case, mixing with the cream comes at a heady price: expect to pay US$20 for a vodka and tonic and up to US$1,500 for a table for ten people.

Where to stay

Lodging in Punta is expensive, but becomes considerably cheaper, even at top-bracket hotels or classic spots like Casapueblo (doubles US$132), if you buy a package through ferry operator Buquebus. **Hotel Conrad** (Parada 4, Playa Mansa, Rambla Claudio Williman, 00 598 42 491111, www.conrad.com.uy, doubles US$180-$300), best known for its bikini fashion shows and cavernous casino, is easily the peninsula's most expensive option. **La Posta del Cangrejo** (La Barra, 00 598 42 770021,

Cactus y Pescados: perfect for lunch.

For sun, sand and solitude, head for the beaches north of **Punta del Este**. *See p246.*

www.lapostadelcangrejo.com, doubles US$120-$170) has a respected kitchen, fine sea view and country-style rooms where George and Barbara Bush and Julio Iglesias have slept (in separate rooms, we hasten to add).

For a relaxed, and informal stay, **Hotel La Bluette** (Ruta 10, Parada 49, 00 598 42 770947, http://hotellabluette.com, doubles US$90-$160) is a delightfully decorated 13-room guest house. The impromptu *parrillas* in the summer and roaring fires in the winter pull together guests for wine and plenty of spirited chat. La Barra's charming **Villa de Mar** (Calle Las Estrellas, 00 598 42 772147, doubles US$80-$200) is a four-star hotel of Italian colonial design, steps from the beach. If cash is running thin, take refuge in six-room **La Ballenera** (Ruta 10, km 162, 00 598 42 771079, www.laballenera.net, doubles US$70-$160), a *Little House on the Prairie*-style wooden abode close to the beach.

Real high-rollers stay at the 100-room **Mantra Resort & Casino** (Ruta 10, km 162, 00 598 42 771100, www.mantraresort.com, doubles from US$200). The luxurious rooms are spacious and the sparkling pool, spa and health centre area second to none. Even closer to La Barra's beach, facing the rolling waves of Playa Montoya, *Miami Vice*-inspired **Esturion de Montoya** (Playa Montoya, 00 598 42 772116, www.esturiondemontoya.com.uy, doubles US$120-$250) regularly hosts post-catwalk parties. If you are willing to pay double for the privilege, the wide, white balconies overlooking the beach are perfect for ogling.

José Ignacio's most scenic hotel is **La Posada del Faro** (Calle de la Bahia, 00 598 48 62110, www.posadadelfaro.com, doubles US$150-$250), with 12 individually designed rooms. British author and ex-pat Martin Amis lives just a few doors down.

Getting there

By air
Aerolíneas Argentinas and Uruguayan airline **Pluna** fly several times daily from BA to Punta (50 mins). Flights depart from BA's Aeropuerto Jorge Newbery and arrive at Punta's **Laguna del Sauce** airport, 16km (10 miles) outside the city centre.

By boat & road
From its Puerto Madero terminal (Av. Cordoba y Madero, www.buquebus.com) in Buenos Aires, **Buquebus** runs at least two boats a day to Montevideo (2hrs 35mins). Buses run from Montevideo to Punta (2hrs 30 mins). Boat and bus round trip costs US$83-$112.

Tourist information

Centro Información Turística
Parada 1, Calle 31, La Mansa (00 598 42 440514). **Open** *Dec-Feb* 8am-10pm daily. *Mar-Nov* 10am-6pm daily.

Directory

Features

Directory

Getting Around

To & from Ezeiza

By air

Ezeiza (Aeropuerto Ministro Pistarini)

Ezeiza, Buenos Aires, 35km (22 miles) from city centre. Recorded flight information or operator, plus listings of airline telephone numbers 5480 6111 (English & Spanish)/www.aa2000.com.ar.
The official name of Buenos Aires' international airport is Aeropuerto Ministro Pistarini, although it is more commonly known by the name of the area in which it is located, Ezeiza. All international flights arrive and depart from here, except those between Buenos Aires and Uruguay (*see below* **Aeroparque Jorge Newbery**). The airport has two interlinked terminals, A and B, in close proximity. Aerolíneas Argentinas uses Terminal B, while all other airlines operate out of Terminal A.
During rush hour allow one hour 20 minutes for travel between downtown BA and Ezeiza. At all other times, plan for 30-40 minutes.

By shuttle bus

Manuel Tienda León

Avenida Eduardo Madero s/n, Retiro (4314 3636/www.tiendaleon.com).
Operates from the airport – with one stand in the arrivals hall and one outside the terminals – and its downtown office (above). Buses leave every 30 minutes from the city centre, from 4am to 10.30pm. From the airport there is a 24-hour service, with buses every 30 minutes. Fares per person: AR$25 one-way, AR$45 return. There's free pick-up and drop-off at hotels, offices or homes in a defined area of the city centre; otherwise, journeys start and finish at the firm's office on Avenida Eduardo Madero.

By *remise* or taxi

Ignore the 'independent' taxi drivers touting for customers in the arrivals area and head for one of the approved operating companies. **Manuel Tiendo León** (4314 3636, AR$72) and **Transfer Express** (4312 8883,

AR$65) both operate from the airport and offer *remise* (minicab) services. Fares are one-way to the centre and include road tolls. Several other *remise* companies accept advance calls on airport pick-ups and drop-offs. Alternatively, call on arrival and they will send a driver within about 15 minutes. Try **Le Coq** (4964 2000, AR$36) or **Recoleta VIP** (4983 0544, AR$48). These fares exclude road tolls (AR$6 one-way).

By city bus

If you have more time than cash on your hands, you can take a *colectivo* (city bus) for just AR$1.35, but allow at least two hours. Bus 86 (make sure you take one that says Aeropuerto Ezeiza) runs to/from La Boca and Avenida de Mayo.

To & from Aeroparque

Aeroparque Jorge Newbery

Avenida Costanera Rafael Obligado, entre La Pampa y Sarmiento, Costanera Norte. Recorded flight information or operator, plus listings of airline telephone numbers 5480 6111 (English & Spanish)/www.aa2000.com.ar.
Map p283 N12.
Aeroparque Jorge Newbery, more commonly known as simply Aeroparque, is the arrival and departure point for all domestic flights, as well as those to and from the Uruguayan cities of Montevideo and Punta del Este. It's conveniently located on the Costanera Norte, beside Palermo park, just 15 minutes from the city centre. **Manuel Tienda León**, (4314 3636/www.tiendaleon.com) has a shuttle bus service to/from Aeroparque every 30 minutes (AR$9 one way), as well as *remise* services. **Transfer Express** (4312 8883), operating from the airport, also has *remise* services to the city centre. *Remises* cost AR$20-$23. Several city buses also serve the airport; the fare is AR80¢. The most useful is the No.33 (make sure it says Aeroparque on the front), from Plaza de Mayo. There is also a taxi rank at the airport entrance. A taxi to a downtown hotel costs AR$12-$15.

Airlines

International

In addition to these airlines, all the major Latin American airlines have services to Buenos Aires.
Aerolíneas Argentinas
0810 222 86527/4139 3000/
www.aerolineas.com.ar
Air Canada
4327 3640/www.aircanada.ca
Air France
0800 222 2600/4317 4700/
www.airfrance.com/ar
Alitalia
4310 9999/www.alitalia.com.ar
American Airlines
4318 1111/www.aa.com
British Airways
4320 6600/www.britishairways.com
Iberia
4131 1000/01/www.iberia.com
KLM
4326 8422/www.klm.com
Lufthansa
4319 0600/www.lufthansa.com
Swiss
4319 0000/www.swiss.com
United Airlines
4316 0777/www.united.com.ar

Domestic

Several of these airlines also offer international routes to neighbouring countries, particularly to Uruguay. Note that non-Argentinian residents pay significantly higher prices for internal flights in Argentina.
Aerolíneas Argentinas
0810 222 86527/4139 3000/
www.aerolineas.com.ar
American Falcon
0810 222 3252/4393 5700/
www.americanfalcon.com.ar
Lade
0810 810 5233/5129 9000/
www.lade.com.ar

Arriving by other methods

By bus

Estación Terminal de Omnibus

Avenida Ramos Mejía 1680, Retiro. Passenger information 4310 0700.

Buenos Aires' bus station is in Retiro, next to the train station. It is on the Subte C line and is served by many *colectivos* (city buses) including the 6, 93, 106, 130 and 152. There are left-luggage lockers in the station (AR$3) but they are not completely secure. Be wary of pickpockets in and around the terminal.

More than 80 long-distance buses operate out of Retiro. Don't panic: they are grouped together by region (i.e. North-west or Patagonia), so it's easy to compare prices and times. There are services to every major destination in Argentina, and also to neighbouring countries.

For most destinations there are two levels of service, known respectively as *común* and *diferencial* or *ejecutiva*. The latter has hosts or hostesses, includes food, and has different types of seat – comfiest is the *coche cama*: larger, almost fully reclining 'bed seats'. Tickets to all destinations must be purchased at the bus station. In high season (December to February, Easter week and July) it is worth buying your ticket in advance.

By sea

Unless you are arriving from Uruguay, across the River Plate, or stopping off on a cruise, it is unlikely that you will arrive in Buenos Aires by boat. Boats from Uruguay arrive at the passenger port in **Dársena Norte**, a few blocks from the city centre at Avenida Córdoba y Avenida Alicia Moreau de Justo. Regular boat services run between BA and Colonia (*see p243*) and Montevideo (*see p245*) in Uruguay. Cruise ships dock at the new **Terminal Benito Quinquela Martín** (4317 0671) at Avenida de los Inmigrantes and Castillo.

Public transport

Getting around Buenos Aires is relatively easy and cheap. *Colectivos* (city buses) run frequently, cover the whole capital and offer a 24-hour service, while the Subte – the small but reliable underground network – is a fast alternative.

Buses

City buses are known as *colectivos*. There are 140 bus lines, many of which run along a variety of routes (*ramales*) through every city *barrio*. The service is very frequent and companies are obliged to provide an all-night service, with at least one

bus every half-hour, although not every line complies.

Bus fares are AR80¢ for journeys within the capital, paid directly into the machine behind the driver – coins only, no notes.

Be warned that the average bus driver imagines himself (it usually is a he) as the reincarnation of Ayrton Senna: very few will come to a complete halt to let passengers on and off, except by mistake. You need to be agile, hold on tight while on board, and be ready to shout at the driver if he tries to leave while you're hanging out the door.

For complaints or information, call freephone 0800 333 0300.

Subte

Buenos Aires' underground train network, operating since 1912, is called the Subte. It's the quickest, cheapest and easiest way to get around the city during the day, though it can be very crowded during morning and evening peak hours. The service runs from 5am to 10.30pm (8am to 10pm on Sundays). Large parts of the city are not served by the network, including some important tourist areas such as Recoleta and Palermo Viejo. A single journey to anywhere on the network costs just AR70¢. Magnetic card tickets, for anything between one and 30 Subte journeys, can be bought at the *boleterías* (ticket offices), located inside the stations.

For complaints or suggestions, call Metrovías on 0800 555 1616. The website www.metrovias.com.ar also has updates about the service.

Trains

Trains connecting the northern suburbs with the city centre are modern and air-conditioned, while those serving the south are more run-down. Trains linking the capital with destinations in Buenos Aires province are not in great nick either, but they do have three classes: *turista* (wooden seats); *primera* (soft seats); and *pullman* (even better seats and air-conditioning).

There are several different private companies running the trains, which can make it difficult to get the times, prices and information you need. These are the main stations:

Constitución

General Hornos 11, Constitución.
Map p280 D8.
Trains from Constitución go south.
Metropolitano (passenger information freephone 0800 122 358736/4018 0719) runs services on the Roca line to Buenos Aires

province, to La Plata, Glew, Ezeiza (20 minutes from the airport by a connecting bus) and Temperley. **Ferrobaires** (passenger information (4306 7919) runs a long-distance service to the BA province coastal destinations of Mar del Plata, Tandil and Bahía Blanca.

Retiro

Ramos Mejía 1508, Retiro.
Map p281 H12.
Trains run north and west from Retiro, actually three stations in one, known by their old names: Mitre, Belgrano and San Martín.

From Mitre, **Trenes de Buenos Aires** (TBA – passenger information 4317 4407/4445) runs services to Tigre, with connections to Capilla del Señor, José León Suárez and Bartolomé Mitre (in Olivos). There is a weekly service to Rosario in Santa Fe province. From Belgrano, **Ferrovías** (passenger information 4511 8833) runs trains to Villa Rosa. From San Martín, **Transportes Metropolitanos** (passenger information 4011 5826) has a service to Pilar.

Taxis & *remises*

Taxis in Buenos Aires are reasonably priced and plentiful (except in rainy rush hours). Travelling by taxi, however, has some risks and visitors need to be wary of being taken for a long ride, or worst of all, being robbed by an unlicensed driver. For this reason, it is recommended that you use only a radio taxi or a *remise* (licensed minicab). Both will come to any destination in the city to collect a passenger. You will need at least a few words of Spanish to call a radio taxi or *remise* company, though staff in hotels and restaurants will usually be happy to help. If you're in a rush and need to hail a cab in the street, you should still try to stop a radio cab (the name of the company and telephone company will be marked on the vehicle).

Taxis run on meters: the initial fare is AR$1.98, plus AR20¢ for every 200 metres or one minute of waiting time. You are not expected to tip taxi drivers and they should give you change to the nearest AR10¢. Change is the perennial problem with taxis. Anything larger than a AR$10 bill is guaranteed to produce a sigh, a AR$20 note may provoke a verbal complaint and you are unlikely to find a driver if you only have a AR$50. And most taxi drivers would rather gargle battery acid than change a AR$100 note. Many radio taxis have a minimum charge of AR$3.50, and a few charge an extra fee for making a pick-up (*adicionales*). Check first.

Directory

Taxis are black and yellow (radio cabs included), with a red *libre* (free) light in the front window. *Remises* look like other private cars and do not run on meters. You should agree a price before setting off. Also, bear in mind that *remises* are often less punctual than radio taxis. It's a good idea to make a second call, ten minutes before pick-up time, to check the *remise* is on its way.

Radio taxis

Pidalo 4956 1200. AR$1.40 call-out. **Radio Taxi Premium** 4374 6666.

Remises

Remises Blue 4777 8888. **Remises Recoleta Vip** 4804 6655.

Driving

Driving in Buenos Aires is the surest way to raise your blood pressure. Chaos rules as buses, taxis and private cars fight it out on the roads. People drive at very high speeds, change lanes with dizzying frequency, and generally bring out the Mr Hyde aspect of their personality while behind the wheel. Setting off slowly at a green light is considered an unpardonable sin by many drivers, who will proceed to honk their horns and run through their full repertoire of hand gesticulations.

Despite the apparent anarchy, there are a few basic rules:

● You have to be 17 to drive (16 with a parent or guardian's permission).

● Front seatbelts are compulsory.

● Under-10s must sit in the back.

● Priority is given to cars crossing other streets from the right. Cars fly out of nowhere on cross streets, so be warned.

● Overtake on the left – that's the principle, anyway. No one respects this rule, and even the law bends a little to say that if the left-hand lane is moving slower than the right-hand one, you can overtake on the right instead.

● On streets (*calles*), the maximum speed is 40kmh; avenues (*avenidas*), maximum 60kmh; semi-motorways (*semiautopistas*), maximum 80kmh; and on motorways (*autopistas*), maximum 100kmh. On main national roads (*rutas nacionales*), signs on different stretches of road indicate minimum and maximum speeds, but the max is never over 130kmh.

Breakdown services

Only members of automobile associations or touring clubs with reciprocal agreements with other regions (FiA in Europe and FITAC in the Americas) can use the breakdown services of the **Automóvil Club Argentino** (ACA, www.aca.org.ar). This includes members of the British AA and RAC. You can use this facility in Argentina for up to 30 days. You will have to present the membership credentials of your local club, showing the FITAC or FiA logo, to the mechanic.

Various companies offer emergency assistance to drivers. The basic call-out price is AR$40-$50. Try **ABA** (4572 6802), **Estrella** (4922 9095) or **Mecánica Móvil** (4925 6000).

Automóvil Club Argentino (ACA)

Information 4808 6200/breakdown service 4803 3333/www.aca.org.ar. FITAC members also get special deals on hotels and car rental.

Parking

Parking restrictions are indicated on street signs, but in general there is no parking in the Microcentro area downtown during working hours (and on some streets, there's no parking at any time). Parking is prohibited in the left lane on streets and avenues throughout the city, unless otherwise indicated.

The easiest option is a private garage (*estacionamiento privado* or *garaje*), signalled by a large blue sign with a white letter 'E' in the middle, costing around AR$3.50 per hour. Some *barrios* still have free on-street parking, though you'll probably be approached by an unofficial *guardacoche* (car-keeper, possibly a child), offering to look after your car while you're gone. You will be expected to pay a couple of pesos on your return. If you're not happy with this arrangement, find somewhere else to park.

Always take all valuables out of your car (stereo included, if possible), close windows and lock all doors.

Vehicle hire

You need to be over 21, with a driver's licence, passport and credit card to hire a car in Buenos Aires. Prices vary greatly – a rough guide is AR$130-$170 per day, depending on required mileage. Major car rental companies will allow you to take the car out of the country if you sign a contract in front of a public notary, which will set you back around

AR$160. You can often return the car to a different office within Argentina. You must have at least third party insurance (*seguro de responsabilidad civil*), but it makes sense to take out fully comprehensive insurance.

Dollar Rent a Car

Marcelo T de Alvear 449, entre Reconquista y San Martín, Retiro (4315 8800/www.dollar.com.ar). Subte C, San Martín/93, 130, 132, 152 bus. **Open** 9am-7pm Mon-Fri; 9am-1pm Sat. **Credit** AmEx, DC, MC, V. **Map** p281 G12.

Hertz Annie Millet

Paraguay 1138, entre Cerrito y Libertad, Tribunales (4816 8001/www.milletrentacar.com.ar). Subte D, Tribunales/10, 17, 59, 132, 152 bus. **Open** 8am-8pm daily. **Credit** AmEx, DC, MC, V. **Map** p281 H10.

Cycling

This ain't Holland. Cycling in Buenos Aires can be a hazardous undertaking, thanks to potholes, sociopathic drivers, pollution and a lack of respect for cycle lanes. However, there are pleasant cycling areas in Palermo, the Reserva Ecológica and the riverside neighbourhoods.

There are bicycle hire stands (open at weekends during daylight hours, and on some weekdays) around the entrance to major parks, including Parque Tres de Febrero and the Reserva Ecológica, the most cycle-friendly areas. For more on circuits and bike hire, *see p212*.

Walking

Walking in Buenos Aires is a pleasure, despite frustrations such as broken pavements and potholes; ongoing street repairs add to the challenge.

Don't give up. Green spaces in Palermo and Recoleta make these ideal *barrios* for a stroll. San Telmo is also a delightful area to explore on foot. For tours in the Microcentro, Palermo parks and Recoleta areas, *see p70, p88* and *p92* **Walk on.**

Resources A-Z

Age restrictions

The law says that to buy alcohol or have sex you must be at least 18; to buy cigarettes you need to be at least 16; and you have to be at least 17 (16 with parental consent) to drive. In general, the law (or at least in the first three of those four cases) is broken.

Attitude & etiquette

Meeting people

Argentinians are gregarious, friendly and usually interested in meeting foreigners. Tactile and physically demonstrative, most exchange kisses (usually a single cheek-to-cheek kiss) on first meeting – men as well as women. If you're meeting someone in a formal context (for example a business meeting), or a senior person, it's safer to shake hands.

Personal contacts and introductions are highly valued. In business, if someone is proving difficult to contact, a quick name-drop can help; or, better still, use a third party for an introduction. When selling, it does no harm, and often a lot of good, to lean on the foreign side of your business background.

It's best to start most conversations with a *buen día* (before noon) or *buenas tardes* (afternoon) and a brief exchange of pleasantries, if your Spanish is up to it. You will find that most business people speak – and are happy to use – at least some English, although this is not true in other environments. Any kind of attempt to speak in Spanish will always be appreciated, regardless of the context.

Don't sweat if you are delayed on your way to an appointment; punctuality is a phenomenon that barely exists. Out of politeness, as the foreigner, it is better if you are on time, but expect to be kept waiting, always.

Dress & manners

Argentinians are usually well presented. The dress code is best classified as smart casual and applies from the boardroom to the bedroom.

Argentina's contradictory quality is never more apparent than in the behaviour of its citizens. On the one hand, they are champions of door opening, friendly salutations and good manners; on the other, they are among the world's greatest perpetrators of shoulder barging and shameless queue jumping.

Business

If you're considering doing business in Argentina, you should first contact the commercial department of your embassy. It's also worth contacting the **Cámara Argentina de Comercio** (Argentinian Chamber of Commerce, Avenida Leandro N Alem 36, 5300 9000).

Conventions & conferences

Many of Buenos Aires' major hotels offer comprehensive convention and conference facilities. The **Sheraton** in Retiro (*see p45*) is a well-located and long-established convention venue that can (in theory) accommodate up to 9,000 people in its 15 conference rooms. A stone's throw from the Obelisco, the **Panamericano** (*see p39*) has 16 event rooms for between six and 1,000 participants, while the **Hilton** in Puerto Madero (*see p57*) has extensive convention facilities for up to 2,000 delegates.

For smaller meetings, lunches or dinners, many restaurants – particularly those in Puerto Madero – offer a private room for business functions. Most do not charge for room hire if you are hosting a meal on their premises.

Couriers & shippers

DHL

Avenida Córdoba 783, entre Esmeralda y Maipú, Microcentro (4314 2996/freephone 0800 222 2345/www.dhl.com.ar). Subte B, Florida/6, 26, 93, 130, 152 bus. **Open** 9am-7pm Mon-Fri; 9am-noon Sat. **Credit** AmEx, DC, MC, V. **Map** p281 G11.
Call two hours ahead to arrange pick-up from your premises at no extra charge, between 9am and 6pm.

FedEx

Maipú 753, entre Córdoba y Viamonte, Microcentro (4393 6139/customer service 4630 0300/www.fedex. com/ar). Subte B, Florida/6, 26, 93, 130, 152 bus. **Open** 9am-7pm Mon-Fri; 9am-1pm Sat. **Credit** AmEx, MC, V. **Map** p281 G11.
International door-to-door express delivery. Home, office or hotel pick-ups costs US$3 extra.

UPS

Bernardo de Irigoyen 974, entre Estados Unidos y Carlos Calvo, San Telmo (freephone 0800 222 2877/ www.ups.com/ar). Subte E, San José/39, 96, 126 bus. **Open** 9am-7pm Mon-Fri. **Credit** AmEx, DC, MC, V. **Map** p281 E9.
International delivery for packages from 0.5-50kg. Free home pick-up.

Office hire & business centres

If you need use of a telephone, fax or internet, your best bet is one of the many *locutorios* (call centres) situated all across town (*see p261* **Telephones**). Charges are from AR$1.50 a page for sending and receiving faxes and around AR$2 for 30 minutes' internet use.

If you need something more permanent (or to give that impression), there are several choices for temporary office hire. Options range from the excellent, upmarket and very expensive international companies such as **Regus** (4590 2227/www.regus.com), to these local choices:

Cerrito Rent-an-Office

2nd Floor, Cerrito 1070, entre Santa Fe y Marcelo T de Alvear, Recoleta (4811 4000/www.rent-an-office. com.ar). Bus 10, 59, 101, 152. **Open** 8am-8pm Mon-Fri. **Credit** AmEx, V. **Map** p281 H11. Temporary office hire by the day, week or month. Monthly rates from AR$800-$2,000. Translators, lawyers, accountants and architects available at extra charge.

SG Oficinas

6th Floor, Maipú 267, entre Sarmiento y Perón, Microcentro (4328 3939/www.sgoficina.com.ar). Subte B, Florida/6, 10, 17, 24, 29 bus. **Open** 9am-7pm Mon-Fri. **No credit cards. Map** p281 F10. Serviced offices from AR$800 per month or from AR$85 per day.

Translators & interpreters

Aleph Translations

6th Floor, Office C, Godoy Cruz 2915, y Juncal, Palermo (4779 0305/www.alephtranslations.com). Bus 15, 39, 152. **Open** 9am-5pm Mon-Fri. **No credit cards. Map** p283 N9. General, technical and legal translations, with an online express service.

Estudio Laura Rosenwaig

3rd Floor, Apartment C, Billinghurst 2467, entre Las Heras y Pacheco de Melo, Recoleta (4801 4536). Subte D, Bulnes/10, 37, 59, 60, 102 bus. **Open** 9am-7pm Mon-Fri. **No credit cards. Map** p282 K10. Simultaneous translation for conferences and written translation work via fax or email.

Interhotel

1st Floor, Office M, Esmeralda 1056, entre Santa Fe y Arenales, Retiro (4311 1615/www.inter-hotel.com.ar). Subte C, San Martín/45, 106, 152 bus. **Open** 9am-6pm Mon-Fri. **No credit cards. Map** p281 H11. Scientific and public translations.

Useful organisations

Ministerio de Relaciones Exteriores, Comercio, Internacional y Culto

Arenales 1212, entre Esmeralda y Suipacha, Retiro (4829 7504/www. mrecic.gov.ar). Subte C, San Martín/ 10, 17, 152 bus. **Open** 9am-6pm Mon-Fri. **Map** p281 H11. The public face of the government arm responsible for international business relations.

Dirección Nacional de Migraciones

Avenida Antártida Argentina 1355, Dársena Norte, Retiro (4317 0200/ www.mininterior.gov.ar). Subte C, Retiro/7, 9, 92, 100 bus. **Open** 7am-9pm Mon-Fri. **Map** p281 G12. For entry visas, student permits and work permits. Three month business visas are also issued here.

Consumer

Dirección General de Defensa y Protección al Consumidor

Esmeralda 340, entre Corrientes y Sarmiento, Microcentro (5382 6200/ www.buenosaires.gov.ar). Subte B, Florida/6, 26, 93, 130, 152 bus. **Open** 9am-5pm Mon-Fri; 9am-1pm Sat. **Map** p281 F10. Receives and investigates consumer complaints and gives advice on what rights and actions are available to consumers (including tourists).

Customs

Entering Argentina from overseas you can bring in the following, without paying import duties: 2 litres of alcoholic drinks, 400 cigarettes, 5kg of foodstuffs, 100ml of perfume. If entering from a neighbouring country, these quantities are halved.

Disabled

Getting around

BA is not known for its efforts to make it easier for those with mobility problems to get around. Pavements are in bad condition and there are often no drop-kerbs – or if there are,

people will have parked in front of them. Using the Subte is practically impossible, as few stations have lift access. An increasing number of *colectivos* (city buses) are *super-bajo* (ultra-low), and just about accessible for accom-panied wheelchair users. Radio taxis and *remises* do what they can to help but are not specially equipped, and many do not have enough space to stash a wheelchair.

There are several companies that specialise in transport and trips for disabled passengers.

Movidisc

4328 6921/www.movidisc-web.com.ar. Specially adapted vans for wheelchair users. City tours also available with advance booking.

QRV – Transportes Especiales

4306 6635/mobile 15 5248 4423. Adapted minibuses for wheelchair users, equipped with microphones and guides. Call to check prices for city tours.

Useful contacts

Red de Discapacidad (REDI)

4706 2769/redi@rumbos.org.ar. Eduardo Joly, a sociologist who has also studied tourism, is a wheelchair user and director of this disabled persons' network, which can provide advice and information.

Electricity

Electricity in Argentina runs on 22 volts. Sockets take either two- or three-pronged European-style plugs. To use US electrical appliances, you'll need a transformer (*transformador*) and an adaptor (*adaptador*); for UK appliances an adaptor only is required. Both can be purchased in hardware stores (*ferreterías*) all over town. Power cuts are occasional, though become more frequent when it rains heavily. Supplies are usually restored within three hours, but can be out for a day or longer.

Embassies & consulates

American Embassy & Consulate

Avenida Colombia 4300, entre Sarmiento y Cerviño, Palermo (5777 4533/http://buenosaires.usembassy.gov). Subte D, Plaza Italia/37, 67, 130 bus. **Open** *Visas* 7.30am-12.30pm Mon-Fri by appointment only. *Information* 8am-noon Mon-Fri. **Map** p283 M10.

Australian Embassy & Consulate

Villanueva 1400, entre Zabala y Teodoro García, Palermo (4779 3500/www.argentina.embassy.gov.au). Bus 59, 63, 67, 152, 194. **Open** 8.30am-12.30pm, 1.30-5.30pm Mon-Thur; 8.30am-1.30pm Fri. **Map** p285 Q8.

British Embassy & Consulate

Luis Agote 2412, entre Libertador y Las Heras, Recoleta (4808 2200/www.britain.org.ar). Bus 37, 60, 102. **Open** *Jan, Feb* 8.45am-2.30pm Mon-Thur; 8.45am-2pm Fri. *Mar-Dec* 8.45am-5.30pm Mon-Thur; 8.45am-2pm Fri. **Map** p282 J11.

Canadian Embassy & Consulate

Tagle 2828, entre Figueroa Alcorta y Juez Tedín, Recoleta (4808 1000). Bus 67, 130. **Open** 8.30am-12.30pm, 1.30-5.30pm Mon-Thur; 8.30am-2pm Fri. **Map** p282 K11.

Irish Embassy

6th Floor, Avenida del Libertador 1068, entre Ayachucho y Callao, Recoleta (5787 0801/www.irlanda.org.ar). Bus 61, 62, 93. **Open** 9.30am-1pm Mon-Fri. **Map** p282 I12.

New Zealand Embassy & Consulate

5th Floor, Carlos Pellegrini 1427, entre Arroyo y Posadas, Retiro (4328 0747/www.nzembassy.com). Subte C, Retiro/10, 59, 130 bus. **Open** 9am-1pm, 2-6pm Mon-Thur; 9am-1pm Fri. **Map** p281 H11.

South African Embassy & Consulate

8th Floor, Marcelo T de Alvear 590, entre San Martín y Florida, Retiro (4317 2900/www.embajadasudafrica.org.ar). Subte C, San Martín/7, 9, 17, 92 bus. **Open** 8.15am-12.30pm, 1.15-5.15pm Mon-Thur; 8.15am-2.15pm Fri. **Map** p281 G12.

Travel advice

For up-to-date information on travel to a specific country – including the latest news on safety and security, health issues, local laws and customs – contact your home country government's department of foreign affairs. Most of them have websites packed with useful advice for would-be travellers.

Australia
www.smartraveller.gov.au

Canada
www.voyage.gc.ca

New Zealand
www.mfat.govt.nz/travel

Republic of Ireland
http://foreignaffairs.gov.ie

UK
www.fco.gov.uk/travel

USA
http://travel.state.gov

Emergencies

All available 24 hours daily.

Fire

100.
For the fire brigade you can also call 4383 2222, 4304 2222 and 4381 2222.

Police

101.
Also 4370 5911 in an emergency.

Defensa Civil

103 or 4956 2110.
For gas leaks, power cuts, floods and other major catastrophes.

Medical emergencies

107.
To call an ambulance.

Emergencias Médicas Náuticas

106.

Gay & lesbian

For more information on advisory and cultural centres, as well as gay accommodation options, *see pp194-9* **Gay & Lesbian**. For HIV/AIDS advice and info, *see below* **Health**. The **Centro Cultural Ricardo Rojas** has a library and archive devoted to gay issues; *see p188.*

Grupo Nexo

4374 4484/www.nexo.org.
Another useful multifaceted cultural centre, offering counselling, information and help. They offer HIV tests free of charge.

Health

No vaccinations are required for BA and the city's tap water is drinkable. Argentina doesn't have reciprocal healthcare agreements with any other countries, however, so you should take out your own medical insurance policy.

Accident & emergency

In case of poisoning, call the **Centro de Intoxicaciones del Hospital Ricardo Gutierrez** on 4962 6666.

Ambulance services are provided by **SAME** (Sistema de Atención Médica de Emergencia) – call 4923 1051 or 107. The specialist burns hospital, the **Hospital de Quemadas**, is at Avenida Pedro Goyena No.369, Caballito (4923 3022 or emergencies 4923 4082).

For public and private hospitals, *see p256.*

Contraception & abortion

Public hospitals will supply the contraceptive pill after an appointment with a doctor. Alternatively, condom machines are found in the

Directory

toilets of most bars, clubs and restaurants and are available over the counter in pharmacies. Abortion is illegal in Argentina.

Dentists

For emergency dental treatment, call the Servicio de Urgencias at 4964 1259.

Hospital Municipal de Odontología Infantil

Pedro de Mendoza 1795, entre Palos y M Rodríguez, La Boca (4301 4834). Bus 29, 53, 64, 152. **Map** p280 A9.
24-hour dental attention for children.

Dr José Zysmilich

1st Floor, Apt C, Salguero 1108, entre Córdoba y Cabrera, Palermo Viejo (4865 2322). Bus 26, 36, 92, 128. **Open** 3-7pm Mon, Wed, Fri. **Map** p278 K5.
English-speaking private dentist: a member of the American Dental Association.

Servicio de Urgencias

Marcelo T de Alvear 2146, entre Junín y Uriburu, Barrio Norte (4964 1259). Subte D, Facultad de Medicina/12, 39, 60, 111, 152 bus. **Map** p282 I9.
Only Argentinians get free treatment at this university dental faculty; foreigners are welcome but are usually asked to pay a small fee of between AR$8 and AR$15.

Hospitals & doctors

For emergency or general non-emergency medical needs, you can see a doctor at one of these hospitals.

Hospital Británico

Pedriel 74, entre Finnochietto y Caseros, Barracas (4309 6400/6500). Bus 59, 67, 100. **Map** p280 D7.
Your best bet is an English speaker is this private, well-equipped and modern hospital. An appointment can be made to see an English-speaking doctor at a cost of AR$45 per appointment. The hospital has several locations; the most central is in Barrio Norte at Marcelo T de Alvear 1573, (4812 0048/49).

Hospital de Clínicas José de San Martín

Avenida Córdoba 2351, entre Uriburu y Azcuénaga, Barrio Norte (5950 8000). Bus 29, 61, 101, 111. **Map** p282 I9.

Buenos Aires' largest, most centrally located public hospital. It has departments for all specialities and the city's main accident and emergency unit. If you don't have insurance, come here.

Hospital de Niños Dr Ricardo Gutiérrez

Sánchez de Bustamante 1330, y Paraguay, Barrio Norte (4962 9232/9229). Bus 29, 92, 111, 128. **Map** p282 K9.
Public paediatric hospital.

Pharmacies

There are always some pharmacies open all night. Go to the nearest; if it's not open, it will post details of the nearest *farmacia de turno*. Mega-pharmacy Farmacity has 24-hour branches across the city – for details, *see p170*.

STDs, HIV & AIDS

Gay information service **Nexo** (*see p255*) runs a phone line for people who are HIV-positive: Linea Positiva 4374 4484.

Pregunte Sida

0800 3333 444. **Open** 9am-10pm Mon-Fri; 9am-4pm Sat-Sun.
Free HIV/AIDS helpline. Also advice on general sexual health issues and where to go for testing or treatment.

Helplines

Although few helplines have English-speaking staff, most will find someone with at least a few words – be ready with your phone number in Spanish in case they need to call back.

Alcohólicos Anónimos

4788 6646.

Centro de Atención a Víctimas de Violencia Sexual

4981 6882/4958 4291.
Support for victims of sex crimes.

Centro de Orientación a la Víctima

4801 4444/8146.
Victim support.

Jugadores Anónimos

4328 0019/15 4412 6745.
Gamblers Anonymous.

Servicio de Orientación en Droga Dependencia

4823 4827.
Support for the drug dependent.

Teleamigo

4304 0061.
Phone support for people in crisis.

ID

By law everyone must carry photo ID. Checks are rare, but if you do get pulled over, you will be expected to show at least a copy of your passport or (photo) driving licence.

Insurance

Argentina is not covered by any reciprocal health insurance schemes, so visitors from all countries are recommended to buy comprehensive private insurance before they travel.

Internet

Downtown and in the more affluent neighbourhoods you'll rarely be more than a block away from a cybercafé or equivalent. Most cybercafés operate around 30 machines with high-speed connections for about AR$2.50 an hour. *Locutorios* (call centres) also provide internet services, though prices are higher than in cybercafés. Most hotels and hostels are hooked up; some throw in the service for free. Local ISPs include FiberTel (www.fibertel.com.ar) and Speedy (www.speedy.com.ar).

Wireless access is just taking off in BA, but most of the high-end hotels have hotspots. Several cafés and bars are also wired for wireless, including Bar 6 in Palermo Viejo (*see p123*) and BN Café in Recoleta (*see p145*).

Legal help

For legal help, contact your consulate or embassy (*see p255*) in the first instance.

Libraries

Buenos Aires has no major English-language lending library, but the **Biblioteca Nacional** (National Library, *see p93*) has a reasonable reference section and the Hemeroteca in the basement is a good resource for newspapers and magazines.

Lost property

Keep a close eye on your belongings at all times. In general, if you've lost it, forget about it. Your chance of recovering any stolen or lost property will depend entirely on the good nature of the person who happens to find your belongings. If you've lost something on public transport, you can call the transport operator, which should hang on to lost property – but don't hold your breath.

This is another good reason to take radio taxis, as you can call the operating company if you leave something in a cab. Always make a mental note of your cab number for just such an eventuality.

Media

Magazines

El Amante del Cine
Reviews of international films and interviews with local filmmakers.

Gente
The bestselling weekly guide to the BA *beau monde*, with a straight-faced, almost reverential take on celebrity and media culture.

Los Inrockuptibles
Funky monthly mag with the word on BA's music scene and gig listings.

Noticias
Popular news weekly, juxtaposing provocative investigative specials and society nonsense.

Time Out Buenos Aires for Visitors
You've bought the book so, ahem, why not pick up the magazine as

well? Published twice yearly and available in all good bookshops and downtown *kioscos*.

Veintitres
Local loudmouth celeb journo Jorge Lanata's anti-establishment organ.

Newspapers

Buenos Aires Herald
English-language daily, read by ex-pats and Argentinians. Sunday edition includes articles from the *New York Times*. The classifieds are a good resource for finding private Spanish teachers.

Clarín
Mass-market daily that's fat with both local and international news. Somehow manages to be high-, middle- and low brow at the same time and so sells loads.

La Nación
BA's grand old daily, beloved of the safe middle classes and conservative on culture, art and lifestyle. Better than *Clarín* for international news. Buy it on Friday for the *Ticket* entertainment listings supplement.

Página 12
Here the word on every article is *'opina'*, as every leftie in the city gives his or her opinion on every subject, squeezing in a bit of news here and there. *Página* flies the flag for independent journalism. The Sunday cultural supplement *Radar* is among the best.

Radio

FM de la Ciudad
92.7FM
Municipal service started in 1990 to ensure that tango, the essential soundtrack to Buenos Aires life, is available all day and all night.

FM La Folklórica
98.7FM
Get your fix of folky strumming and *gaucho* choirs to help you slow down in the big brash city.

Mega – Puro Rock Nacional
98.3FM
No chat, only music, and *rock nacional* at that. One of the most listened to stations by young people.

Metrodance
95.1FM
By day, hip variety shows and news; by night and on weekends, even hipper dance and electronic music.

Rock & Pop
95.9FM
Brought *rock nacional* and rock culture in general to the fore. Mario Pergolini's morning show is the soundtrack young office workers wake up to city-wide.

Television

These are the free-to-air channels available in Argentina; most hotels and homes also have cable and satellite channels.

América TV
Shows live football from the Argentinian *primera*, plus soaps and countless late-night talk shows.

Canal 7
The only state-run TV channel, and thus the one that can afford not to play the ratings game. Programming is big on local culture and music.

Canal 9
Sex, scandals, sex, alien abductions and more sex are the hallmarks of BA's lowest of low brow channels.

Canal 13
The most watched channel with the best series. Good nightly news.

Telefe – Canal 11
Big channel, fronted by big personalities like national treasure Susana Giménez . Also soaps and imports such as *The Simpsons*.

Money

The Argentinian currency is the peso. After the old convertibility system which pegged the peso to the US dollar at 1:1 was abandoned in January 2002, the currency was allowed to float freely and consequently devalue. Its value has since remained largely stable, at AR$2.75-$3 to one US dollar. At time of going to press the headline inflation rate stands at a worrying, but hardly cataclysmic, ten per cent per annum.

The peso is divided into *centavos*. Coins are the silver and yellowy-gold one peso coin, 50, 25, ten and five centavos. Some 50- and 25-*centavo* coins are the same size

Directory

and colour (yellow-gold) so hard to differentiate. Newer 25-*centavo* coins are silver. Notes come in denominations of 100 (purple), 50 (dark grey), 20 (red), ten (brown), five (green) and two (blue) pesos, and in every kind of condition.

Beware of fake money. There are many falsified notes and coins in circulation, so check your change, especially in cabs. False bills are generally quite detectable, as the colours tend to lack the precision of authentic notes and the texture has a plasticky feel. Fake coins (predominantly 50 *centavos*) are commonplace: they're lighter in both colour and weight than the legal tender, so easy to spot.

Also avoid the illegal money changers (known as *arbolitos*, or little trees) lining Florida and its adjacent streets. They are the ones who are most likely to sting you with fake pesos and give a low rate of exchange.

ATMs

Most banks have ATMs, signalled by a 'Banelco' or 'Link' sign. They distribute pesos only and usually charge a fee (US$1-$5). Some are only for clients of the bank in question, so look for a machine showing the symbol of your card company. If withdrawing large sums, do so discreetly and be careful taking a cab: either walk several blocks first or call a radio taxi.

Banks

It's extremely difficult to open an Argentinian bank account if you are a foreigner. Banks ask for endless paperwork, including wage slips and a local ID. To compound the situation, most banks won't accept a transfer unless you have an account. To receive money, use Forexcambio, who can also cash foreign cheques

or bankers' drafts, or Western Union. Charges vary according to the state of the market. In late 2005, Forexcambio was charging a minimum of US$55 per transfer, while Western Union was charging US$18 for a US$50 transfer and US$60 for a US$1,000 transfer.

Forexcambio

Marcelo T de Alvear 540, entre Florida y San Martín, Retiro (4010 2000). Subte C, San Martin/26, 61, 93, 152 bus. **Open** 10am-3pm Mon-Fri. **Map** p281 G12.

Western Union

Córdoba 975, entre Suipacha y Carlos Pellegrini, Microcentro (freephone 0800 8003030). Subte C, Lavalle/10, 59, 111 bus. **Open** 9am-8pm Mon-Fri. **Map** p2817 G11.

Travellers' cheques & bureaux de change

Travellers' cheques are often refused by business establishments and can be difficult and expensive to change in banks.

There are various bureaux de change in the city centre which will change travellers' cheques. Commission is usually around two per cent, with a minimum charge of US$5. Many are situated around the intersection of Sarmiento and Reconquista streets. Usual opening hours are 9am-6pm.

American Express

Arenales 707, y Maipú, Retiro (4310 3000). Subte C, San Martin/10, 17, 70, 152 bus. **Open** 10am-3pm Mon-Fri. **Map** p277 G11. Will change AmEx travellers' cheques without charge.

Credit cards

Credit cards are accepted in most outlets; photo ID is usually required. Visa (V), MasterCard (MC) and American Express (AmEx) are the most accepted cards. Diners Club (DC) is also valid in a number of places, but check first.

Lost & stolen cards

American Express 0810 5552639.
Diners Club 0810 4442484.
MasterCard 4348 7070.
Visa 4379 3333.

Tax

Local sales tax is called IVA, aka Impuestos a Valor Agregado. It's a whopping 21 per cent, though as a rule it's always added on the bill or pricetag. The exception is hotel rack rates that are generally listed without IVA in more expensive hotels. However, in our **Where to Stay** chapter (*see pp35-58*) we have quoted all prices with IVA included, so there's no nasty shock on the final bill.

Natural hazards

Apart from a volatile economy, Argentina is largely free of natural hazards. The only blip comes when a strong wind from the south – *La Sudestada* – brings torrential rain and flash flooding to Palermo, Belgrano and La Boca. *Sudestadas* are more common from June to October.

Opening hours

Opening hours are extremely variable, but here are some general guidelines:

Banks

Generally open from 10am-3pm weekdays, although some branches open an hour earlier, and some close an hour later.

Bars

Most bars in Buenos Aires don't get busy until after midnight and many are open round the clock. Pubs, or evening bars, open around 6pm for happy hour (known here as 'after office'), or 8pm out of the centre, and most stay open till the crowds thin out.

Business hours

Ordinary office hours are 9am-6pm, with a lunchbreak from 1-2pm.

Post offices

The Correo Central (**Central Post Office**; *see below*) is open 8am-8pm Mon-Fri and 8am-1pm Sat. Other branch post offices are open weekdays from 9am-6pm. Many telephone centres (*locutorios*) also have postal services and are often open until midnight.

Shops

Most malls open 10am-10pm, though there can be one hour's variation. The food court and cinemas stay open after the other shops. Shops on the street open around 9am or 10am and close at around 7pm.

Police stations

Public safety in the capital is the responsibility of the Policía Federal, divided into 53 *comisarías* (at least one per *barrio*), with a central police station. Tourists needing to report a crime should go to the **Comisaría del Turista**. Alternatively, you can head to the station in the *barrio* in which the incident occurred. *See p255* for emergency telephone numbers.

Comisaría del Turista

Avenida Corrientes 436, entre San Martín y Reconquista, Microcentro (0800 999 5000). Subte B, Florida/ 10, 93, 99 bus. **Open** 24 hrs daily **Map** p281 F11.
English-speaking staff are on hand to help and offer advice to tourists who need to report a crime.

Departamento Central de Policía

Moreno 1550, entre Luis Sáenz Peña y Virrey Cevallos, Congreso (4370 5800 24hrs). Subte A, Sáenz Peña/39, 64, 86 bus. **Map** p281 F9.
The police stations listed below are in central areas,

be we still recommend you use the Comisaría del Turista.

Comisaría 1ª (Centro)

Lavalle 451, entre Reconquista y San Martín, Microcentro (4322 8033). Subte B, Florida/10, 93, 99 bus. **Map** p277 F11.

Comisaría 2ª (San Telmo)

Perú 1050, entre Carlos Calvo y Humberto 1°, San Telmo (4361 8054). Bus 24, 126, 30, 152. **Map** p276 D9.

Comisaría 17ª (Recoleta)

Avenida Las Heras 1861, entre Callao y Ayacucho, Recoleta (4801 3333). Bus 10, 59, 60, 124. **Map** p278 I11.

Postal services

Numerous competitors offer postal, courier and other express delivery services, though not all can provide international postal facilities. Nor does increased competition appear to have brought many price benefits since Correo Argentino is still the cheapest for domestic mail.

A letter weighing up to 20 grams costs AR$1; from 20 to 100 grams costs AR$3.50. To neighbouring countries, a letter of up to 20 grams costs AR$4, to other countries in the Americas and other, worldwide destinations, AR$5.

Registered post (essential for any document of value) costs a minimum of AR$8.50 for up to 20 grams nationally, and from AR$11.50 for up to 20 grams internationally.

There are Correo Argentino branches throughout the city, and many larger *locutorios* offer their postal services.

If you want to receive post in Buenos Aires, get it sent directly to your hotel or to a private address if you have contacts here and then cross your fingers: post doesn't always make it to the final destination, and packages or parcels of any value tend to go permanently astray. There is

a poste restante service at the Correo Central; it costs AR$4.50 to collect each piece of mail, which should be sent to:

Recipient's name,
Lista de Correos,
Correo Central,
Sarmiento 189,
(1003) Capital Federal,
Argentina.

Correo Central

Sarmiento 151, entre Leandro N Alem y Bouchard, Microcentro (4891 9191). Subte B, LN Alem/ 26, 93, 99, 152 bus. **Open** 8am-8pm Mon-Fri; 8am-1pm Sat. **Map** p281 F11.

Religion

Argentina is a secular country; the constitution insists on the separation of church and state and guarantees freedom of worship for citizens. Roman Catholicism is the official state religion, though only about 20 per cent of Argentinians attend church regularly. There are many synagogues in Once, and many other evangelical gatherings which occur in converted stores around BA. Here are a few addresses of places of worship around the city. For a more complete listing, check the local *Yellow Pages*.

Anglican

Catedral Anglicana de San Juan Bautista *25 de Mayo 282, y Sarmiento, Microcentro (4342 4618). Bus 126, 130, 146, 152.* **Services** *English* 9.30am Sun. *Spanish* 11am Sun. **Map** p281 F11.

Buddhist

Templo Budista Honpa-Hongwanji *Sarandi 951, entre Carlos Calvo y Estados Unidos, San Cristobal (4941 0262). Subte E, Entre Rios/12, 37, 126, 168 bus.* **Service** 5pm Sun. **Map** p281 F7.

Roman Catholic

Catedral Metropolitana *Avenida Rivadavia 412, y San Martin, Microcentro (4331 2845). Subte A, Plaza de Mayo or D, Catedral or E, Bolívar/24, 29, 64, 86 bus.* **Services** Spanish only 9am, 11am, 12.30pm, 6pm Mon-Fri; 11am, 6pm Sat; 11am, noon, 1pm, 6pm Sun. **Map** p281 F10.

Directory

Jewish

Gran Templo de la Asociación Comunidad Israelita Sefardí
Camargo 870, entre Gurruchaga y Serrano, Villa Crespo. Subte B, Malabia/15, 24, 57, 106 110 bus. **Services** 7.10am, 6.45pm Mon-Fri; 9am, 5.30pm Sat; 8am, 6.30pm Sun. Map p279 M3

Muslim

Centro Islámico Ray Fahd
Avenida Bullrich 55, y Libertador, Palermo (4899 0201). Subte D, Palermo/39, 60, 64, 130, 152 bus. Map p283 N10.

Presbyterian

Presbyterian Scottish Church of Saint Andrew *Avenida Belgrano 579, entre Bolívar y Perú, Monserrat (4331 0308). Subte E, Piedras/24, 29, 86, 126 bus.* **Services** *English* 10am Sun. *Spanish* 11.30am Sun. Map p281 E10.

Safety

Over the last ten years, BA's reputation as one of the world's safest capitals has taken a bruising. As poverty has increased, crime rates have risen. *La inseguridad* now ranks above government corruption and the private lives of soap stars as *the* water-cooler conversation topic for *porteños*.

But with a little common sense and a few basic precautions, visitors to Buenos Aires will avoid most crime. Don't display eye-catching jewellery, cameras or clothes synonymous with the typical tourist. Keep an eye on belongings on public transport and always use radio taxis. Check your bills carefully, as forgeries abound. The latest trick is for taxi drivers to accept your 100 peso bill, switch it surreptitiously, and hand you back a forged bill saying they can't change your money.

Remember that while most tourist areas remain safe, more care should be taken in the *barrios* of La Boca and Constitucion, and to a slightly lesser extent in San Telmo and Palermo. Anywhere in the city, avoid pulling out a wallet stacked with bills. If you are

actually threatened, hand over your goods calmly: BA has a gun problem.

Street aggression is most commonly of the verbal kind, especially for women. The best response is to ignore someone – if he's really annoying, walk into a shop or lose him in the nearest ladies' toilet.

If you need to report a crime, head first to the city's centrally located **Comisaría del Turista** (*see p259*) where knowledgeable English-speaking staff are on hand.

Smoking

Argentinians love a fag, so don't expect many no-smoking places. Despite an ambitious effort to change public opinion, the bottom line remains the same: nicotine is in. With the exceptions of public transport, cinemas and some restaurant areas, smoking is permitted. A new law in early 2006 outlawed smoking in most public buildings; thus far it has been scrupulously ignored.

Study

Language classes

Every year new institutes open, offering Spanish for foreigners. There are huge ranges in price and quality.

To organise an *intercambio* or language exchange, check noticeboards in universities and student travel agencies. There are usually lots of willing partners. Check, too, the ads in the *Buenos Aires Herald*; most language institutes and private teachers advertise there. Or try:

Latin Immersion

Virrey Arredondo 2416, entre Cabildo y Ciudad de Paz, Colegiales (1-866 577 8693/www.latinimmersion.com). Subte D, José Hernandez/41, 59, 60, 68, 152 bus. **Open** 8.30am-6pm Mon-Fri. **Rates** *Group classes* US$170 20hrs per wk. *Private classes* US$270 20hrs per wk. **Credit** MC, V. Map p285 Q8.

UBA – Laboratorio de Idiomas, Facultad de Filosofía y Letras

25 de Mayo 221, entre Perón y Sarmiento, Centro (4343 5981/ 1196/www.idiomas.filo.uba.ar). Bus 126, 130, 146, 152. **Open** 9am-9pm Mon-Fri. **Rates** *Group classes* from AR$600 4hrs per wk for 17 wks or 8hrs per wk for 8 wks. **No credit cards.** Map p281 F11.

Students' unions

FUBA (Federación Universitaria de Buenos Aires)

3rd Floor, Azcuénaga 280, entre Sarmiento y Perón, Once (4952 8080). Subte A, Alberti/24, 26, 101, 105 bus. **Open** 9am-8pm Mon-Fri. Map p282 I8.

Universities

There is both state-run and private university education available in Buenos Aires. The **Universidad de Buenos Aires** (or UBA, state run) is, in general, the most academically respected. Study at UBA is free. Private universities tend to have greater numbers of classes throughout the year, and better facilities. Teachers and technical staff at Argentinian universities are scandalously underpaid; many are young volunteers or assistants.

UBA (Departamento de Títulos y Planes)

Uriburu 950, entre Paraguay y Marcelo T de Alvear, Barrio Norte (4951 0634 ext 100 or 101). Subte D, Facultad de Medicina/39, 60, 51, 132, 152, 194 bus. **Open** noon-4pm Mon, Thur. Map p282 I9.
If you want to study at UBA, contact this department or go in person to the Centro Cultural Ricardo Rojas (*see p188*), which has general information for the university.

Universidad Argentina de la Empresa

Lima 717, entre Independencia y Chile, San Telmo (4372 5454/ www. uade.edu.ar). Subte E, Independencia/ 17, 59, 67, 105 bus. **Open** 9am-8pm Mon-Fri. Map p281 E9.
A business school with agreements with universities in the US, Chile, Brazil and Germany, among others.

Universidad de Palermo

Avenida Córdoba 3501, entre Mario Bravo y Bulnes, Palermo Viejo (4964 4600/www.palermo.edu.ar). Bus 26, 36, 92, 128. **Open** 9am-8pm Mon-Fri. **Map** p282 K8.

Useful organisations

www.delestudiante. com

Listings of every university, degree and postgrad offered.

www.studyabroad.com

Information in English on studying around the world; includes Argentina.

Asatej

3rd Floor, Office 320, Florida 835, entre Córdoba y Paraguay, Microcentro (4511 8700/www.al mundo.com). Subte B, Florida/ 10, 26, 93, 130, 152 bus. **Open** 9am-7pm Mon-Fri. **Map** p281 G11.
Student travel agency, with locations across town. ISIC cards issued here.

Telephones

Dialling & codes

All land-line numbers within Bueno Aires begin with either 4, 5 or 6 and consist of eight digits. To call a cellphone number, 15 must be added to the front of an eight-digit number. From overseas, dial your country's international dialling code followed by 54 11 and the eight-digit number. To call cellphones from overseas, dial 54 9 11 and leave out the 15. To dial overseas from BA, dial 00 followed by the country code and number (Australia 61, Canada 1, Ireland 353, New Zealand 64, UK 44, USA 1).

Other useful numbers:

Directory information 110
International operator 000
National operator 19
Repair service 114
Talking clock 113
Telecom/Telefónica commercial services 112
Telelectura 121. This is a free, 24hr service, which tells you the call charges within a billing period.

Call centres

BA is awash with *locutorios* (call centres), generally run by Telefónica or Telecom. Calls cost a few *centavos* more than from a public phone, but for a seat, air-con and the guarantee that your last coin won't be gobbled, it's worth it. They offer fax services and often net access and post services.

Public phones are coin- or card-operated, sometimes both. Phonecards can be bought from kiosks.

Mobile phones

CDMA/TDMA is the predominant system, though it's cheaper to rent locally than bring your own phone. Most UK cellphones will not work.

Phonerental

San Martín 945, entre Paraguay y Marcelo T de Alvear, Retiro (24hr hotline 4311 2933/www.phonerental. com.ar). Subte C, San Martín/10, 93, 30, 152 bus. **Open** 9am-6pm Mon-Fri. **Map** p281 G11.
Free phone rental, AR$1.25 per min air-time charge, no minimum.

Time

The clocks have been known to go back and forward by an hour in a rather arbitrary manner, although in recent years, winter and summer time have remained the same. Thus, Argentina is three hours behind GMT during the southern hemisphere summer, and four hours behind GMT during the southern winter.

Tipping

Tips tend to be left in the same quantities as most developed countries. As a rule of thumb, leave ten to 15 per cent in a bar, restaurant, or for any delivery service; in a cab, just round off a fare. In hotels, bellboys expect AR$1.50-$2 for helping with your bags. Ushers in cinemas expect the same. When checking out, it's normal to leave a small tip for the maids.

Toilets

You're probably more likely to be struck by lightning in Bueno Aires than stumble upon a clean and functioning public convenience. However, most bars and restaurants accept – albeit rather grudgingly – the role of offering evacuatory relief to the public. All shopping centres have clean public toilets. And, of course, bathroom use is one of the few advantages conferred on the world by fast-food outlets.

Tourist information

The tourist board website is www.buenosaires.gov/turismo. These are the official city tourist information points:
Abasto de Buenos Aires *Avenida Corrientes y Agüero, Abasto (4959 3507). Subte B, Carlos Gardel/bus 24, 26, 124, 168.* **Open** 11am-9pm daily. **Map** p282 J8.
Florida *Avenida Roque Sáenz Peña y Florida, Microcentro (no phone). Subte D, Catedral/bus 24, 130, 103, 152.* **Open** 9am-6pm Mon-Fri; 10am-3pm Sat. **Map** p281 F10.
Recoleta *Avenida Quintana y Ortiz (no phone). Bus 17, 67, 124, 130.* **Open** 10am-8pm daily. **Map** p282 J11.
Retiro *Terminal de Ómnibus, Avenida Antártida Argentina y Calle 10 (4311 0528). Subte C, Retiro/Bus 92, 130, 152.* **Open** 7.30am-1pm Mon-Sat. **Map** p281 H12.
Puerto Madero *Dique 4, AM de Justo al 200 (4313 0187). Bus 4, 130, 152.* **Open** noon-6pm Mon-Fri; 10am-8pm Sat, Sun. **Map** p281 F12.
San Telmo *Defensa 1250, entre San Juan y Cochabamba (no phone). Bus 29, 64, 86, 130, 152.* **Open** noon-6pm Mon-Fri; 10am-7pm Sat, Sun. **Map** p280 D9.
San Isidro Turístico *Ituzaingó 608, y Libertador, San Isidro (4512 3209). Train Mitre or de la Costa to San Isidro/660, 168 bus.* **Open** 8.30-5pm Mon-Fri; 10am-5pm Sat, Sun.
For national tourist info, go to:
Secretaría de Turismo de la Nación *Avenida Santa Fe 883, entre Suipacha y Esmeralda, Retiro (4312 5611/15). Subte C, San Martín/Bus 59, 111, 132, 152.* **Open** 9am-5pm Mon-Fri. **Map** p281 G11.
Freephone information line (8am-8pm Mon-Fri) 0800 555 0016.

Visas

Visas are not required by members of the European Community or citizens of the USA and Canada. Immigration grants you a 90-day visa on entry that can be extended by a quick exit out of the country – to Uruguay for example – or via the immigration service for AR$100. The fine for overstaying is AR$50; if you do overstay, arrive at the airport early so you can pay the fine.

More information about longer-stay visas for students or business travellers can be obtained from your nearest Argentinian Embassy.

Weights & measures

Argentina uses the metric system, though a few old measures still stand good in the countryside: horses are measured by *manos* (hands) and distances are sometimes measured by *leguas* (leagues).

When to go

Climate

Summer is December to March, and the winter season is July to October. The proximity to the River Plate and sea-level location make the city humid, so the summer heat and winter chill are felt more acutely.

You'll also hear plenty about a local obsession: *sensación térmica*. This isn't the real temperature, but how hot it feels; so prepare yourself for a midsummer day and being told that it is 44ºC (111ºF)!

Spring and autumn are ideal times to visit Buenos Aires – gorgeous weather and lots going on. At any time of year, be prepared for rain; heavy storms or a day or so of solid downpour are common. For meteorological information within BA, phone 4514 4253.

Public holidays

The following *feriados*, or public holidays, are fixed from year to year:
1 January (New Year's Day); **Jueves Santo** (Thursday before Easter); **Viernes Santo** (Good Friday); **1 May** (Labour Day); **25 May** (May Revolution Day); **9 July** (Independence Day); **8 December** (Day of the Immaculate Conception); **25 December** (Christmas).
For the following, the day of the holiday moves to the Monday before if it falls on a Tuesday or Wednesday, or to the Monday following if it falls Thursday to Sunday: **2 April** (Falklands/Malvinas War Veterans' Day); **20 June** (Flag Day); **17 August** (San Martín Memorial Day); **12 October** (Columbus Day).

Women

Argentinian men can be macho and flirtatious, but seldom behave agressively, making BA one of the safest cities for female travellers in Latin America.

0800 666 8537 is a 24-hour, city-run hotline to assist women in violent situations, with a network of organisations where they can seek counselling and legal advice. The **Dirección General de la Mujer** (7th Floor, Carlos Pellegrini 211, Microcentro, 4393 6466) is a city-run commission charged with promoting women's welfare – it's not a help desk.

Working in BA

Finding work as an English teacher is not difficult, but opportunities dry up from December to February when everyone goes on holiday. Pay averages AR$20-$30 an hour.

Apart from mixing cocktails or bussing tables, most other job opportunities are published in the *Buenos Aires Herald*, which also occasionally hires novice journalists.

Work permits

Most foreigners work on tourist visas, hopping to Uruguay and back every three months, though, strictly speaking, it's illegal.

To obtain a work permit, you need translated birth, police and medical certificates, sponsorship from an employer, bags of patience and at least AR$400. To facilitate the procedure, *escribanos* (notaries) will act on your behalf for a fee of AR$300-$500. Once your papers are in order, you have to exit the country in order to make the official application. Permits are valid for a year; renewal costs another AR$200.

Weather report

Month	Average high	Average low
January	30.4°C (87°F)	20.4°C (69°F)
February	28.7°C (84°F)	19.4°C (67°F)
March	26.4°C (80°F)	17°C (63°F)
April	22.7°C (73°F)	13.7°C (57°F)
May	19°C (66°F)	10.3°C (51°F)
June	15.6°C (60°F)	7.6°C (46°F)
July	14.9°C (59°F)	7.4°C (45°F)
August	17.3°C (63°F)	8.9°C (48°F)
September	18.9°C (66°F)	9.9°C (50°F)
October	22.5°C (73°F)	13°C (55°F)
November	25.3°C (78°F)	15.9°C (61°F)
December	28.1°C (83°F)	18.4°C (65°F)

Directory

Language & Vocabulary

Porteños living and working in tourist areas usually have some knowledge of English and generally welcome the opportunity to practise it with foreigners. However, a bit of Spanish goes a long way and making the effort to use even a few phrases and expressions will be greatly appreciated.

As in other Latin languages, there is more than one form of the second person (you) to be used according to the formality or informality of the situation. The most polite form is *usted*, and though it's not used among young people, it may be safer for a foreigner to err on the side of politeness. The local variant of the informal, the *voseo*, differs from the *tú* that you may know from European Spanish. Both forms are given here, *usted* first, then *vos*.

Pronunciation

Spanish is easier than some languages to get a basic grasp of, as pronunciation is largely phonetic. Look at the word and pronounce every letter, and the chances are you will be understood. As a rule, stress in a word falls on the penultimate syllable, otherwise an accent indicates stress. Accents are omitted on capital letters, though still pronounced. The key to learning Argentinian Spanish is to master the correct pronunciation of a few letters and vowels.

Vowels

Each vowel is pronounced separately and consistently, except in certain vowel combinations known as diphthongs, where they combine as a single syllable. There are strong vowels: a, e and o, and weak vowels: i and u. Two weak vowels, as in *ruido* (noise), or one strong and one weak, as in *piel* (skin), form a diphthong. Two strong vowels next to each other are pronounced as separate syllables (as in *poeta*, poet).

a is pronounced like the **a** in **a**pple.
e is pronounced like the **a** in s**a**y.
i is pronounced like the **ee** in b**ee**t.
o is pronounced like the **o** in t**o**p.
u is pronounced like the **oo** in m**oo**d.
y is usually a consonant, except when it is alone or at the end of the word, in which case it is pronounced like the Spanish **i**.

Consonants

Pronunciation of the letters **f, k, l, n, p, q, s** and **t** is similar to English. **y** and **ll** are generally pronounced like the French *'je'*, in contrast to the European Spanish pronunciation. **ch** and **ll** have separate dictionary entries. **ch** is pronounced as in the English **ch**air.
b is pronounced like its English equivalent, and is not distinguishable from the letter **v**. Both are referred to as **be** as in English be**t**. **b** is **long b** (called *b larga* in Spanish), **v** is known as **short b** (*b corta*).
c is pronounced like the **s** in s**e**a when before **e** or **i** and like the English **k** in all others.
g is pronounced like a guttural English **h** like the **ch** in lo**ch** when before **e** and **i** and as a hard **g** like **g** in **g**oat otherwise.
h at the beginning of a word is silent.
j is also pronounced like a guttural English **h** and the letter is referred to as **jota** as in English ho**tt**er.
ñ is the letter **n** with a tilde and is pronounced like **ni** in English o**ni**on.
r is pronounced like the English **r** but is rolled at the beginning of a word, and **rr** is pronounced like the English **r** but is strongly rolled.
x is pronounced like the **x** in ta**x**i in most cases, although in some it sounds like the Spanish **j**, for instance in Xavier.

Basics

hello *hola*
good morning *buenos días*
good afternoon *buenas tardes*
good evening/night *buenas noches*
OK *está bien*
yes *sí*
no *no*
maybe *tal vez/quizá(s)*
how are you? *¿cómo le va?* or *¿cómo te va?*
how's it going *¿cómo anda?* or *¿cómo andás?*
Sir/Mr *Señor*; **Madam/Mrs** *Señora*
please *por favor*
thanks *gracias*; **thank you very much** *muchas gracias*
you're welcome *de nada*
sorry *perdón*
excuse me *permiso*
do you speak English *¿habla inglés?* or *¿hablás inglés?*
I don't speak Spanish *no hablo castellano*
I don't understand *no entiendo*
speak more slowly, please *hable más despacio, por favor* or *habla más despacio, por favor*
leave me alone (quite forceful) *¡déjese!* or *¡déjame!*
have you got change *¿tiene cambio?* or *¿tenés cambio?*
there is/there are *hay/no hay*
good/well *bien*
bad/badly *mal*
small *pequeño/chico*
big *grande*
beautiful *hermoso/lindo*
a bit *un poco*; **a lot/very** *mucho*
with *con*; **without** *sin*
also *también*
this *este*; **that** *ese*
and *y*; **or** *o*
because *porque*; **if** *si*
what? *¿qué?*; **who?** *¿quién?*; **when?** *¿cuándo?*; **which?** *¿cuál?*; **why?** *¿por qué?*; **how?** *¿cómo?*; **where?** *¿dónde?*; **where to?** *¿hacia dónde?*
where from? *¿de dónde?*
where are you from? *¿de dónde es?* or *¿de dónde sos?*
I am English *soy inglés* (man) or *inglesa* (woman); **Irish** *irlandés*; **American** *americano/norteamericano/estadounidense*; **Canadian** *canadiense*; **Australian** *australiano*; **a New Zealander** *neocelandés*
at what time/when? *¿a qué hora?/¿cuándo?*
forbidden *prohibido*
out of order *no funciona*
bank *banco*
post office *correo*
stamp *estampilla*

Emergencies

Help! *¡auxilio! ¡ayuda!*
I'm sick *estoy enfermo*
I need a doctor/policeman/hospital *necesito un médico/un policía/un hospital*
there's a fire! *¡hay un incendio!*

On the phone

hello *hola*
who's calling? *¿quién habla?*
hold the line *espere en línea*

Getting around

airport *aeropuerto*
station *estación*
train *tren*
ticket *boleto*
single *ida*
return *ida y vuelta*
platform *plataforma/andén*
bus/coach station *terminal de colectivos/omnibús/micros*
entrance *entrada*
exit *salida*
left *izquierda*
right *derecha*
straight on *derecho*
street *calle*; avenue *avenida*;
motorway *autopista*
street map *mapa callejero*;
road map *mapa carretero*
no parking *prohibido estacionar*
toll *peaje*
speed limit *límite de velocidad*
petrol *nafta*; unleaded *sin plomo*

Sightseeing

museum *museo*
church *iglesia*
exhibition *exhibición*
ticket *boleto*
open *abierto*
closed *cerrado*
free *gratis*
reduced *rebajado/con descuento*
except Sunday *excepto los domingos*

Accommodation

hotel *hotel*; bed & breakfast *pensión con desayuno*
do you have a room (for this evening/for two people)? *¿tiene una habitación (para esta noche/para dos personas)?*
no vacancy *completo/no hay habitación libre*; vacancy *desocupado/vacante*
room *habitación*
bed *cama*; double bed *cama matrimonial*
a room with twin beds *una habitación con dos camas*
a room with a bathroom/shower *una habitación con baño/ducha*
breakfast *desayuno*; included *incluido*
lift *ascensor*
air-conditioned *con aire acondicionado*

Shopping

I would like... *me gustaría...*
Is there a/are there any? *¿hay/habrá?*
how much? *¿cuánto?*
how many? *¿cuántos?*
expensive *caro*
cheap *barato*

with VAT *con IVA* (21 per cent valued added tax)
without VAT *sin IVA*
what size? *¿qué talle?*
can I try it on? *¿me lo puedo probar?*

Numbers

0 *cero*
1 *uno*
2 *dos*
3 *tres*
4 *cuatro*
5 *cinco*
6 *seis*
7 *siete*
8 *ocho*
9 *nueve*
10 *diez*
11 *once*; 12 *doce*; 13 *trece*; 14 *catorce*; 15 *quince*; 16 *dieciséis*; 17 *dieciete*; 18 *dieciocho*; 19 *diecinueve*; 20 *veinte*; 21 *veintiuno*; 22 *veintidós*
30 *treinta*
40 *cuarenta*
50 *cincuenta*
60 *sesenta*
70 *setenta*
80 *ochenta*
90 *noventa*
100 *cien*
1,000 *mil*
1,000,000 *un millón*

Days, months & seasons

morning *la mañana*
noon *mediodía*;
afternoon/evening *la tarde*
night *la noche*
Monday *lunes*
Tuesday *martes*
Wednesday *miércoles*
Thursday *jueves*
Friday *viernes*
Saturday *sábado*
Sunday *domingo*
January *enero*; February *febrero*; March *marzo*; April *abril*; May *mayo*; June *junio*; July *julio*; August *agosto*; September *septiembre*; October *octubre*; November *noviembre*; December *diciembre*
spring *primavera*
summer *verano*
autumn/fall *otoño*
winter *invierno*

Others

Argentina is Spanish-speaking. But as anyone arriving from Spain or Mexico can attest, the expressive, Italian-laced street slang of Buenos Aires known as *lunfardo*, can, at times, make communicating a confusing if not comical experience.

Talking among friends, *porteños* will start every few sentences with '*che*' ('hey, you' or 'mate') in the monotonous way Southern California skateboarders say 'dude'. Of course, the most famous '*che*', and everybody's buddy, was Ernesto 'Che' Guevara.

The real fun begins, though, when you start sifting through the more than 1,000 *lunfardo* words and expressions with which *porteños* liven up even the most mundane conversation. Many of them have their origins in the tango underworld at the beginning of the 20th century, but now are used even by presidents to get messages across in a typically straight-shooting manner.

A few choice words or expressions you might hear only in Argentina (and Uruguay) include: *laburo* (work), *piola* (cool), *cana* (police, jail), *chabón* (man, guy), *mina* (girl/chick), *faso* or *pucho* (cigarette), *chamuyar* (sweet talk, bullshit), *chapita* (crazy), *limado* (incapacitated by drugs), *birra* (beer), *bocha* (large quantity, as in money). Although many of the words have a macho connotation, as in *boludo* or *pelotudo* (big balls, used as an insult or to kid a friend), they also, illogically, can take a feminine form as in *boluda* or *pelotuda*.

Some local terms are so out of whack with traditional Spanish that using them incorrectly runs a risk of public ridicule. For example, in Mexico when you ask for a *paja*, you'd be given a straw, whereas to do the same in Argentina would be to confess you want a wank. Meanwhile, the Spanish verb *coger* (to take, or catch, as in a bus) means to fuck in Buenos Aires, inappropriate no matter what you think of public transport. Better to *tomar* a bus instead.

Further Reference

Books

Non-fiction

Jimmy Burns *The Land That Lost Its Heroes: Argentina, the Falklands, and Alfonsin* The essential analysis of *that* conflict.
S Collier, A Cooper, MS Azzi and R Martin *¡Tango!* Currently the definitive guide to tango in English, lavishly illustrated and lovingly collated by the late Simon Collier.
Ronald Dworkin (introduction) *Nunca Más: The Report of the Argentine National Commission on the Disappeared* Still awful to read, the necessary accounts of torture and murder perpetrated by the 1976-83 dictatorship.
Robert Farris Thompson *Tango: the Art History of Love* In this impassioned attempt to challenge the widely held assumption that tango is a white European musical form, Thompson traces the aetiology of those twisting thighs and swaying torsos back to sub-Saharan Africa.
Miranda France *Bad Times in Buenos Aires: A Writer's Adventures in Argentina* Insightful travelogue that has fun with the big Argentinian myths: shrinks, sex and machismo.
Uki Goñi *The Real Odessa* How Perón helped his Nazi mates find homes in Argentina after the war.
Diego Armando Maradona *El Diego* In Spanish – the best No.10 in his own inimitable words.
Gabriela Nouzeille and **Graciela Montaldo** (eds) *The Argentina Reader* Great collection of primary texts from 16th-century journals to sociological analyses of soccer.
VS Naipaul *The Return of Eva Perón* Old-style travel writing, full of sharp political observations on Argentina in the 1970s.
Richard W Slatta *Gauchos and the Vanishing Frontier* Puts the cowboys of the Argentinian countryside in their historical context.
Jason Wilson *Buenos Aires: A Cultural and Literary Companion* Open your eyes to the roots and remains of literary greats and their influence on the city.

Literature

Jorge Luis Borges *Selected Poems* Buenos Aires conjured up through the exquisitely crafted words of Argentina's literary hero.
Julio Cortázar *Hopscotch* The king of experiment's masterpiece jumps between BA and Paris.

Graham Greene *The Honorary Consul* Mainly set in northern Argentina in the 1970s, Greene's novel successfully captures the conflicting currents of Argentinian society.
José Hernández *Martín Fierro* Epic 19th-century poem following the hoof prints of a persecuted *gaucho*.
Alejandro López *Die Lady Die* Camp, crossdressing and cumbia dominate this picaresque tale of a Ricky Martin-obsessed provincial girl let loose in big, bad Buenos Aires.
Tomás Eloy Martínez *Santa Evita* A gripping tale of the afterlife of Eva Perón's corpse. Brilliantly revealing on the blurred boundaries between history and fiction in Argentina.
Manuel Vázquez Montalbán *The Buenos Aires Quintet* Detective Pepe Carvalho tries to find a relative in the city of the disappeared.
Ernesto Sábato *The Tunnel* The definitive existentialist portrait of Buenos Aires, with plenty of gloom and urban alienation.
Domingo Faustino Sarmiento *Facundo: Or, Civilization and Barbarism* A subjective assessment of the country during the era of Rosas and the provincial *caudillos*.

Film

Alejandro Agresti *Buenos Aires viceversa* Earthy but plot-driven Ken Loach-like work from one of the best young film directors around.
Tristán Bauer *Iluminados por el fuego* Award-winning drama about a Falklands War veteran who returns to the islands after one of his combat buddies commits suicide.
Fabián Belinsky *Nueve reinas* Two con-artists try to make a fast buck on the streets of Buenos Aires.
Daniel Burman *Derecho de familia* Comedy drama about a thirty-something *porteño* coming to terms with the trials of fatherhood
Adrián Caetano and **Bruno Stagnaro** *Pizza, birra, faso* Down and out in Buenos Aires with a gang of street urchins.
Juan Carlos Desanzo *Eva Perón* Esther Goris and Victor Laplace star in this local, no-frills biopic.
Lucrecia Martel *La niña santa* The story of the sexual awakening of a 16-year-old Catholic choir girl.
Alan Parker *Evita* Madonna, Jonathan Pryce, Antonio Banderas and Jimmy Nail… go on, you know you want to.
John Reinhardt *El día que me quieras* A 1935 black-and-white classic: Gardel goes to Hollywood.

Carlos Sorin *Bombon el perro* A warm, dead-pan take on the everyday foibles of the human condition.

Music

Charly García *Piano Bar* A solo work, considered by many to be the *porteño* rock icon's best.
Carlos Gardel *20 grandes exitos* An absolute gem; the voice still comes through as the finest in tango and every track is a classic.
León Gieco *De ushuaia a la quiaca* A rocker's anthropological adventure in regional folk music.
Manal *Manal* The first, and perhaps, best blues disc in Spanish.
Daniel Melingo *Tangos bajos* Tom Waits meets the tango traditions of Edmundo Rivero.
Miranda *Sin restricciones* The album that catapulted the masters of catchy pop into the big time in 2005.
Astor Piazzolla *Buenos Aires: zero hour* Late, subtle, stirring tango from the postmodern maestro.
Soda Stereo *Canción animal* Finest hour from the stadium-filling trio who conquered Latin America.
Mercedes Sosa *Mujeres argentinas* The young voice of 'la Sosa'. Songs like 'Juana Azurduy' made history.
Sui Generis *Obras cumbres* A double album of rock-folk tracks from the legendary teaming of Charlie Garcia and Nito Mestre.
Carlos Libedinsky *Narcotango* Sexier than the Gotan Project, *tango electrónica* for dancers, dark bars and horizontal coupling too.
Yerba Brava *Corriendo la coneja* One of the best *cumbia villera* albums – rude, lewd, crude and shrewd.
Atahualpa Yupanqui *El payador perseguido* Master work from the folk poet and guitarist.

Websites

www.argentinesoccer.com Everything you need to know about the national obsession.
www.buenosaires.gov.ar The city government's site, includes details of cultural events.
www.buenosaliens.com Dance music and clubbing in the city.
www.cinenacional.com Spanish-only Argentinian cinema site.
www.guiaoleo.com.ar Listings for almost every restaurant in town.
www.www.vinosdeargentina.com Official site for viticulture and the booming local wine scene.
http://argentina.indymedia.org/ Good for getting the lowdown on new politics and protest.

Index

Note: Page numbers in **bold** indicate section(s) giving key information on a topic; *italics* indicate photos.

Advertisers' Index

KEY TO MAPS

Place of interest and/ or entertainment	⬛
Railway station	⬛
Railway	▬
Park	⬛
Church	✚
Synagogue	✡
Hospital	✚
Tourist information	🛈
Subte	●●●●
Line H (under construction)	-----
Area	NUÑEZ
Hotels	❶
Restaurants	❶
Bars	❶

Maps

Trips Out of Town

SANTA FE PROVINCE

Santa Fe
Paraná

ENTRE RÍOS PROVINCE

Embalse Salto Grande

Concordia • Salto

Santana do Livramento
Rivera

Colón
Paysandú

U R U G U A Y

Rosario

San Nicolás de los Arroyos

Gualeguaychú

14

Fray Bentos · Mercedes

12

San Pedro

Colón

Carmelo (p244)

Zárate

San Antonio de Areco (p235)

Campana

(Arg.)

Belén de Escobar

Colonia del Sacramento (p243)

Canelones

Minas

Rocha

Carmen de Areco

Capilla del Señor

9

Tigre (p231)

1

La Paloma

Junín **7**

San Andrés de Giles
Mercedes

Pilar

BUENOS AIRES See p276-7

MONTEVIDEO (p245)

Piriápolis

Maldonado

Luján

Chivilcoy

LA PLATA

1

Punta del Este (p246)

Lobos

RÍO DE LA PLATA

Saladillo

San Miguel del Monte

Chascomús

3

Las Flores

BUENOS AIRES PROVINCE

Límite del lecho y subsuelo

11

Límite exterior del Río de la Plata

San Clemente del Tuyú

Azul

Olavarría

A R G E N T I N A

Límite lateral marítimo argentino-uruguayo

11

Tandil

Pinamar (p241)

Villa Gesell

Mar de las Pampas (p242)

Laprida

Mar Azul

2

Tres Arroyos

11

Mar del Plata (p240)

Miramar

3

Necochea

ATLANTIC OCEAN

Monte Hermoso

| 0 | | 100 miles |
| 0 | | 200 km |

© Copyright Time Out Group 2006

VENEZUELA
GUYANA
SURINAM
COLOMBIA
GUAYANA FRANCESA
ECUADOR
PERU
BRAZIL
BOLIVIA
PARAGUAY
Puerto Iguazú (p233)
URUGUAY
Buenos Aires
ARGENTINA
CHILE

| 0 | 1000 miles |
| 0 | 1000 km |

Tigre & Zona Norte

Parque de la Costa
TIGRE
DELTA
Río de la Reconquista
Arroyo Abra Vieja
CANAL SAN FERNANDO
TIGRE
Yacht Club Río de la Plata
Club Náutico Belgrano
AVENIDA J B JUSTO
CARUPA
Río Luján
TREN DE LA COSTA
ALVEAR
Canal de Vinculación
Arroyo Anguilas
Delta del Paraná
Arroyo Pacú
Club San Fernando
SAN FERNANDO
Yacht Club Argentino
SAN FERNANDO
AVENIDA HIPOLITO YRIGOYEN
AVENIDA ARNOLD
CHACABUCO
AVENIDA DEL LIBERTADOR
AVENIDA AVELLANEDA
VIRREYES
SAN FERNANDO
DEL ARCA
AVENIDA PERON
2200
3000
Marina Norte
Puerto Chico
MARINA NUEVA

0   2.5 miles
0   5 km
© Copyright Time Out Group 2006

Cementerio de
San Fernando
MALVINAS ARGENTINAS
URUGUAY.
SOBREMONTE
AVENIDA ROLON
AVENIDA SUCRE
JOSE INGENIEROS
NEYER
Club Hípico
del Norte
INTENDENTE TOMKINSON
NICOLAS AVELLANEDA
SAN
ISIDRO
Lomas de
San Isidro
DON BOSCO
AVENIDA FERNANDEZ
Golf Club
San Isidro
AVENIDA BERNABE MARQUEZ (CAMINO DE CINTURA)
Campo
de Golf
Jockey Club
de Buenos Aires
DARDO ROCHA
AVENIDA DE LA UNION NACIONAL
AVENIDA SIR ALEXANDER FLEMING
DIAGONAL SALTA
DIAGONAL TUCUMAN
CATAMARCA
TOMAS EDISON
Unicenter
3200
DEBENEDETTI
SAN LORENZO
CASEROS
MARIANO PELLIZA
GOBERNADOR UGARTE
AVENIDA USAL
ITALIA
HIPOLITO YRIGOYEN
VICENTE LOPEZ

Marina Punta Chica
PUNTA CHICA
RÍO DE LA PLATA
BECCAR
Club Náutico San Isidro
T B A (EX MITRE)
AVENIDA CENTENARIO
ESPAÑA
17900
17700
7200
1800
3800
3900
17900
TREN DE LA COSTA
Museo Biblioteca y Archivo Histórico Municipal
SAN ISIDRO
Museo Histórico Municipal
Juan Martín de Pueyrredón
SAN ISIDRO
Museo del Rugby
Catedral
de San
Isidro
Reserva Ecológica Municipal
Perú Beach
LAS BARRANCAS
Hipódromo
de San Isidro
PERU
ACASSUSO
100
800
AVENIDA SANTA FE
MARTINEZ
700
Parque Ecológico
ANCHORENA
13400
AVENIDA DEL LIBERTADOR
13000
300
AVENIDA PARANA
1400
2700
2000
4000
0
LA LUCILA
LIBERTADOR
3000
3000
BORGES
Club Náutico
MAIPU
OLIVOS
Puerto de Olivos
2400
MITRE
Residencia
Presidencial
AVENIDA MAIPU
2200
1800
CETRANGOLO
VICENTE LOPEZ
1000
VICENTE LOPEZ
AVENIDA SAN MARTIN

9
4
ACCESO NORTE
RAMAL TIGRE

Tigre
BUENOS
AIRES
PROVINCE
Vicente López
BUENOS
AIRES
CITY
0   10 miles
0   10 km

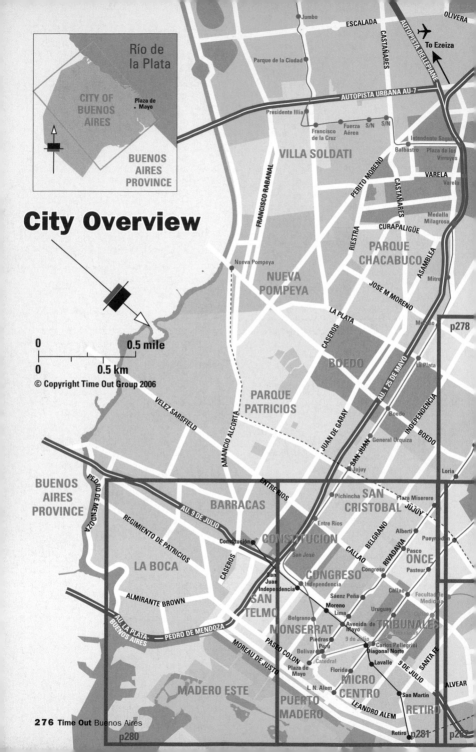

City Overview

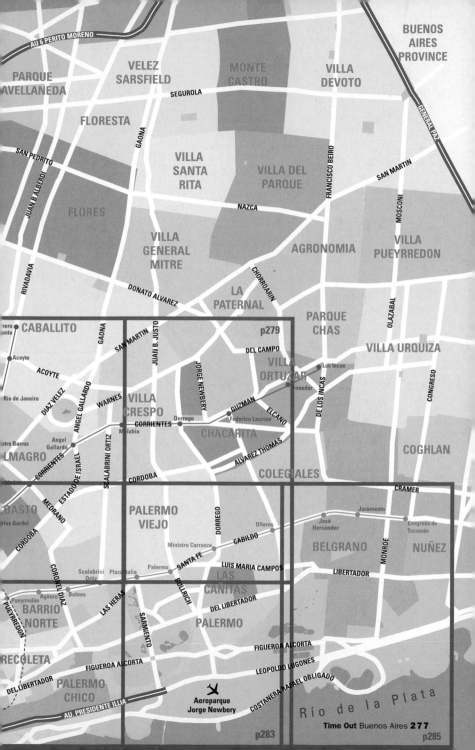

AU 6 PERITO MORENO

BUENOS
AIRES
PROVINCE

PARQUE
AVELLANEDA

VELEZ
SARSFIELD

MONTE
CASTRO

VILLA
DEVOTO

GENERAL PAZ

SEGUROLA

FLORESTA

SAN PEDRITO

GAONA

VILLA
SANTA
RITA

VILLA DEL
PARQUE

FRANCISCO BEIRO

SAN MARTIN

JUAN B. ALBERDI

NAZCA

MOSCONI

FLORES

RIVADAVIA

VILLA
GENERAL
MITRE

AGRONOMIA

VILLA
PUEYRREDON

OLAZABAL

DONATO ALVAREZ

CHORROARIN

LA
PATERNAL

PARQUE
CHAS

CABALLITO

nera
unta

Acoyte

GAONA

SAN MARTIN

JUAN B. JUSTO

DEL CAMPO

p279

VILLA URQUIZA

VILLA
ORTUZAR

Los Incas

ACOYTE

JORGE NEWBERY

Coronador

Río de Janeiro

DIAZ VELEZ

ANGEL GALLARDO

WARNES

VILLA
CRESPO

GUZMAN

ELCANO

DE LOS INCAS

CONGRESO

stro Barros

Angel
Gallardo

CORRIENTES

ESTADO DE ISRAEL

SCALABRINI ORTIZ

Dorrego

Malabia

Federico Lacroze

CHACARITA

COGHLAN

LMAGRO

CORRIENTES

CORDOBA

ALVAREZ THOMAS

COLEGIALES

CRAMER

BASTO

MEDRANO

PALERMO
VIEJO

DORREGO

Olleros

José
Hernández

Juramento

Congreso de
Tucumán

rlos Gardel

CORDOBA

Ministro Carranza

CABILDO

BELGRANO

MONROE

NUÑEZ

CORONEL DIAZ

Palermo

SANTA FE

LUIS MARIA CAMPOS

LIBERTADOR

Scalabrini
Ortiz

Plaza Italia

BARRIO
NORTE

Aguero

Bulnes

LAS HERAS

BULLRICH

LAS
CAÑITAS

Pueyrredón

PUEYRREDON

SARMIENTO

DEL LIBERTADOR

PALERMO

RECOLETA

FIGUEROA ALCORTA

LEOPOLDO LUGONES

DEL LIBERTADOR

PALERMO
CHICO

FIGUEROA ALCORTA

COSTANERA RAFAEL OBLIGADO

Río de la Plata

AU. PRESIDENTE ILLIA

Aeroparque
Jorge Newbery

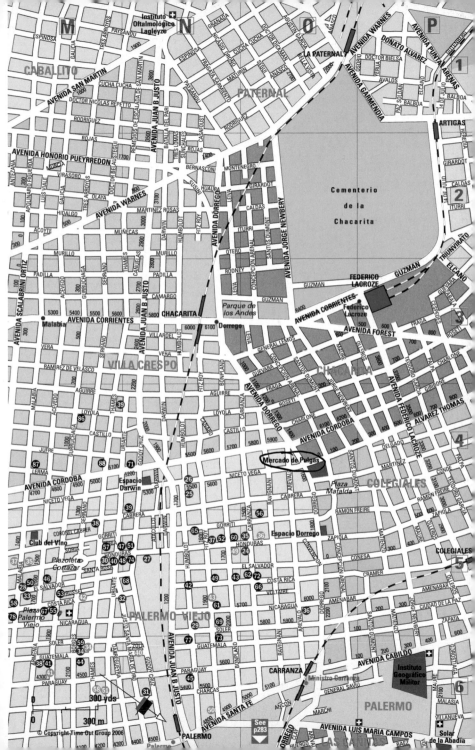

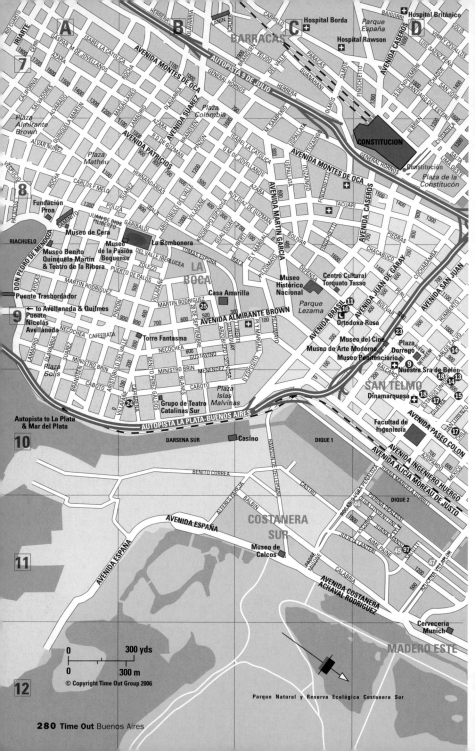

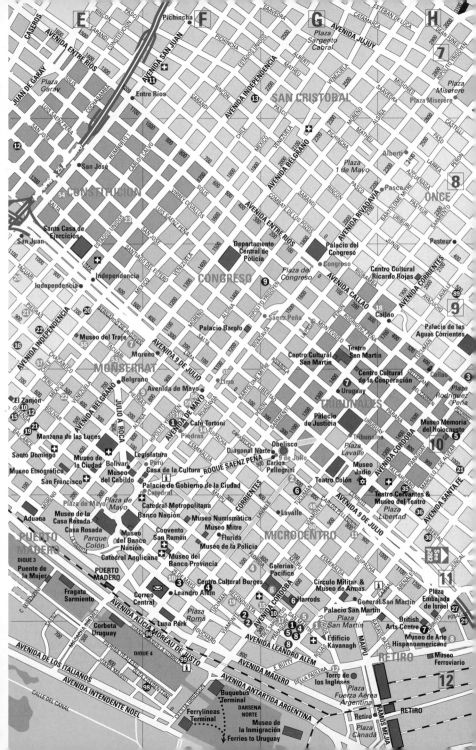

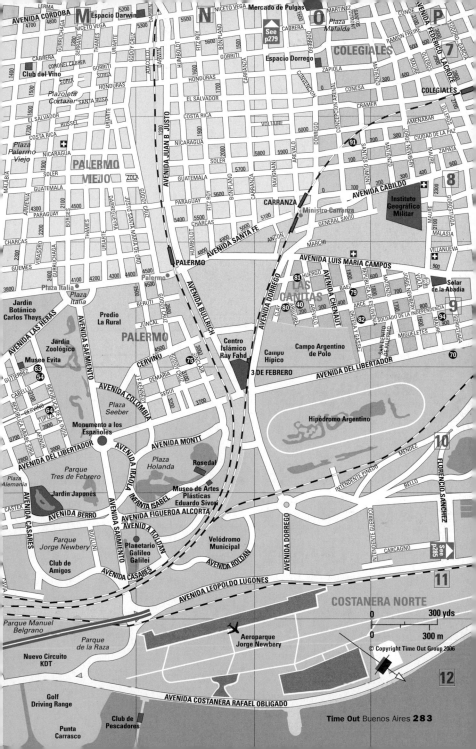

THE WORLD'S YOUR OYSTER

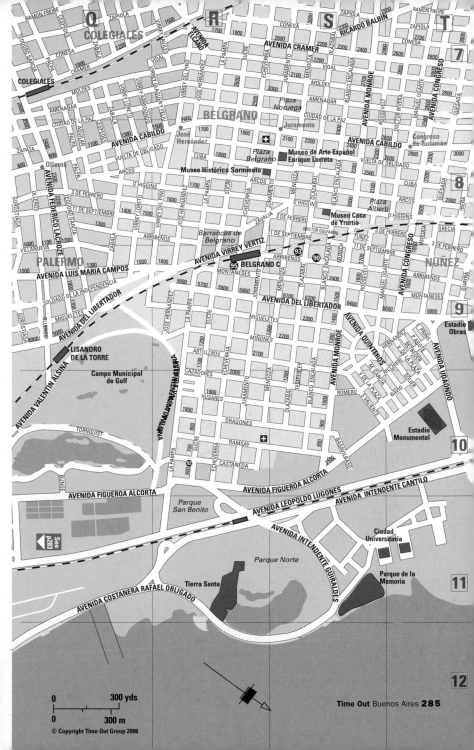

© Copyright Time Out Group 2006

Street Index